Memory and Identity

The Carolina Lowcountry and the Atlantic World

Sponsored by the Lowcountry and Atlantic Studies Program
of the College of Charleston

Money, Trade, and Power
Edited by Jack P. Greene, Rosemary Brana-Shute, and Randy J. Sparks

The Impact of the Haitian Revolution in the Atlantic World
Edited by David P. Geggus

London Booksellers and American Customers
James Raven

Memory and Identity
Edited by Bertrand Van Ruymbeke and Randy J. Sparks

Memory and Identity

The Huguenots in France and the Atlantic Diaspora

Edited by

Bertrand Van Ruymbeke
and Randy J. Sparks

UNIVERSITY OF SOUTH CAROLINA PRESS

© 2003 University of South Carolina

Published in Columbia, South Carolina, by the
University of South Carolina Press

Manufactured in the United States of America

07 06 05 04 03   5 4 3 2 1

Library of Congress Cataloging-in-Publication Data

Memory and identity : the Huguenots in France and the Atlantic Diaspora
/ edited by Bertrand Van Ruymbeke and Randy J. Sparks.
    p. cm. — (The Carolina lowcountry and the Atlantic world)
  Includes bibliographical references and index.
  ISBN 1-57003-484-2 (alk. paper)
  1. Huguenots—History—Congresses. 2. Religious
refugees—History—Congresses. 3. Huguenots—History—17th
century—Congresses. 4. Religious refugees—History—17th
century—Congresses. I. Van Ruymbeke, Bertrand, 1962–
II. Sparks, Randy J. III. Series.
BX9454.3 .M46 2003
284'.5'09—dc21

                                                    2003003578

In memory of Hilda M. Kenner
(1940–2002)

Contents

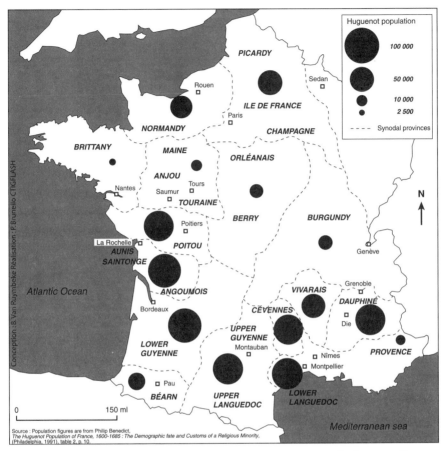

Huguenot population

- 100 000
- 50 000
- 10 000
- 2 500
- --- Synodal provinces

PICARDY

Rouen □

Sedan □

ILE DE FRANCE

Paris □

CHAMPAGNE

NORMANDY

BRITTANY

MAINE

ORLÉANAIS

ANJOU

Nantes □

Tours □

Saumur □

TOURAINE

Poitiers □

BERRY

BURGUNDY

Genève □

La Rochelle □

POITOU

AUNIS
SAINTONGE

VIVARAIS

Grenoble □

DAUPHINÉ

Atlantic Ocean

ANGOUMOIS

CÉVENNES

Die □

Bordeaux □

UPPER
GUYENNE

Montauban □

Nîmes □

PROVENCE

LOWER
GUYENNE

Montpellier □

Pau □

BÉARN

UPPER
LANGUEDOC

LOWER
LANGUEDOC

Mediterranean sea

0   150 ml

N
↑

Source : Population figures are from Philip Benedict,
The Huguenot Population of France, 1600-1685 : The Demographic fate and Customs of a Religious Minority,
(Philadelphia, 1991), table 2, p. 10.

Conception :B. Van Ruymbeke Réalisation : P. Brunello CTIGFLASH

Huguenot Population and Synodal Provinces in Seventeenth-Century France

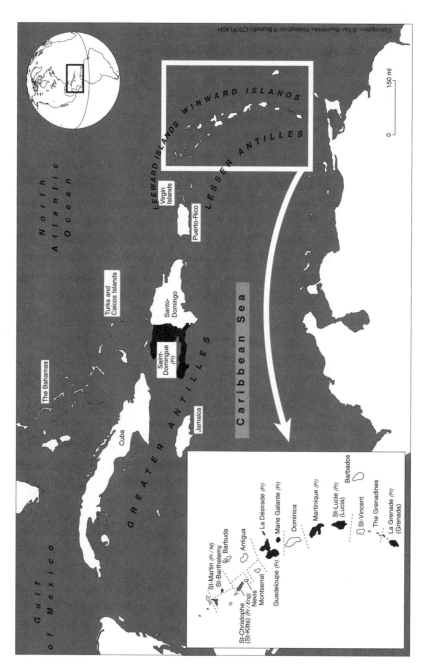

French Islands in the West Indies in the Late Seventeenth Century

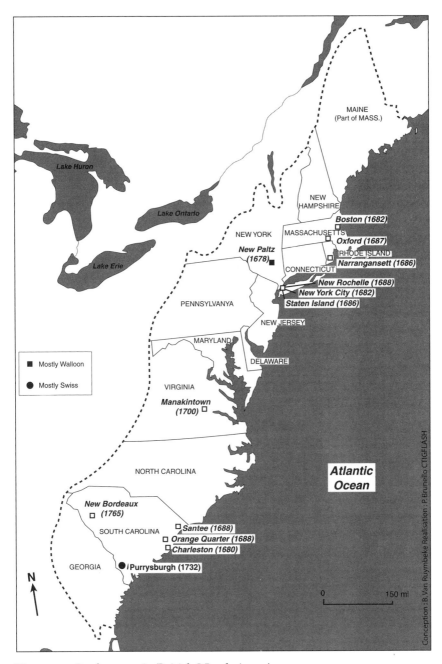

Huguenot Settlements in British North America

Chronology of Huguenot History
in France and in the Diaspora

1559   First national synod

1562–1598   Wars of Religion

1562–1565   Huguenot attempts to settle La Florida

1572   Saint-Bartholomew's Day massacres

1598   Promulgation of the Edict of Nantes

1621–1622/   Huguenot rebellions
1625–1629

1624   Arrival of Walloon settlers in New Netherland

1627–1628   Siege of La Rochelle

1627   Huguenots prohibited from settling in New France

1629   Peace of Alès

1659   Last national synod before Revocation

1680   Arrival of Huguenots in South Carolina

1680–1702   Huguenot migration to British North America

1681   First *Dragonnade* (Poitou)

1682   Arrival of Huguenots in New York and New England

1685   Black Code (*Code Noir*) outlaws Protestantism and
Judaism in the French West Indies (March)

Revocation of the Edict of Nantes (October)

1685–1687   Peak years of Huguenot exodus from France

1687–1689   Huguenot emigration to South Africa

1700   Arrival of Huguenots in Virginia

1702–1704   War of the Cévennes

1715   First underground national synod

1787   Edict of Toleration

1802   Reorganization of the Huguenot Church under
       Napoléon Bonaparte

1852   Founding of the *Société de l'Histoire du Protestantisme
       Français*

1872   First official national synod since 1659

1878   Founding of the Dutch Walloon Society (*Commission pour
       l'Histoire des Eglises Wallones*)

1883   Founding of the Huguenot Society of America in New
       York

1885   First commemoration of the Revocation

       Founding of the Huguenot Society of London
       (Huguenot Society of Great Britain and Ireland since
       1987) and of the Huguenot Society of South Carolina

1890   Founding of the German Huguenot Society (*Deutsche
       Hugenotten-Gesellschaft* since 1997)

1922   Founding of the Huguenot Society of the Founders of
       Manakin in the Colony of Virginia

1953   Founding of the Huguenot Society of South Africa

1975   Founding of the Huguenot Society of the Netherlands
       (*Nederlandse Huguenoten Stichting*)

Minority Survival

The Huguenot Paradigm in France and the Diaspora

Bertrand Van Ruymbeke

If ethnic and religious groups are to sustain themselves, they must do so as purely voluntary associations. This means that they are more at risk from the indifference of their own members than from the intolerance of the others

Michael Walzer, *On Toleration* (1997)

I regard this refuge of England as the best heritage I can bequeath to [my children]

Jean-François de Portal's will (1704)

I believe I should tell you [my dear children] from whom you are descended, and who are your relatives, so that the history you write may be a sequel to mine

Jacques Fontaine's *Memoirs* (1722)

This edited volume contains fourteen of the thirty-five papers that were presented at the 1997 international symposium "Out of New Babylon: The Huguenots and their Diaspora" held at the College of Charleston, South Carolina, and sponsored by the Program in the Carolina Lowcountry and the Atlantic World.[1] It is not just simply another book on the Huguenots, but a collective work that sheds new light on crucial aspects of the Protestant experience both in and out of France. Indeed, the study of the Refuge, or Huguenot diaspora has for too long been dissociated from the history of the Huguenots in France.[2] Even within the diaspora, studies of refugee communities in Europe and the Atlantic world are not usually juxtaposed in the same volume.[3] *Memory and Identity* offers a novel comparative perspective on Huguenot communities in pre-Revocation France, French America (the French West Indies and New France), and in the Premier (ca. 1530s–ca. 1660s) and Second (ca. 1670s–ca. 1710s)

Refuges in continental Europe and around the Atlantic world (the German states, the Netherlands, England, South Carolina, New York, and South Africa).[4] Topically, these essays focus on the Huguenot experience as a minority in France as well as in the different host societies into which they immigrated in Europe and around the Atlantic world. They also explore the diverse means the Huguenots used to preserve an identity in pre-Revocation France and in the diaspora. Finally, some authors describe the emergence of a late nineteenth-century Huguenot revival which constructed a group identity born of a mythically glorified self-perception of their history.

Minority status or *le fait minoritaire* is an inescapable feature of the Huguenot experience in France and the diaspora. In his introduction to *Minorities in History*, A. C. Hepburn defined a cross classification of the concept of "minority" based on its nature and its objectives. Following this dual typology, a minority belongs to three main and, at times overlapping, categories: religious, racial, and "a looser group labelled at different times cultural, ethnic, linguistic or national." It is also either of an "American-type" when "it seeks unqualified assimilation into the majority" or a "European-type" when "it wishes to preserve its separate status from attack or erosion by the majority community."[5] From this perspective, the Huguenots were a religious and, to some extent, socio-cultural minority of a "European-type" in France, and became, in the diasporic process, a religious, linguistic, and ethnic (rather than national) minority of the "American-type."[6] Interestingly enough, whereas in France they resisted assimilation within the French Catholic majority group, in the Refuge they lost their distinctive traits in a matter of two or three generations. The pace of this integration, which proceeded without steadfast and deliberate external pressure (except in South Africa) varied depending on the more or less latitudinarian policies of the host government, the assimilationist tendencies of the host society, and the geographic isolation of the place of refuge (i.e., its distance from France), but not so much, as might be expected, on the size of the refugee communities.

A Minority at Home
The Edict of Nantes and the Marginalization of French Protestantism

Although, as Elisabeth Labrousse stressed, the Huguenots were "proud to be French" and regarded foreigners "with tacit condescension," they nonetheless were "French in a particular way."[7] Except in a few areas, they never formed more than a numerically small minority. Even when in the 1560s, in the wake of the Calvinist reformation, the Huguenot population reached its all-time high watermark at about 1.5 million, it scarcely represented 10 percent of the French population.[8] In the seventeenth century, their numbers inexorably declined and leveled off at about 730,000, or 4 percent of the population, in the years preceding the Revocation.[9] Geographically, if in the sixteenth century Huguenot churches were located everywhere in the kingdom, even in thoroughly Catholic provinces such as Brittany, Burgundy, and Provence, in the following century they were circumscribed to the famed "Huguenot crescent or triangle," which extended from Alpine Dauphiny to Atlantic Aunis.[10]

From a religious standpoint, the presbyterianism of Huguenot ecclesiology embodied in the institution of the consistory, "the focal point of the Reformed Church polity," according to Raymond Mentzer, further isolated the French Protestants from their (Catholic) countrymen. Controlled by lay parishioners, consistories ran the congregations, supervised the communicants, and, as Mentzer and Diane Margolf explain in their essays, offered the Huguenots an alternative to the partisan royal courts of justice. French Protestants were also somewhat culturally marginalized as they did not take part in the eminently Catholic feasts and parades celebrating patron saints of towns and trades. Finally, except in rural Cévennes, Vivarais, and parts of Poitou where the peasantry adopted Calvinism en masse, the Huguenots tended to be more urban and literate than the rest of the French population.[11]

After 1598, this Huguenot minority was protected by the religious, civil, judicial, and military clauses of the Edict of Nantes. As Margolf states, "the Edict remained a key element in the Huguenots' definition of themselves and in others' views of them." Under the Edict, the Huguenots enjoyed freedom of worship (not to be confused with freedom of religion, as it was limited to certain localities), unrestricted access to civil positions and to special (theoretically bipartisan) courts of justice, funds to maintain their pastors, and subsidized garrisons in the towns that they controlled.[12] However, after more than thirty years of intense fighting during which both sides alternatively enjoyed the military upper hand, the Edict explicitly restored Catholicism as the official religion of France, and in so doing, permanently relegated Calvinism to the margins of French society. Protestantism officially became the religion of a protected and privileged minority.

The Edict thus guaranteed the Huguenots legal recognition and protection, which were justified by the pressing need for peace and the strength of the Huguenot military. Over the course of the seventeenth century, however, in the eyes of the Catholic majority, the Huguenots gradually appeared to be an excessively and unjustifiably privileged group.[13] Beyond the religious and legal privileges it offered the Huguenots, the Edict of Nantes actually preserved Protestantism in a fragile cocoon since the advantages that the Crown had granted could be easily revoked by the same authority. As Margolf writes, with the Edict "the Huguenots' assertions of collective identity remained entangled with the issue of their obedience to the French Crown." When it signed the Peace of Alès in 1629, which concluded the last and unequivocally unsuccessful Huguenot rebellion, the Crown not surprisingly refused to renew the temporary military and political clauses of the Edict contained in the appendices known as the *brevets*.[14] Consequently, the Huguenots lost the right to form political assemblies and to hold fortified towns.[15]

Once Louis XIV assumed personal control of French affairs in 1660, the Huguenots gradually lost their civil, judicial, and religious privileges. This increasing marginalization forced the Protestants to develop strategies for survival. As the royal *commissaires* traversed France in the 1660s investigating the legitimacy of congregations following formal complaints by the local Catholic clergy, the Huguenots did not hesitate to take court action to challenge the *commissaires'* unfavorable decisions. When the courts rejected their appeals, banned worship services, and demolished temples, the Huguenots still met in the chapel of a local seigneur, joined other congregations, or simply gathered where their churches once stood.

In his essay on Huguenot and Catholic cemeteries in Poitou, Keith Luria explores other Huguenot strategies to preserve their Calvinist identity either through coexistence or separation. In some cases, they resisted the building of a dividing wall or used the Catholic cemetery by force, and in others they accepted partitioning, "provided it did not lead to their exclusion from the community." Clearly, from the 1630s to the 1670s, the Huguenots avoided confrontation as much as possible and managed to live as French subjects among Catholics as long as this coexistence did not infringe on their Calvinism. As John Locke reported when he was staying in Montpellier, "They & the papist[s] live together friendly enough in these parts."[16] Thus, echoing the work of Gregory Hanlon on mixed communities in Aquitaine, Luria describes this peaceful coexistence between Catholics and Huguenots as a "cooperative atmosphere [born of] a pragmatic interest in avoiding conflict."[17]

In the 1670s, however, the desire to avoid confrontation with the monarchy led an increasing number of Huguenots down the path of Catholic conversion. Lured by the state's financial rewards and tax exemptions or simply eager to gain social promotion, *nouveaux catholiques* or *nouveaux convertis* left the group to gain what they thought was their due place in French society.[18] As Hanlon emphasizes, "The alacrity [of those who converted] was often proportionate to the compensation they expected in return."[19] Consequently, conversion was most meaningful to those who had something to lose in remaining Calvinists and was inevitably predominant in the upper strata of Huguenot society. However, with the launching of the *dragonnades* in 1681, converting to Catholicism took on a whole new meaning. These individual and mass conversions obtained through terror were most often nominal, as they merely represented a temporary escape from brutality. The Crown was well aware of this phenomenon and legislation against *relapses* (*nouveaux catholiques* who returned to the Huguenot church) was particularly harsh.

Survival through conversion turned out to be the choice of most Huguenots at the time of the Revocation in 1685. Although France had suddenly become, following Pierre Bayle's famous phrase, "toute catholique," close to 600,000 Huguenots still lived within the kingdom.[20] The Revocation put an arbitrary end to the official existence of France's most important religious minority but failed to completely eradicate Calvinism. The three-generation conversion pattern (i.e., the first clung to the Huguenot faith, the second practiced a Catholicism *de façade*, while the third was truly Catholic), delineated by Gérard Lafleur and Lucien Abénon in the French Antilles, also applies to France. It is undeniable, however, that although seriously undermined, French Protestantism survived as the church went underground, and a significant number of individuals devised ways to maintain their faith. All in all, the repressive royal policy proved, as the Revocation itself, largely unsuccessful.[21] In 1715, there were enough Huguenots and clandestine congregations for the meeting of an underground national synod.[22] In 1726, a seminary was even opened in Lausanne, Switzerland, which by mid-century had sent ninety pastors to serve the Huguenot congregations in France.[23] By the first quarter of the eighteenth century, the Huguenot church was born again, and by 1760, France had a Calvinist population of about half a million.[24]

A Minority Abroad
Survival through Acculturation

For about a third of the Huguenots living in France in 1685, survival involved immigration to a Protestant country. From the early decades of the sixteenth century, and particularly in the wake of the Saint Bartholomew's Day massacre in 1572, Huguenots had always resorted to (im)migration, temporary or permanent, as a means to preserve their Calvinism in the face of royal persecution.[25] Historians estimate that about 20,000 Huguenots left France before the 1660s.[26] The systematic use of force and the actual Revocation of the Edict of Nantes, which, ironically, was more irrevocable than the "perpetual" edict itself, led a far higher number of Huguenots to seek a permanent refuge in more distant places.[27] Its short duration (1680–1710) and magnitude (about 200,000 individuals) makes the Huguenot exodus, often called *le Grand Refuge* or Second Refuge in opposition to previous immigration outbursts or simply *le Refuge*, was the third largest one-shot migration in early modern Europe after the expulsion of the Jews and the Moriscos from Spain in 1492 and 1609, respectively.[28]

Apart from the number of individuals involved, the Premier differed from the Second Refuge in three ways: most refugees were not Huguenots but Walloons, the geographic scope of the migration was limited, and emigration was not always permanent.[29] Charles Littleton explains that in the second half of the sixteenth century most "strangers" who settled in London were Walloons from the southern French-speaking provinces of the Low Countries (Artois, Hainaut, southern Brabant, and Walloon Flanders). In turn, these French-speaking refugees were also very few in comparison to the Dutch Calvinists fleeing the Spanish-controlled Netherlands. John Miller has found, for example, that in Norwich "Dutch outnumbered Walloons by more than three to one in 1568 and four to one in 1571." In this Premier Refuge, the Huguenots, therefore, as Timothy Felher explains in the case of the German East

Frisian town of Emden, only constituted "a minority among the minorities." The scope of this migration was also limited to the Netherlands, the Rhineland, the Swiss Cantons, and England. Huguenots migrated to neighboring countries, cities, especially Strasburg and Geneva, and principalities because they hoped to return to France once the Crown reverted to a more tolerant religious policy. Thus, as regards the cases discussed in this volume, Norwich had well-established ties with the neighboring Low Countries, Canterbury and London are just a short sea-crossing away from northern France and Flanders, and Emden is near the Dutch-German northern border.

Beyond these factual distinctions, however, both Refuges offer a fundamental similarity. In both cases, migrants faced the problem of maintaining a distinct group identity within their host societies. The fundamental aspect of Huguenot life back in France, *le fait minoritaire*, followed the Huguenots in their flight. Everywhere they went, they constituted a minority. Once again they devised survival strategies, sometimes in the face of new adversity as in South Africa, and episodically in England and its North American dependencies. In both Refuges, Huguenot group identity became defined by church organization, language, kinship, and, in the sixteenth century, by regional origins (Huguenots from France as opposed to Walloons from the southern Netherlands).

The capacity or incapacity to transfer a durable and distinctly French Reformed ecclesiastical structure turned out to be a key element in succeeding or failing to preserve a Huguenot identity abroad. In the sixteenth century, refugee churches were divided along linguistic lines as the French and Walloons shared the same churches apart from the Dutch. In Emden, as Tim Fehler explains, the French-speaking refugees, who were few in number, nonetheless were granted the privilege to have their own congregation "because of obvious linguistic necessities." By the time massive waves of Huguenots left France in the 1680s and 1690s, these "French" churches lost their Walloon element (the Walloon emigration having dried up by mid-century), and truly became Huguenot refugee congregations, although as Willem Frijhoff explains in the case of the Netherlands they were still called "Walloon churches." The existence of these French churches played a crucial role in providing a Calvinist structure for the Huguenots of the Second Refuge particularly in the

Netherlands and in England. As Frijhoff puts it, "Seen from the Second Refuge, the most important achievement of the First Refuge was the elaboration of a stable network of institutions where French-speaking refugees could find appropriate help, shelter, and support: the local congregations of the Walloon Church." In England, as Miller explains, whereas the Norwich "French" church shrank because it was almost exclusively Walloon, the one in Canterbury remained substantial until the 1680s, when it grew even larger with the new influx of Huguenots. Even in South Africa, Philippe Denis found that the refugees fought hard to obtain "a special status, comparable to the one they had in France before the Revocation of the Edict of Nantes or of that of the Walloon Church in the Netherlands," so that they could worship in French and follow the French Reformed tradition.

In his study of the London Threadneedle Street Church, Littleton shows that although second-generation refugees "felt increasingly comfortable in English society," they still paid "homage to [their] continental roots through membership in the Stranger Church." This "successful straddling of the French and English worlds, and of the continental Reformed and English episcopalian religious traditions" illustrates a crucial aspect of the refugees' capacity to adapt to their new religious and cultural environment. If the continuous—albeit sometimes infinitesimal —flow of Calvinists out of France enabled the sixteenth-century Huguenot churches located in the main refugee centers of London, Amsterdam, Geneva, and Frankfurt-am-Main to maintain a substantial membership until they were once again overwhelmed with refugees, after 1710 refugee churches had to become self-sustaining in order to survive. The unusual example of "forced assimilation" of the Huguenot community in South Africa is, in that respect, a case in point. In order to force the French refugees to integrate within the Dutch population, the Lords XVII simply decided to put an end to their emigration to the colony.

Although the need to preserve their Calvinism was a prime factor in their decision to emigrate, nowhere were the Huguenots able to maintain an active French Protestant congregation beyond the 1730s. Second and third generation Huguenots, as Butler points out, turned towards religious pluralism, and at best kept an occasional membership in the local French church while being a full-fledged member of another denomination. The case, evoked by Littleton, of Pierre Delaune, the author of the first French translation of the Anglican *Book of Common Prayer,* who became rector of Redendall while still being involved in the French church in Norwich is emblematic of the refugees' effort to conciliate their aspiration to fully integrate into their new society without completely abandoning the religion of their "heroic" ancestors. One may wonder, however, to what extent this attachment to French Calvinism was not actually cultural, and even familial, rather than truly religious. What seemed to matter more was maintaining an emotional, and personal, tie to what had been so central to their ancestors' experience both in France and in the Refuge than observing Huguenot religious ways. English legal reformer, Samuel Romilly, a third-generation refugee, thus recalled that attending the French church was "a kind of homage which [his family] paid to faith of [their] ancestors."[30] With time, however, this effort proved nearly impossible to sustain. This was especially the case in overseas refugee locations, such as in New York City, where, as Joyce Goodfriend has shown, the Huguenot community was plagued by a high death rate and familial dispersion as economic opportunities lured second and third-generation Huguenots away from the City. Every congregation in exile, it seems, had "their last Huguenot," such as John Pintard in New York City who died in 1844 after an exceptionally long personal devotion to the French church.[31] By the late 1700s almost everywhere refugee churches had either closed or become showcases of past suffering.

Beyond the passage of time, which predictably eroded the vitality of the refugees' Calvinism, the incapacity of the Huguenots to form, what Butler has called "a denomination-in-exile,"[32] condemned the Huguenot churches to extinction. Surely, Huguenot refugee congregations maintained ties between themselves, especially between London and the churches scattered throughout the English-speaking world in England, Ireland, and North America, but these were informal. Huguenot refugee congregations were isolated, and nothing in the 1680s vaguely resembled the meetings or *coetus* which united, in a Calvinist synodal fashion, representatives of the Dutch and French/Walloon churches in sixteenth-century England. Only in the Netherlands did the well-established Walloon Synod provide the Huguenots a viable denominational structure to sustain an independent Calvinist ecclesiastical life through most of the eighteenth century.

Next to their brand of Calvinism, the French language was an essential defining element of the Huguenot group identity in the Refuge. In Emden, the French and Walloon refugees obtained the privilege of organizing an independent Calvinist congregation only because they spoke French, and not surprisingly, the church lost its special status once the mother tongue of most members was no longer French. Similarly, at the turn of the eighteenth century, the South Carolina Huguenot conformist parish of St. Denis became what Butler has called a unique "linguistically defined Anglican parish,"[33] and ceased to exist once the need to have a French-speaking minister to officiate there disappeared. In South Africa, the right to use French for the divine service was obtained by Pierre Simond, pastor and leader of the Huguenot refugees, through hard negotiations, and was withdrawn immediately after Simond's departure from the colony. Following this decision, as Denis writes, "there was nothing which could prevent the rapid assimilation of the French refugees into the Dutch settler population."

Although this linguistic change is difficult to document, except with rare letters, second-generation Huguenots were undoubtedly bilingual, officially interacting in the language of the host society but using French as the medium of oral and written communication with their relatives and fellow refugees. By the late eighteenth century, however, most Huguenot descendants no longer spoke their ancestors' native tongue. The La Rochefoucauld family, described in Carolyn Lougee's essay, is a case in point. Whereas the refugee Marie never bothered to learn German, her grandson, Saint-Surin, was an adamant Prussian patriot.

Because kinship ties transcended religious, linguistic, and national barriers, they remained a unifying thread among the descendants of the refugees. Lougee describes how Monsieur de Champagné, an Irish Anglican Dean, and the Baron de Saint-Surin, a Prussian junker, both grandsons of Marie de la Rochefoucauld were "united in a sincere friendship [through] the ties of blood and epistolary commerce." Although they were of different nationalities and religions, wrote in mutually unintelligible languages, and, as Lougee adroitly puts it, "spoke in culturally specific voices," they were cognizant of belonging to a specific kinship network. This familial dimension of the Huguenot diaspora also had a financial raison d'être as in the case of Champagné and Saint-Surin, who were co-heirs to their grandmother's portfolio of investments.

Family ties played an equally vital role in the commercial endeavors of the first-generation Carolina Huguenot merchants studied by R. C. Nash. These merchants used family-based trading networks to prosper, and formed "ethnic associations" among themselves, though less systematically than the refugees who settled in New York City and Boston discussed by John F. Bosher in his article on the Huguenot merchants and the protestant international.[34] In his essay, however, Nash has shown that ethnicity gradually ceased to be a determining factor, and by the mid-eighteenth century, most Huguenot merchants had deserted the Charleston French church, intermarried and formed partnerships with non-French mercantile families. At that point social endogamy prevailed over ethnic cohesion.

An Invisible Minority
The Huguenot Diaspora in the Atlantic World

Nash's essay on the involvement of the Huguenot merchants in the Anglo-Carolinian trade sheds new light on a crucial—although under-studied—outcome of the Second Refuge: the creation of a Huguenot Atlantic world. Although Huguenots attempted to found settlements in La Florida and in Brazil in the mid-1500s, and Walloons settled in New Netherland in the 1620s, the geographic scope of the Premier Refuge did not encompass the Atlantic. A Huguenot Atlantic assuredly existed in the sixteenth and early seventeenth centuries, but it was the world of navigators, explorers, privateers, and high seas fishermen, not that of families and congregations.

At the time of the Revocation, however, Huguenots spread around the Atlantic to Ireland, New England, New York, Virginia, South Carolina, English and Dutch West Indian islands, Surinam, and South Africa. As Voltaire emphatically noted in his *Siècle de Louis XIV,* "The French [i.e., Huguenots] were dispersed farther away than the Jews."[35] Thus, a Huguenot Atlantic world integrated into a larger Protestant Anglo-Dutch-American space, which tied together families, congregations, pastors, intellectuals, and merchants, emerged in the 1680s and 1690s. For instance, the London Threadneedle Street Church recommended pastors to the Boston and Charleston Huguenot congregations and South Carolina families regularly corresponded with relatives in Dublin. Huguenot Rochelais merchants exiled in London traded with partners in Charleston, New York, and Boston.[36]

A case in point is the well-known New England Faneuil family. André and his nephew Pierre emigrated to Boston whereas Benjamin, André's brother, settled in New York City. Pierre's maternal grandfather, François Bureau, was in New England, but two of his brothers were in London. Finally, the New England Faneuils also had a cousin in the Netherlands.[37] Spread between Boston, New York, London, and Rotterdam, this familial diaspora is a noteworthy example of a kin network well integrated into the North Atlantic world. The Simond family, coincidentally discussed in Denis' and Nash's essays, offers another fascinating—yet somewhat different—example of an Atlantic-wide family diaspora. Pierre Simond was the pastor of the Huguenot church at the Cape from 1687 to 1702. His son, born in South Africa and educated in Amsterdam, was a London-based merchant who, with his brother, operated a company involved in the Anglo–West Indian, Anglo-Georgian, and Anglo–South Carolinian trades. Specializing in the rice and naval stores trades, Pierre Jr. eventually acquired extensive land grants in the South Carolina Swiss-Huguenot settlement of Purrysburgh.[38]

These Huguenot mercantile, religious, and familial ties, which Lougee aptly describes as "layers of superimposed networks," literally formed what can be called *un Refuge atlantique*. Indeed, recent historiography on early modern European expansion, with its focus on the interactive Atlantic world instead of its national components, forces us to reconsider the traditional spatial interpretation of the Huguenot diaspora. Instead of the usual Europe/colonies dichotomy, historians must distinguish an *Atlantic* from a *continental* refugee space. The first comprises the British Isles, the coastal Netherlands, the continental and Caribbean North American colonies, and the Dutch settlement of the Cape. The second encompasses central and eastern Netherlands, the German states, and Switzerland. The line of demarcation, so to speak, between these two refugee spaces is not in the middle of the Atlantic, but in the middle of the Netherlands, itself being divided between a coastal Refuge open to the ocean and another to the continent. The numerical ratio between the two refugee worlds was nearly half or about 80,000 (Atlantic) to slightly over half or about 100,000 (continental).[39] Needless to say, the Atlantic refugee space did not exist in isolation but interacted with its continental counterpart through the coastal provinces of the Netherlands, which constituted an intermediary zone of contact and passage between the two Refuges.[40]

Most interestingly, the migration and mercantile routes of the Atlantic Refuge overlapped those of the French Atlantic. Although officially banned from settling in France's overseas colonies, Huguenots emigrated there in relatively significant numbers. Whereas in New France, as Leslie Choquette explains, they were officially tolerated only as "temporary" immigrants, in the West Indian islands they established plantations or *habitations* without official impediment. Lafleur and Abénon even found that, in the 1670s, the Huguenots and the Dutch Protestants, who left Brazil in the mid-seventeenth century and with whom the Huguenots intermarried extensively, controlled between 25 and 30 percent of the French West Indian sugar production. Whether in New France or in the West Indies, these Huguenots, who often hailed from La Rochelle, Dieppe, and Bordeaux, had urban and Atlantic origins. The geographic recruitment of the Atlantic Refuge is strikingly similar as, in the case of South Carolina, for example, La Rochelle and Dieppe were the single most represented French cities.[41]

The predominance of La Rochelle particularly stands out. It can be explained by the involvement of the city's Huguenot merchants in the French transatlantic trade, and by the fact that before the Revocation these merchants also maintained regular and illicit trade ties with Boston and New York via London.[42] At the time of the Revocation, Huguenots living in or near French ports active in the colonial trade chose to emigrate to Atlantic destinations, whether it be England, Ireland, the coastal Netherlands, or British North America.[43] Similarly, the French Protestants who escaped from the West Indian islands used well-known trade routes which linked Martinique and Guadeloupe to New York and Boston.

From Survival to Revival
The Nineteenth-Century Huguenot Renaissance

Whether the refugees settled around the Atlantic or in Northern Europe, a common and oft-described feature of the Huguenot diaspora is their rapid integration into the various host societies they encountered. As we have seen earlier, except for South Africa where they were forced to "assimilate" among the Dutch settlers, everywhere else the refugees gradually distanced themselves from their Huguenot churches, ceased to speak French, and married outside the group without manifest external pressure. Yet, the Huguenots did not disappear altogether. A latent and diffuse identity persisted until it was publicly revived throughout the Refuge in the second half of the nineteenth century. In the wake of the foundation of the Paris-based *Société de l'Histoire du Protestantisme Français*

(S.H.P.F.) in 1852, which literally became, to use a corporate metaphor, a sort of *maison mère* (parent society), national and regional Huguenot Societies appeared in Great Britain, Germany, New York, and South Carolina in the 1880s and the 1890s (see chronology).[44] This Huguenot renaissance, born of an intense need to celebrate the past and of a sense of sharing the same heritage, led the Huguenots, as Butler writes, to reestablish "a group identity . . . through the cultivation of genealogy." Huguenot societies, which in some places are very exclusive, seek, as in the case of the one in South Carolina discussed in Bernard Cottret's essay, to "perpetuate the memory . . . and promote" the so-called "principle and virtues of the Huguenots." To that purpose, they erect markers and monuments to the glory of the first-generation refugees, establish genealogical libraries, publish journals, and organize live reenactments on the occasion of anniversaries which Society members relish.[45] No doubt descendants of Huguenot refugees perfectly fit Pierre Nora's description of "certain minorities [that] create protected enclaves as preserves of memory to be jealously safeguarded . . . [through] commemorative vigilance [without which] history would soon sweep them away."[46]

The key words of this "self-celebration," as Cottret calls it, are heritage or legacy, heroism, pride, and faith. Consciously or not, Huguenot descendants always seem aware that despite its obvious value as an historical phenomenon and object of study, the Refuge was not a world-history shaping event. Therefore, the contribution of the Huguenot refugees to their host societies, albeit undeniable, is always exaggerated. A standard claim, for example, is that Huguenot achievements and influence far surpass the actual number of refugees. This is especially true, of course, in remote places such as South Carolina and South Africa, but also in Northern Europe, where the refugees emigrated en masse. Thus, among other well-known contributions, the Huguenots founded the Bank of England, resurrected Prussia from the devastation of the Thirty Years' War, secured William III's military success in Ireland, and brought freedom of religion to America.[47] The most important dimension of this oft-heralded legacy though, is, as South African academics emphasize, "less tangible." Huguenot refugees are hailed as models of what Denis rightfully terms "Christian heroism." The Huguenots were persecuted, but they held onto their beliefs, left their material belongings and sometimes their beloved friends and relatives behind them in their flight, and prospered in their new homes. As nineteenth-century French historian

Jules Michelet, who was one of the first to reincorporate Huguenot history into mainstream French history, once wrote, contrasting the royalist *émigré* to the Huguenot refugee, "the *émigré* of [17]93 wanted to save his life; the [refugee] of 1685 wanted to save his conscience."[48]

A remarkable aspect of the biased and introspective Huguenot memory, which, it is worthy of note, managed to absorb and eclipse Walloon memory, except perhaps in the Netherlands where Walloons were more numerous and where their settlement had a more lasting impact, is the way it has blended in different and at times antagonistic national and local historical traditions. This is particularly striking in the case of the North and the South in the American Civil War, Britain and Germany during World War I, and apartheid and post-apartheid South Africa.[49] In this last instance as Denis explains, for better or for worse, the Huguenot legacy helped define the Afrikaner, that is the dominating white identity, and the Refuge retroactively became another Great Trek. This is an important aspect of what has been aptly referred to as "the Calvinist paradigm of Afrikaner history."[50] Accordingly, although the Huguenots constitute less than 15 percent of their ethnic makeup, twentieth-century Afrikaners "speak of all the Afrikaans settlers as having settled in South Africa to escape religious persecution."[51] However, in his foreword to a 1996 publication on French travelers to the Cape of Good Hope, two years after "the birth of a new South Africa," Nelson Mandela, in a eulogy to the ideals of the 1789 French Revolution, praised the "French Huguenots [who] brought [to the Cape of Good Hope] a culture enriched by their own struggle for human rights."[52]

In North America, the Huguenot immigrant experience was incorporated into the White Anglo-Saxon Protestant model, and the French Protestant, according to the South Carolina chronicler quoted in Cottret's essay, became "a French Puritan, substantially identical with the English Puritans. . . , [who] was not essentially different from a Catholic Frenchman, except that he averaged higher." Thus, the Huguenot saga admirably contributes to "the most enduring American myth," which purports that America was "peopled largely by settlers fleeing religious persecution and yearning for the opportunity to worship openly and without fear."[53]

This Huguenot contribution to the alleged essence of the American national character extends beyond religion though. As a prominent local journalist emphatically exclaimed in an editorial published in a

Charleston newspaper on the occasion of the 305th anniversary of the Revocation in 1990, "the Huguenots are the essence of what America is all about."[54] The French Protestants, "the brothers of the Puritans" as Michelet dubbed them, embodied characteristics commonly perceived as eminently American such as religious freedom, economic success, perseverance, and entrepreneurial spirit.[55] However, the capacity of Huguenot history to espouse national and local cultural models is not exclusive to the Refuge. Even in France, where, as Philippe Joutard observes, "the memory of the Protestant minority has not been at odds with national memory since the nineteenth century," the renaissance of French Protestantism is widely perceived as related to the emergence of the modern republican values.[56] As Cottret explains, "[French] Protestantism has fulfilled its historical mission by transmitting its values to the rest of society" unless "French society acculturated Calvinism." In turn, these observations lead one to wonder whether Huguenot memory is particularly adaptable or irresistibly appealing.

The nineteenth-century Huguenot revival is remarkably reminiscent of Eric Hobsbawm's description of "invented traditions." Of the three overlapping types that Hobsbawm defines, the Huguenot tradition clearly belongs to types A and B, namely, "those establishing or symbolizing social cohesion or the membership of groups, real or artificial communities," and "those whose main purpose [is] socialization, the inculcation of beliefs, value systems and convention of behaviour."[57] Indeed, especially in the far-away locations where the refugees were few in number and arrived in the founding decades of a settlement, Huguenot societies tend to be exclusive groups promoting a set of values allegedly carried over by their ancestors. They have their by-laws, admission rules, codified ceremonies, and "emotionally and symbolically charged signs of club membership."[58] The Huguenot cross stands out as the most revealing of these signs. Although a Huguenot cross was indeed designed in Nîmes in the 1680s, never was it in France the *symbole de reconnaissance* it later became for the descendants of the Huguenot refugees in the last third of the nineteenth century.

These groups further follow Hobsbawm's pattern as they "foster the corporate sense of *superiority* of elites—particularly when these had to be recruited from those who did not already possess it by birth."[59] Nineteenth- and twentieth-century Huguenot descendants cultivated minority status to the point of exclusivity, a sort of ethno-nobility or *noblesse ethnique.*[60] Not everyone can claim a Huguenot refugee, usually of noble lineage, as an ancestor.[61] Whether in London, Dublin, Cape Town, New York, or Charleston, a thinly disguised pride, sometimes verging on snobbery, is associated with having a *French* Protestant ancestor who fled his dragooned home hidden in a wine cask on an English or Dutch ship.[62] In the United States, the Huguenot pedigree duplicates the mythicized lineages of the Massachusetts Pilgrims and of Pocahontas and John Rolfe in Virginia recently studied by Ann Abrams. Though these are better known and more central to American history than the Huguenot myth, all share a central characteristic: "Stripped of the rich royal heritage of the British Empire, the United States had to create its own aristocracy [whose] determining factor was the date of an ancestor's arrival."[63] Abrams's analysis perfectly fits the Huguenot paradigm of ancestor glorification, not only in South Carolina and New York but also in South Africa and even Prussia.

As in the case of the New England Pilgrims, the pride of the descendants of French refugees, an unequivocal expression of what may be called Huguenot exceptionalism, is utterly Calvinistic since, in the eyes of Huguenot chroniclers, then and now, the Refuge was evidently a selective migration. The equation is simplistic yet powerfully convincing: emigration equals selection, which in turn means election. As André Du Toit describes in the case of South Africa, Afrikaans nationalists extended "the Calvinist notion of *predestination* with its concomitant concept of the *elect*" to "collective election." In other words, Calvinist values permeated Afrikaans nationalism so deeply that Afrikaners conceived of themselves as "a chosen and covenanted people."[64] In the eyes of their descendants, and of those who claimed to have collectively inherited their "values," the Huguenots who fled France were the most devoted to and uncompromising in their faith, the most courageous, and the most enterprising. Clearly, their survival was heroic, not to say edifying.

Fundamentally defined by its minority status, French Protestantism paradoxically survived in the diaspora by losing its core identity, i.e., its Gallican Calvinism and French language, while espousing the religious and cultural traits prevailing in the host societies it encountered. Back in France, it weathered the storm until the united forces of royalism and Catholicism lost their grip on French society, which allowed the emergence of political and cultural values that were loosely associated with "Protestantism." Clearly, in France and abroad, the familial nature of

Huguenot memory, wrongly perceived as a structural weakness, actually constituted its greatest strength. Families, genealogists, and amateur historians preserved an embellished individual and collective memory while saving it from total oblivion until academics offered it a perennial future by securing it a place in history. In sum, Huguenot identity, in France and in the Refuge, is rooted in the gray area where memory and history overlap.

Notes

Epigraphs are from the following sources: Michael Walzer, *On Toleration*, (New Haven: Yale University Press, 1997), 31; Jean-François de Portal's will quoted in Tessa Murdoch, "The Quiet Conquest. The Huguenots, 1685–1985," *History Today* 35 (May 1985): 30; and Jacques Fontaine, *Memoirs*, ed. Dianne W. Ressinger (Ashford: printed by the Invicta Press for the Huguenot Society of Great Britain and Ireland, 1992), 25. The author wishes to thank Randy Sparks, Bernard Cottret, Diane Margolf, and Lou Roper for their comments.

1. The fifteenth essay, "Uncertain Brotherhood: The Huguenots in the Dutch Republic," contributed by Willem Frijhoff, was not presented at the symposium. In the wake of the Charleston symposium, two international conferences on the Huguenot Refuge were organized in London (2000) and Stellenbosch, South Africa (2001). For the proceedings see respectively Randolph Vigne and Charles Littleton, eds. *From Strangers to Citizens. The Integration of Immigrant Communities in Britain, Ireland, and Colonial America, 1550–1750* (Brighton: Sussex Academic Press, 2001) and *Handlinge van die 3de Internasionale Hugenote-Konferensie/Proceedings of the 3rd International Huguenot Conference* (Frankchhoek: Hugenote-Vereniging van Suid-Afrika, 2002).

2. The Huguenot exodus has not traditionally been called a diaspora or included in diaspora studies. See, for example, Gérard Chaliand and Jean-Pierre Rageau, *The Penguin Atlas of Diasporas*, trans. A. M. Berrett (New York: Penguin Books, 1995, [*Atlas des Diasporas*, Paris, 1991]) and Robin Cohen, *Global Diasporas: An Introduction* (London: UCL Press, 1997). This is most unfortunate because as Philippe Joutard, who first and daringly used the terms Huguenot diaspora in 1979, and Chantal Bordes-Benayoun have shown respectively in their foreword and conclusion to a recent volume edited by Eckart Birnstiel, the Refuge undeniably belongs to the Jewish diasporic paradigm. Eckart Birnstiel, ed., *La diaspora des huguenots. Les réfugiés protestants de France et leur dispersion dans le monde (XVIe–XVIIIe siècles)* (Paris: Honoré Champion, 2001), 11–13, 141–47; Philippe Joutard, "La diaspora des Huguenots," *Le Monde dimanche*, October 28, 1979: xvi; reprinted in *DIASPORAS* 1 (2002), "Terres promises, terres rêvées," documents, 115–21.

3. One noteworthy exception and a sign that the historiography of the Huguenot diaspora may be going into new directions is the above-cited volume of essays *La diaspora des huguenots*, which contains a comparative essay by Birnstiel on the Huguenot settlements in South Africa and British North America.

4. On the mutual interdependence of these notions of memory and identity in the context of national histories, see John R. Gillis, "Memory and Identity: The History of a Relationship," in *Commemorations: The Politics of National Identity*, ed. John R. Gillis (Princeton: Princeton University Press, 1994), 3–24.

5. The terms "American" and "European" are conceptual, not geographical, as they referred to definitions. The "American-type" is "concerned primarily with the problem of assimilation" in a host society, whereas the "'European type' . . . finds itself overtaken by historical development." Anthony C. Hepburn, ed., *Minorities in History* (New York: St. Martin's Press, 1978), 1–2. Needless to say, minority status, which by definition presupposes numerical inferiority, does not necessarily imply a negative *rapport de force* (power struggle) as in the case, for instance, of colonization. See for example, Nicholas Canny, "Dominant Minorities: English Settlers in Ireland and Virginia, 1550–1650," in ibid., 51–67.

6. On the issue of Huguenot ethnicity in the context of American immigration history, see Bertrand Van Ruymbeke, "From Ethnicity to Assimilation: The Huguenots and the American Immigration History Paradigm," in *From Strangers to Citizens*, 332–41.

7. "*Des Français particuliers.*" Elisabeth Labrousse, "*Une foi, une loi, un roi?*" *Essai sur la Révocation de l'Édit de Nantes* (Geneva: Labor et Fides, 1985), 77.

8. Philip Benedict, "*Un roi, une loi, deux fois:* Parameters for the History of Catholic-Reformed Co-Existence in France, 1555–1685," in *Tolerance and Intolerance in the European Reformation*, ed. Ole Peter Grell and Bob Scribner (New York: Cambridge University Press, 1996), 66.

9. Philip Benedict, *The Huguenot Population of France, 1600–1685: The Demographic Fate and Customs of a Religious Minority* (Philadelphia: The American Philosophical Society, 1991), 75. In comparison, the Catholics in England, who numbered about 60,000 in 1660, constituted 1.2 percent of the total population. John Miller, *Popery and Politics in England, 1660–1688* (New York: Cambridge University Press, 1973), 11; John Bossy, *The English Catholic Community, 1570–1850* (London: Darton, Longman, and Todd, 1975), 189.

10. In 1660, 83 percent of the Huguenots lived in the southern provinces, and the ratio of congregations and people between the south and the north was four to one. Benedict, *The Huguenot Population of France*, 10.

11. For an interesting essay that described the Huguenot experience in France from the angle of the minority status with comparisons to English Puritans, see David Parker, "The Huguenots in Seventeenth-Century France," in Hepburn, ed.,

Minorities in History, 10–30. For a broader comparative European perspective see, John Miller, "Les minorités calvinistes," in Miller, ed., *L'Europe protestante aux XVIe et XVIIe siècles* (Paris: Belin, 1997), 258–67.

12. Mack P. Holt, *The French Wars of Religion, 1562–1629* (New York: Cambridge University Press, 1995), 164–65.

13. Incidentally, the Huguenots also constituted a privileged group in the Calvinist sense of the term as they saw themselves as the chosen people. This self-perception, as Elisabeth Labrousse points out, was reinforced by their minority status. "Au temps du Roi soleil," in *Du christianisme flamboyant à l'aube des Lumières, XIVe-XVIIIe siècle*, ed. François Lebrun, vol. 2, *Histoire de la France religieuse*, gen. ed. Jacques Le Goff and René Rémond (Paris: Seuil, 1988–1992), 470.

14. Holt, *The French Wars of Religion*, 186–87.

15. These political assemblies must not be confused with the Huguenot synods which met nationally (on condition of royal approval) until 1659 and regionally until 1685. Ironically, because of their minority status, the Huguenots enjoyed a greater liberty than, for example, the Dutch Calvinists, and were able to call more synods between 1559 and 1659 (twenty-nine) than their Dutch brethren (six). Jonathan N. Gerstner, *The Thousand Generation Covenant: Dutch Reformed Covenant Theology and Group Identity in Colonial South Africa, 1652–1819* (Leiden: E. J. Brill, 1991), 221–22.

16. John Lough, ed., *Locke's Travels in France, 1675–1679*, (1953; reprint, New York: Cambridge University Press, 1984), 28.

17. Gregory Hanlon, *Confession and Community in Seventeenth-Century France: Catholic and Protestant Coexistence in Aquitaine* (Philadelphia: University of Pennsylvania Press, 1993). For a brief nationwide overview see Benedict, "*Une loi, un roi, deux fois*," 65–93.

18. Some of these converts were also known, ironically, as *non-catholiques*.

19. Hanlon, *Confession and Community*, 259.

20. Pierre Bayle, *Ce que c'est que la France toute Catholique* (Saint-Omer: Chez Jean Pierre, 1686).

21. What Elisabeth Labrousse calls *le fiasco de la Révocation*. Labrousse, "*Une foi, une loi, un roi?*," 224.

22. Daniel Ligou, *Le protestantisme en France de 1598 à 1715* (Paris: SEDES, 1968), 256; Geoffrey Adams, *The Huguenots and French Opinion, 1685–1787: The Enlightenment Debate on Toleration* (Waterloo, Ontario: The Wilfrid Laurier University Press, 1991), 38–39.

23. Adams, *The Huguenots and French Opinion*, 39.

24. Daniel Ligou and Philippe Joutard, "Les Déserts," in *Histoire des Protestants en France*, ed. Robert Mandrou et al. (Toulouse: Privat, 1977), 244.

25. Bernard Cottret, *The Huguenots in England: Immigration and Settlement, c. 1550–1700* (Cambridge: Cambridge University Press, 1991), 7–17.

26. Jean-Pierre Poussou, "Mobilité et migrations," in *De la renaissance à 1789*, vol. 2 of *Histoire de la population française*, ed. Jacques Dupâquier et al. (Paris: Presses Universitaires de France, 1995), 130.

27. On the contemporaneous and historiographic misconstruction of the "perpetual and irrevocable" character of the Edict of Nantes, see Mario Turchetti, "Une question mal posée: la qualification de 'perpétuel et irrévocable' appliquée à l'Édit de Nantes (1598)," *Bulletin de la Société de l'Histoire du Protestantisme Français* 139 (1993): 41–78.

28. On the expulsions of the Jews and the Moriscos, see Erna Paris, *The End of Days. A Story of Tolerance, Tyranny, and the Expulsion of the Jews from Spain* (Amherst, N.Y.: Prometheus Books, 1995) and Norman Roth, *Conversos, Inquisition, and the Expulsion of Jews from Spain* (Madison: University of Wisconsin Press, 1995); Antonio Domínguez Ortiz and Bernard Vincent, *Historia de los moriscos. Vida y tragedia de una minoría* (1978; reprint, Madrid: Alianza Editorial, 1997) and Pierre Chaunu, "Minorités et conjoncture. L'expulsion des Moresques en 1609," *Revue Historique* 225 (1961): 81–98.

29. Walloons were French-speaking Calvinists living in the southern Netherlands provinces of Walloon Flanders (Lille), Artois, southern or Walloon Brabant, Hainaut, western Luxemburg, and the Prince-bishopric of Liège. Some or part of these would later be conquered by France but were under Spanish rule at the time of the Walloon migrations. Jonathan I. Israel, *The Dutch Republic. Its Rise, Greatness, and Fall, 1477–1806* (Oxford: Clarendon Press, 1998 [1995]), 36 and 782 (maps); Paul Dibon, "Le Refuge Wallon, précurseur du Refuge huguenot," *Dix-Septième Siècle* 76–77 (1967): 53–74. Bertrand Van Ruymbeke, "The Walloon and Huguenot Elements in New Netherland and Seventeenth-Century New York: Identity, History, and Memory," paper presented at New Netherland at the Millennium: The State of New World Dutch Studies (New York, 2001).

30. Quoted in Robin D. Gwynn, "England's First Refugees," *History Today* 35 (May 1985): 25–26.

31. Joyce D. Goodfriend, "The Last of the Huguenots: John Pintard and the Memory of the Diaspora in the Early American Republic," *Journal of Presbyterian History* 78 (2000): 181–92. Etienne Thomas (1750–1839) is similarly referred to as the last South Carolina Huguenot. Marguerite C. Steedman, *A Short History of the French Protestant (Huguenot) Church of Charleston, South Carolina* (Charleston: The Nelson Printing Corporation, 1983 [1970]), 9.

32. Jon Butler, *The Huguenots in America: A Refugee People in New World Society* (Cambridge: Cambridge University Press, 1983), 212.

33. Ibid., 115.

34. John F. Bosher, "Huguenot Merchants and the Protestant International in the Seventeenth Century," *William and Mary Quarterly* 52 (January 1995): 77–102.

35. Voltaire, *Le Siècle de Louis XIV,* 2 vols. (Paris: Garnier-Flammarion, 1966), 2:101.

36. Bosher, "Huguenot Merchants and the Protestant International," 90–92.

37. Ibid.

38. On Pierre Simond, the elder, see Randolph Vigne, "South Africa's First Published Work of Literature and Its Author, Pierre Simond," *South African Historical Journal* 39 (November 1998): 3–16. For other examples of transatlantic Huguenot familial webs, see Maurice Boucher, "Huguenot Refugees: Some Links Between the Cape, France and England in the Early Eighteenth Century," *Historia* [South Africa] 1 (1975): 55–62.

39. For the period 1680–1710, the breakdown for the Atlantic Refuge is (rough estimates): England (50,000), Ireland (5,000), North America (3,000), the Cape (200), plus about half the number of refugees who settled in the Netherlands (20,000).

40. On the issue of Atlantic Refuge, see Bertrand Van Ruymbeke, "Le refuge atlantique: la diaspora huguenote et l'Atlantique anglo-américain," in *D'un rivage à l'autre. Villes et protestantisme dans l'aire atlantique XVIe-XVIIIe siècles,* ed. Guy Martinière, Didier Poton, and François Souty (Paris: Imprimerie Nationale, 1999), 195–204.

41. Bertrand Van Ruymbeke, "The Huguenots of Proprietary South Carolina: Patterns of Migration and Integration," in *Money, Trade, and Power: The Evolution of South Carolina's Plantation System* ed. Jack P. Greene, Rosemary Brana-Shute, and Randy J. Sparks (Columbia: University of South Carolina Press, 2001), 29–32.

42. Bosher, "Huguenot Merchants and the Protestant International," 82–83.

43. The South African case departs from this trend as most refugees who settled in the Cape were from provinces unconnected to the Atlantic world, such as Provence and Artois. This is likely explained by the fact that in the 1680s South Africa was not yet fully integrated into the Atlantic maritime economy.

44. On the context surrounding the foundation of the S.H.P.F. and its founders' original objectives, see Philippe Joutard, "The Museum of the Desert: The Protestant Minority," in *Conflicts and Divisions,* vol. 1 of *Realms of Memory: Rethinking the French Past.,* gen. ed. Pierre Nora, American ed. Lawrence D. Kritzman, trans. Arthur Goldhammer, 3 vols. (Paris, 1992; reprint, New York: Columbia University Press, 1996), 357–62; on its history see Patrick Harismendy, "'Post Tenebras Lux' ou cent ans de la *Societé de l'Histoire du Protestantisme Français,*" *Revue de l'Eglise de France* 86 (2000): 717–33. See also the Bulletin anniversary issue: 1852–2002. Numéro spécial du cent-cinquantenaire de la S.H.P.F., *Bulletin de la Societé de l'Histoire du Protestantisme Français* 148 (2002).

45. An example is the reenactment organized in 1930 by the Huguenot Society of South Carolina and the Charleston Huguenot church, with the help of the

Dramatic Society of the College of Charleston, to commemorate the 250th anniversary of "the arrival of the first group of Huguenots at Charles Town, Province of Carolina, April, 1680." The short play featured people "of Huguenot descent, though two only . . . were descendants of members of the original group," and college and high school students. A commemorative service was also held at the church. "Pageant of the Richmond," *Huguenot Society of South Carolina Transactions* 35 (1930): 9–17; "Program of the Service at the Huguenot Church, April 13th, 1930," (Charleston, S. C.: The French Protestant Church, 1930). The *Richmond* is, of course, the *Mayflower* of the Carolina Huguenots. For South Carolina Huguenot settlement markers, see *The Huguenot Crosses of South Carolina* (Columbia, S.C.: State Printing Company for the Huguenot Society of South Carolina, 2001).

46. Pierre Nora, "General Introduction: Between Memory and History," in Nora, gen. ed., *Realms of Memory*, 1:7.

47. Rudolf von Thadden, "Du réfugié pour sa foi au patriote prussien," in *Le Refuge huguenot*, ed. von Thadden and Michèle Magdelaine (Paris: Armand Colin, 1985), 219–20; Charles C. Ludington, "Between Myth and Margin: The Huguenots in Irish History," *Bulletin of the Institute of Historical Research* 73 (2000): 4–6. In the case of the Bank of England, Huguenot holdings never exceeded 10 percent, reaching an all-time peak of 9.6 percent in 1697, and out of the twenty-four "Huguenot" directors during the bank's first half-century, thirteen were descendants of Walloon immigrants and only five were of recent French origins. F. M. Crouzet, "Walloons, Huguenots, and the Bank of England," *Huguenot Society of Great Britain and Ireland Proceedings* 25 (1990): 170–74. See also ibid., "The Huguenots and the English Financial Revolution," chap. 1 in *Britain, France and International Commerce. From Louis XIV to Victoria* (Aldershot: Variorum, 1996), 221–66. For a divergent opinion that stresses Huguenot participation in the early years of the bank, see Alice C. Carter, "The Huguenot Contribution to the Early Years of the Funded Debt, 1694–1714," chap. 7 in *Getting, Spending and Investing in Early Modern Times: Essays on Dutch, English and Huguenot Economic History* (Assen: Van Gorcum, 1975), 76–90.

48. Jules Michelet, *De la Révocation de l'Édit de Nantes à la Guerre des Cévennes, 1685–1704* (1860; reprint, Montpellier: Presses du Languedoc, 1985), 87. See also Paul Viallaneix, "Michelet et la légende huguenote," in *The Huguenots and Ireland. Anatomy of an Emigration*, ed. C. E. J. Caldicott, H. Gough, and J. P. Pittion (Dun Laoghaire: Glendale Press, 1987), 399–415.

49. See also, in the case of Ireland, Ludington, "Between Myth and Margin," 1–19. Huguenot heroism also admirably blends in the American collective memory of the Revolution and the settling of the trans-Appalachian frontier in Daniel Trabue's 1827 memoirs. Chester R. Young, ed., *Westward into Kentucky: The Narrative of Daniel Trabue*, (Lexington: University Press of Kentucky, 1981) and

Marco Sioli, "Huguenot Traditions in the Mountains of Kentucky: Daniel Trabue's Memories," *Journal of American History* 84 (March 1998): 1313–33.

50. André Du Toit, "No Chosen People: The Myth of the Calvinist Origins of Afrikaner Nationalism and Racial Ideology," *The American Historical Review* 88, no. 4 (October 1983): 920–21. See also Gilles Teulié, "L'Église réformée hollandaise d'Afrique du Sud: Une histoire du calvinisme afrikaner, 1652–2002" *Etudes Théologiques et Religieuses* 77 (2002): 537–62.

51. Gerstner, *The Thousand Generation Covenant*, 219.

52. Xavier Beguin Billecocq, foreword to *Des voyageurs français au Cap de Bonne Espérance* (French Travelers to the Cape of Good Hope) (Paris: Relations Internationales et Culture, 1996), 9. In the post-apartheid South African context, the name "Good Hope" has acquired a renewed symbolic significance.

53. John M. Murrin, "Religion and Politics in America from the First Settlements to the Civil War," in *Religion and American Politics. From the Colonial Period to the 1980s*, ed. Mark A. Noll (New York: Oxford University Press, 1990), 19.

54. John Burbage, "Huguenots: The Essence of What America Is All About," *News and Courier*, 15 October 1990, sec. B.

55. Michelet, *De la Révocation de l'Édit de Nantes*, 147.

56. Joutard, "The Museum of the Desert," 372. On this point, see also the amazingly high attention the 1998 anniversary of the Edict of Nantes—somewhat unexpectedly—received in France in a most consensual context described by Olivier Christin in "L'Édit de Nantes. Bilan historiographique," *Revue Historique* 301 (1999): 128–35. See also Hubert Bost, "Les 400 ans de l'Édit de Nantes: oubli civique et mémoire historique," in *L'Édit de Nantes revisité. Actes de la journée d'étude de Waldegg (30 octobre 1998)*, ed. Lucienne Hubler, Jean-Daniel Candaux, and Christophe Chalamet (Geneva: Droz, 2000), 55–77. Regarding Michelet's works, Viallaneix even writes of "a republican history of the Revocation" ("Michelet et la légende huguenote," 410).

57. Eric Hobsbawm, "Introduction: Inventing Traditions," in *The Invention of Tradition*, ed. Eric Hobsbawm and Terence Ranger (New York: Cambridge University Press, 1983), 9. On individual and collective constructed memories, see also David Thelen, "Memory and American History," *Journal of American History* 75 (March 1989): 1117–29.

58. Hobsbawm, "Introduction: Inventing Traditions," 11.

59. Ibid., 10.

60. For a similar illustration of ethnic and genealogical exclusivity and ancestor glorification, see the case of the New York Holland Society, founded in 1886, in Willem Frijhoff, "Reinventing an Old Fatherland: The Management of Dutch Identity in Early Modern America," in *Managing Ethnicity. Perspectives from Folklore Studies, History, and Anthropology*, ed. Regina Bendix and Herman Roodenburg (Amsterdam: Het Spinhuis, 2000), 121–41.

61. The case of the famed backcountry-born South Carolina Unionist, James Louis Petigru, who "Huguenotted" his name from Petigrew to Petigru in honor of his maternal grandfather, Jean-Louis Gibert, and in "rejection of the Scots-Irish frontier culture of his father for the education and relative security of his mother's family" provides a compelling illustration of the social prestige associated with a Huguenot lineage in South Carolina. William H. Pease and Jane H. Pease, *James Louis Petigru: Southern Conservative, Southern Dissenter* (Athens: University of Georgia Press, 1995), 14–18.

62. In a footnote to his memoirs, fifth-generation South Carolina Huguenot Paul Trapier typically explained that his great-great-grandfather's wife had escaped France "concealed in a hogshead marked 'Poterie,' & then conveyed on board the vessel in which she reached America." Slann L. Simmons, ed., "Notices of Ancestors and Relatives, Paternal and Maternal by the Reverend Paul Trapier," *Huguenot Society of South Carolina Transactions* 58 (1953): 30.

63. Ann U. Abrams, *The Pilgrims and Pocahontas: Rival Myths of American Origin* (Boulder, Colo.: Westview Press, 1999), 12.

64. Du Toit, "No Chosen People," 920, 925 (quote).

ONE

Identity, Law, and the Huguenots of Early Modern France

Diane C. Margolf

In his book *The Huguenots in America*, Jon Butler explores the rapid assimilation of French Calvinist immigrants to North American colonies in the later seventeenth and eighteenth centuries. He argues that the Huguenots' ability to adapt to their new social and cultural surroundings resulted in "their swift disappearance as a cohesive refugee group."[1] Moreover, this phenomenon was directly tied to the Huguenots' history in seventeenth-century France, prior to their immigration:

> The earlier Huguenots' experience rang with antagonisms, insecurities, and internal tensions only poorly constrained within the social interstices of the Ancien Régime. . . . Nowhere did the Huguenots escape the burdens of their past.[2]

Butler cites several features of seventeenth-century French Calvinism which account for the Huguenots' lack of cohesion as refugees: the restriction of ecclesiastical governance to the local and provincial level, which made the Huguenots ill equipped to establish and govern a unified church overseas; the dominance of Huguenot ministers in church affairs, which left the laity unprepared for such leadership in exile; and the Huguenots' habit of bowing to government authority, even when such submission compromised the collective safety of their community in France.[3] According to this analysis, then, the Huguenots' fragmented history helps to explain their inability to retain a distinctive social or religious identity, both in Europe and the New World.

Historians of religion and society in early modern France have long been preoccupied with the study of those "antagonisms, insecurities, and internal tensions" which beset the Huguenots during the seventeenth century. The Huguenots' decline has been analyzed in demographic terms, using parish and census records spanning the period 1600–1685.[4] Commemorating the three-hundredth anniversary of the Edict of Nantes' revocation inspired studies of that event and of the Huguenots' experiences both before and after 1685.[5] More recently, scholars have emphasized studying the Huguenots in relation to their Catholic contemporaries of both the sixteenth and seventeenth centuries, examining confessional relations in terms of coexistence as well as conflict.[6] Such studies have approached the issues which Butler raises—cohesion, assimilation, identity—from a different perspective. Instead of examining the Huguenots' ability to disappear completely into a new social, religious, and cultural setting, they have focused on the Huguenots' survival as a Calvinist minority in Catholic France. Rather than probing the weaknesses of Huguenot collective identity, they have implicitly or explicitly asked how the Huguenots maintained any sense of identity or community at all in the face of persecution by secular and religious authorities. Yet Butler himself has suggested one factor which bridges all of these approaches to the Huguenots' history: in ancien régime France, he states, "the law may have stimulated a cohesion that was not inherent in the community."[7]

Whether one is tracing the Huguenots' survival in France or their assimilation overseas, law clearly plays an important role in the story. We have perhaps come to take for granted how much law has shaped the trajectory of the Huguenots' history. The Wars of Religion which engulfed France during the second half of the sixteenth century were interrupted periodically by peace treaties among the Catholic and Huguenot factions and the French Crown. Many of these agreements gave the Huguenots varying degrees of legal permission to exercise their religion publicly. The last and most famous of these peace treaties, the Edict of Nantes, marked the end of military hostilities and promised a regime of peaceful coexistence for the future. A strict legal interpretation of the Edict of Nantes, however, also helped to undermine the Huguenots' position in France throughout the seventeenth century. In the 1660s, a series of royal decrees imposed significant limitations on the Huguenots' participation in French society by forbidding them access to offices and professions, restricting their public worship and assemblies, and threatening their ability to control the religious education of their children. Louis XIV's revocation of the Edict of Nantes in 1685 spurred many Huguenots to seek refuge elsewhere in Europe, in Africa, and in the Americas, providing another benchmark in the Huguenots' history—the diaspora which is the subject of this book. Laws issued by French monarchs during the late sixteenth and seventeenth centuries thus played a double role in the Huguenots' history, sometimes preserving the religious minority through royal protection and at other times providing a weapon to be used against the group. In either case, law essentially helped to define the Huguenots' changing position within French society and the state.

Connections among law, history, and identity form the principal theme of this essay. How did law shape the Huguenots' sense of themselves, their past, and their future in France during the seventeenth century? To what extent did law support or undermine the Huguenots' cohesion as a social and religious group through royal edicts and judicial decisions? What part did law and litigation play in the Huguenots' struggle to balance allegiance to their religious faith and community with obedience to the central government, as embodied in the French monarchy? I propose to offer some answers to these questions by focusing on one specific arena where these struggles took place: the Paris Chambre de l'Édit, or "chamber of the edict," a special law court mandated by the Edict of Nantes to hear lawsuits between Huguenots and Catholics. Though attached to the *parlement* of Paris and staffed predominantly by Catholic magistrates, the Chambre de l'Édit attracted complaints of all kinds involving Huguenots throughout the seventeenth century. The records (*minutes d'arrêt*) of criminal lawsuits adjudicated by the court reveal the Huguenots' efforts to assert and defend themselves according to the law, often with specific reference to the Edict of Nantes. Such lawsuits also show the Huguenots airing grievances and protesting unfairness even as they submitted to the authority of royal justice. Most of all, the court's records demonstrate the battle over political and religious identity which raged throughout early modern France for Huguenots and Catholics alike.

The touchstone of Huguenot appeals for protection throughout the seventeenth century, as well as their protests against mistreatment, was the Edict of Nantes, issued by Henry IV in April 1598. In fact, the Edict of Nantes was not one document but four. The general edict of pacification outlined the terms under which the Huguenot minority would coexist with French Catholics; two *brevets* dealt with financial compensation and military protection for the Huguenots, and a set of secret articles further specified and modified some of the general edict's provisions. Unlike the other documents, however, the general edict was ultimately ratified by France's *parlements* and therefore represented more than a decree based on royal authority alone.[8] Its preamble declared Henry IV's intention of providing his Catholic and Huguenot subjects with "a general, clear and absolute law, by which they may be governed regarding all disputes which have occurred between them in the past [concerning religion], and which may yet occur."[9] Far from being "general, clear and absolute," the edict immediately and continually fostered disorders of its own, as lawyers, litigants, magistrates, and other officials debated the interpretation and implementation of the law's provisions.

The Edict of Nantes clearly did not represent a broad declaration of religious toleration or freedom of conscience. Instead, the edict extended specific privileges to Huguenots regarding their ability to hold public religious services, to bury their dead, to gain access to civic posts and professions, and even to print books concerning *la religion prétendue réformée* ("the so-called reformed religion")—the legal designation for French Calvinism.[10] The edict upheld the Huguenots' ecclesiastical organization of consistories, colloquies, and synods, but the secret articles restricted such assemblies to places where public Calvinist worship was legally sanctioned by the general edict. National synods could only occur with the king's approval.[11] The Huguenots' political organization, composed of local and provincial assemblies and councils, was dissolved by the edict's provisions.[12] Moreover, the same edict which extended privileges to the Huguenots also restored Catholicism as the official religion of France. Huguenots had to acknowledge the Catholic Church's calendar of religious holidays and the authority of canon law in matters of marriage and consanguinity, as well as pay church taxes.[13] While the Edict of Nantes transformed the Huguenots from a heretical sect into a legally sanctioned religious minority, it did so through specific privileges rather than broad legal principles. These privileges themselves constituted real limitations on the Huguenots' activities and status in France, and they would become a fertile source of legal dispute.

Another source of debate (among both contemporaries and later historians) concerned the intentions behind the edict which gave it meaning beyond its particular provisions. The Huguenots tended to regard the

Edict of Nantes as a kind of contract between themselves and their ruler—a guarantee of protection and favor in return for loyalty and good behavior. The text of article 6 seemed to suggest such a *quid pro quo:*

> We [Henry IV] have permitted and permit those of the so-called reformed religion to live and dwell in all the towns and areas of our kingdom and lands under our authority, without being investigated, vexed, molested or forced to do anything against their consciences concerning religion, nor for this to be sought out in their homes and residences, comporting themselves for the rest according to the contents of this our present edict.[14]

Huguenots also regarded the Edict of Nantes as a permanent agreement, an inviolable promise which Henry IV and his successors were obligated to maintain through the force of royal authority.[15] After all, the preamble stated, "for our part, we promise to have it observed to the letter, without allowing it to be in any way contravened."[16] Scholarly analysis has demonstrated that this document was the product of lengthy negotiations and that it was rooted in peace treaties of the past, yet the text itself reads like an act of royal fiat.[17] The edict's language emphasizes obedience, rather than reciprocity:

> We implore and await God's divine goodness . . . that His grace will make our subjects understand well that in the observation of this our ordinance lies (after their duty toward God and toward all) the principal foundation of their union, concord, tranquility and repose, and of the entire state's return to its first splendor, opulence and strength.[18]

Read in this light, the entire edict's underlying aim was to restore peace, order and strength to France under the aegis of royal authority. The success of such a policy depended upon Catholics and Huguenots alike obeying the king's law.

Consolidating the French Crown's judicial authority formed an important part of Henry IV's effort to strengthen his kingdom after decades of civil war and to maintain peace among his divided subjects. Not surprisingly, over one-third of the Edict of Nantes' articles dealt with the organization and fair administration of justice in France. During the Wars of Religion, Huguenots complained that the *parlements*—the highest royal law courts in the French judicial hierarchy—were composed of predominantly Catholic magistrates and were therefore inherently hostile to Huguenot litigants. Huguenots demanded special tribunals (or at least the inclusion of Huguenot judges in royal law courts) in order to assure a fair hearing of their legal disputes, along with the share of political power and social status which accompanied judicial office. Such arrangements had a complex and troubled history during the later sixteenth century; in 1598, the Edict of Nantes provided a new legal foundation for the Huguenots' access to royal justice. The edict established three bipartisan law courts affiliated with the *parlements* of Toulouse, Bordeaux, and Grenoble. These were known as *chambres mi-parties* because they comprised equal numbers of Huguenot and Catholic judges. A fourth court— the Paris Chambre de l'Édit—received only one of the four Huguenot magistrates who were supposed to hold offices in the Paris parlement. The chamber's president and remaining fifteen councilors would be drawn from the ranks of the parlement's Catholic judges.[19]

The Edict of Nantes defined these special law courts, including the Paris Chambre de l'Édit, as both part of and yet separate from the parlements, not only in terms of their composition but also their jurisdiction. The Chambre de l'Édit's geographical reach matched that of the Paris parlement itself, covering Picardy, Champagne, Touraine, Poitou, Anjou, and Saintonge as well as Île-de-France and the areas immediately surrounding Paris; it also temporarily included Normandy and Brittany. The Paris chamber was further authorized to hear legal disputes for which the provincial *chambres mi-parties* had rendered split decisions.[20] As sovereign courts of appeal, the Paris Chambre de l'Édit and its provincial counterparts could adjudicate virtually all civil and criminal lawsuits in which one or both parties were Huguenots, including cases which dealt with infractions of the Edict of Nantes itself. In establishing these tribunals, the Edict of Nantes thus created a concrete judicial institution with the authority to resolve disputes that might arise about the Huguenots' status or activities. Appealing for justice from these chambers constituted yet another privilege which the law accorded to the Huguenots.

The Paris Chambre de l'Édit and the *chambres mi-parties*, however, also highlighted the ambiguous legacy which the Edict of Nantes imparted to the Huguenots. On the one hand, the Huguenots' legal privileges —including access to royal justice through these tribunals—promoted a kind of cohesion by designating the Huguenots as a group specially protected by royal authority. Yet the Huguenots were dependent upon the French Crown to maintain their safe but limited legal status; exercising their privileges under the law reinforced this dependency. The special law courts created for the Huguenots' use were embedded within a judicial system which the Huguenots still tended to view as prejudiced against them. As the Paris Chambre de l'Édit's records of criminal lawsuits illustrate, enforcing the Edict of Nantes was no easy task. The law itself contained contradictions and paradoxes, and the whole process of litigation presented opportunities for delays, diversions, and deceits, as well as the quest for justice, order, and truth. Litigants and lawyers presented information before the court in an effort to fit their claims to the law's requirements and to win a favorable verdict from the magistrates. Let us turn to an example of this complex process: lawsuits concerning the remembrance of things past and the Huguenots' recent history.

One of the Edict of Nantes' most provocative elements was its attempt to regulate past as well as future relations among members of the two religious confessions. In seeking to redress injustices committed against Huguenots by French law courts during the Wars of Religion, the edict overturned previous judicial verdicts, actions and resolutions. For example, article 89 restored Huguenot nobles and their followers to their rightful titles, property, and privileges. All sentences, proceedings, and seizures decreed against Huguenots, including those who had fled the kingdom since Henry II's death in 1559, were revoked. Huguenots and Catholics alike were declared exempt from legal prosecution for military captures and nearly all war-related activities.[21] Most of all, the edict's opening article declared that in the name of peace for the future, the wartime past was to be forgotten:

> The memory of everything which occurred on one side or the other since the beginning of March 1585 until our accession to the throne and during the other preceding troubles, and because of them, will remain extinguished and suppressed, as things which did not happen.[22]

Despite the sweeping language of this statement, certain acts remained open to prosecution: rape, violations of safeguards and passports, unbounded violence and pillage, and any destruction which had been committed for personal vengeance or profit, rather than as part of the general military hostilities.[23] The Edict of Nantes thus established a legal distinction between acts of war and crimes committed during wartime. This not only prevented the past from being forgotten but actually encouraged its remembrance through litigation.

Lawsuits concerning incidents which had occurred during the Wars of Religion represented a total of only fifty-seven cases brought before the Paris Chambre de l'Édit during the period 1600–1610. The number of such cases clearly declined over the course of the decade: the court heard fourteen lawsuits of this sort in 1600, but the number dropped to three in 1609, and none at all appear in the records for 1610. In twenty-five out of the fifty-seven lawsuits, the court effectively dismissed the charges by declaring the matter "abolished," "extinguished," or "covered" by the royal edicts of pacification. Sixteen cases were remanded to other jurisdictions or were unresolved, while in the remaining cases the court acquitted or convicted one of the litigants. When disputing about past events and *oubliance* (forgetting), plaintiffs, defendants, and their lawyers described such events as either exploits of war or deeds of personal hatred and revenge. Each party sought to turn the edict's provisions to its advantage. In presenting their competing histories before the court, litigants challenged each other's versions of the past, as well as each other's obedience to the law of *oubliance* in the present.

Individual cases clearly reveal the opposing parties' efforts to depict each other as present-day criminals in their pursuit of judicial redress for past wrongs. François Delahaye and Gilles Chaudet petitioned the Chambre de l'Édit in September 1600 for restitution of the ransom and goods which Jacques de La Ferrière had seized from them nine years earlier while he was commanding a garrison in Anjou for Henry IV. Claiming that they were innocent civilians at the time, Delahaye and Chaudet argued that La Ferrière's conduct was not covered by the policy of *oubliance*, which excused such incidents as acts of war. La Ferrière's lawyer, of course, argued just the opposite:

> During the troubles . . . he only did what was permitted by the ordinary usage and practice in military discipline for protecting Vezins, an important stronghold for the king, against those who made war on him and held an allegiance contrary to his service.[24]

The chamber magistrates accepted La Ferrière's legal claim to be exempt from punishment and dismissed the appeal against him.

Less than a year later, however, La Ferrière found himself before the court in a similar dispute with another set of accusers from his wartime past: Hillaire Ogeron, Jacques Demazières, and Renée Letheulle, widow of Claude Ogeron. They accused him of having attacked them one night in the spring of 1594, pillaging their homes and then transporting them to the Vezins garrison, where they were held for ransom. They emphasized the unfairness of this act, "given their status, not making war and paying the king's taxes, and all the same constrained by force and violence against their persons to pay ransom."[25] They had obtained La Ferrière's conviction for this crime from the seneschal of Anjou in August 1599, but La Ferrière appealed to the Chambre de l'Édit for a reversal of that sentence. He reiterated his earlier arguments about service to the king in wartime and the law's prohibition of such complaints against former soldiers. He also noted that in 1594 one of his accusers had had two sons in the service of a local member of the Catholic League, thus associating his accusers with his wartime enemies and challenging their claims to have been only peaceful taxpayers. Once again, the Chambre de l'Édit dismissed the case without costs.[26] For the magistrates, La Ferrière's portrayal of himself as a loyal soldier fighting the king's enemies and their civilian supporters apparently won out over his accusers' claims to have been victims of the commander's personal rapacity.

In attempting to enforce the Edict of Nantes' complex requirements about remembrance and *oubliance*, the chamber magistrates frequently dealt with the relatives or descendants of those who had actually committed the crimes—or their victims. In such cases, family members often sought restitution of property, revision of earlier judicial verdicts, and restoration of the individual's and the family's good name and reputation, regardless of how much time had passed since the original incident. In 1606, widow Margueritte Poussard, dame Du Breuil Goullard, and her son successfully appealed a judicial sentence delivered against her husband in December 1584 *par contumace* (that is, in his absence), along with the seizure of their goods. The Chambre de l'Édit annulled the sentence and condemned Poussard's opponents—the children and heirs of François de La Tousche, sieur de Montagues—to repay any monies received as a result of the earlier verdict, along with costs and damages.[27] In 1602, six men from three different families sued René Hervé, sieur de Ruffé, and his accomplices for robbery and murder committed in 1576. The three victims—Henri Cavelier, Clement Lefebvre, and Pierre de Couldraye—had been merchants from Rouen whose sons and heirs now sought justice before the Paris Chambre de l'Édit. The six plaintiffs claimed that it had been impossible for them to pursue their fathers' killers twenty-six years earlier because "they had been minors and under aged, lacking resources and under the authority of guardians who neglected them."[28] Now that they could act on their own behalf, the merchants' sons declared that they were ready to summon the widows and heirs of their fathers' murderers to answer for the deed, if the guilty men themselves were no longer living. After two years of litigation, the Chambre de l'Édit rejected the case and declared the matter closed.[29] In each case, lawsuits about the past involved the Huguenots' posterity, literally represented by the widows and children of those whose actions had caused the legal dispute.

Attempting to settle the conflicting claims of remembrance and *oubliance* sometimes meant destroying physical evidence of past injustices, something which the Edict of Nantes had also mandated. Article 58 called for judicial sentences, confiscations, and decrees against Huguenots to be removed from the records of sovereign and inferior courts, and for "all marks, vestiges and monuments of the said executions . . . against their persons, memory and posterity" to be removed and effaced.[30] The Chambre de l'Édit's records show that litigants were willing to invoke this element of *oubliance*. Benjamin Girault, sieur de La Mothe Charente, and his sister Anne petitioned the court in 1602 to have all judicial proceedings and sentences against their late father, Thomas Girault, expunged from all court records. They based their request on "the edicts accorded to those of the so-called reformed religion, which the suppliants' father professed" and on letters patent from Henry IV himself which supported their claims.[31] The king's letter explained that Thomas Girault had been executed and his property confiscated after he had attacked Angoulême on Henry's behalf; when Henry reconciled with his cousin King Henry III in 1589, Girault was among those whose "memory" was restored—an arrangement which the Edict of Nantes reinforced. As a result, Girault's heirs "could not be marked by any stain of dishonor" and could inherit his property, which had been appropriated by the canons of the Church of Saint André in Angoulême.[32] The children of Pierre Denyau, sieur de La Seicherie, protested the presence of an effigy of their father which had been hung on a gibbet in the town of Ollonne in Poitou. The Chambre de l'Édit had already dismissed the case brought against him, which had involved accusations of excessive violence committed against a monastery in 1568. The effigy, however, represented a concrete reminder of the criminal allegations which were supposed to be forgotten. In response to the Denyau family's appeal, the court ordered the effigy to be quietly removed.[33]

A final example from the *minutes d'arrêt* for January 1601 illustrates the court's policy on *oubliance* and restoring family property and reputation. The family of a man named Jullart claimed that he had been unjustly seized and executed in 1592. In appealing to the Chambre de l'Édit, the defendants cited "the edicts of pacification of the troubles which have covered, extinguished and abolished all that happened during the said troubles."[34] Although the chamber magistrates agreed with this interpretation of *oubliance*, they invoked other elements of the law to protect Jullart's reputation and relatives:

> [The court] forbids all persons to reproach the appellants and their posterity, and orders that the said sentence [against Jullart] will be struck from the registers at Rochefort and the fines adjudged by that court, if any have been paid, will be given to the appellants.[35]

The Chambre de l'Édit thus interpreted the edict's mandate to forget the wartime past selectively, responding to royal letters of pardon as well as family appeals for justice. Moreover, the court sometimes ordered reminders of that past, in the form of legal records and effigies, to be literally obliterated in the interests of keeping peace in the present.

These cases adjudicated by the Paris Chambre de l'Édit reveal a complex relationship between remembrance and *oubliance* which stemmed from the ambiguity of those concepts in the law itself. The Edict of Nantes required that Huguenots and Catholics forget their recent history of conflict and violence, but it also included exceptions to this rule. By overturning legal actions taken against Huguenots during the Wars of Religion, the edict effectively reopened such cases and made it possible for litigants to pursue a different outcome for past legal disputes—in a sense, to revise history. Such efforts to correct or change the historical record, however, would have to be done in a public judicial forum and not through private, violent means of redress. The Edict of Nantes had strictly forbidden all of the king's subjects "to dispute, contest, quarrel, insult, or offend each other by deed or word; but to contain themselves and live peaceably together as brothers, friends and fellow citizens."[36] Most of all, lawsuits about wartime events could not be allowed to jeopardize the immediate task of restoring peace among the king's Catholic and Huguenot subjects. Although litigants sometimes succeeded in revising history through judicial appeal, the chamber magistrates usually acted to relegate wartime disputes to the past.[37]

The Edict of Nantes remained a key element in the Huguenots' definition of themselves and in others' views of them throughout the seventeenth century. While lawsuits concerning the Wars of Religion, memory and *oubliance* quickly faded from the Paris Chambre de l'Édit's records after 1610, Huguenots continued to appeal to the court for justice on a variety of other matters: clandestine marriages, disputed inheritances, thefts, insults, physical violence, forgery, murder, and reports of misconduct by local judicial officials. Huguenots thus exercised their privilege of judicial appeal before the Chambre de l'Édit even as the monarchy and the central government became increasingly suspicious of this privilege. In the Code Michaud, a royal ordinance issued in 1629 to reform French legal procedures, Huguenots were accused of becoming parties in lawsuits in which they had no real interest. Their true motive was to direct litigation to their special law courts and away from more appropriate tribunals, a practice which caused "great disorder in justice."[38] The Code Michaud also cited instances of Catholics pretending to be Huguenots to pursue their litigation in the Huguenots' law courts, a further abuse of legal privilege. All judges were ordered to insist upon formal written attestations of religious affiliation from Huguenots, as well as notarized statements from Catholic converts to the Reformed faith.[39] The Code Michaud thus depicted the Huguenots, their law courts and their legal privileges as a source of disorder in the judicial system and a threat to justice within the realm. Such accusations were frequently echoed by the French Catholic clergy and members of the laity who saw the Huguenots as an affront to Counter-Reformation Catholicism, unworthy of either legal or royal protection.[40]

The Huguenots themselves, of course, viewed the situation quite differently. When deliberating in national synods or presenting *cahiers* of grievances to the Crown, Huguenot leaders expressed concern about the vulnerability of their special law courts, not their strength or their disruptiveness. Huguenots complained that Catholic judicial officers, ranging from local court clerks to parlement magistrates, interfered with the work of the *chambres mi-parties* and the Paris Chambre de l'Édit.[41] They struggled to establish a boundary between the jurisdiction of the local consistory, whose members were responsible for maintaining concord and discipline within Reformed communities, and that of the king's law courts. Though they tenaciously defended their legal privileges and their special law courts, Huguenot leaders also expressed ambivalence about taking their disputes to court at all. In 1644, the synod of Charenton recommended that Huguenots resolve their conflicts within their own ranks:

> They of the religion, which have processes and differences as well
> civill as criminall, shall be seriously exhorted by the Pastours to
> indeavour an accord between themselves by the arbitrement of them
> which are of the Religion without going to law.[42]

By the middle of the seventeenth century, the Huguenots had discovered that legal proceedings and royal decrees—even the Edict of Nantes itself—did not necessarily guarantee the safety and stability of their communities. To the extent that the Huguenots' collective identity and protected status were based upon law and royal favor, their position became increasingly precarious during the seventeenth century.[43]

Ironically, this did not stop them from "going to law," and the Chambre de l'Édit's records reveal the Huguenots' continued reliance on royal justice for redress of their grievances. Indeed, Huguenot litigants defined themselves as loyal, law-abiding subjects despite the problems associated with their legal privileges. As an illustration of this pattern, consider the petition which four Huguenots presented to the court in May 1645. They complained of threats and abusive treatment by their overlord, the seigneur of Houday Sainte Croix, which were intended to drive them from the seigneury and which stemmed from hostility toward their religion. The seigneur had assaulted one plaintiff, Nicollas Barbichon, in public on the day after Easter, telling Barbichon that "he had the plague and wanted to haunt respectable people; he forbade [Barbichon] to appear in public in the future and ordered him to stay closed up in his house."[44] Another plaintiff, Viban Desbordes, described how the local priest had summoned him to his home at dusk one day. Though their discussion of religion began on civil terms, it ended with the priest throwing Desbordes to the ground and whipping him. Moreover, the plaintiffs accused the priest of pressuring the seigneury's Catholic inhabitants to take oaths and sign agreements promising "that they would not associate with the suppliants in the future for any reason whatsoever." Barbichon, Desbordes, and the others protested that all of these actions violated "the edicts of pacification" and unfairly oppressed them as "subjects of the King."[45] Attacked physically, verbally, and legally by local authorities, described as carriers of an infectious disease because of their religion, and ordered to isolate themselves from the rest of the community, the four men invoked the law and their status as royal subjects to assert that they indeed belonged in Houday Sainte Croix. As in earlier cases concerning memory and *oubliance*, these Huguenots claimed that the law entitled them to royal protection and made them part of French society, despite religious difference.

Other petitions presented before the Paris Chambre de l'Édit invoked the court's and the king's protection, although less explicitly than the Huguenots of Houday Sainte Croix. Simon Leclerc, a Parisian ribbon maker, and his wife protested the abduction of their daughter Marguerite in May 1654. They accused a neighbor of seizing the girl in an effort to convert her to Catholicism, though she "had never indicated by word or otherwise or thought of changing [her] religion."[46] The court granted the parents' request to pursue the matter further with the *procureur général du roi*—the royal prosecutor who acted as the king's legal representative in the parlement. In September 1660, a widow named Sara Buffier complained that the two men who had killed her husband had been "wrested from the hands of justice with open force" and had managed to obtain promise of a royal pardon within the year.[47] Witnesses had been frightened into silence regarding the crime, and the two men were free to roam the country and insult Buffier at every opportunity. This was unjust, she argued, "and against the King's intention and the court's orders."[48] The chamber magistrates responded by ordering the two men brought to the Conciergerie, the Paris parlement's prison. Like Buffier and Leclerc, many Huguenot litigants who encountered hostility, abuse, or miscarriages of justice claimed the king's and the court's protection under the law.

This discussion of the Huguenots and their litigation before the Paris Chambre de l'Édit seems to confirm the notion that law helped to develop a sense of cohesion among the Huguenots of early modern France. Yet this cohesion proved to be fragile at best because of ambiguities in the laws themselves and in the process of living under them. After the Wars of Religion, the Huguenots' legal privileges and identity were inscribed in the Edict of Nantes, a law which was intended to cloak the past in *oubliance* and to provide a measure of legal protection for the Reformed minority in the future. With the historian's gift of hindsight, however, we know how little protection awaited the Huguenots: the promises and privileges of 1598 would be followed by the fitful rebellions of the 1620s, the vicissitudes of royal and ministerial favor in the 1640s, and the increasingly rigorous repression of the 1660s. While these events were certainly shaped by considerations of domestic policy, foreign relations, public sentiment, and royal will, the law served as a potent shield for the Huguenots—and a powerful weapon which was used against them even during the reign of Henry IV. Interpreting the law, especially the Edict of Nantes, became a new battleground for the Huguenots, Catholics, and the French Crown, and many such battles were fought before the magistrates of the Paris Chambre de l'Édit.

Throughout the seventeenth century, the Huguenots' assertion of collective identity remained entangled with the issue of their obedience to the French Crown. Whenever they invoked the Edict of Nantes and appealed to the Chambre de l'Édit for justice, they also submitted to the authority of the state and especially of the monarchy, on which enforcement of the law and their legal privileges depended. The Huguenots implicitly and continually acknowledged the magistrates' and the king's authority over them, yet their own churches, consistories, and communities also claimed a share of their allegiance. If law helped to promote cohesiveness among the Huguenots, it also exacerbated fundamental tensions surrounding their place and identity within Catholic France. To the French government, the French clergy, and many ordinary French men and women, the Huguenots' adherence to their faith and to each other clearly conflicted with their claims to be obedient, trustworthy subjects who were fully integrated into French society and the state. In short, they were anything but the "brothers, friends and fellow citizens" which the Edict of Nantes had declared them to be. Caught between the community of Calvinist religious confession and an emerging French national consciousness, the Huguenots ended the seventeenth century as *nouveaux convertis* in France, as *émigrés* to more hospitable countries in Europe, or —as Jon Butler has shown—as immigrants to the New World, in search of new identities and communities.[49]

Notes

1. Jon Butler, *The Huguenots in America: A Refugee People in New World Society* (Cambridge: Cambridge University Press, 1983), 7.

2. Ibid., 8.

3. Ibid., 212–14.

4. Philip Benedict, *The Huguenot Population of France, 1600–1685: The Demographic Fate and Customs of a Religious Minority*, Transactions of the American Philosophical Society 81 (Philadelphia: American Philosophical Society, 1991), 5.

5. Elisabeth Labrousse, *"Une Foi, une loi, un roi?" Essai sur la la Révocation de l'Édit de Nantes* (Geneva: Labor et Fides, 1985); Janine Garrisson, *L'Édit de Nantes et sa révocation: Histoire d'une intolérance* (Paris: Seuil, 1985); Roger Zuber and Laurent Theis, ed., *La Révocation de l'Édit de Nantes et le protestantisme en 1685: Actes du colloque de Paris, 15–19 Octobre 1985* (Paris: Société de l'Histoire du Protestantisme Français, 1986).

6. Gregory Hanlon, *Confession and Community in Seventeenth-Century France: Catholic and Protestant Coexistence in Aquitaine* (Philadelphia: University of Pennsylvania Press, 1993); Barbara Diefendorf, *Beneath the Cross: Catholics and Huguenots in Sixteenth-Century Paris* (Oxford: Oxford University Press, 1991); Raymond A. Mentzer Jr., *Blood and Belief: Family Survival and Confessional Identity Among the Provincial Huguenot Nobility* (West Lafayette, Ind.: Purdue University Press, 1994).

7. Butler, *The Huguenots in America*, 25.

8. For a summary analysis of the Edict of Nantes' provisions, see Daniel Ligou, *Le Protestantisme en France de 1598 à 1715* (Paris: S.E.D.E.S., 1968), 23–25 and Mack P. Holt, *The French Wars of Religion, 1562–1629* (Cambridge: Cambridge University Press, 1995), 162–72.

9. Quoted from the text of the Edict of Nantes as reprinted in Roland Mousnier, *L'Assassinat d'Henri IV* (Paris: Gallimard, 1964), 296: "une loy générale, claire, nette et absolue, par laquelle ils soient réglez sur tous les différens qui sont cy-devant sur ce survenus entr'eux, et y pourront encore survenir cy-après." All translations are mine unless otherwise noted; original spelling has been retained but some punctuation and accents have been added for clarity.

10. Mousnier, 298–99 (articles 7–11) and 300–301 (articles 13–14, 21).

11. Ibid., 325 (article 34).

12. Ibid., 317 (article 82) and 314–15 (article 76).

13. Ibid., 297 (article 3) and 301 (articles 20 and 24).

14. Ibid., 298 (article 6): "[nous] avons permis et permettons à ceux de ladite religion prétendue réformée vivre et demeurer par toutes les villes et lieux, de celluy nôtre royaume et pais de nôtre obéissance, sans être enquis, vexez, molestez, ni astraints à faire chose pour le fait de la religion contre leur conscience, ne pour raison d'icelle être recherchez és maisons et lieux où ils voudront habiter, en se comportant au rest selon qu'il est contenu en nôtre present edit."

15. See Mario Turchetti, "Une question mal posée: La qualification de 'perpétuel et irrévocable' appliquée à l'Édit de Nantes (1598)," *Bulletin de la Société de l'Histoire du Protestantisme Français* 139, no. 1 (1993): 41–78.

16. Mousnier, 296 (preamble): "de nôtre part, nous promettons de la faire exactement observer, sans souffrir qu'il y soit aucunement contrevenu."

17. See N. M. Sutherland, *The Huguenot Struggle for Recognition* (New Haven: Yale University Press, 1980).

18. Mousnier, 296 (preamble): "Nous implorons et attendons de sa divine bonté . . . qu'elle face [fasse] la grace à nosdits sujets de bien comprendre, qu'en l'observation de cette nôtre ordonnance consiste (après ce qui est de leur devoir envers Dieu et envers tous) le principal fondement de leur union, concorde, tranquilité et repos, et du rétablissement de tout cet Etat en sa première splendeur, opulence et force."

19. Ibid., 302–3 (article 30).

20. Ibid., 306–7 (article 47).

21. Ibid., 309–10 (articles 58–60) and 317–19 (articles 83–89).

22. Ibid., 296 (article 1): "La mémoire de toutes choses passées d'une part et d'autre, depuis le commencement du mois de mars 1585 jusques à nôtre avènement à la couronne, et durant les aultres troubles précédens, et à l'occasion d'iceux, demeurera éteinte et assoupie, comme de chose non advenue."

23. Ibid., 318 (article 86).

24. Archives Nationales (hereafter AN) X2b 196 (6 September 1600): "Durant les troubles . . . il n'aye faict que ce que luy a esté permis par l'usage et pratique ordinaire en discipline militaire pour la conservation de la place de Vesins important au service du Roy contre tous ceux qui luy faisoient la guerre et prestoient faveur contraire à son service."

25. AN X2b 201 (20 June 1601): "attendu leur qualités, ne faisans la guerre et paiant les tailles au Roy et touttefois par force et viollances exercées sur leurs personnes auroient esté contraincts à paier Rançon."

26. AN X2b 201 (20 June 1601).

27. AN X2b 231 (5 May 1606).

28. AN X2b 210 (7 December 1602): "ils ont tousjours esté mineurs et en bas âge, desimé de moyens et soubs la puissance de tuteurs qui les ont négligés."

29. AN X2b 217 (11 February 1604).

30. Mousnier, 309 (article 58): "nous voulons aussi être ôtées et effacées toutes marques, vestiges et monumens desdites executions . . . contre leurs personnes, mémoire, et posterité." The beginning of the article refers to legal actions taken "contre ceux de la religion prétendue réformée, tant vivans que morts."

31. AN X2b 209 (30 August 1602): "lesd[its] procedures et sentences estoient cassés tant par les edicts accordés à ceux de la Religion prétendue réformée dont led[it] deffunt . . . père desd[its] suppliants faisoit profession que par lesd[its] lettres [du roy]."

32. AN X2b 204 (11 July 1601): "ne peult ester marqué d'aulcune tasche de deshonneur." The letter was officially registered by the Paris chamber in December 1601.

33. AN X2b 206 (19 March 1602).

34. AN X2b 199 (31 January 1601): "les edicts de pacification des troubles qui ont couvert, exteinct et aboly tout ce qui s'est passé durant desdicts troubles."

35. AN X2b 199 (31 January 1601): "[la cour] faictes deffences à toutes personnes d'en rien improperer aux appellans et à leur posterité, ordonne que ladite sentence sera rayée des registres de Rochefort et les amendes adjugés par icelle si aucunes ont été payees seront rendues aux appellans."

36. Mousnier, 296–97 (article 2): "[Défendons à tous nos sujets] . . . d'en disputer, contester, quereller, ni s'outrager, ou s'offenser de fait ou de parole; mais se contenir et vivre paisiblement ensemble comme frères, amis et concitoyens."

37. See also Diane C. Margolf, "Adjudicating Memory: Law and Religious Difference in Early Seventeenth-Century France," *Sixteenth Century Journal* 27, no. 2 (1996): 399–418; Elisabeth Labrousse, "The Wars of Religion in Seventeenth-Century French Thought," in *The Massacre of Saint Bartholomew: Reappraisals and Documents*, ed. Alfred Soman (The Hague: M. Nijhoff, 1974): 243–51; David Parker, "The Huguenots in Seventeenth-Century France," in *Minorities in History*, ed. Anthony C. Hepburn (New York: St. Martin's Press, 1979): 11–30; and Elizabeth I. Perry, *From Theology to History: French Religious Controversy and the Revocation of the Edict of Nantes* (The Hague: M. Nijhoff, 1973).

38. Code Michaud, article 105: "un grand desordre en la justice." Quoted from text reprinted in François-André Isambert, et al., *Recueil général des anciennes lois françaises* (Paris, 1822–33; reprint, Farnborough: Gregg Press, 1966), vol. 16 (1610–1643), 257–58.

39. Code Michaud, articles 106 and 108, in Isambert, vol. 16, 258–59.

40. See Bernard Dompnier, *Le Venin de l'hérésie: Image du protestantisme et combat catholique au XVIIe siècle* (Paris: Centurion, 1990).

41. Such complaints appear in *Decisions royales sur les principales difficultez de l'Edict de Nantes. Par Responses et Expressions faites et ordonnées au Conseil d'Estat, sur les*

Cayers des plaints et remonstrances qui en ont esté presentées au Roy (Paris, 1643), 76 (August 1606); 104–5 (July 1611); 141–42 (August 1617).

42. *The Generall and Particular Acts and Articles of the Late National Synod of the Reformed Churches of France, Assembled by the Permission of the King at Charenton near Paris, beginning the 26th of December 1644* (London, 1645), 42.

43. See Ruth Kleinman, "Changing Interpretations of the Edict of Nantes: The Administrative Aspect, 1643–1661," *French Historical Studies* 10 (1978): 541–71, and Philip Benedict, "*Un roi, une loi, deux fois*: Parameters for the History of Catholic-Reformed Co-Existence in France, 1555–1685," in *Tolerance and Intolerance in the European Reformation*, ed. Ole Peter Grell and Bob Scribner (Cambridge: Cambridge University Press, 1996), 65–93.

44. AN X2b 485 (11 May 1645): "luy disant qu'il avoit la peste et qu'il vouloit hanter des gens de bien, qu'il luy deffendoit de se trouver à l'advenir en compagnie et luy enjoignoit de se tenir reclus en sa maison."

45. AN X2b 485 (11 May 1645): "qu'ils s'obligent [ ] ne [plus] frequanter doresnavant les suppliants pour quelque occasion que ce soit, toutes lesquelles procedures sont aultant des contraventions aux edicts de pacification et une oppression contre les subjects du Roy." The court ordered the matter heard before the *lieutenant criminel* at Vitry-le-François.

46. AN X1b 4397 (8 June 1654): "ceste fille . . . n'avoit jamais tesmoigné de parolle ny aultrement ny songé à changer de religion."

47. AN X2b 632 (6 September 1660): "les coupables ont esté arrachés d'entre les mains de la justice à force ouverte."

48. AN X2b 632 (6 September 1660): "[ils] sont dans le pais aussy triomphent de leurs crimes et luy font Insultes . . . ce qui n'est poinct juste et ce qui est contre l'intention du Roy et contre les arrests de la cour."

49. Butler, 215. Connections between memory, history, and national identity in France with reference to the Huguenots are explored in Myriam Yardeni, *La Conscience nationale en France pendant les guerres de religion, 1559–1598* (Louvain: Editions Nauwelaerts, 1971); Labrousse, "The Wars of Religion in Seventeenth-Century French Thought"; and Margolf, "Adjudicating Memory." For a broader perspective on French national consciousness, see David A. Bell, "Recent Works on Early Modern French National Identity," *Journal of Modern History* 68 (1996): 84–113, and ibid., *The Cult of the Nation in France: Inventing Nationalism, 1680–1800* (Cambridge, Mass.: Harvard University Press, 2001).

TWO

Sociability and Culpability

Conventions of Mediation and Reconciliation within the Sixteenth-Century Huguenot Community

Raymond A. Mentzer

What was the meaning of the Protestant Reformation for those who joined its ranks in sixteenth-century France? How did these Huguenots go about setting up and regulating their church as well as their community? What was their understanding of the place and nature of the sacred within the larger social and cultural structure? As historians formulate responses to these and related queries, they must increasingly take account of an insistence that social discipline—the meticulous reform and supervision of all aspects of communal life—was as important to the Reformation as traditional considerations such as the rethinking of theological positions or the revision of prayer and the liturgy. Indeed, the concept of social discipline is probably the most striking interpretative framework to emerge on this subject during the past decade or so. This reading of the sixteenth century insists that Protestants, especially those operating within a Reformed tradition that drew inspiration from Calvin's Genevan model, worked above all to foster confessional identity and establish ecclesiastical discipline.

Following Calvin's lead, Reformed Protestants throughout France labored to institute a forceful church polity whose focal point was a supervisory body known as the consistory. The pastors, lay elders, and deacons who sat on the consistory gathered weekly to organize and guide the religious life of the congregation. They shared, in immediate and direct fashion, collective responsibility for handling the everyday affairs of the local church, attending to the material welfare of the less fortunate among them, and watching over the spiritual and moral life of the entire body of the faithful.

As part of their longer-term strategic objectives, the Huguenots aspired to concentrate people's attention on the sermon service and celebration of the Lord's Supper, while simultaneously repudiating in no uncertain terms the "abuses of the Mass" and other papal "superstitions." The pastors and elders conducted catechism lessons for the edification of villagers and city dwellers who often had but the vaguest notion of Christian belief. They fashioned an elaborate social assistance agency, which delivered substantial religious and social guidance even as it aided the poor economically. These Protestants also mounted a furious offensive against "sins" such as Sabbath breach, quarreling, dancing, adultery, and gambling. In all of these various facets of their conduct, the members of the consistory consciously tried to redirect behavior and regulate the tangle of human associations that centered on fundamental issues of aid and aggression, sharing and strife. Close examination of the endeavor can tell us a great deal about the overall character of the Huguenot experience as well as the profound cultural reverberations which accompanied the Reformation everywhere in early modern Europe.

Historians have too long viewed the consistory as a coercive body, one which summoned and punished those who committed fornication, got drunk, profaned the Lord's name, and so forth. More recent scholarship accentuates the positive aspects of the consistory's operation, pointing out that pastors and elders also acted to ameliorate social relationships by resolving marital difficulties, counseling families, and in general looking after the well being of all members of the community.[1] These suggestions can, I think, be usefully applied to the consistory's tireless efforts to settle conflict, lessen tensions, and foster public peace. My own work in France has found the consistory's role in communal affairs an exceptional source for exploring the contours of social dynamics and, in particular, what we today label conflict resolution. Accordingly, I should like to examine briefly the issues surrounding disputes and their mediation in drawing upon the consistory records of more than a dozen Huguenot communities spread across southern France.[2]

Their historic reputation not withstanding, the Protestant reformers, leastways the Huguenots, displayed a marked preference for peacemaking rather than punishment. Within the institutional framework of the consistory, local church officers strove to direct and discipline the community —to promote virtue and repress vice. A large measure of the consistory's task as moral watchdog entailed defusing discord. The role of the church as mediator was certainly not new. Already in the late imperial age, Christian bishops regularly performed public service along these lines, presiding over what amounted to small-claims courts. By the sixteenth century, the lay elders who so dominated the Reformed consistories played an equally critical role in what might be loosely termed the process of sociability. Their intense, sustained involvement in the identification and resolution of discord within the community is striking. Even a cursory reading of the consistory minutes makes clear that the settlement of conflict among members of the congregation was the single largest chore to which church officials applied themselves.

Quarrels, both verbal squabbles and the physical brawls frequently associated with such strife, appear to have been widespread and incessant. Some scholars have suggested that early modern Europeans were everywhere disputatious, disorderly, and undisciplined.[3] And there is ample evidence to support their claims. At the same time, it is clear that consistorial predilection also operated here. Reformed ecclesiastical officials were determined to identify and correct fractious behavior. It was, in their minds, a serious and endemic problem that required close, continuing attention.

Although the incidence of verbal and physical disputes as a percentage of all behavioral offenses examined by French pastors and elders varied from one community to another, quarrels almost always constituted the single largest category among morals offenses. There was typically a greater incidence of disagreements and brawls than, say, sexual wrongdoing which came to the consistory's attention. At Montauban, a town of some 17,000 inhabitants, disputes accounted for roughly one fourth of all transgressions examined by the pastors and elders during the mid-1590s. The investigation of adultery and fornication amounted to no more than 7.5 percent of offenses. A similar pattern held for the much smaller nearby community of Cardaillac. At Castelmoron, yet another neighboring village, quarreling was a third of the morals offenses investigated by consistory officials. To the east at Nîmes, aggressive and insulting behavior amounted to fully half of all misconduct investigated by the local consistory. The same was true in the rural world of the Cévennes mountains. At Bédarieux, for example, strife and discord amounted to slightly more than 40 percent of all cases handled by the pastors and elders, while at

Meyrueis the rate approached 56 percent.[4] The consistory undoubtedly believed that discord among members of the community was a major problem and that it had an obligation to remedy the matter.

What precisely was the nature of these seemingly incessant oral and physical conflicts among members of the community? Let us begin by examining the conventions of defamatory language and abusive remarks. Insults appear to have varied dramatically according to gender. Men were often called thief (*larron* and *voleur*), cheat (*trompeur*) or forger, a reflection on their trustworthiness and honesty in economic dealings. Affronts such as "coward" (*poltron*) or "false noble" challenged other obvious aspects of masculine honor and reputation. Detractors also characterized men as slow-witted and dumb (*bête*) or as a dumb animal such as a horse, ass, or pig. Occasionally, their sexual abilities were called into question when suggestions of cuckold were bandied about.[5]

Female insults, predictably enough, tended to concentrate on a woman's sexual virtue.[6] A pastor's widow slandered her neighbor, intimating that the woman had several pregnancies prior to her marriage.[7] Other slurs were more direct: women were called sluts, whores, filthy whores, and innumerable variations thereof.[8] On other occasions, verbal affronts were directed against maternal competence. Thus a woman at Montauban insulted her neighbor, asking if her daughter, who was about to be married, "pisse encore au lit."[9] Another recurrent smear against women was drunkard, an affront that was apparently related to accusations of being a rotten housekeeper. Finally, there were the usual misogynistic attacks such as old hag and gossip.[10]

Verbal invective sometimes gave way to physical abuse. In about onefourth of these cases and especially those involving men, people raised fists, threw stones, brandished sticks and swords, and drew pistols. At Layrac, a man threatened a stable boy with a lighted torch. Another constant troublemaker from the same town bashed a neighbor with his sword (probably with the flat of the sword or with it still in the scabbard). Jean Bere clubbed David Gimet on the head. A barber-surgeon whacked a widow in the stomach and on the head with his shoe. A fellow clubbed his sister-in-law with a heavy stick. A woman yanked with all her might on a man's beard, if only to stop him from the beating that he was administering to her son. The disagreement between two businessmen escalated from words to fists, and from there to swords before the consistory intervened. A soldier beat a pregnant woman from Pont-de-Camarès so brutally that she aborted the fetus.[11]

What were the circumstances of these disputes? Not unexpectedly, many were fought at close quarters—within the family. Jacques Rémond, an inhabitant of Nîmes, surprised his daughter in the act of robbing his house. When he objected, she sent him to the floor with a quick punch to the stomach. The same man's son-in-law reportedly threatened him repeatedly with a knife.[12] A miller beat his wife so severely that he broke her bones in several places. A cobbler and his mother-in-law got into a violent row. She tried to dump a pot of hot soup on his head but he attacked first, hitting her with a broom.[13] There were also disagreements among neighbors and business people or between local clans and cliques. Some were part of long-standing feuds; others seem to have been spontaneous flare-ups. Bernard de Jonas and Pierre Lartigue fought over five sacks of grain left outstanding in a contract. Two other men vehemently argued over a barrel of wine and yet another pair quarreled over leasing arrangements.[14] Other squabbles focused on pots and pans, goats and donkeys, unpaid wages, disputed inheritances, and outstanding dowries.[15]

Even the issue of who sat where in the temple became cause for endless bickering. Two notaries complained bitterly to the consistory of Saint-Jean-du-Bruel in February 1596. Someone had hacked to pieces the pew belonging to their wives. Upon investigation, ecclesiastical officials learned that the bench, which had only recently been built and installed in the temple, deeply offended a prominent woman in the congregation. Her pew stood immediately to the right of the new one. More to the point, the carpenter had moved the bench on which the woman's daughters sat in order to accommodate the notaries' wives. The perceived slight led to "highly passionate" exchanges and considerable murmuring around town. It so enraged mother and daughters that they hired some local hooligans to destroy the upstarts' seats.[16]

Another mother and daughter, members of one of the foremost families at Aimargues, physically attacked the pastor's wife whom they held responsible for moving their bench to a less prominent spot within the town's temple. The pair "rudely shoved and insulted" the minister's spouse and was accused of having pulled her hair and scratched her throat and upper chest. The consistory, anxious to reestablish public peace, called upon two pastors from neighboring towns to settle the quarrel and restore communal harmony. These mediators, following considerable posturing by both sides, eventually assigned the women to benches at opposite ends of the temple. It was years, however, before the two families could forget the various affronts and put their disagreement to rest.[17] The wrangling over pewing arrangements, furthermore, did not seem to lessen with time. In the mid-1650s, several judicial officers from Castres became entangled in a similarly tiresome feud over who had priority in the seating within the temple. The consistory found the parties so intractable that it finally compelled them to submit to outside arbitration.[18]

Healing the wounds and repairing injured dignity was, of course, of paramount concern. The resolution of conflict through mediation was critical to proper and amicable relations within a small, tightly knit group of people. Communal authorities as well as close neighbors wished ideally to conclude disputes without acrimony. Mediated settlements had to be congenial and capable of reconciling the feuding parties.[19] Litigation and court settlements ran the risk of leaving rivals in dangerous animosity. The judicial process was often better at fostering grievance than understanding. It assessed blame but could not as readily promote a sense of community. Indeed, lawsuits tended to exacerbate conflicts rather than ease them.[20] What was needed were mechanisms to encourage harmony and agreement.

Officials of the Reformed churches everywhere in France went to great lengths to settle differences. They wished to reduce conflict, maintain harmony, and foster cohesion within society. Again, a rough survey of the surviving archival materials indicates that they generally attempted to pacify bickering persons with symbolic handshakes. Pastors and elders demanded solemn promises that the feuding parties would forget past differences and live henceforth in peace and friendship. Occasionally, persons made up in the presence of those who witnessed their quarrel or on the site where the clash had taken place. When necessary, the authorities appointed arbiters rather than allow a dispute to become a full-blown legal battle.

Perhaps the most common remedy applied by the consistory was its demand that feuding parties "extend the hand of friendship" or the "hand of reconciliation." Others "touched" one another's hand as a sign of their promise to live in peace and friendship. Some disputants were told to "forget the past," reconcile, and shake hands. Jean Gautier and Moïse Lafont gave "witness" to the settlement of their enmity "par touchement de mains."[21] In this regard, it appears that early modern society, in general, and the consistory, in particular, used the handshake less as a conventional salutation—a form of greeting upon arrival or departure—than as a gesture for sealing agreement and concord.[22] Invoking the imagery of hands in a slightly different way, the consistory urged others to place their disputes "in the hands of God." The consistory of Nîmes varied the ritual forms once more when it asked persons to "kiss" one another's hands. It restored harmony, for instance, between two women who had slandered one another with vile names and baseless accusations; their agreement was cemented by the kissing of hands. Europeans had, of course, long understood the kiss as a symbol of peace and instrument of reconciliation.[23]

The language of conciliation accentuated ideals of Christian love and fellowship. According to the ecclesiastical officers at Layrac, the faithful needed to renounce their animosities and hatreds; they must instead behave properly and live together as good friends and good neighbors, good companions and good Christians.[24] Other churches employed similar words. At Meyrueis, several women promised to live in neighborly peace and friendship; two men forgave one another and agreed to live as "good brothers."[25] Etienne Sabatier and Jean Birot, residents of Pont-de-Camarès, had fought with both words and fists. When they reconciled, the consistory demanded that they accept one another as "good brothers and friends," while simultaneously dismissing "all appetite for vengeance."[26]

The consistory especially wished to deter members of the congregation from lawsuits. Thus, the pastors and elders of Montauban urged Gerard Suc and Pierre Laboysse along with their wives to abandon the criminal suit between them and to live in peace and friendship. There were minor exceptions. Two prominent gentlemen were allowed to continue their judicial contest, but pointedly told to avoid animosity and bitterness.[27] As a rule, however, suits reflected badly on the community; they gave cause for scandal. And frankly, French Calvinists were not always interested in recourse to justice dispensed by the state, especially one controlled by Catholics, for the resolution of disputes and avoidance of unauthorized violence.

The consistory sometimes found it necessary to win agreement from the two sides that they would submit their differences to arbitration. This was most likely in instances where the quarrel had some economic basis. The process was informal in the sense that it took place outside a court of law. The ideal arbitrators were persons of experience and integrity. They were individuals who possessed adequate authority to act independently and were sufficiently familiar with the particular circumstances of the parties to arrange a salutary settlement. In truth, the consistory's role in these procedures was theoretically limited by the *Discipline*. The members were not supposed to name the arbiters, nor were they to act themselves in this capacity except as private persons.[28] Only occasionally did elders serve as arbiters. An elder of Layrac acted as such in a case involving a father and son who fell out over disputed provisions in a marriage contract.[29] The norm was for combatants to place their "affair" in the hands of two impartial non-ecclesiastical persons for resolution. In most conflicts, the consistory permitted each side to nominate an arbiter, typically a judge, attorney, notary, or someone otherwise versed in the law or prominent within the community, and the two appointees then hammered out a settlement.[30]

When all else failed and the consistory was unable to bring bickering parties to settle their differences, the obstinate principals could be excommunicated and thereby cut off from the sacraments, above all, the Lord's Supper, as well as normal economic and social relationships with other members of the community. Not surprisingly, feuds and quarrels were the single greatest reasons for excommunication in the French Reformed churches during the sixteenth century.[31]

Some faithful eventually came to view the consistory as a body to which they could have recourse for righting an injury and repairing their honor. Take the example of Anne Amalrique, a servant in the house of Damoiselle Anne Pairine, wife of the first consul of Saint-Amans. The servant woman had been dismissed from the household due to her alleged theft of some linens. Convinced that her honor had been unjustly damaged and that back wages were still owed her, she appealed to the consistory, which eventually sorted out the rival claims and patched things up.[32] In a slightly different sort of case, an apprentice apothecary of Nîmes felt that his advance had been blocked. He petitioned the elders of the consistory in June 1580 and asked them to speak with the town's master apothecaries. He wished specifically to be examined, presumably to demonstrate his proficiency and allowed, in turn, to practice his profession fully.[33] In this regard, the consistory may well have served the needs of less-affluent persons who could rarely afford exorbitant legal battles. When the cost of going to court was beyond their means, they could turn to the consistory for less formal yet apparently acceptable justice.

◆ ◆ ◆

An earlier generation of scholars, sociologists such as Max Weber and Norbert Elias,[34] saw in the Reformed offensive against usury or fornication the expression of characteristically bourgeois concerns with money and sexuality. They emphasized these issues as salient features in the gradual emergence of modern western culture. In fact, there were very few usury cases which came before the French consistories, and the number of persons who trespassed upon consistorial notions of proper sexual comportment was far less than those summoned for dancing. At the same time, the strong interest in pacifying society, controlling violence, and quelling strife fits well within the conceptual parameters of the construction of a bourgeois morality. The elders were, after all, educated and literate laypersons, members of a middling professional elite, who strove to regulate business affairs, control sexual behavior and, as we have seen, suppress disruptive discord within the community.

Historians such as Heinz Schilling have modified and in some ways rejuvenated these interpretations. He and others of similar inclination describe the shifts that took place over the course of the Reformation as a process of confessionalization and social discipline which involved a sweeping metamorphosis. It included the spread of bourgeois values, the reinforcement of family structures, and rigid redefinition of sexual boundaries.[35] Again, the pacification of an admittedly disputatious society accords nicely with these ideas. It is clear, moreover, that the French Reformed churches were not unique in their efforts. The Amsterdam Calvinist Church, to take but one example, worked diligently toward the settlement of differences and establishment of concord among the members of its congregation. The Dutch consistory had concerns similar to those of the Huguenots in France, employed almost identical language, and applied analogous remedies.[36]

Social discipline, in particular, led to the internalization of restraint based on decorum and piety, and the suppression, or at least the redirection, of violence and anger. The changes embraced the individual as well as society as a whole, touching all aspects of public and private life. Because religion and politics, church and state were structurally linked in preindustrial Europe, the processes of change reached beyond the confines of ecclesiastical life. Social discipline affected every aspect of community existence, redefining its basis and radically reshaping it. Still, I think that, despite the broad appeal of these general models, there are additional interpretative frameworks which strike closer to contemporary interest in collective religious experience.

I would like to suggest that, without discarding notions of social discipline, we must also take account of the announced goals of the Reformed movement itself in assigning meaning to the consistory's actions. The sustained interest displayed by the Reformed church and its consistory in the identification and resolution of communal discord goes to the very nature of the "godly" society, which the Huguenots sought to establish. Their reconceptualization and implementation of proper communal relations aimed ideally at a pacified and amicable world in which the faithful cooperated closely for the achievement of mutually agreed spiritual and moral goals. The pastors and elders sought to create a society based on the prescriptions of Holy Writ and permeated by the principals of the New Jerusalem as they understood them. Reforming the individual and reforming society meant that battles over economic resources, points of personal honor, and breaches of the social code had to be suppressed. In this effort, the Reformed churches of France emphasized the determined involvement of all members of the community. Together, they were to join in the ordering of social relationships as well as the elaboration of new mechanisms for conflict resolution. The church, even as it counseled the contentious to cease their destructive bickering, called upon others in the congregation to serve, for example, as arbiters. Strengthening of the bonds of sociability, mediating conflict, and promoting harmony proved an arduous communal task, which required the full participation of all the faithful.

Notes

The author thanks the National Endowment for the Humanities and Montana State University for their continuing support of his research.

1. Robert M. Kingdon, *Adultery and Divorce in Calvin's Geneva* (Cambridge, Mass.: Harvard University Press, 1995), 4.

2. The towns include Aimargues, Bédarieux, Cardaillac, Castelmoron, Ganges, Layrac, Meyrueis, Montauban, Nîmes, Pont-de-Camarès, Saint-Amans, Saint-Gervais, and Saint-Jean-du-Bruel.

3. The remarks of Robert Muchembled, *La violence au village (XVe–XVIIe siècle)* (Paris: Brepols, 1989) or Lawrence Stone, *The Family, Sex, and Marriage in England, 1500–1800* (New York: Harper and Row, 1977), 93–96 are representative.

4. Janine Estèbe and Bernard Vogler, "La genèse d'une société protestante: étude comparée de quelques registres consistoriaux languedociens et palatins vers 1600," *Annales: économies, sociétés, civilisations* 31 (1976): 378–79. Raymond A. Mentzer, "*Disciplina nervus ecclesiae*: The Calvinist Reform of Morals at Nîmes," *Sixteenth Century Journal* 18 (1987): 100–103, 109; idem, "Le consistoire et la pacification du monde rural," *Bulletin de la Société de l'Histoire du Protestantisme Français* (hereafter *BSHPF*) 135 (1989): 379, 381–82.

5. Archives Départementales (hereafter AD), Gers, 23067 (27 mars 1587). AD, Tarn-et-Garonne, I 1, fols. 355–356. Bibliothèque Nationale (hereafter BN), MS fr [Manuscrit Français] 8666, fols. 100–100v, 121–122v, 123v, 154v, 156v, 168v, 191v, 192v–193; MS fr 8667, fols. 124v, 166, 170, 223v, 227v, 236v, 252v, 256v. Bibliothèque de l'Arsenal, MS 6563, fols. 78v-80, 65–66v. Bibliothèque de la Société de l'Histoire du Protestantisme Français (hereafter Bibliothèque de la SHPF), MS 222/1, fols. 14, 42v. Estèbe and Vogler, "La genèse," 378. Mentzer, "Le consistoire," 381–82.

6. See the remarks of Malcolm Greenshields, *An Economy of Violence in Early Modern France: Crime and Justice in the Haute Auvergne, 1587–1664* (University Park: The Pennsylvania State University Press, 1994), 90; that women's honor was "calculated, insulted, and defended in sexual and physical terms."

7. AD, Gers, 23067 (12 août 1588).

8. AD, Gers, 23067 (21 avril 1622). AD, Tarn-et-Garonne, I 1, fols. 340v. BN, MS fr 8666, fols. 100, 123v, 147, 154v, 156v, 162v, 180v; MS fr 8667, fols. 7v, 30v, 101, 123v–124, 145v, 153, 184, 193, 195, 199, 202v, 203, 209, 224, 227, 236v, 292, 348v.

9. Estèbe and Vogler, "La genèse," 378.

10. BN, MS fr 8666, fols. 100, 144v, 154, 154v; MS fr 8667, fols. 19, 43, 153, 187, 202v, 223v, 227, 227v, 229, 244v, 325v, 335.

11. AD, Gers, 23067, février, 31 juillet 1587 (10 mars, 6 juillet 1606). Bibliothèque de l'Arsenal, MS 6563, fols. 58–58v, 69–70, 89–89v. Bibliothèque de la SHPF, MS 222/1, fol. 42v. Philippe Chareyre, "'The Great Difficulties One Must Bear to Follow Jesus Christ': Morality at Sixteenth-Century Nîmes," in *Sin and the Calvinists: Morals Control and the Consistory in the Reformed Tradition*, ed. Raymond A. Mentzer (Kirksville, Mo.: Sixteenth Century Journal Publishers, 1994), 80.

12. Chareyre, "The Great Difficulties," in *Sin and the Calvinists*, 77.

13. BN, MS fr 8667, fols. 37v, 146–146v, 183v, 337–337v.

14. AD, Gers, 23067 (26 avril 1591, octobre 1594, 18 juillet 1606).

15. Bibliothèque de l'Arsenal, MS 6563, fol. 10. Bibliothèque de la SHPF, MS 222/1, fols. 13, 97. Mentzer, *"Disciplina,"* 101.

16. Archives Nationales, TT 270, dossier 13, 779–81.

17. Archives Municipales, Aimargues (deposited at AD, Gard), GG 57, fols. 66–77v, 86v–87.

18. AD, Tarn, I, 1, fols. 1212–13.

19. For the importance of mediation and arbitration in early modern England, see Steve Hindle, "The Keeping of the Public Peace," in *The Experience of Authority in Early Modern England*, ed. Paul Griffiths, Adam Fox, and Steve Hindle (London and New York: Macmillan, 1996), 213–48.

20. Alfred Soman and Elisabeth Labrousse, "Le registre consistorial de Coutras, 1582–1584," *BSHPF* 126 (1980): 194.

21. AD, Gers, 23067, (19 novembre 1604). AD, Tarn-et-Garonne, I 1, fol. 350. Bibliothèque de la SHPF, MS 222/1, fols. 9, 13, 15, 23v, 25v, 40, 41, 61, 90v–91.

22. A helpful recent study on this subject is Herman Roodenburg, "The 'Hand of Friendship': Shaking Hands and Other Gestures in the Dutch Republic," in *A Cultural History of Gesture. From Antiquity to the Present Day*, ed. Jan Bremmer and Herman Roodenburg (Cambridge: Polity Press, 1991), 152–89.

23. BN, MS fr 8667, fol. 187. John Bossy, "The Mass as a Social Institution," *Past and Present* 100 (August 1983): 29–61. Willem Frijhoff, "The Kiss Sacred and Profane: Reflections on a Cross-Cultural Confrontation," in *A Cultural History of Gesture*, 210–36.

24. AD, Gers, 23067 (7 août 1587, 8 avril 1588, 25 juin 1603, 24 mars, 13 août 1604, 18 juillet 1606, 13 avril 1607, 28 mars, 18 juin 1608, 1er janvier, 28 mai 1610).

25. Bibliothèque de la SHPF, MS 453, fols. 53v, 56, 61, 75.

26. Bibliothèque de l'Arsenal, MS 6563, fols. 49–49v.

27. AD, Tarn, I, 1, fols. 308v, 314.

28. François Méjan, *Discipline de l'Eglise Réformée de France annotée et précédée d'une introduction historique* (Paris: Editions "Je Sers," 1947), 232.

29. AD, Gers, 23067, (11 février 1611). Elders served as arbiters elsewhere, too. See: Bibliothèque de la SHPF, MS 222/1, fol. 5v.

30. AD, Gers, 23067 (15 septembre 1584, 20 août, 8 octobre 1604, 31 mars, 5, 12 avril, 29 décembre 1606, 2 juin 1623).

31. Raymond A. Mentzer, "Marking the Taboo: Excommunication in the French Reformed Churches," in *Sin and the Calvinists*, 105–7.

32. AD, Tarn, I, 8 (7, 16 et 19 décembre 1590, and 9, 10 janvier 1591).

33. BN, MS fr 8667, fol. 27. I am indebted to D. C. H. Morris of the University of Leeds for this reference.

34. Max Weber, *The Protestant Ethic and the Spirit of Capitalism*, trans. Talcott Parsons (London: Allen and Unwin, 1930). Norbert Elias, *The Civilizing Process: The History of Manners and State Formation and Civilization*, trans. Edmund Jephcottt (Oxford: Blackwell, 1994).

35. For a fuller explanation of confessionalization see Heinz Schilling, "Confessionalization in the Empire," in idem, *Religion, Political Culture, and the Emergence of Early Modern Society* (Leiden: E. J. Brill, 1992), 205–46.

36. Herman Roodenburg, *Onder Censuur: De kerkelijke tucht in de gereformeerde gemeente van Amsterdam, 1578–1700* (Hilversum: Verloren, 1990), 207–8, 248–49, 352–53, 359.

THREE

Cemeteries, Religious Difference, and the Creation of Cultural Boundaries in Seventeenth-Century French Communities

Keith P. Luria

The study of religious harmony is only starting to catch up with work on religious violence in early-modern France.[1] Violence appears so inevitably the result of sixteenth-century religious divisions that coexistence seems startling. Yet recent work on the seventeenth century has shown that coexistence was not exceptional.[2] Despite long years of rivalry and bloody conflict, Huguenots and Catholics—living in confessionally mixed communities under the Edict of Nantes—intermarried, worked together, shared civic responsibilities, participated in each others' ceremonies, and sometimes even told their clergy that people could be saved in either faith. Frequently they also buried their dead in common cemeteries.

Evidence from the western province of Poitou during the seventeenth-century largely confirms the view of widespread coexistence. In this province with its sizable, powerful, Huguenot minority living amidst a Catholic majority, a pragmatic interest in avoiding conflict contributed to the cooperative atmosphere.[3] The attitude was similar to what Bob Scribner has described for Germany as the "tolerance of practical rationality." "This was," he suggests, "very much the tolerance of ordinary people, a tolerance found frequently in daily life which made little fuss about difference in belief and accepted it as a normal state of affairs." It was "frequently manifested during the Reformation upheavals in a good-natured acceptance that common folk could hardly be expected to agree on matters of belief since theologians could not reach any form of agreement."[4] But what also encouraged this coexistence was the common concern among Protestants and Catholics for matters such as familial honor and advancement, rank, neighborliness, communal solidarity, and the exercise of local power. These considerations often led people of different faiths to construct the religious boundary in ways quite different from that which the clergy preferred.

Local people delineated the communal religious boundary in at least three ways. First, it could be indistinct if people differentiated themselves less by religion than by other social distinctions—family, occupation, rank, and privilege. When parents of one faith chose godparents of the other for their children, or when families of different religions joined their offspring in marriage, the sense of different confessions did not entirely disappear. But it did seem less important than the social alliances achieved and familial interests served. Or, second, a clear demarcation could define the position of each group and "contribute . . . to the conditions that made possible the continued existence" of both in the same communities.[5] Consider the militia companies assembled in some Poitevin towns in the 1620s, a time of renewed religious war. The militias had strictly equal numbers of Catholic and Huguenot members and officers.[6] They integrated both groups into the community by carefully articulating the place of each in an important civic institution. The companies did not efface religious difference; indeed, they accentuated it in enumerating the militiamen of both faiths. We cannot assume that separations always gave each side an equal part, but they did not exclude members of either religion.

Maintaining boundaries thus could create distinction and separation between the groups without necessarily implying rejection and exclusion. But the creation of greater separation did eventually overshadow coexistence and toleration. The boundary could be constructed in a third way that drove Huguenots out, symbolically and then literally, from the communities they shared with Catholics. Although we should not think of these three possibilities as necessarily succeeding each other in chronological sequence, it is clear that the last, persecutory one did become increasingly apparent in Poitevin communities from the 1630s on. The stricter boundary was, to a large degree, the work of the French state and the Catholic Church, culminating in the Revocation of the Edict of Nantes in 1685. But what we still need to understand is how the redefining was carried out, how greater distinction and separation between the communal religious groups was constructed.[7]

Through cemeteries we can trace the construction of boundaries. As the anthropologist Lawrence J. Taylor has pointed out, for cultures "death is not only a problem, but also an opportunity—an occasion for furthering social, cultural, and political ends."[8] The work of Natalie Davis, Denis Crouzet, and Barbara Diefendorf on sixteenth-century religious violence has shown that cemeteries presented an opportunity for demonstrating doctrinal differences and the seemingly inevitable conflict between the faiths.[9] Protestants suffered the exhumation and desecration of Huguenot corpses; Catholics endured the destruction of relics and the profanation of consecrated space.[10] Yet in confessionally mixed communities of the seventeenth century, burial grounds were among the most surprising areas of local coexistence and boundary crossing.

For Catholics, cemeteries were sacred ground, hallowed by the bones of the faithful buried within them. Protestant denial of the sacredness of cemeteries and of human remains was anathema. Jean Filleau, a seventeenth-century Poitevin magistrate and ardent anti-Huguenot campaigner, made the Catholic view clear:

> The false beliefs of the *religionnaires* [Huguenots] concerning the prayers for the dead and purgatory render them unworthy of burial in Catholic cemeteries. . . . [These false beliefs] alone are enough to distance them from our churches and cemeteries. . . . It is therefore unreasonable that sacred ground, destined only to receive the bodies of those who died in the true belief of the Church, remain open and profaned by the reception of the bodies of those who separated themselves from the Church and, while alive, condemned the mysteries and holiness of it.[11]

Catholics surrounded the cult of the dead with an elaborate structure of practices (e.g., masses for the dead, testamentary alms giving, indulgences) and of physical signs (e.g., tombs, chapels, crosses). Calvinists, who believed that one was saved or damned immediately upon death, saw no point to the elaborate and costly rituals aimed at rescuing souls from purgatory. They rejected Catholic funeral and memorial customs as superstitions that served the power and enrichment of the clergy. As Pierre Du Moulin, a leading seventeenth-century Huguenot theologian, succinctly put the matter, "We don't fleece people for burials."[12] Nor were cemeteries sacred; "we are," wrote Huguenot historian Elie Benoist, "not so obstinate as to continue to believe the vain prejudice that one piece of land is holier than another."[13]

The Edict of Nantes sought to set aside such conflicts. Article twenty-eight addressed the provocative issue of cemeteries: "For the interment of the dead of those of the said religion . . . officers, magistrates, and commissioners in all places . . . will promptly provide them with the most convenient place possible. And those cemeteries which they formerly held but which were taken from them during the troubles will be returned to them, except in cases in which they are occupied by edifices and buildings, no matter of what sort. In these cases another cemetery will be provided for them for free."[14]

Thus, the Edict ordered separate Protestant and Catholic cemeteries. Royal officials were to provide Huguenots with their own burial ground, though at whose expense was not made clear. Indeed, this terse article could not begin to deal with the confusion over cemeteries. Problems arose from conditions in which separate burial grounds for Protestants were neither practical nor even desirable for communities. Local people, concerned with economic necessity, neighborliness, kinship, and power relations, often ignored the law and the supposed chasm between the confessions on matters concerning the dead.

Throughout France, Catholic and Huguenot neighbors shared parish cemeteries, either by burying the dead indiscriminately or by dividing old burial grounds with each group taking a portion. Over eighty parishes had such collective cemeteries in Poitou.[15] Reasons for the sharing are not hard to find. Protestants interpreted the provisions of the Edict of Nantes as ordering the whole community to pay for their new cemetery when they lost the use of an old parish one.[16] They also insisted that Henry IV's intention was to allow them to continue sharing Catholic cemeteries until provided with new burial grounds.[17] Catholic anti-Protestant campaigners followed the lead of the magistrate Jacques Talon, who argued before the Paris *parlement* in 1622 that the king had never intended to permit Protestants to continue burials in Catholic cemeteries, only that they not be prosecuted for earlier interments. Furthermore, he insisted that they were to pay for their own new burial grounds.[18]

In the early decades of the seventeenth century, royal commissioners frequently sided with the Protestants. Where they found shared cemeteries, they often ordered communities to pay for separate ones. But many financially strapped localities simply could not bear the expense. And so they divided up the old cemetery and gave the part furthest from the church to the Protestants. The division would be signified by a sign, a ditch, or perhaps a wall if the inhabitants could afford it.[19]

The complete separation of burial space was also difficult because of the desire of Protestants (especially nobles) to continue to use tombs in which their Catholic ancestors were buried.[20] Protestant seigneurs claimed a right of burial in chapels of which their families were patrons by "ancient foundations; others had longstanding rights over tombs in parish churches."[21] They insisted on being buried with their kin, even Catholic kin.[22] The tombs in chapels and churches were strong symbols of familial power, status, and continuity over time, all aspects of a noble ethos that defied Protestant denials of significance to burial grounds and Catholic objections to the profanation of cemeteries by heretics. The clerical deputies of the Estates General in 1614 asked for a prohibition on Protestant patrons and founders enjoying their prerogatives over Catholic cemeteries.[23] A patron's interests might be "so considerable that the church is obliged to" honor them. Nonetheless, if a patron was a Protestant, "and if he died without having abjured, he could not be buried" in a Catholic tomb.[24]

Financial necessity and aristocratic power thus overrode doctrinal differences. So did the need to establish peace. After the religious wars, carefully constructed agreements to keep peace in communities often insured the common use of cemeteries. In a 1619 court case, the Protestants of Latillé claimed that royal commissioners had previously approved an arrangement by which the parish cemetery remained common to both religions in return for which the Protestants had agreed to contribute to the cost of repairing the parish church. The agreement, they said, had never provoked any dispute among the inhabitants, but now the Catholics claimed the cemetery was too small for both confessions and wanted the Protestants provided with another. The two groups reached another agreement. The curé offered a piece of land belonging to the parish church at no cost. The Protestants accepted under the condition that if their possession of the new cemetery were ever challenged, they would regain their rights in the old cemetery. The arrangement seemed perfectly acceptable to the people of Latillé—even to the Catholic priest.[25]

Similarily, in 1634, the Protestant response to the decisions of the court of the Grand Jours convened in Poitiers—one of whose principle purposes was to hear Catholic grievances against Protestants—objected to the separation of cemeteries in which the dead of the two religions had been buried "promiscuously." If that practice continued in some parishes, it was only by a "convention particuliere [*sic*]" between the inhabitants of the two religions, authorized in many cases by royal commissioners. "No one had complained about them until now, . . . and Catholics had in no way suffered."[26] Documents from lawsuits speak of the communal consent to sharing and even to the "amitié ancienne" that had governed cemetery use. When the Catholics of Saint-Maixent accused their Huguenot neighbors in 1635 of trying to aggrandize the Protestant portion of a cemetery, they referred to the "amitié ancienne" between the groups that the Huguenots had recently forsaken.[27] In the same year, the Protestants of Cherveux insisted that Catholics had formerly consented to sharing the cemetery and now both groups were willing to divide it. The curé, however, obstructed the agreement because a Catholic was buried in what would become the Protestant portion. He wanted the Huguenot cemetery moved elsewhere.[28]

As these cases make clear, Catholic and Protestant neighbors were not the only parties to agreements for sharing or partitioning cemeteries. Royal commissioners adjudicating disputes under the Edict of Nantes lent the agreements the king's authority. When the Catholics of Loudun complained in 1611 that the Protestants had usurped their cemeteries, the commissioners ruled that Catholic graveyards would be returned to them except for the parish cemetery of Saint Pierre Du Marché. Here Catholics and Protestants had been buried "indifferently." The commissioners ordered this ground to be divided in two. The Protestants would receive a portion with the condition that they not touch a cross that stood on their side.[29]

Sharing a cemetery indiscriminately and partitioning one into two separate but adjacent parts reflect different senses of the confessional boundary. Separation bespeaks an awareness of religious difference that is less clear in the case of indiscriminate sharing. Such divisions created distinct boundaries that could weaken coexistence and disadvantage the religious minority. Conscious of this change, Protestants might object to separate but adjacent cemeteries. In 1612, the Huguenots of Saint-Maixent resisted the construction of a wall dividing their cemetery from that of the Catholics.[30] In Melle, Protestants continued to use the Catholic cemetery by force after having received a separate one.[31]

But Huguenots did not necessarily object to separation. While mixed burial grounds imply the greatest commonality between the confessions, the partitioning of cemeteries, either by communal agreement or by obeying royal officials, still suggests a willingness on the part of people to live together, despite confessional difference. After all, partitioning not only met the concerns of Catholics apprehensive about the profanation of cemeteries. It also met the concerns of Protestants, especially ministers, eager to avoid the mixing of their funerals with the "superstitious" practices of their papist neighbors. They wanted separation of the faiths just as much as their Catholic rivals, providing it did not lead to their exclusion from the community. And so, in general, the Protestant clergy was content with a community's provision of a separate burial ground for the Protestants: "There seemed something perfectly equitable in a regulation that left Catholics masters of their cemeteries on the condition that they gave others" to the Protestants.[32]

Such arrangements would be entirely unacceptable to Catholic, anti-Protestant campaigners. Protestants could not usurp cemeteries older than their religion, according to Filleau, even if the commissioners had granted them portions. He reported with approval a case from Couhé in which government officials had partitioned the cemetery, and local Catholics and Protestants had lived with the arrangement until royal policy changed in the 1630s. Then the Grands Jours court disrupted the agreement by prohibiting the community's Huguenots from using their section. Filleau also praised the bishop of Poitiers, Henri-Louis Chasteigner de La Rocheposay, for prosecuting the Huguenots of La Mothe-Sainte-Héray, Vouillé, Nanteuil, and other places, who held parts of Catholic cemeteries by permission of royal commissioners.[33] Even old cemeteries in parishes that had no Catholics could not be turned over to Protestants. After all, the fate in purgatory of those already interred was still endangered by the profanation of burying heretics next to them.[34]

Catholic campaigners would work hard to move Huguenot burial grounds some distance from the old ones, often outside the walls of cities and towns. Doing so would not only make funerals more inconvenient for the Huguenots but also deny them an important symbol of their place in the community.[35] A cemetery outside the walls might be a perfectly suitable burial ground, but it could leave local Protestants with the sense that their dead, and hence they as well, were being exiled from the community.

The assault on the symbol of a shared cemetery undermined the position of Protestants in communities. Elie Benoist pointed out that since Catholics were prohibited from burying in their cemeteries anyone whom the "councils or popes had declared a heretic," Protestants had to demand "with great insistence that they share the same cemeteries with Catholics." Protestants "could not suffer a distinction in burials that would mark them with an odious stain"; to accept a distinct and distant burial ground would be to accept that they were heretics. Because, according to Benoist, the Edict of Nantes did not treat them as heretics, they should not be denied burial in the same ground as Catholics. "Protestants could never live in peace with those who were allowed to carry hatred for them beyond the grave. . . . One could not treat without contempt, or frequent without horror, people whose corpses, one believed, profaned the ground in which they were buried."[36]

For Catholic authorities, however, complete separation in death could foster complete separation in life. And so Catholic authorities worked hard to get rid of shared or even divided cemeteries. The major attack on shared cemeteries in Poitou came with the opening of the court of the Grands Jours in 1634. Over two years, the court ordered the separation of cemeteries in sixty-nine parishes in the province.[37] Those that escaped would face lawsuits in later years. Protestants had to find other burial grounds and often pay the expense themselves. They faced fines starting at 1,000 livres for any further burials in Catholic cemeteries, and they would have to disinter the bodies.[38] So as not to obstruct the daily activities of local Catholics, new Protestant graveyards required express approval from royal officials, now less sympathetic to the Huguenots or less worried about conflict than the earlier commissioners. This stipulation was intended to cause Huguenots maximum inconvenience and to push their cemeteries as far as possible from the center of communal life.[39]

The attempt to instill a strong sense of the differences between Protestant and Catholic understandings of cemeteries would be an uphill battle. Authorities had to combat the powerful notion of a cemetery as common ground used by all members of a community either through division or by burying the dead near relatives rather than dividing them by religion.[40] The sharing of cemeteries depended on the values and practices central to French local culture and social relations—custom, kinship, lineage, patronage, neighborliness, communal sentiment, seigneurial rights. Sharing by means of separated but adjacent cemeteries also depended on the enforcement of the Edict of Nantes. Distinct and distant cemeteries resulted from a redirection of royal policy starting in the 1630s and intensifying under Louis XIV. But royal policy worked in tandem with the religious divisions and tensions in local society, and it helped further them. An increasingly hard and fast boundary between the faiths progressively made religion a primary means of differentiation in a society crisscrossed by other distinctions—corporate privileges, class tensions, family rivalries, and so forth. Increasingly, the only means to efface the boundary was through conversion.

By the 1680s, Poitou Protestants were rapidly losing ground, literally and figuratively. In 1684, a magistrate ordered a new cemetery for the Huguenots of Chenay. But what they lost was not access to an old Catholic burial ground; that issue had long since been decided in this region's communities. Instead, they lost their own cemetery to those who had formerly been of their faith. According to the official investigation, Chenay had thirteen remaining Protestant families as opposed to the 170 who had converted.[41] The magistrate ordered a division of the cemetery that would leave the Protestants with only one-fifteenth of the original. The new Catholics, led by their curé, could no longer suffer burial in profaned ground, and presumably a purification rite, not specified in the report, would sanctify their new portion despite the presence in it of their Protestant predecessors. Sharing, even discriminatory sharing such as this, was, however, a doomed option, as the Revocation of the Edict of Nantes made clear the next year. The Revocation set off another round in the battle over cemeteries, corpses, and the meaning of both. Now those Huguenots, whose abjurations only covered the clandestine continuation of Protestant practice, sought to avoid burial with their Catholic neighbors. Those who could had quiet burials on private property, away from priests' prying eyes. This was not the sort of separation the Catholic clergy had envisioned, but it did follow directly from a century-long conflict over cemeteries and the dead.

Notes

I would like to thank the organizers of the "Out of New Babylon" conference, and I would like to express my gratitude to Mary D. Sheriff for her comments on this essay. All translations are my own unless otherwise indicated.

1. This comment refers to studies of the coexistence of French Catholic and Reformed communities. The intellectual history of religious toleration has a much

longer tradition. See the classic work by Joseph Lecler, *Histoire de la tolérance au siècle de la Réforme*, 2 vols. (Paris: Editions Montaigne, 1955) and translated into English as *Toleration and the Reformation*, 2 vols. (New York: Association Press, 1960). For recent discussions of this issue, see Hans R. Guggisberg, Frank Lestringant, and Jean-Claude Margolin, ed., *La Liberté de conscience (XVIe–XVIIe siècles): Actes du Colloque de Mulhouse et Bâle, 1989* (Geneva: Librairie Droz, 1991) and Ole Peter Grell and Bob Scribner, ed., *Tolerance and Intolerance in the European Reformation* (Cambridge: Cambridge University Press, 1996), and for France specifically the essay by Philip Benedict, "*Un roi, une loi, deux fois:* Parameters for the History of Catholic-Reformed Co-Existence in France, 1555–1685," 65–93.

2. For the sixteenth century see, despite the differences among them, Natalie Zemon Davis, "The Rites of Violence," in *Society and Culture in Early Modern France* (Stanford: Stanford University Press, 1975), 152–87; Denis Crouzet, *Les Guerriers de Dieu: La Violence au temps des troubles de religion, vers 1525–vers 1610*, 2 vols. (Seyssel: Champ Vallon, 1990); and Barbara B. Diefendorf, *Beneath the Cross: Catholics and Huguenots in Sixteenth-Century Paris* (New York: Oxford University Press, 1991). For the seventeenth century, the work of Elisabeth Labrousse, contained in numerous articles, has been crucial in exploring local relations, but her ideas are briefly described in *"Une foi, une loi, un roi?" Essai sur La Révocation de l'Édit de Nantes* (Paris: Payot, 1985), chap. 4. See also Robert Sauzet, *Contre-réforme et réforme catholique en Bas-Languedoc: Le Diocèse de Nîmes au XVIIe siècle* (Louvain: Nauwelaerts, 1979), chap. 5.; and Gregory Hanlon, *Confession and Community in Seventeenth-Century France: Catholic and Protestant Coexistence in Aquitaine* (Philadelphia: University of Pennsylvania Press, 1993). Hanlon, in particular has signaled the lack of attention to the study of coexistence (see the introduction). None of these historians of the seventeenth century, however, deny the continued existence, or the continued possibility, of communal violence.

3. I have discussed the situation of coexistence in the Poitou in Keith P. Luria, "Rituals of Conversion: Catholics and Protestants in Seventeenth-Century Poitou," in *Culture and Identity in Early Modern Europe (1500–1800): Essays in Honor of Natalie Z. Davis*, ed. Barbara B. Diefendorf and Carla Hesse (Ann Arbor: University of Michigan Press, 1993), 65–81, and "The Politics of Protestant Conversion to Catholicism in Seventeenth-Century France" in *Conversion to Modernities: The Globalization of Christianity*, ed. Peter van der Veer (New York: Routledge, 1996), 23–46.

4. Bob Scribner, "Preconditions of Tolerance and Intolerance in Sixteenth-Century Germany," in Grell and Scribner, *Tolerance and Intolerance*, 32–47, esp. 38. This definition, in its description both of irenicism and suspicion of theologians' disputes, probably characterizes much pragmatic coexistence in France as well as Germany. But it is important to note that, whatever the pragmatic toleration

found in local society, it did not always preclude the eruption of intolerance and violence.

5. David Nirenberg, *Communities of Violence: Persecution of Minorities in the Middle Ages* (Princeton: Princeton University Press, 1996), 228. Nirenberg treats the relations between minority Jews and Muslims and majority Christians in medieval Spain. Thus the context of his analysis is quite different from mine. And he focuses on issues of sexual relations and ritualized violence. But his notion of rituals, which both keep religious groups separate and integrate them into communities, opens possibilities for thinking about the boundaries constructed between Catholics and Protestants later in France as well.

6. "Establissements des gardes de la ville de Niort au service du roi, 30 juin 1621 and 23 janvier 1625," Bibliothèque municipale de Poitiers, (BMP), Fonds Fonteneau, vol. 68, 357–59, 431.

7. For sociological examinations of other processes of "boundary work," see the essays in Michèle Lamont and Marcel Fournier, ed., *Cultivating Differences: Symbolic Boundaries and the Making of Inequality* (Chicago: University of Chicago Press, 1992).

8. Lawrence J. Taylor, "Introduction: The Uses of Death in Europe," *Anthropological Quarterly* (special issue on "The Uses of Death in Europe") 62, no. 4 (October, 1989): 149–53, quotation from 149.

9. See Davis, "Rites of Violence," 179, on the desecration of corpses; Crouzet, *Guerriers de Dieu*, on the issue of pollution (where he takes issue with Davis), 1:253–54, on the desecration of corpses, 1:256, and on violence over cemeteries, 1:414–15; and Diefendorf, *Beneath the Cross*, on cemetery violence and disinterments, 53, 62, 73.

10. Benoist's work contains numerous accounts of exhumations and desecrations from the last stages of the Wars of Religion, but also from later periods. Elie Benoist, *Histoire de l'Édit de Nantes contenant les choses les plus remarquables qui se sont passées en France avant & après sa publication. . .* , 5 vols. (Delft: Adrien Beman, 1693–94), esp. vol. 1.

11. *Décisions catholiques ou recueil des arrests rendus dans toutes les cours souveraines de France en exécution ou interpretation des edits qui concernent l'exercice de la Religion Pretendue Reformee . . .* par Messire Jean Filleau, chevalier de l'Ordre du Roy, conseiller en ses conseils d'estat, son premier et ancien avocat au siege présidial, et doyen des docteurs regens és droits en l'Université de Poictiers, 2 vols. (Poitiers, 1668), 263, 290. Filleau was an *avocat au siège presidial*, associate of Poitiers Company of the Blessed Sacrament, brother of Poitiers's vicar-general, and indefatigable anti-Protestant campaigner. On him, see Elisabeth Labrousse, "*Une foi, une loi, un roi?*" 130–31.

12. Quoted in Paul de Félice, *Les Protestants d'autrefois: Vie intérieure des églises, moeurs et usages*, 4 vols. (Paris, 1896–1902), 1:272. "Nous ne tondons point sur les

sépulchres." In what might almost seem a response to Du Moulin, the Catholic clergy and lay elite of Poitiers started, in 1643, the practice of accompanying to the cemetery the bodies of the poor who died in the local hospital. Previously, only the hospital's chaplain had been present. Several years later the practice was formalized with the start of a congregation devoted to Saint Charles Borromeo, who was remembered for his own efforts among the poor of Milan, especially during the plague. The practice is reported by the lawyer Jean Denesde in "Journal d'Antoine Denesde et de Marie Barré, sa femme (1628–1687)," in *Archives historiques du Poitou* vol. 15 (Poitiers, 1885), 51–332, see 125.

13. Benoist, *Histoire de l'Édit de Nantes*, 1:232.

14. The text of the edict is in Catherine Bergeal and Antoine Durrelman, ed., *Protestantisme et libertés en France au 17e siècle de l'édit de Nantes à sa révocation, 1598–1685* (Carrières-sous-Poissy: La Cause, 1985). These articles are found on 23–24. The edict's provisions were based on those of earlier pieces of legislation enacted during the religious wars. "From 1570 onward, successive edicts obliged the Protestants to obtain their own burial grounds, forbade Catholic attempts to interfere with their doing so, and sought to spell out procedures whereby Huguenot corpses might be taken to these burial grounds without creating 'scandal' or 'tumult.'" Benedict, "Catholic-Reformed Co-Existence," 80.

15. This number comes from the lawsuits enumerated by André Benoist in "Catholiques et Protestants en 'Moyen-Poitou' jusqu'à la Révocation de l'Édit de Nantes, 1534–1685," *Bulletin de la Société Historique et Scientifique des Deux-Sèvres*, 2d series, 16 (1983): 235–439, especially 343–44. See also his "Les populations rurales du 'Moyen-Poitou protestant' de 1640–1789: Économie, religion, et société dans un groupe de paroisses de l'élection de Saint-Maixent," 4 vols. (Thèse pour le doctorat de troisième cycle, Université de Poitiers, 1983), 2:326. Further information comes from Filleau, *Décisions catholiques*, 26, 162–63, 234–322; Archives départmentales de Vienne (hereafter ADV) C 49; Bibliothèque municipale de Poitiers (BMP) Fonds Fonteneau, vol. 64:673 and vol. 78:407, 415; Bibliothèque de la Société de l'Histoire du Protestantisme Français (hereafter BSHPF) Ms. 869 (1), 870 (1); A.-F. Lièvre, *Histoire des protestants et des églises réformées du Poitou*, 3 vols. (Paris: Grassart, 1856), 1:301–6; P. Raoul de Sceaux, *Histoire des frères mineurs capucins de la province de Paris* (1601–1660) (Blois: Editions Notre-Dame de la Trinité, 1965), 455; and J. Durand, "La Réforme à Lusignan en Poitou des origines à la Révolution (1559–1789)," (Thèse, La Faculté Libre de Théologie Protestante de Paris, 1907), 43–44. In the Moyen-Poitou with its large Huguenot population, only Niort seems to have had clearly separate Protestant and Catholic cemeteries in the early decades of the century. Protestants acquired a cemetery in 1621. Benoist, "Populations rurales," 326; Archives Nationales (hereafter AN) T T 260 (10), 1161–62; BMP Fonds Fonteneau, vol. 78:407, 415; and Lièvre, *Histoire des protestants*, 1:304.

16. Pierre Dez, *Histoire des protestants et des églises réformées du Poitou* (La Rochelle: Imprimerie de l'Ouest, 1936), 235–36. Despite this understanding of the edict, the Protestants of Fontenay-le-Comte purchased their own burial ground in 1600.

17. A 1606 royal response to the grievances of the Protestant deputy general seemed to support them. Elie Benoist gives the Protestant interpretation of the appropriate articles, of the debate over them during the negotiations for the Edict of Nantes, and of the 1606 response to the deputy general in *Histoire de l'Édit de Nantes*, 1:287–89, 436.

18. For Talon's arguments and later cases, see Filleau, *Décisions catholiques*, 283–95.

19. At least the Huguenot historian Elie Benoist saw this reason as explaining the frequency of separated but adjacent cemeteries. *Histoire de l'Édit de Nantes*, 1:364.

20. A complete list of Poitevin Protestant seigneurs who continued to use familial tombs in churches, chapels, or Catholic cemeteries is not available. But Filleau provides a couple of examples—Louis de Saint-Georges, Sieur de Boissec of Exoudun and the Dame de La Tarbarrière of Chantonnay (*Décisions catholiques*, 163).

21. Benoist, *Histoire de l'Édit de Nantes*, 1:364, also 1:232.

22. Perhaps this is why a Huguenot noble broke down a church door in Luçon in 1613 to bury one of his co-religionists. BMP Fonds Fonteneau vol. 14, 233. "Deposition des [*sic*] la rupture d'une porte de l'eglise de Boufferé par des gentilhommes protestants pour faire l'inhumation d'une religionnaire, 27 mai 1613." Copy in the BSHPF MS 870(l).

23. BMP Fonds Fonteneau, vol. 79 (1), 281–88. "Les articles proposez . . . deputtez du clergé." Already in 1606, the king had responded to the Assembly of the Clergy with an edict forbidding Protestant burials in Catholic cemeteries as well as in churches, even if Protestants could claim a right of patronage. Benoist, *Histoire de l'Édit de Nantes*, 1:431. This edict appears to disagree with the royal response to Protestant grievances of the same year that seemed to allow Huguenots to continue using Catholic cemeteries until they were provided with new ones. See above note 18.

24. Filleau, *Décisions catholiques*, 279.

25. The arrangement would be overturned three decades later because it established a Protestant cemetery on church-owned land. Filleau, *Décisions catholiques*, 293–95.

26. ADV C 49, "Sommaire des raisons que ceux qui font profession de la religion réformée ont de se plaindre de l'arrest du 16 septembre 1634 donné par [les] Grands Jours . . ." (1634), 1.

27. The curé and *fabrique* [vestry] of Saint-Maixent brought suit against the Protestants for constructing a new wall that would increase the size of the Protestant portion of the cemetery. The plaintiffs wanted the wall reconstructed in its old place and Huguenot graves outside of it moved inside. Obviously the use of the phrase "amitié ancienne" in this context might have exaggerated the previous friendship between the groups in order to cast the Catholics as victims. Nonetheless, it does suggest that some previous sense of agreement had been transgressed, even if we cannot be sure that the Protestants were at fault. After the Catholics won the suit, they resanctified their part of the cemetery with a procession during which the ground was "purgé et lustré" [purged and cleaned]. They erected a large cross, and the Capuchin Etienne de Bourges preached under it. The ceremony and the preaching suggest that any *amitié* which might have once existed within the cemetery was, in the 1630s, under severe strain. Information on the case comes from André Benoist, "Catholiques et Protestants," 343.

28. Archives départmentales des Deux-Sèvres (hereafter ADDS) B, Siège royal Saint-Maixent 13 septembre 1635 cited in Benoist, "Catholiques et Protestants," 344 and note 115.

29. BSHPF MS 869(1), Extracts of the consistory register of Loudun, "Articles contenants les plaintes des habitants catholiques de la ville de Loudun pour estre presentés à M. M. les commissaires députés pour l'exécution des Edits" (1611). The later curé of this parish, Urbain Grandier, would be at the center of the famous case of the possessed Ursuline nuns.

30. BMP Fonds Fonteneau, vol. 16, p. 505, "Requête des maires, échevins, bourgeois et habitants catholiques de la ville de Saint-Maixent . . . au sujet de la révolte et violence des religionnaires (1612)," copy in BSHPF MS 870(1); Archives de la Société des Antiquaires de l'Ouest, No. 81, copy in BSHPF MS 869(1). This wall is presumably the one Protestants tried to move in the 1630s, provoking the Catholic suit discussed above. See note 28. For more on this case, see Filleau, *Décisions catholiques*, 276–77.

31. Or so they were accused by an *arrêt* of the Grands Jours in 1634. Filleau, *Décisions catholiques*, 278.

32. Benoist, *Histoire de l'Édit de Nantes*, 1:289–90. Benedict also discusses how "elements within both churches worked through the seventeenth century to limit or eliminate certain social practices that blurred the boundaries between the two groups." He includes attending the ceremonies of the rival faith, god-parentage, intermarriage, socializing with religious rivals, and the sending of Protestant children to Catholic schools. "Catholic-Reformed Co-Existence," 88–90.

33. Filleau, *Décisions catholiques*, 321–23. This bishop's tenure had ended in 1651. Filleau had assisted with the prosecutions.

34. Ibid., 283, 296. Filleau argued that the presence of crosses and relics (by which he dignified the remains of any Catholic) rendered a piece of ground venerable. Even Protestant burials in places where crosses or chapels had formerly stood must be prohibited. He also argued that Protestants could not have a cemetery on any piece of land which had an ecclesiastical seigneur. See 298.

35. The same sort of campaign was carried on against Huguenot temples. See Solange Deyon, "La destruction des temples," in *La Révocation de l'Édit de Nantes et le protestantisme français en 1685: Actes du colloque de Paris (15–19 octobre 1985),* ed. Roger Zuber and Laurent Theis (Paris: Société de l'Histoire du Protestantisme Français, 1986), 239–59.

36. Benoist, *Histoire de l'Édit de Nantes,* 1:232, 364.

37. Benoist, "Catholiques et Protestants," 343. The author also lists nine decisions by the *Siège royal* court of Saint-Maixent for 1635 as well as four from other years.

38. Filleau, *Décisions catholiques,* 26. In some cases the fines were much larger.

39. Ibid., 297. Catholic authorities also sought to increase the Catholics' suspicion of their Protestant neighbors. Official permission was necessary, Filleau argued, because without close surveillance, new, separate cemeteries might provide Protestants with a means to hide murdered corpses. What more could one expect from people who conducted their funerals at night with so little ceremony (this despite the fact that Catholics insisted on Protestants conducting their funerals under such conditions)?

40. Natalie Z. Davis describes both the differences and the slowness with which a sense of them took hold in "Ghosts, Kin, and Progeny: Some Features of Family Life in Early Modern France," *Daedalus* (spring 1977): 87–114, esp. 92–96. Benedict reminds us of the gap that existed between the letter of the law, which governed relations between the religious groups, and its implementation. "Catholic-Reformed Co-Existence," 75.

41. The new Catholics' request to the intendant Lamoignon de Basville claimed that only three or four Protestant families remained in the parish, but the report of the investigator put the number at thirteen. Both are found in ADV C49 (10 juin 1684).

FOUR

The French Congregation's Struggle for Acceptance in Emden, Germany

Timothy Fehler

In 1894, the year after Emden's French Reformed church joined the German Huguenot Alliance, the pastor would write that his congregation was, next to Frankfurt-am-Main's, the oldest of all continuously surviving foreign Huguenot churches.[1] Ironically, following Pastor Pleines' death two years later, the Emden Huguenot church would be formally dissolved in 1897 by the regional Reformed Presbytery and merged into Emden's German-speaking Reformed church. In many ways, the almost three-and-a-half-century survival of the Walloon and Huguenot congregation in the city was emblematic of Emden's historic significance as an exile center. Indeed, it was to this history that the French congregation appealed as they were facing dissolution last century—ultimately to no avail. This essay will examine the early history of the French refugee community in Emden, focusing primarily on theological, social, and political issues that were raised by their existence as one of several refugee groups in the town and also how these issues affected the congregation's role in the town and their acceptance by both local residents and other refugee groups.

Introduction—Emden
A City of Refuge

First, a bit of background information on the city of Emden is in order. The city is located in the territory of East Frisia in the far northwestern corner of Germany, at the mouth of the Ems River on the North Sea, and on the border of the Netherlands. Although the extent of Emden's sixteenth-century significance has only recently attracted the attention of scholars, its prominence was not overlooked by contemporaries. Indeed, Christopher Marlowe's Doctor Faustus responded to the Bad Angel's entreaty to think only of honor and wealth by saying, "Of Wealth! Why, the signiory of Embden shall be mine. When Mephistophilis shall stand by me, what god can hurt thee, Faustus? Thou art safe."[2] One study has placed the shipping capacity of the fleet of ships registered in Emden in 1570 as greater than that of the entire Kingdom of England.[3] Of course, this had not always been the case (nor would it be for long, hence the reason that Emden has seemingly slipped from memory); just a couple of decades earlier, around 1550, Emden had been a moderate-sized town of 3,000 to 5,000 inhabitants with an important, if small, trade with the German hinterland, especially the Baltic grain trade with Westphalia.[4] Emden's economic boom lasted only a matter of decades, and during the seventeenth and eighteenth centuries, economic stagnation reduced Emden's relative importance.

During the first half of the sixteenth century, Emden had already undergone significant religious changes relating to Protestantism. Yet, in the 1550s the velocity of the changes increased dramatically. The most significant phenomenon in Emden's development was the arrival of thousands of Dutch refugees fleeing the war against Spain in the Netherlands. Over the next twenty years, Emden underwent a social, economic, and demographic boom as an enormous number of Dutch refugees entered the city's gates.[5] Emden's population increased from 5,000 to at least 10,000, and at the height of the immigration in 1572 might have been as high as 20,000–25,000.[6] In the 1560s, about one-third of Emden's population were Dutch refugees; the proportion climbed to no less than half by the 1570s.[7]

Of course, the flood of exiles affected not only Emden's economy. Virtually all of the Dutch refugees who came to Emden were members of the Reformed church, fleeing their homelands to escape religious persecution. Emden's significance for the development of Reformed Protestantism in the Netherlands—as a city of refuge, a missionary center, and a hub of printing, propaganda, and advice—led to its designation as "Mother Church" (*Moederkerk*).[8] Its influence on the Netherlands may be compared to Geneva's influence on France; indeed, toward the end of the century Emden had the nickname "Geneva of the North."[9]

The Arrival of the Exiles

The spring of 1554 brought the first significant arrival of refugees. This hardy group of 175 under the leadership of Johannes a Lasco had been on a half-year odyssey following the accession to the English throne of Mary Tudor and the subsequent expulsion of the foreign Protestant congregations who had been in English exile under Edward VI. Throughout a harsh Baltic winter, the group was expelled from city after city in Denmark and northern Germany before being welcomed into Lasco's former stomping grounds of Emden.[10] These early exiles came predominantly from the southern Netherlands (for instance, Lille, Valenciennes, Antwerp) and especially out of the city of Ghent.[11] One of the leaders of the community, also from Ghent, the noblemen Jan Utenhove (originally Du Jardin), composed a fascinating narrative of their tumultuous journey which culminates with their arrival in Emden: "After our difficult wanderings the Lord God . . . gave us places with the illustrious dowager, the Countess of East Friesland; both the ministers and citizens of Emden lavished on us every courtesy of humane hospitality. And thus, for the sake of his fatherly goodness, God is wont to give peace to the church after fierce and stormy trials."[12]

Two of the initial concerns of the countess, Utenhove's "illustrious dowager," and of the congregation involved the economic and religious conditions of the refugees. Countess Anna required as a condition of her admission grant to the refugees that they were to care for their own poor and not burden the local poor relief.[13] The second concern, over the religious organization of the refugees, related to the various linguistic needs of the exiles: because of the linguistic proximity of Emden's dialect with Dutch, the Dutch-speaking refugees were to participate in Emden's local church services and council, while the countess authorized the French-speaking Walloon exiles and the English to have their own church officials.[14] The French also founded a school.[15]

It was this special status which fostered some of the problems of acceptance for the French congregation throughout its existence in Emden. In some ways, the French congregation had the character of a "free" or "voluntary" church. Although the Emden church consistory was granted the right to oversee emergencies in the French church, the congregation nevertheless had its own ministers, elders, deacons, church council, and school.[16] The Dutch-speaking refugees, on the other hand, despite the fact that they would ultimately make up the vast majority of refugees in Emden, were not allowed their own church institutions, with the exception of a well-developed Dutch diaconate (deacons of the *Fremdlingen Armen*) to care for the poor. The Emden church leadership refused to allow an official, autonomous gathering of a Dutch refugee consistory. In addition to Emden's ministers' concerns about losing their own authority over religious affairs in the city, the consistory also took account of the political implications of giving the Dutch refugees too much influence or recognition during the Dutch Revolt when Emden and East Frisia had supposedly claimed neutrality.[17] The French congregation, because of their much smaller numbers and because of obvious linguistic necessities, did not pose the same problems for Emden's local officials as far as recognition of a special status. Although French refugees continued to arrive in Emden throughout the sixteenth century, particularly in the aftermath of the St. Bartholomew's Day massacre in 1572, the French remained a minority among the minorities.

Emden's "Small and Quarrelsome" French Church

Unfortunately, the exact form of the Walloon church organization is not clear from the surviving sources: the church's protocol book goes back only to 1611, when the minister Samuel de La Vigne reorganized the Walloon congregation with a new "Confession" and a new "Discipline."[18] The French congregation's consistory clearly handled most quarrels and discipline problems, but several heated controversies that split the French consistory have made it into the records of the local consistory. Because of the local consistory's oversight responsibility, representatives of the French church did appear frequently before Emden's consistory—usually in attempts to settle disputes relating to either theological or poor relief controversies; and these appearances provide us with some idea of the early Walloon organization in Emden. This much is clear: the French church had its own consistory, a minister, and at least four elders and two deacons.[19]

The representatives of the French-speaking congregation underscored their modest size when faced with an overwhelming poor relief problem in 1568. Following the Duke of Alba's smashing victory against the Dutch rebel forces on East Frisian soil in nearby Jemgum on 21 July, many people were terrified that Alba would continue his march northward to Emden, which to that point had been openly supportive of the Dutch cause against Spain. In the event, Alba turned back toward the Netherlands, giving Emden's church the opportunity to give prayers of thanksgiving "for the deliverance for a time from the bloody tyrant." But the city faced a steady stream of poor and wounded soldiers from the battle. A considerable number of soldiers were French-speaking, and on 4 August, the French congregation presented its concerns to the consistory regarding its limited ability to provide poor relief to the wounded soldiers.[20] The disproportionate number of French-speaking soldiers made the relief responsibilities of the French church's deacons impossible since "their wealth, because of their small congregation, is very small." The French church "hoped that one would not impose upon them the entire burden of their nation." They asked for assistance in providing special relief—at the least, for a provision that the soldiers be cared for "without distinction according to nation."[21] The Walloon congregation wanted the burden of poor relief to be shared by the entire refugee community in Emden.

Although the Walloon community was comparatively small, a number of influential and wealthy refugees were members of the congregation. Most important were the rich grain merchants who were members of the grain cartel run by the Commelin and Du Gardin families.[22] While such members added an important level of prestige to the French exile community, they could also stir up animosities both within and especially without the congregation; the latter—creating anger among the local community—can be especially devastating as a group struggles for acceptance in a foreign setting. Indeed, the activities of some of the leaders of the Walloon grain cartel caused such problems in 1563. A rise in refugee immigration into Emden in 1562 and 1563 had both created an economic strain and raised tensions between the exiles and local residents.[23] Perhaps in recognition of the need to preserve local acceptance of the refugees, the Emden consistory stepped in and began to make rulings regarding business practices, in this case against the immoral business practices of some of the members of the Walloon grain cartel. The consistory accused them of selling tainted grain (and mixing it with good grain) and of seeking undue profit during a time of scarcity. In order to stem the tide of complaints against these foreign merchants (and any connected animosity against the immigrant community as a whole), the consistory ordered them to provide restitution as well as additional money for the poor.[24]

French Theological Disputes and Theological Importance
Perhaps the most significant of the quarrelsome French congregation's disputes arbitrated by the Emden consistory, at least from the standpoint

of Emden's church history, were those involving theological controversies. Indeed, the theological leanings of Emden's church seem to have paralleled or perhaps been influenced by the French congregation. The Emden consistory spent much time and energy in the mid-1560s and mid-1570s attempting to resolve some major theological controversies which had split the French congregation. The enmity raised by such disputes can be illustrated by Mathias Jansen, a congregant in the French congregation, who appeared before the Emden consistory stating that he wanted to participate in communion with the Emden congregation: with the French congregation he wanted "to hold no further fellowship, neither in the Word, nor in communion, nor in alms."[25]

Disputes involving the French ministers began with André Gorin, who was pastor of Emden's Walloon church from 1561 to 1568. Gorin had alienated part of the congregation with his tolerant position regarding Anabaptists; he had also sponsored the publication of a book by the Spanish spiritualist Juan de Valdés and apparently argued in favor of brothels in order to prevent more widespread evil. All of these supposed positions are in addition to his criticisms of Calvin.[26] A split occurred in the French congregation when Gorin apparently put forth too little energy disciplining a day-laborer who had criticized Calvin; in fact, Gorin's response included the declaration that he himself could not believe at least twelve articles in Calvin's Catechism so how could he condemn the man.[27] Throughout 1565 and 1566, the French congregation was embroiled this controversy involving its "anti-Calvinist" or "Libertine" pastor Gorin and some of his influential supporters in the Walloon grain cartel. Gorin's critics appealed to the Emden ministers, but when the consistory refused to condemn him the critics sought help from farther afield, appealing even to the Walloon church in Antwerp and to Theodore Beza in Geneva. Both of these urged the dismissal of Gorin, but the Emden ministers stood by him until he left the city in 1568.[28] This dispute uncovers for us both the international Calvinist connections that Emden's Walloon church utilized as well as the fact that Gorin and his so-called "anti-Calvinist" leanings could find support in an Emden church which had not yet been fully "Calvinized" in the 1560s.

A decade later, however, the religious climate in Emden had completely changed. As the long-running friction within the French congregation continued under the firm Calvinist minister Jean Polyander, the

Emden church leadership now supported the French church's strict Calvinists in an interesting controversy that led to the excommunication of the "Libertines" who had been victorious a decade earlier.[29] Polyander promptly angered many of Gorin's former supporters, men like Commelin and Du Gardin, the leading figures of the French grain cartel. The conflict dominates Emden's church consistory minutes as it came to a head in 1575–1576, just as Menso Alting, a strict Calvinist minister from the Palatinate, arrived in Emden to serve as the leading minister in the city's congregation, which would begin what one scholar has called the "calvinization" of Emden in the last quarter of the century.[30] Polyander heated up the dispute by selecting as elder one of Gorin's fierce opponents. This action caused another split in the French congregation. Both sides appealed to Menso who obtained pledges from all parties to abide by his decision; after nearly six months, Menso held both sides responsible and ordered public repentance. In the end this became a stunning victory for both Polyander and especially for Menso since Polyander's opponents refused to comply and were excommunicated by Alting.[31] For the rest of the French pastor's life, his relationship with Alting was quite close as Alting utilized the strong Calvinist leanings of the French congregation to modify the Emden church which had not been as "Calvinist" up to this point. The close relationship between the two pastors can be seen, for instance, in 1585 when Menso helped the French congregation get a suitable place for their services which did not "frustrate" them.[32] The French congregation, though small, played an important role in Emden's Calvinist ministers' victories in the city and territory during this age of "calvinization."

Finally, the theological significance of the French congregation can be demonstrated by its participation in the Emden Synod of 1571. This first General Synod of the Dutch Churches could not take place on Dutch soil because of the turmoil of the Revolt; yet the synod laid the theological groundwork for the presbyterial/synodal principle of church organization, citing the Gallican and Belgic Confessions (1559 and 1561). At the Emden Synod, delegates adopted the Genevan Catechism (1545) for the French-speaking churches and the Heidelberg Catechism (1563) for the German. Although the synod was one of the single most important events in the organizational development of the Dutch Reformed church, the officials of Emden's "Mother Church"—due primarily to political pressures—played no visible role either in its planning or in the synod itself which took place within its city walls. It seems that Emden wanted to avoid the appearance of too close a connection with affairs of the Dutch rebels. Emden officials realized that they would probably have been at the Duke of Alba's mercy had he chosen to exact retribution from the city a couple of years earlier. Although the city continued to receive and support refugees, local and territorial officials wanted to avoid any appearance of breaking their stand of neutrality in the Revolt; interestingly, even the consistory minutes from the time of the synod were silent about the important meeting taking place in Emden. The participation in the synod of the French congregation as a small "free church" with little connection to the official local church leadership appears, therefore, to have been of little concern to Emden's officials. Of the twenty-nine signatories of the synodal acts, only three were from Emden: all of them from the small French congregation, namely the new minister Jean Polyander, who served as secretary, and two of the French elders.[33]

Disputes over Poor Relief
We can learn even more about the French congregation and especially about the relationships between the various refugee groups in Emden by looking briefly at a less obvious issue: poor relief. The following two controversies involving poor relief provide insights regarding the acceptance of the French-speaking congregation by other refugees in the town. The Dutch-speaking refugees seem to have emphasized as much as anyone else the linguistic differences of the French-speaking refugee community. As mentioned earlier, the Dutch-speaking refugees assimilated into the local congregation; indeed, they were explicitly prohibited by the Emden consistory from forming their own official Dutch exile consistory.[34] Thus, the only separate institution that the Dutch refugees formed was a special diaconate, for their social welfare administration: a diaconate which at the height of the Dutch Revolt recorded poor relief expenditures 400–700 percent greater than those of Emden's local deacons![35] Generally, any recorded problems in the French church's poor relief involved jurisdictional disputes with the Dutch-speaking deacons.

The Walloon church, though much smaller, was very similar in both religious confession and refugee status to the other Dutch exiles. Yet, the French-speaking congregation had established a complete church organization in Emden while the Dutch had not been allowed to do so. Both groups had their own deacons to provide relief to their respective members, and jurisdictional disputes arose as rivalries increased between these similar refugee communities who were each looking for competitive advantage in their exile home.

The jurisdictional problem was best illustrated in a case before the Emden consistory in November 1568.[36] Four deacons—two from the French congregation and two from the Dutch—asked the Emden consistory to settle a dispute. The complication arose over the provision of poor relief for two orphans of a French lace-maker named Mathys. It seems that Mathys, "although born a Frenchman," had taken part not in the French congregation but rather in the Dutch. Now that he had died, the French deacons did not want to support his orphaned children from their purse as he had not participated with their congregation. The Dutch deacons, on the other hand, argued that the French should support their own poor just as the Dutch must support theirs.

The consistory's response was both interesting and important in establishing a precedent in dealing with minority groups. In order to prevent future disputes, the consistory argued that the deacons should hold to what they called "the oldest rule of all" and decide jurisdictional disputes on the basis of the "tongue" of the recipient. This rule would be especially important in determining the responsible poor relief party in cases involving orphans of refugees since the parents might not have been active in or faithful to any congregation. In the case of Mathys, the consistory exhorted the deacons of both congregations "to the liberal collection of alms" in order to ensure that the two children were provided for by the refugee deacons—because "it was definitely unproved that [Mathys] was in our congregation, but it is certain that he was from their community." Whatever the resolution of this particular conflict, the Emden consistory was certain that the care of these refugee orphans should not be the responsibility of the local deacons.

Another interesting jurisdictional dispute between these two "foreign diaconates" arose in the aftermath of the new Huguenot influx following the St. Bartholomew's Day massacre in 1572. Hans de Brander and his wife Mary had determined in their testament that fifty gulden would be given to the "foreign" poor upon the death of the first spouse.[37] The problem emerged after Mary's death in 1574 when the Dutch deacons requested the fifty gulden; indeed, the wording of the testament had earmarked the money to the "expelled foreign poor of the German congregation in Emden," in other words, the Dutch-speaking community. Yet, when asked about the wording, Hans complained that the testament had not been written properly because it had in fact been the desire of both himself and his wife that both the Dutch and the Walloon poor divide the fifty gulden; it was simply through carelessness that the Walloon poor had been forgotten. He backed up his claim by pointing out that his wife had been from the French congregation and he was from the Dutch.

The position of each of the minority groups was so rigid and the arguing so fierce that the Emden consistory thought it most useful for both sides to present their cases before two impartial legal scholars. Both sides then made their arguments before the arbitrators.[38] The French deacons argued that they should receive half of the bequeathed fifty gulden on the basis of Hans' verbal confirmation; moreover, they claimed, the fact that Hans belonged to the Dutch congregation added credence to the impartiality of his statement. While the French church wanted the case settled with "justice and love according to the conscience," the Dutch deacons argued for "the letter of the testament"—one cannot simply go around changing testaments; with the death of the testatrix, they argued, the testament was fixed and could not thereafter be modified.

That so much acrimony developed over the relatively small sum of twenty-five gulden is immediately striking.[39] The available resources of the smaller French congregation probably did increase the importance of each contribution. Still, however, the intense positions and the willingness even to go to legal arbitration suggest that underlying issues were at stake for these minority groups. Most importantly, this case demonstrates deep-seeded friction between the Dutch and the French refugee churches. The Dutch deacons had no desire to share even a portion of the bequest with the French congregation. Of course, there was always competition between poor relief institutions—especially over bequests in testaments—but the fighting was fiercest between the most closely related institutions. The Dutch deacons did not consider the separate institutions and congregation of the French to be legitimate. Despite the religious and refugee similarities between the French and Dutch exiles in Emden, the "special" minority status of the French congregation gave it an atmosphere of a voluntary church, outside the structure of the city congregation. Since the Dutch refugees had assimilated into the Emden congregation, they began to ostracize their French-speaking fellow exiles and did not want to encourage the continued "special status" of the French congregation. The Dutch-speaking refugees used their sole autonomous institution, the diaconate, to stress the distinctions with the French congregation.

In the end, the legal decision came down in favor of the Dutch deacons, and they received the full fifty gulden.[40] When the French deacons next appeared before Emden's consistory to ask about Hans de Brander's bequest and a second testament in question, the consistory softly explained to them the decision of the jurists, and promised to consider their request regarding the other testament.[41] This new testament had left its bequest to the "foreign poor" to be divided "according to the executors" of the will. In this case, the consistory decided "according to their best wisdom" to distribute the entire bequest to the French congregation. This complete exchange then reveals not only the tension between the refugee communities, but also the local authorities' desires to moderate between them and to avoid any outright disturbances among the minority groups. Perhaps the consistory tried to soothe hurt feelings and even things out after the legal decision in Hans de Brander's case. If that was their intention, they were largely successful as the consistory minutes report that "the brothers of the French congregation were contented," although the French deacons did express the reservation that they wished to be informed when future deliberations in the Emden consistory should concern them.[42]

The Survival and End of Emden's Huguenot Congregation

The turbulence of the early decades seems to have lessened along with the tensions of the Dutch Revolt, and the French community's struggle for acceptance by the local authorities and citizenry was largely successful. In 1611, the French minister Samuel de La Vigne reorganized the consistory of the French church, which had some of the leading figures in the Emden magistracy sign its "Confession" and "Discipline" during the seventeenth and eighteenth centuries.[43] At the end of his life, Pastor de La Vigne (1611–1621) served in official roles for both the French and local congregations, demonstrating the widespread acceptance of the French. The Huguenot church would continue to survive throughout the next three centuries.

This survival was fostered in part by additional outbreaks of persecution against French Protestants. For instance, in the aftermath of the Revocation of the Edict of Nantes (1685) the number of members of Emden's Huguenot congregation climbed so high that a second pastor was hired and two additional weekly worship services were held for the next two decades.[44] Although the congregation's size soon fell again, Emden's Huguenot community had a lasting effect on the politics of the city and territory throughout recent centuries—a look at city officials from secretary through Senator and Bürgermeister reveals numerous members and descendants of members of the Huguenot church.

While the French church might have been viewed positively and apparently been accepted into the civic community, this historic "special status" continued to haunt it, perhaps leading to jealousy among those who disliked its "free church" character. Emden's Huguenot congregation had a certain prestige in the town, and some looked with suspicion at the small church, making accusations that the French congregation proselytized members from the sister German Reformed congregations in the city. In the 1840s, there were increasing rumblings from the regional Reformed Presbytery against the Huguenot congregation because of its small size and lack of resources.[45] The regional Presbytery reported the following about Emden's French congregation in 1840, a statement which carries with it a certain disdain:

> Most of the current members [of the French congregation] belonged originally to the German Reformed congregations and went over primarily because they do not like the worship service, among other [reasons] because of the prestige of the French congregation and out of dread of burdensome service in the "mother-congregation" as well as due to the allure of the French lessons given by the French pastor. For all members [of the French Church], either German or Dutch is the "mother language" and French is merely an acquired language. . . . The more influential members of the German Reformed congregation are withdrawing in order to be received into the French Church. With jealous eyes, therefore, the German Reformed congregation is accustomed to looking at the sister congregation, which especially because of its smallness can never stay free of the suspicion that they mean to create such converts.[46]

The Presbytery wanted to mandate the merger of the French into the German Reformed congregations in Emden—basically arguing that if there was ever any ground for a special status of the church it was linguistic, and now that reason was gone. Because they had no substantive theological argument against the proposed merger, the French congregation countered primarily with a historical argument: "One should not destroy such an old ornament of the city without an emergency."[47] For the next half-century, the Huguenot congregation prevailed. The second half of the nineteenth century was dominated by activities which emphasized the French congregation's tradition, including the celebration of the 300th anniversary in 1854, articles written by Pastor Pleines on the congregation's history and importance (which, incidentally, mention none of the quarrels or controversies which dominated the early years), and joining the German Huguenot Alliance in 1893. In the end, though, the claim of history and tradition was to no avail. One year after Pastor Pleines' death in 1896, the Emden Huguenot congregation, having lost its historic *function* as a refugee church, ceased to exist.

Notes

1. Menno Smid, *Ostfriesische Kirchengeschichte* (Deichacht Krummhörn, Pewsum: Selbstverlag, 1974), 495; J. N. Pleines, "Die französisch reformirte Kirche in Emden," *Geschichtsblätter des Deutschen Hugenotten-Vereins* (1894): 4. Nicolaus Pleines was the French minister in Emden from 1842 until 1896. See also Jean Charles Montigny, "Die Französisch-reformierte Kirche zu Emden. Vor 100 Jahren endete die Geschichte der Hugenottengemeinde," *Der Deutsche Hugenott* 61 (1997): 130–42.

2. Christopher Marlowe, "The Tragical History of Dr. Faustus, Scene V," in *A Treasury of the Theatre*, ed. John Gassner, 3d ed., (New York: Simon and Schuster, 1967), 226. Marlowe's *Dr. Faustus* was first performed successfully in England in the winter of 1588–89. For an example of the close economic connections between England and Emden/East Frisia, see G. D. Ramsay, *The Politics of a Tudor Merchant Adventurer: A Letter to the Earls of East Friesland* (Manchester: Manchester University Press, 1979) and his *The City of London in International Politics at the Accession of Elizabeth Tudor* (Manchester: Manchester University Press, 1975), 240.

3. Bernd Hagedorn, *Ostfrieslands Handel und Schiffahrt im 16. Jahrhundert* (Berlin, 1910), 251. Of course, many merchants from across Europe, not just from the Netherlands, took advantage of Emden's neutrality to move their base of operations and sail under Emden's banner; not all were necessarily Emden citizens,

and as soon as the Dutch ports were again fully open, most would quickly leave Emden.

4. Hermann de Buhr, "Die Entwicklung Emdens in der zweiten Hälfte des 16. Jahrhunderts," (Ph.D. diss., Universität Hamburg, 1967), 53.

5. On the Dutch refugees in the sixteenth century, especially in Emden, see Andrew Pettegree, *Emden and the Dutch Revolt. Exile and the Development of Reformed Protestantism* (Oxford: Oxford University Press, 1992); Heinz Schilling, *Niederländische Exulanten im 16. Jahrhundert* (Gütersloh: Gütersloher Verlagshaus G. Mohn, 1972); Aart Arnout van Schelven, *De nederduitsche vluchtelingenkerken der XVIe eeuw in Engeland en Duitschland in hunne beteekenis voor de reformatie in de Nederlanden* (The Hague, 1908).

6. Heinz Schilling, *Civic Calvinism in Northwest Germany and the Netherlands: Sixteenth to Nineteenth Centuries* (Kirksville, Mo: Sixteenth Century Journal Publishers, 1992), 21.

7. Schilling, *Niederländische Exulanten*, 66.

8. On this issue, see Pettegree's comprehensive study *Emden and the Dutch Revolt.*

9. Hermann Klugkist Hesse, *Menso Alting: Eine Gestalt aus der Kampfzeit der calvinischen Kirche* (Berlin: Furche-Verlag, 1928), 86, 88.

10. Menno Smid, "Jan Laski," *Theologische Realenzyklopädie*, vol. 20 (Berlin: Walter de Gruyter, 1990): 448–51. Lasco had been superintendent of the East Frisian churches from 1543–1548 until he was forced to leave during the Augsburg Interim. Invited to England by Archbishop Cranmer, Lasco became superintendent of the exile churches in London.

11. Indeed, we can find names from the leading families of Ghent's magistracy among Emden's exiles: Herlyn, van Wingene, de Pottère; Pleines, "Die französisch reformirte kirche in Emden," 7.

12. Jan Utenhove, *Simplex et fidelis narratio de instituta ac demum dispatat Belgarum, aliorumque peregrinorum in Anglia ecclesia* (Basle, 1560); a copy is available in the Johannes a Lasco Bibliothek in Emden. This has been reprinted in the *Bibliotheca Reformatoria Neerlandica*, ed. S. Cramer and F. Pijper, vol. 9 (The Hague: M. Nijhoff, 1912), 29–186 (here 148).

13. Among the initial refugees were "many poor and common handworkers"; the countess required an assurance that the local poor would not be overburdened by the maintenance of "these newly arriving foreign poor," Staatsarchiv Aurich, MSC, Rep. 241, A190, 581–83; J. J. van Toorenenbergen, *Stukken betreffende de Diaconie der Vreemdelingen te Emden, 1560–1576* (Utrecht: Kemink en Zoon, 1876), 1–5.

14. The confirmation from 1554 no longer survives, but following the Countess Anna's death in 1575, her son the count Johann issued an edict which reads in

part, "Since our dear mother had gracefully consented in 1554 and allowed that the Walloon and other foreign nations [namely the English] might have their own special church officials within the city of Emden . . . we confirm and allow this now as before"; Stadtarchiv Emden, I. Reg., 405, fol. 1: Acta Miscellanea der Französisch-Reformierten Gemeinde zu Emden.

15. The Emden magistracy published an ordinance regulating the German and French schools in 1582; the text of the "Ordnung der dueitschen schoelen und der franzosischer schoelen" is edited in Emil Sehling, *Die evangelischen Kirchenordnungen des XVI. Jahrhunderts*, vol. 7, part 2 (Tübingen: Mohr, 1963), 514–16. The city's school ordinances of 1596 limit the number of French schools to two (one in the old city and one in Emden's Faldern suburbs) to be supported by the French church; ibid., 526.

16. This privilege was apparently granted in Countess Anna's confirmation; Hesse, 128.

17. For example, the 1 May 1567 minutes of Emden's church council recorded that the brothers of the consistory found the suggestion of the creation of a Dutch refugee consistory "troublesome on account of our Counts, who indeed greatly fear the Burgundians"; *Die Kirchenratsprotokolle der reformierten Gemeinde Emden, 1557–1620*, ed. Heinz Schilling and Klaus-Dieter Schreiber, 2 vols. (Cologne: Böhlau, 1989–92), 1:277–78 (hereafter cited as *KRP*).

18. The "Confession de Foy" and "La discipline ecclesiasticque observée en l'eglise françoise redressée a Embde" are kept in the Archive of the Johannes a Lasco Bibliothek (hereafter cited as JALB) #1100. The consistory protocols of the French church 1611–1718 are in JALB #1090. The first page of the protocol named four elders and four deacons for the French congregation.

19. *KRP*, 1:496 (15 February 1574). On the jurisdiction of the French consistory, compare *KRP*, 2:584: on 23 December 1575, the Emden consistory instructed a supplicant "as a member of the Walloon congregation" to bring his complaint "first before the Walloon consistory."

20. My use of the term "consistory" in the text will always refer to the local Emden church consistory unless specifically noted otherwise.

21. *KRP*, 1:319 (2 and 4 August 1568).

22. Hagedorn, *Ostfrieslands Handel und Schiffahrt im 16. Jahrhundert*, 125f.

23. The rise of violent events in 1562 and 1563 in the Netherlands involving the Dutch Protestants (particularly the beginnings of armed preaching) had provoked a crackdown against many evangelical groups and inspired new groups of exiles to make their way out of the Netherlands and into Emden.

24. *KRP*, 1:160–61 (29 March 1563); that the merchants in question were members of the Walloon grain cartel: Pettegree, 52.

25. *KRP*, 2:563 (6 June 1575).

26. *KRP,* 1:229–30 (19 January 1566).

27. Hesse, *Menso Alting,* 126; *KRP,* 1:230 (19 January 1566), the long-running dispute is included throughout the consistory minutes of 1565–1566.

28. Beza's letters to Countess Anna (22 January, 2 September 1566) in *Correspondance de Bèze,* ed. Hyppolyte Aubert, et al. vol. 7 (Geneva: Droz, 1973–), 37–38, 220. The Antwerp church not only ruled against Gorin, they wrote that he should respond himself in Antwerp; *KRP,* 1:238, 240 (28 February, 11 March 1566).

29. Polyander, who had studied with Calvin in Geneva, was the French minister from 1571–1598.

30. Schilling, *Civic Calvinism,* 9. Schilling, uses the term "calvinization" to describe Emden's developments of the last quarter of the sixteenth century under the Alting's leadership.

31. Hesse, *Menso Alting,* 126–33.

32. *KRP,* 2:813*f*. Also when Polyander died in 1598, Menso quickly secured the position for Jean's son Jacques.

33. *Die Akten der Synode der Niederländischen Kirchen zu Emden vom 4.-13. Oktober 1571,* ed. J. F. Gerhard Goeters (Neukirchen-Vluyn: Neukirchener Verlag, 1971); the synodal acts are printed on pages 14–87; the list of signatories is on page 88.

34. See note 17, above.

35. Compare the account books of the local (*Haussitzenden*) deacons, JALB #1117–18, 3001; also the accounts of the Dutch (*Fremdlingen*) deacons, JALB (no number).

36. *KRP,* 1:330 (29 November 1568).

37. Hans supposedly served both as a local [*Haussitzenden*] deacon and later as a Dutch refugee [*Fremdlingen*] deacon; he was the only person to do that in the sixteenth or early seventeenth century. He was a *Haussitzenden* deacon in 1582–1583 and perhaps later (compare, JALB #3194, 259*f*.); J. Mülder, *Die Diakonie der Fremdlingen-Armen, 1558–1858* (Emden, 1858), lists him as a *Fremdlingen* deacon in 1589, but no surviving records document this service. It seems unlikely that the *Fremdlingen* deacons would want him to serve given the amount of bitterness that developed in this dispute.

38. *KRP,* 1:498 (1 March 1574). The legal *Questio* drawn up for the legal arbitration describing both sides in the dispute is in JALB #320B, 15.

39. The income of the Dutch deacons in 1574 exceeded 3,300 gulden; they received 464 gulden from testaments alone; compare the second account book of the *Fremdlingen* deacons in JALB (no number), 423–30 (also van Toorenenbergen, *Stukken betreffende de Diaconie,* 44–50).

40. They received the full fifty gulden on 16 March; second *Fremdlingen* account book, 427; van Toorenenbergen, *Stukken betreffende de Diaconie,* 47.

41. *KRP,* 1:501 (5 April 1574).

42. *KRP,* 1:505 (7 June 1574); the consistory agreed to inform them in the future.

43. JALB #1090.

44. Normally the French minister held services on Sundays and holidays; Smid, *Ostfriesische Kirchengeschichte,* 494. From 1686–1708, the extra services were held on Sunday afternoon and during the week; Pleines, "Die französisch reformirte kirche in Emden," 15. At the end of the eighteenth century, several Reformed nobles fled to Emden during the French Revolution; Montigny, "Die französisch reformirte kirche in Emden," 133.

45. Overall in Emden's Reformed congregations, including the French, there were 6,000 to 7,000 members and seven pastors: the French Reformed church with its eighty-two members had one of those pastors; Smid, *Ostfriesische Kirchengeschichte,* 494f. Interestingly, in the first half of the nineteenth century, six of Emden's Reformed ministers were from the Netherlands; only one was German, which demonstrates how close Emden's cultural ties were with the Netherlands.

46. An 1840 report of the Aurich Konsistorium, quoted in Smid, *Ostfriesische Kirchengeschichte,* 495.

47. Ibid.

FIVE

Acculturation and the French Church of London, 1600–circa 1640

Charles Littleton

During the second half of the sixteenth century, at the height of the religious wars on the continent, well over 10,000 Protestants from northwest Europe fled to neighboring England to seek refuge from the persecution and warfare in their home countries. Most of those immigrants who settled in the capital London at this time were in fact from the war-ravaged Low Countries, and particularly from the southern provinces of Flanders, Hainaut, Artois, Walloon Flanders, and Brabant. In the English capital these immigrants, or "strangers" as they were known to the English, could become members of one of the so-called "Stranger churches," the "Dutch church" for Dutch and Flemish speakers, and the "French church" for Francophones from France and the Walloon territories. These churches were ecclesiastically autonomous Reformed presbyterian churches which had been established in 1550, and reestablished in 1560, to minister to these many Protestant refugees in the capital according to their own Protestant rites and ceremonies. During this period of the late sixteenth century, the Stranger churches were populous, at about 2,000 members each, and vibrant, with a congregation and ministry actively committed to the Protestant cause in their homelands and to the maintenance of a Calvinist church and discipline in the heart of an English episcopalian church government.

The size, importance, and vitality of the Stranger churches in the reign of Elizabeth I has long been recognized, and has most recently been successfully reiterated by Andrew Pettegree.[1] In this paper, though, I would like to look at the years of the early seventeenth century in the history of one of these churches, the French church on Threadneedle Street, the institution that would so effectively receive the many Huguenot refugees later in the century. The history of the continental immigrants and their descendants in the first half of the seventeenth century has been sorely neglected, except by Ole Grell, who has written on the Dutch congregation in the early Stuart years.[2] This was a critical period for the French church as well, for at the turn of the seventeenth century the members of the Francophone community in London were becoming rapidly integrated into English society, due principally to a decline in immigration because of the uneasy peace in the continental religious wars, and to the growing predominance of the English-born second generation of immigrants in the stranger population. It is true that this core of second- and third-generation church members was supplemented in the 1620s and 1630s by continental refugees from the Thirty Years' War and the Huguenot revolts in France—but their numbers were nothing like those the churches had faced in the 1570s and 1580s. Indeed, according to a government census of aliens in London, already in May 1593 an overwhelming majority of the children among the 7,000–strong stranger community had been born in England—2,543 had been born in the realm compared to 514 born abroad.[3] Forty years later, in 1634, only about a third of the heads of household attending the Stranger churches were reported to be stranger-born, a figure which Archbishop Laud emphasized when he insisted that the English birth, and thus the English subjecthood, of these second- and third-generation immigrants required them to abandon the Stranger churches and attend their local English parish churches.[4]

In these conditions, it could be supposed that during the first half of the seventeenth century the French church went into a decline from its glory days of the Elizabethan period, both in numbers and influence. The situation, however, was actually far more complicated. There is indeed a wide array of evidence, from the consistory minutes to the church's own registers, to suggest that the church's members began to feel more comfortable in English society at this time and were less exclusively committed to the society of the French church and the doctrinaire Calvinism it represented. Yet there is also ample evidence that the church itself remained populous, active, yet also highly committed to the Calvinist discipline, even at the expense of alienating some of its assimilated members. The church did not really decline in influence in these years, but its meaning did change for its increasingly anglicized members, as did their exclusive loyalty to it. Members now felt free to attend both the French church and Church of England, as these immigrants and their children now could move easily back and forth between the native English and the immigrant "French" worlds they inhabited. Yet among all these changes, the French church's own commitment to orthodox Calvinism and the enforcement of the ecclesiastical discipline, which made it so distinctive in early modern London, always remained constant. It was the strength of the church's commitment to Calvinism and its discipline which helped it to survive the troubled years of the midseventeenth century and prepared it for its new role later in the century of accepting and integrating the flood of Huguenots fleeing Louis XIV's efforts to suppress the Protestant religion in France.

The Population of the French Church in the Seventeenth Century

The early seventeenth century saw a fairly steady decline in the number of strangers in the metropolis in general. The only Jacobean census of the alien population, made in 1618, counts only 1,281 aliens in the City wards, Southwark, and some of its adjoining parishes in Surrey. Unfortunately, this survey does not include aliens living in the sprawling northern and eastern suburbs of the metropolis, in which areas strangers had been settling in large numbers since the late sixteenth century.[5] A later return from 1635 indicates that there were then approximately 3,622 aliens living in the wards of the City, Westminster, Middlesex, and Surrey.[6] This latter figure is made even more difficult to interpret for our purposes by the fact that the majority of these French aliens are recorded as luxury craftsmen living in Westminster and were most likely Catholic servants of Charles I's French queen, Henrietta Maria. Despite the inevitable imprecision of these numbers, both show a precipitous drop in the stranger population from the late sixteenth century, at which time it had stood at about 7,000.

It is even more difficult to calculate the size of the French church congregation at this time, as various sources give highly conflicting figures. More fundamentally, this exercise raises the larger question of what we mean by a "member of the church" at this period. The baptismal registers of the French church of London show that there was an average of 125 baptisms per year in the period from 1600 to 1640. Assuming that at this period there were 35 births per 1,000 members of the population, this would suggest that in the first half of the seventeenth century the congregation of the French church hovered at around 3,400 people (see table 1).[7] This seems like an impossibly high number compared with the size of approximately 2,000 people that the French church seems to have attained in the late sixteenth century. Indeed, other sources do suggest a much smaller, and indeed declining, congregation. The minister of the Walloon church in Canterbury, John Bulteel, calculated that in 1635 the size of the French church of London congregation stood at 1,400 men, women, and children, at a period when the annual number of baptisms as recorded in the registers was higher than it had been in the preceding decades (in 1635 alone there were 213 baptisms performed in the French church, the highest number of any year). However, this may very well be a purposeful under-estimation, as one of Bulteel's goals in producing this figure was to counter the age-old claim that London was flooded with too many strangers.[8]

In addition, the same church registers which provide us with such high baptism figures also give us some indication of the low level of institutional loyalty among the second-generation immigrants, whose membership was vital to the survival of the church. Unlike their baptism, the English-born children of church members could choose whether to marry in the French church. Assimilated members, or those disgruntled

TABLE 1: *French Church Congregation Population, 1600–1640*

	AVERAGE BAPTISMS PER YEAR	CONG. SIZE
1600–1604	98	2,800
1605–1609	103	2,943
1610–1604	97	2,771
1615–1619	103	2,943
1620–1624	114	3,257
1625–1629	128	3,657
1630–1634	173	4,943
1635–1639	187	5,343
1600–1639	125	3,571

Source: William J. C. Moens, ed., *The Registers of the French Church, Threadneedle Street, London*, (Huguenot Society Publications, Series 9, 1896)

with the church and its demands, always had the option of marrying in a nearby English parish church. It would therefore be revealing to see whether members of the second generation continued to marry in the French church and whom they married there. This project is possible as the French church's marriage registers note where each party to the marriage was born, or, in the terms of the registers, was *natif* (or *native*) of. Table 2 shows the result of an analysis of the origins of parties marrying in the French church and recorded in its registers for the period 1600–1640. Two sets of figures are given. The first column counts the number of actual marriages recorded for a five-year period, while the second shows the number out of those total marriages in which one of the parties to the marriage is described as *natif(ve)* of an English city.[9] The third column shows the number of actual individuals marrying (obviously, double the first column), while the fourth column shows the number of those individual parties born in England. A comparison of the second and fourth columns can also show how many of the second generation married fellow English-born strangers and how many married "true" strangers from abroad.

These figures show us that throughout the first half of the seventeenth century English-born second-generation immigrants made up only one-third of the people married in the French church, and that they

TABLE 2: *English-born Children of Strangers Marrying in FC, 1600–1640*

	TOTAL MARRIAGES	MARRIAGES W/ENG. PARTY	TOTAL PARTIES	ENGLISH PARTIES
1600–1604	110	58 (53%)	220	68 (31%)
1605–1609	125	62 (50%)	250	78 (31%)
1610–1614	110	71 (65%)	220	94 (43%)
1615–1619	93	44 (47%)	186	57 (31%)
1620–1624	93	50 (54%)	186	60 (32%)
1625–1629	160	81 (51%)	320	107 (33%)
1630–1634	103	45 (44%)	206	55 (27%)
1635–1639	149	47 (32%)	298	57 (19%)

Source: Moens, ed., *The Registers of the French Church*.

were always outnumbered by the stranger-born. Indeed, a comparison of columns two and four shows that those born in England who did marry in the French church most frequently married spouses born overseas, rather than a fellow English "native." It would appear then that such services of the church did not appeal greatly to the more numerous offspring of the original Elizabethan immigrants, who could so easily marry in their local English parish churches. This conclusion is further corroborated by a comparison of the baptismal and marriage records of the church. Out of the one hundred infants born in England baptized in the French church in 1600, only two are recorded as marrying in that church years later (Marie Lescaillet, married in 1623, and Marie Roussel, married in 1626).[10]

The minutes of the consistory of the church reveal much the same trend. A number of members of the French church evidently felt increasingly comfortable in English society, and even chose to identify themselves as "English." In 1615, Adrian Marie, the brother of the minister of the church, Nathaniel Marie, was admonished for marrying without the consent of his brother or his mother. In response he demanded that he be received in the church "as an Englishman," which in fact he was, as he and his minister brother had both been born in England.[11] These members who considered themselves English and who did not wish to follow the directives of the French church could join their English parish churches to escape the discipline. This had always been a problem for the consistory to face, but such defections became increasingly common in the seventeenth century and caused grave problems for the administration of the church's ecclesiastical discipline. When Jehan Honoré was remonstrated with for absenting himself from the French church's services, he explained that he had been attending the sermons of English ministers instead, "which he brusquely said are as good as ours." Sibille Croisarde was censured in 1612 for marrying a papist in the parish of St. Mary Savoy, but she replied that she "had not done anything except according to her duty and the order of the English Church," and when threatened with excommunication, "she responded that if we did not wish to receive her here, she will retire to the English Church, which she considers just as good as ours."[12]

Sibille Croisarde's offense also reveals that the Francophone immigrants of the seventeenth century and their English-born children could show a disturbing lack of concern over the vital distinctions between papists and "those of the Religion." Like Croisarde, Antoinette Canon, Judith le Sage, and Anne Sulin were all censured for marrying Catholics against the wishes of both the consistory and their own mothers.[13] The consistory also strenuously opposed Marie Boufant's impending marriage to the Catholic Robert Achilles, even though both Marie and her mother insisted that he had agreed to be married in the French church, "although he does not wish to leave his religion or heresy." Matters became more embroiled when the couple consummated their relation before the marriage ceremony and Marie became pregnant. After several more months of negotiation, the church only grudgingly agreed to baptize her child in February 1611 because her Catholic husband provided a written agreement promising that the child would be raised as a Protestant.[14] Perhaps such unions arose from a more frequent socialization of Francophone people of differing faiths in Jacobean London, as the temporary religious peace on the continent was translated to the relations between immigrants in their new homes across the Channel. However, the consistory could only frown upon this growing coexistence. Indeed, in February 1615, it decided that the elders should tell the members of the congregation to desist from their frequent practice of lodging papists in their houses.[15]

How then do we reconcile the large population figures extrapolated from the baptism registers with the evidence from the marriage registers and consistory acts of a declining congregation and the departure of the second generation? I suspect that a solution relies a great deal on how we define a "member" of the congregation. Perhaps membership in the French church meant something different to many of the anglicized second-generation immigrants than it had done to their parents. Probably for many, occasional participation in the French church's services was primarily a means of maintaining an emotional attachment to their parents' homelands and to the "Cause" which had originally prompted their emigration, while in their daily lives they participated more fully in the neighborhood life of their local English parishes and looked to that institution for the provision of preaching and other religious services. By the same token, though, we should not assume that an alien's membership in his or her local English parish church necessarily signified a rejection of the French church or even a break with Reformed presbyterian

Calvinism. One could function as an assimilated member of English society and yet still pay homage to one's continental roots through membership in a Stranger church. Indeed, it appears that dual membership in both ecclesiastical institutions was common, perhaps even the norm, at this time. In his defense to Charles I of the continued separate existence of the Stranger churches, the minister John Bulteel claimed that the members of these churches also attended their local English parish churches, "making profession with them of one and the same Religion and beliefe, they joyn themselves often in that which concerneth the Liturgy and divine service; but besides, they come themselves with liberty amongst those of their owne tongue, to maintaine unity among them, and to provide for the entertainment of the ministry, as also for the relieving of the poore and needy."[16]

Case Study—Guillaume Delaune and His Children

Such a successful straddling of the French and English worlds, and of the continental Reformed and English episcopalian religious traditions, can best be seen through the experiences of one prominent Huguenot family in London, the Delaunes. The remarkably wealthy and successful Delaunes are certainly not representative of most immigrants in early Stuart London, but precisely because of their success their lives are far better documented than those of the many immigrant silk weavers in London and are able to throw into high relief some salient aspects of the immigrant experience in the first half of the century. Most significantly, the experience of the Delaunes reveals that rapid and successful integration into English society did not necessarily entail for these immigrants and their children a concomitant abandonment of the French church and the community it represented.

The Norman physician and Reformed minister Guillaume Delaune fled France with his wife and three sons at the time of the St. Bartholomew's Day massacre in 1572, and quickly settled in the precinct of Blackfriars in London.[17] He served both as a minister of the French church of London, even publishing an epitome of passages from Calvin's *Institutes* through the refugee printer Thomas Vautrollier, and as a physician licensed by the Royal College of Physicians.[18] By the time of his death in 1611, he had become an established and wealthy member of the Blackfriars community, leasing seven large rooms in the building that was eventually to become the second Blackfriars Theatre, and being able to call on the services of three English neighbors to act as witnesses for his will in 1611.[19]

The executor of his will was his eldest son Gideon Delaune, who later became a fabulously wealthy apothecary in Blackfriars and at the Royal Court, where he served as apothecary for Anne of Denmark. He was a founding member of the Society of Apothecaries in 1617, for which he also headed the first Court of Assistants, and later, after the City had made him a freeman of London in 1623, served as under warden from 1624 to 1625, upper warden in 1627, and master from 1628 to 1629 and again from 1636 to 1637. He even contributed the land in Blackfriars on which Apothecaries' Hall was built and still stands.[20] Gideon was indeed very closely connected with Blackfriars parish, and by 1618 had served as churchwarden twice, for which service the church vestry gave him and his family the second pew from the pulpit as a mark of their esteem.[21] It is true that his alien birth could at times impede his participation in the political and economic life of London—as it did in January 1626 when he had to step down from the office of alderman of Dowgate Ward to which he had been elected—but by the time of his death at the great age of ninety-four, he had been able to travel very far into the ranks of the English elite. It was reported that at his death in 1659 he was worth £90,000, and in his will of that year he left £1,000 for his burial, which was to be conducted by the College of Arms following the ceremony usually reserved for an alderman of London.[22] His long will further details his extensive bequests to his two surviving children, both of them married to members of the English gentry, and the disposition of his substantial property holdings in Blackfriars, Kent, Bedfordshire—and Virginia and Bermuda.

Yet throughout all the time of his involvement at Court, Blackfriars, and in the Society of Apothecaries, he maintained a strong identification with his French ancestry and Calvinist religious background through his continued and active membership of the French church, which he served intermittently as deacon and elder from at least 1593.[23] His will bequeathed the large amount of £100 to the poor of that institution, while it only gave £20 to the poor of Blackfriars.[24] He was obviously equally involved in both worlds. In June 1621, the consistory of the French church sent to the Privy Council a letter insisting that they had not excommunicated the Blackfriars physician Simon Du Val from their midst simply because of his participation in the services of the Church of England. The letter, written in English, claims, "We are so farre from blaming anyone that conformeth himself to the English Church, that most of our Company are members thereof and have borne offices in the same and conformed ourselves to the discipline of the said Church."[25] Significantly, the signature of Gideon Delaune, who had indeed served as churchwarden in the parish church of St. Anne's Blackfriars and was now acting as elder in the French church, heads the list of thirteen elders who signed this petition.

Gideon's younger brother Paul was also a medical man. He became a fellow of the College of Physicians in 1618 and went on to serve in Dublin as personal physician to Lord Falkland, lord deputy of Ireland. He only returned to London in 1642, at which point he was made an elect of the College of Physicians, professor of physic at Gresham College, and a physician for the Earl of Essex's Parliamentary troops. In 1654, ousted from his position at Gresham College, Delaune was offered the post of physician-general for the fleet that was about to embark for Jamaica, during which campaign he was lost at sea.[26] Unlike his brother Gideon, Paul Delaune had been born in England, and was thus an English subject. Certainly he was well integrated into the medical and political circles of mid-seventeenth century England. Yet late in his life, even after spending many years away in Ireland and while fulfilling the prestigious post at Gresham College, he still saw fit to serve as an elder of the French church, from 1651 until he set off to sea in 1654. And in his will of 1654, written just before he was to set sail on his fateful trip to the Americas, he still bequeathed to the poor of the French church the token sum of twenty shillings, the same amount he left for the poor of his own English parish of St. Anne's Blackfriars (unlike his brother Gideon, Paul never became rich).[27]

Another of Gideon's younger brothers, Pierre Delaune, served as minister to the French and Walloon congregation in Norwich from 1601 to about 1655.[28] In 1616, he translated the English Book of Common Prayer into French, an influential work which was to serve as the basis for John Durel's translation of 1661. His links with the Church of England only grew tighter when he was appointed rector of Redenhall near Norwich in 1629, a remarkable posting as he had only ever undergone a

Reformed laying on of hands in Leiden and had never received episcopal ordination. Later, he received more honor and recognition from the church of England when he was awarded a Doctor of Divinity from Cambridge in 1636 for his renowned translation of the Book of Common Prayer. In other words, this Reformed minister, the son of a refugee Calvinist minister, worked diligently to put the alien liturgy of the Church of England into the language spoken in his separate Reformed church and even aspired to be simultaneously both a Reformed pastor of the French church of Norwich and a beneficed Anglican clergyman. Like his brothers, Pierre was able to participate successfully in the professional life of English society while also actively maintaining his involvement with the ecclesiastical institutions that represented his recent ancestry in the Huguenot communities of France.

We have seen from the above discussion that the bequests in the aliens' wills can often serve as an indicator of their attachment to the English and immigrant communities. If it is found that there are significant bequests to the parish churches in the aliens' wills, we can perhaps conclude from this that these immigrants recognized, even if in a rather formulaic manner, some connection or responsibility to the inhabitants of the English communities in which they lived.[29] From an examination of 105 wills of members of the French church proved between 1560 and 1625, I have found that all but one of these wills leave some bequest to the poor of the French church. Only seventeen, that is sixteen percent of the total, include a bequest to the English parish poor, and these donations are on average a fifth to a tenth of the amounts left to the French church. For example, a generous widow who gave £100 to the French church in 1624 left to the churchwardens of her parish of St. Mildred Poultry a scant £2.[30] However, the majority of the wills which include donations to the English parish churches, that is, eleven of the seventeen, were written and proved after 1600. Thus, these bequests to the English localities are more common in the wills of immigrants who had remained settled in the capital for a long time, or in those of the original immigrants' children. More significantly, though, this analysis shows that even for those many second- and third-generation immigrants who may have been highly integrated into the life of their English parish, providing for the poor of the French church could be an important symbolic means of expressing their connection with the Francophone Protestant community which was a major part of their ancestry.

The Maintenance of a Calvinist French Church, 1600–1625

The greatest danger to the continued survival of the Stranger churches in the seventeenth century thus did not come from a supposedly declining and assimilating congregation. Instead, it came from the immigrants' own hosts in the episcopalian Church of England. Certainly the relations between the French church and the Church of England had always been complex and ambivalent. Above all, there was a wealth of jurisdictional problems that complicated their relations. The consistory had no effective means, apart from the censures of the Calvinist ecclesiastical discipline, to prevent people from making use of the services of the undisciplined Church of England, or worse, fleeing to it to escape the discipline. Certainly any attempt to force its members back into the French fold, or censure them for participating in English services, could be seen as an implicit criticism of the validity of the host church and its ecclesiastical order and could earn the Stranger churches a stinging rebuke from the Privy Council.

There could also be conflict between the French and English ecclesiastical officials, as they both competed for the loyalties of the many immigrants in London. In August 1592, for example, the consistory felt it necessary to send a delegation to Robert Heas, the minister at St. Botolph's Aldgate, to ask him to stop marrying so many of the church's members without the consistory's knowledge or approval.[31] But for every Robert Heas surreptitiously marrying the church's members outside the city's walls, there were numerous parish ministers who cooperated with the consistory and worked with it to enforce the discipline. The many Huguenots of the French church who settled in St. Anne's Blackfriars, such as the large Delaune clan, would have found a sympathetic welcome from Stephen Egerton and William Gouge, the parish's two successive incumbents from 1585 to 1653 and two of the leading lights in the English Puritan movement.[32] Such members of the London clergy who insisted on the further reformation of their own church were only too happy to collaborate with the French church in bringing offenders under the eye of a discipline they themselves so admired.

Although the French church had long informally cooperated with the English clergy in reining in alien troublemakers in the London parishes, in the early seventeenth century, as members frequently attended services at both institutions, these relations appear to have become more formal.

In particular, members were supplied with testimonials (*témoignages*) from either the French or English ministers which they could show to be admitted into the communion of the other church. In the consistory minutes for 1615 there is a transcription of such a formal certificate. It attests that the signer, the French minister Nathaniel Marie, has talked to the minister of the parish of St. Botolph's Bishopsgate, who told him that he would permit a young man of his parish named Bois (the first name is left purposely blank in the transcript) and his wife to communicate at the French church. Similarly, when Pierre Priere wished to join the French church so that he could marry another member of the church, he was told to bring a suitable *témoignage* from his own parish minister. On the other hand, Marie Henry, the wife of the Englishman Richard West, requested a *témoignage* from the French church so that she could join her English parish church. The former church member Helene de La Noe also produced a *témoignage* from her parish minister so that she could always have the option of occasionally communicating at the French church if she so wished.[33]

Nevertheless, many of the old conflicts remained, and in fact increased, as the boundaries between the two institutions became more blurred. In 1612, the consistory saw fit to remonstrate with Abraham Chamberlen for his denigration of the crucifixes carried by "several pious English ministers" (the consistory secretary's judgment). Chamberlen had further publicly insisted that he did not wish to follow "the ridiculous ceremonies of the Anglican Church" and had even previously asked his local parish minister to forego these ceremonies, which the English minister had refused to do.[34] This entry suggests that at the same time as Chamberlen (a brother-in-law of Gideon Delaune) was lamenting the "ridiculous" ceremonies of the Church of England, he was also a regular attender of services in his local church and was well known to the parish minister. How else would he have known about these ceremonies? In fact, at the same consistory session in which he was censured for his insults to the English ministers, Chamberlen, who was at that time an elder of the consistory, was also admonished for having his child baptized in an English parish church instead of in the French, an offense he had committed previously as well.[35] Despite his dual loyalties, then, he felt free to disparage the liturgy of the Church of England, and was still very much aware of the differences separating the rites of the episcopalian host church from those of the Reformed presbyterian French church—and it is clear which ones this assimilated wealthy merchant preferred. And while Chamberlen condemned the rites of the church in which he had had his children baptized, the consistory defended the crucifixes of the "pious English ministers" while condemning Chamberlen for having his children baptized in their church. These people were not being inconsistent or hypocritical. They were just trying to make some sense of the ambiguity that surrounded the French church's place in English society. The consistory of the French church, like Chamberlen himself, was aware that it and the Church of England were ostensibly united in the same faith, and thus had to coexist and cooperate. Yet it was also very well aware of the differences which made the French church unique, and in their eyes better and more "reformed."

During this entire period, though, the officers of the French church were absolutely insistent on maintaining the church's ecclesiastical distinctness, and especially the rigorous Calvinist discipline that had been at the heart of the church since its foundation in 1550. Although the French church may have allowed its members to attend the services of the church of England, that was only with its express permission and contingent on their good behavior, as expressed in the testimonials exchanged between the churches. The consistory certainly was not willing to let its members escape the censures of the ecclesiastical discipline by joining their undisciplined parish churches. This could happen all too easily, and appears to have become a major problem in the early seventeenth century. It came to a head in the early 1620s, when the consistory began its long battle with Simon Du Val and the bishop of London on precisely this point. In 1621, the consistory demanded that the physician Simon Du Val make a public repentance before the assembled French congregation for his various misdeeds. In response to this censure, he left the church to attend his parish church in St. Anne's Blackfriars. The consistory proceeded nevertheless publicly to excommunicate him for his faults, in retaliation to which Du Val wrote a damaging letter to the Privy Council claiming that the French church had excommunicated him merely because he had left to join his local English parish church. This apparent open contempt for the ecclesiastical order in England greatly angered the Privy Council, and it made its displeasure clear to the consistory. That prompted the letter from the consistory which has already been quoted, in which Gideon Delaune and the other elders professed their own loyalty to and participation in the Church of England. The Council was largely placated by such assurances, but the new bishop of London, George Mountain, decided to pursue the matter and further insisted that Du Val was to be reinstated into the church community without having to undergo any sort of public repentance. The consistory absolutely refused to do this, and proceeded to engage in a three-year standoff on this issue with the bishop and his belligerent chancellor. Throughout, the church insisted on its ecclesiastical privilege to enforce the discipline unimpeded, but the bishop questioned and even threatened to abolish that privilege. This was the most serious run-in the London church had yet had with the English ecclesiastical authorities, and the closest they had yet come to having their autonomy removed. Finally, in June 1623, after the consistory had enlisted the services at court of archbishop Abbot, the royal physician Théodore Turquet de Mayerne, and the theologian John Cameron, a compromise was reached with the bishop whereby Du Val would be able to rejoin the community after a vague public statement was read for him from the church's pulpit. The minister Abraham Aureli found even this compromise in the church's discipline so offensive that he pointedly refused to read the statement himself and left it to his friend John Cameron to readmit Du Val into the congregation.[36]

At his accession in 1625, the new king Charles I promised the Stranger churches his continued protection, as all his predecessors had done. Yet despite these assurances, the rapid rise and influence of William Laud in Charles's reign only led to further crises for the churches. When Laud became archbishop of Canterbury in 1633, the Stranger churches in Canterbury, Maidstone, and Sandwich were among the first targets of his diocesan visitation of 1633. In 1634, the archbishop demanded two things of these Stranger churches. First, he insisted that they have the liturgy of the Church of England translated into French and Dutch and used in the churches. We have seen that Pierre Delaune had already translated the Book of Common Prayer into French by this time and had thus only facilitated Laud's attack on his own church. Secondly, the archbishop ordered that all those members of the Stranger churches who were "natives," that is born in England, were to start attending their English parish churches as of the beginning of 1635. The churches complained that such a demand would ruin them, as they claimed that the churches were largely supported by the contributions of the wealthier second-generation immigrants. The period between April 1634 and the publication of the injunctions in the churches in October 1635 saw these churches in Kent trying to mitigate these demands through a flurry of petitions to and audiences with the Archbishop and the King and consultations with the other Stranger churches and supporters at Court, such as the earl of Pembroke, the countess of Southampton, Théodore Turquet de Mayerne, and Benjamin Rohan, the duc de Soubise. A detailed account of the events of this campaign has been recently supplied by Ole Grell.[37] Here it is enough to know that the churches fought tooth and nail against the injunctions, and that when these, after several delays and emendations, were officially promulgated in the Stranger churches of Kent, they were largely ineffective in practice.

This episode demonstrates both the tenacity of the Stranger churches in defending their ecclesiastical autonomy, and the continuing popular support for the international Protestant struggle among the English people. Laud's apologist Peter Heylyn later ascribed the failure of the injunctions to the support the Stranger churches received from sympathetic English supporters. He complained that "the leading men of the Geneva faction in most parts of the Realm, did secretly solicit them [the Stranger churches] not to be too forward in conforming to the said Injunctions, assuring them of such assistances as might save them harmless, and flattering them with this Opinion of themselves, that the liberty of the Gospel, and the most desireable freedom of the Church from Episcopal Tyranny, depended chiefly on their Courage and Resolution."[38] Indeed, his persecution of the Stranger churches was held against Laud at the time of his trial, and the wording of the actual charge against him is revealing of the significance the Stranger churches in England still retained for the leaders of the Parliamentary Cause at this time. Laud, it was charged, "hath traiterously indevored to cause division and discord betwixt the Church of England and other Reformed churches; And to that end hath supprest and abrogated the Priviledges and Immunities which have been by his Majestie and his Royal Ancestors granted to the Dutch and French churches in this Kingdome."[39] Even in the 1640s, when the immigration of religious refugees had slowed down considerably, the Stranger churches were still valued for their symbolic connection with the Reformed churches on the continent—not just among the descendants of the original refugees themselves, who flocked in such numbers to the church to have their children baptized, but among the churches' many English supporters as well.

The evidence from the church registers and consistory minutes suggests that by the mid-seventeenth century many of the members of the French church, largely English-born children of the original immigrants, were less exclusively tied to the institution of the French church than their forebears had been. This was dangerous for the continued survival of the church, for now recalcitrant members were more comfortable with English society than their parents had been, and could more easily assume an "English" identity to escape the constraints of the French church and its discipline. We have seen, through the examples of Gideon Delaune and Abraham Chamberlen, that the extent of this potentially damaging assimilation even reached high into the ranks of the church's officials. Indeed, the principal ministers of the church during the first half of the seventeenth century—Aaron Cappel (1591–1619), Abraham Aureli (1605–1631), Nathaniel Marie (1601–1642), and Gilbert Primerose (1623–1642)—had all been born and bred in England (or Scotland, in the case of Primerose), and were highly integrated into English society.

Yet at no time did any of these church officials attempt to weaken the church's commitment to orthodox Calvinism and its discipline, even at the expense of alienating other assimilated church members or members of the English episcopate. The French church held on to the discipline that had been an integral part of its original foundation because among an increasingly assimilated congregation it made the church distinct and true to its Reformed origins. The church's identity, and thus the identity of its members, was not centered around being "French," as that distinction was slowly being eroded away (and was itself problematic to define in a congregation with Francophones from so many regions of Europe), but was concentrated on the Reformed discipline that the church insisted on maintaining vigorously, rigorously, and without exception among its congregation throughout all these years, both among the recently arrived battle-scarred Protestant refugees of the sixteenth century and the assimilating "English" children of those refugees.

And the second- and third-generation immigrants appear to have responded to this desire to maintain the Reformed core of the church. They may not have been willing to obey the strictures of the discipline when put into practice against them, but in their desire to have their children baptized in the church, their continued participation in the church even while attending their local English services, and their many testamentary donations to the church poor, they still expressed a commitment to the church and the Protestant "Cause" that it symbolized and that had originally brought their parents to England. This was important for the future. When the Huguenot refugees from Louis XIV's France began to flood into London in the 1680s, they were greeted by a functioning and well-administered Reformed church which had not disappeared from sight during the years of sparse immigration in the mid-seventeenth century and which still played an important role for the increasingly anglicized descendants of the original immigrants. Its officers, many well-established in English society but still committed to the church and the cause for which it stood, were vitally important for the peaceful reception, maintenance, and integration of the thousands of Huguenots who washed up on English shores in the Second Refuge. This meant that those Huguenots who decided to stay in London could freely practice their Reformed faith in safety, despite the Anglican backlash of the Restoration religious settlement. The French church of London had become, after over one hundred years in existence, an accepted part of the landscape which had already proven its resilience and could not be easily suppressed. This was a privilege that was harder to obtain for those Huguenots who moved on to other British settlements in Ireland or North America, where there was not the same tradition of a long-functioning and vibrant Stranger church.

Notes

1. Andrew Pettegree, *Foreign Protestant Communities in Sixteenth-Century London* (Oxford: Clarendon Press, 1986).

2. Ole Peter Grell, *Dutch Calvinists in Early Stuart London: The Dutch Church in Austin Friars, 1603–42* (Leiden: E. J. Brill, 1989); idem, *Calvinist Exiles in Tudor and Stuart England* (Aldershot: Scolar Press, 1996).

3. Irene Scouloudi, ed., *Returns of Strangers Living in the Metropolis, 1593, 1627, 1635, 1639*, Huguenot Society Publications Series, vol. 57 (London: Huguenot Society of Great Britain and Ireland, 1985), 90.

4. John Bulteel, *A Relation of the Troubles of the Three Forraign Churches in Kent* (London: Printed for Samuel Enderbie, 1645), 3, and passim.

5. R. E. G. and Ernest F. Kirk., ed., *Returns of Aliens Dwelling in the City and Suburbs of London*, Huguenot Society Publications Series 10, 3 vols. (Aberdeen: Huguenot Society of London), 3:180–231.

6. Scouloudi, *Returns of Strangers*, 100.

7. William J. C. Moens, ed., *The Registers of the French Church, Threadneedle Street. Vol. 1: 1600–36* Huguenot Society Publications Series 9 (Lymington: Huguenot Society of London, 1896).

8. Bulteel, *A Relation of the Troubles*, 22.

9. Not all the "English" strangers marrying in the French church of London were actually born in London. A large number, perhaps almost on a par with those from London, were natives of Canterbury, and secondarily from Norwich. This shows that there was also a great deal of mobility between the different Francophone communities in the southeast of England.

10. Moens, *Registers of the French Church*, 21, 37.

11. The French Protestant Church of London, Ms. 4 (Actes du consistoire, 1588–1615) (hereafter FPC 4), fols. 520v, 521v (12 January, 20 April 1615).

12. Honoré: FPC 4, fol. 473r (8 March 1610). Croisarde: ibid., fol. 490v (27 February 1612).

13. Canon: ibid., fol. 457r (1 October 1607). Le Sage: ibid., fol. 478r (13 December 1610). Sulin: ibid., fol. 485r (20 June 1611).

14. Ibid., fols. 474v, 477v, 482r–v, 485r, 486r (14 June, 4–22 October 1610, 10 February–18 July 1611).

15. Ibid., fol. 521r (9 February 1615).

16. Bulteel, *A Relation of the Troubles*, 21.

17. On Guillaume Delaune, see Frederick N. L. Poynter, *Gideon Delaune and His Family Circle*, The Gideon Delaune Lecture for 1964 (London: The Wellcome Historical Medical Library, 1965).

18. The French Protestant Church of London, Ms. 3 (Actes du consistoire, 1578–88) (hereafter FPC 3), fols. 76, 78 (16–27 March 1581); Guillaume Delaune, *Institutionis Christianae Religionis a Joanne Calvino . . . Epitome* (London, by Thomas Vautrollier, 1582).

19. Public Record Office (hereafter PRO), Prerogative Court of Canterbury wills (hereafter PCC) 23 Wood, dated 27 November 1610 and proved 12 March 1611.

20. On Gideon Delaune, see Poynter, *Gideon Delaune and His Family Circle*; Cecil Wall and H. Charles Cameron, *History of the Worshipful Society of Apothecaries. Vol. 1: 1617–1815*, revised and edited by E. Ashworth Underwood (Oxford: Oxford University Press, 1963); Leslie G. Mathews, "London's Immigrant Apothecaries, 1600–1800," *Medical History* 18 (1974): 262–74; Brian Burch, "The Parish of St. Anne's Blackfriars, London, to 1665," *Guildhall Miscellany* 3 (1969): 9, 17.

21. Brian Burch, "The Parish of St. Anne's Blackfriars," 17.

22. Thomas Delaune, *Angliae Metropolis; or, The Present State of London* (London, 1690), 329–30; PRO, PCC 380 Pell, written in 1654, and proved in 1659.

23. FPC 4, fols. 177 (18 July 1593), 254 (29 June 1596); French Protestant Church of London, Ms. 5 (Actes du consistoire, 1615–80), fols. 52, 56 (5 July, 23–28 October 1621).

24. PRO, PCC 3 80 Pell.

25. PRO, State Papers (hereafter SP) 14/121/81.

26. On Paul Delaune, see Poynter, *Gideon Delaune and His Family Circle*; A. H. T. Robb-Smith, "Cambridge Medicine," in *Medicine in Seventeenth-Century England* ed. Allen G. Debus (Berkeley: University of California Press, 1974), 361–62, 366; William Munk, *Roll of the College of Physicians of London*, 3 vols. (London: Royal College of Physicians, 1878) 1:108, 160–62; John Ward, *Lives of the Professors of Gresham College* (London, 1740), 266–67.

27. PRO, PCC 248 Ruthen, dated 13 December 1654 and proved 6 June 1657.

28. On Pierre Delaune: Poynter, *Gideon Delaune and His Family Circle*; William J. C. Moens, *The Walloons and their Church at Norwich, their History and Register, 1565–1832*, Huguenot Society Publications Series 1 (Lymington: Huguenot Society of London, 1888), 230–31; David N. Griffiths, "The French Translations of the English Book of Common Prayer," *Proceedings of the Huguenot Society of Great Britain and Ireland* 22, no. 2 (1972): 90–95.

29. For another example of this exercise, see Andrew Pettegree, "'Thirty Years On': Progress towards Integration amongst the Immigrant Population of Elizabethan London," in *English Rural Society, 1550–1800*, ed. John Chartres and David Hey (Cambridge: Cambridge University Press, 1990), 297–312.

30. Gillette de Willem: PRO, PCC 3 Bryde, proved 17 January 1624.

31. FPC 4, fol. 154 (31 August 1592); George Hennessy, *Novum Repertorium Ecclesiasticum Parochiale Londinense* (London: Swan, Sonnenschein and Son, 1898), 106.

32. Brian Burch, "The Parish of St. Anne's Blackfriars," appendix.

33. Bois: FPC 5, fol. 33r (September 1615). Priere: FPC 4, fol. 473v (22 March 1610). Henry: ibid., fol. 481r (4 April 1611). De la Noe: *"quelle communique avec nous quelquefois."* ibid., fol. 488r (28 November 1611).

34. FPC 4, fol. 496r (30 August 1612).

35. Ibid., fols. 415r (21 October 1602), 496r (30 August 1612).

36. PRO, SP 14/121/81; FPC 5, fols. 52r (5 July 1621); 56r (11–28 October 1621); 66r–70r; Fernand de Schickler, *Les Églises du Refuge en Angleterre*, 3 vols. (Paris: Librairie Fischbacher, 1892) 1:409–12.

37. Grell, *Dutch Calvinists in Early Stuart London*, chap. 6; Grell, *Calvinist Exiles in Tudor and Stuart England*, 78–84.

38. Grell, *Calvinist Exiles*, 82.

39. Bulteel, *A Relation of the Troubles*, sig. A3.

SIX

The Fortunes of the Strangers in Norwich and Canterbury, 1565–1700

John Miller

This paper attempts to reconstruct the composition and assess the con-trasting fortunes of two stranger communities. That of Norwich grew rapidly under Elizabeth I but declined almost to nothing in the seven-teenth century, while that of Canterbury was repeatedly replenished by new influxes from the continent. I shall also consider the fortunes of the strangers in terms of residential patterns and wealth and their relations with their English neighbors.

Evidence of stranger numbers is of two types: "snapshots," based on censuses or tax records (aliens were charged double for the only direct tax before 1643, the subsidy); and estimates, based on the record of baptisms, which make it possible to measure trends over time. The former have sev-eral weaknesses. The censuses often cover only men (or women who were self-supporting, usually widows). The subsidy returns are probably more reliable for the few who were taxed on goods valued at £1 or more than for the many who were taxed by the poll (or head); they also contain few women, usually only the wives and daughters of the wealthy. The latter rest on the assumption that baptisms were fully and accurately recorded (which is questionable for both communities in the 1640s and 1650s)[1] and that the birth rate among the strangers was roughly similar to that for the rest of the population. In addition, there is the problem for Norwich that the first type of evidence relates to all strangers, French- and Dutch-speaking, while the latter relates to the Walloon church only.

The letters patent of 1565 which allowed strangers to settle, work, and trade in Norwich set a limit of 300, but this was quickly exceeded. In 1568, the bishop claimed that there were 1,132 Dutch and 339 Walloons[2]; a year later the mayor gave a figure of 2,826[3]; and a census of 1571 gave almost 4,000.[4] By 1583, the number had risen to 4,679, despite stranger mortality estimated at 2,500 in the plague epidemic of 1579–1580.[5] Numbers may have continued to rise. Estimates based on baptisms for the period 1596–1605 suggest that the French congregation numbered over 2,000 and the Dutch congregation may have been larger: Dutch outnumbered Walloons by more than three to one in 1568 and four to one in 1571.[6]

The baptismal estimates suggest that after 1605 numbers in the Walloon church declined, with a brief recovery in the early 1630s; an apparent recovery in the 1650s is probably due to under-recording in the 1640s. The estimates fall from over 2,000 in the later 1590s to under 1,000 in the late 1620s, under 500 after the Restoration and under 200 in the late 1680s. The fall continued after the Revocation of the Edict of Nantes, when few refugees came to Norwich: the *actes* of the consistory show two *témoignages* from 1669 and four from 1685.[7] Two Norwich women married Frenchmen, one from Poitou and the other from "Montauban, en France."[8] Other evidence supports this picture of decline. The 1571 census produced two lists, giving totals of 1,054 and 1,071 men. The number of aliens (most, but not all of them men) on the subsidy rolls declined from 997 in 1581 to 740 in 1598 and 225 in 1624; the census of 1622 revealed a total of 331, again mostly men.[9] The 1571 census would suggest that men comprised just under one quarter of the stranger community; the figure from the 1581 subsidy roll (997) was 21 percent of the total for 1583 (4,679). That would suggest a stranger population of a little over 3,000 in 1598 and almost 1,500 in the early 1620s, in which case the baptismal estimates are probably too high. They would certainly be far too high if the Dutch continued to outnumber the Walloons as heavily as they had done initially. However, an estimate from 1635 gives 396 Walloon communicants and 363 Dutch.[10]

Whatever the weaknesses of the figures, there can be no doubting that the Norwich stranger community shrank in the seventeenth century. The French church at Canterbury, however, was sustained by repeated waves of immigration—in the Huguenot wars of the 1620s, in the Franco-Spanish war (with much fighting in Flanders and northern France) in the 1630s and 1640s and above all in the aftermath of the *dragonnades*. The consistory estimated the size of the congregation as 1,679 in 1582 and 2,068 in 1597.[11] A census of 1622 revealed exactly 300 men, suggesting an overall population of 1,200–1,500. Figures prepared for Archbishop Laud in 1635 gave the number of communicants as 900 (although the consistory's own figure was 1,068).[12] All of this would suggests that the baptismal estimates are a little high; however, two separate estimates for the later 1670s numbered the congregation at 2,500, rather above the figure in the estimates.[13]

A clue as to how Canterbury maintained its numbers can be found in the censuses of 1622, which distinguished between those born in England of stranger parents and those born overseas. In the case of Norwich, the numbers were almost equal: 168 and 163. At Canterbury, those born abroad were twice as numerous as those born in England—194 as against 94—thanks to a continuing influx.[14] In 1641, the burghmote (city council) agreed to admit those who were genuine religious refugees and who would submit to the government of the city and the consistory.[15] The influx of the 1680s was much larger: in 1695, the church claimed to have received between 1,400 and 1,500 refugees, many of them destitute, in the last ten years.[16] This decade saw the highest level of baptisms since the 1590s, suggesting a congregation in excess of 3,000.

Under Elizabeth I, virtually all the Norwich strangers came from the Netherlands, particularly Flanders. Of sixty-nine Walloons in 1568, forty-one came from Flanders, ten from Hainault, and eight from Artois; only three came from outside the southern Netherlands and only one from France.[17] The great majority of the Dutch church came from Flanders, with significant contingents from Brabant and Zeeland. The remainder came from Holland (five), Friesland (two), and Picardy (one).[18] The picture from Canterbury was similar. Those marrying between 1590 and 1627 included some from France (notably Calais and Amiens), but the great majority hailed from Artois and above all what was then Walloon Flanders, from a cluster of textile towns running from Armentières through Lille, Tourcoing, and St. Amand down to Tournai, Cambrai, and Valenciennes.[19] In the seventeenth century, the pattern changed. The incomers of the 1630s and 1640s came mostly from the region between Dunkirk and Boulogne.[20] In the 1680s, most of the refugees came from around Calais and above all Guisnes, which had had the last surviving temple in the area; some were Walloon textile-workers, encouraged to settle by the governor of Calais, but the majority were French.[21]

Why did the flood of refugees dry up at Norwich, but not at Canterbury? One reason must be geography: Norwich had well-established links with the Low Countries, whereas Canterbury's were with northern France, and especially Picardy. (For similar reasons, some Huguenots from southwestern France settled in Bristol and Plymouth.)[22] Moreover, the fact that the French community in Canterbury remained substantial ensured that many incomers would have friends or relations there; there are also signs that the French-speakers at Canterbury continued to trade with their homeland on a large scale.[23] By contrast, Norwich's attenuated Walloon community had good reason not to draw attention to its Frenchness, as we shall see.

The composition of the original immigrant communities was shaped in large part by the policies of town governments, who sought economically valuable skills, above all in cloth-making: Norwich needed to revive its flagging industry; Canterbury wished to develop one. They also wished to prevent the strangers from competing with the natives. The agreements under which they were allowed to settle restricted them to certain (textile) trades: the only exceptions were for those who supplied equipment for wool-combing and weaving or who supplied necessities to the immigrant community of the sort that they had been used to at home: bakers, tailors, and (more contentiously) aqua-vita makers. (Both Walloons and Dutch had a reputation for drinking too much.) The strangers were allowed to sell only wholesale, at least in and around the city. As the mayor of Norwich wrote in 1571: "Others some here be of artisans, men of honest conversation, yet not needful in this commonwealth"—such as tailors, shoemakers, bakers, and joiners—"which be offensive to some of our citizens (being of like occupation) whereupon we have taken order to the pacification thereof."[24]

At both Canterbury and Norwich, there were repeated complaints that the strangers were selling goods by retail, trading in other commodities (such as grain or butter), and depriving the natives of their livelihoods. However, occupational surveys show that the great majority were textile-workers. Of 325 persons in the Dutch Church in Norwich in 1568 whose trades are given (including 13 women), at least 221 were involved in textiles (including 151 wool combers and 54 weavers). There were also 17 tailors and 23 "merchants," many of whom no doubt dealt in cloth or yarn.[25] Among the Walloons, of 74 whose trades were given, 59 were involved in textiles, plus 4 merchants.[26] Nor did the proportion change over time, unlike at Sandwich and Maidstone, where the strangers abandoned cloth-making.[27] The Norwich census of 1622 showed that nearly 80 percent of the strangers—259 out of 331—were involved in textiles, not including 8 tailors and 11 merchants, 1 of whom was described as "merchant and hosier" and 2 as "merchant and draper." There were 111 weavers, 81 combers (79 of them concentrated in the two "petty wards" of Colegate and Fyebridge), 22 "twisterers" or spinners, and 28 hosiers.[28] (It is unclear whether the strangers introduced the hosiery trade into Norwich; it certainly became important in the course of the seventeenth century.)[29] For Canterbury, no occupational census appears to survive, but it is clear that the strangers built up a textile industry based first on woollens and then, when that declined, on silk. By the 1680s, it was estimated that there were 1,000 silk looms in and around the city. Soon after, the silk industry collapsed in the face of foreign competition: in 1710, it was claimed that where once 2,700 people had been employed, there were now only 334. Even so, the corporation repeatedly stated that the strangers provided work for hundreds of people and enabled an impoverished city to maintain its poor.[30]

When assessing the prosperity of the strangers, there is little but anecdotal evidence for Canterbury. In 1622 and 1637, the mayor and aldermen wrote that trade was much decayed. The strangers complained that the influx of penniless refugees after 1685 imposed an impossible financial strain. However, in 1672, a group of freemen complained that the strangers were growing rich at the expense of the natives, thanks to unfair trading practices.[31]

For Norwich, there is more evidence, enabling us to gain an impression of residential patterns and the strangers' wealth. It is often assumed that immigrants, being poor, tend to settle in the poorest areas. This does not seem to be the case for Norwich (or for London: the East End in the later seventeenth century enjoyed a modest prosperity, with few slums).[32] The census of 1571 shows that 77 percent of the strangers lived in two of the four "great wards," Wymer and Over the Water (1,729 and 1,325 respectively). These were not the poorest areas: Wymer (along with Mancroft Ward) contained some of the wealthiest and most fashionable parishes of the city, while the poorest ward (Conesford) contained only 15 percent of the strangers (595).[33] The strangers settled in Wymer and Over the Water probably because these were traditionally the main manufacturing areas in the city. Easy access to the river was no doubt also useful (for washing and scouring), and accommodation may have been easy to find: it was claimed in 1582 that 653 strangers lived in the "petty ward" of Colegate (in Over the Water), mostly in houses which had stood empty (presumably since the decline in the worsted industry earlier in the century).[34]

The next half-century saw two significant developments. First, the strangers were increasingly concentrated in Wymer and, above all, Over the Water; second, Over the Water became more prosperous and fashionable. We can follow this using the number of those appearing in the subsidy rolls and the 1622 census.

WARD	SUBSIDY ROLLS		CENSUS	
	1581	1597	1624	1622
Conesford	120	52	9	10
Mancroft	64	71	7	9
Wymer	409	250	80	116
Over the Water	404	367	129	196
TOTAL	997	740	225	331[35]

These figures are not wholly reliable for reasons given earlier, but they clearly indicate a decline in stranger numbers and a geographical shift northwards. Conesford and Mancroft contained 23 percent of the stranger community in 1571 but only 6 or 7 percent (depending on which figures one uses) in the 1620s. Conversely, Over the Water was home to just over 33 percent of those in the 1571 census, but 57 or 59 percent in the 1620s.

The growing prosperity of Over the Water—as indicated by subsidy and hearth tax returns and the number of large houses—reflected the growth of the cloth industry, after the sixteenth-century slump. Although the "wet and greasy" Dutch cloths failed to establish themselves in the long term, the lighter, colorful "French" cloths became very popular, at home and abroad. Although the Walloons introduced the new techniques, English cloth-workers followed their lead. Worsted-weaving became the most widely practiced trade in the seventeenth century, and worsted-weavers increasingly figured among the city's business and political elite: yeomen, clergy, even gentry apprenticed their sons to worsted-weavers. Whereas Norwich owed much of its Elizabethan prosperity to its role as a marketing center and "county capital," in the seventeenth century it again became an important manufacturing center. As industry remained predominantly domestic, Over the Water, the venue of much of this manufacturing, grew in prosperity.[36]

Although it is clear that strangers increasingly became concentrated in one of the more prosperous parts of the city—albeit not as prosperous as parts of Mancroft or Wymer—it does not follow that they themselves were prosperous. Tax levels or numbers of hearths are necessarily averages. Norwich was not, overall, a wealthy city: in the 1670s, 60 percent of households were exempt from paying the hearth tax on the grounds of poverty—as compared with just over 20 percent in Bristol.[37] Moreover, in both Bristol and the City of London there were great differences of wealth *within* parishes, with large houses on the main streets, smaller houses on side streets, and shacks and hovels in back alleys and courts. The pattern seems similar in Norwich, with thoroughfares like Colegate and Magdalen Street becoming fashionable irrespective of the parishes they were in.[38] It may be that the strangers moved into cramped, below-standard accommodation in a moderately prosperous area; the fact that there was only a limited amount of new building between 1560 and 1700, while the population more than doubled, suggests that there was much subdivision and multi-occupancy, so that moving north of the river may have brought no improvement in their condition.[39]

We need a more direct indicator of wealth and the subsidy rolls offer the best source. The poor were taxed by the head, but the better-off paid according to the assessed value of their goods, from £1 upwards. The table gives the number of those assessed for goods and for poll only in the three subsidies used earlier.

	1581		1597		1624	
WARD	GOODS	POLL	GOODS	POLL	GOODS	POLL
Conesford	14	106	8	44	1	8
Mancroft	12	52	14	57	1	6
Wymer	77	332	46	204	33	47
Over the Water	59	345	56	31	66	63
TOTAL	162	835	124	616	101	124[40]

The percentage of strangers assessed for goods rose from 16 in 1581 to 17 in 1597 to 45 in 1624. This might reflect a growing carelessness in collecting 8d from those too poor to be assessed for goods, but even if one takes the 1622 census as giving a more accurate account of the stranger community, the 101 paying on goods would still amount to 30 percent of the total. An even more reliable indicator is the number paying on goods worth £3 or more. The figures are as follows:

WARD	1581	1597	1624
Conesford	-	3	-
Mancroft	4	4	-
Wymer	13	12	22
Over the Water	12	9	22
TOTAL	29	28	44

Considered in percentage terms, those taxed on goods valued at £3 or more increased from 3 percent in 1581 to 4 percent in 1597 to almost 20 percent in 1622. (Even if one uses the 1622 census figure one still comes out with 13 percent.) Nor can these changes be explained by an increasing rigor of assessment: there is compelling evidence of increasing *under*-assessment of the subsidy under the early Stuarts, with one subsidy bringing in half as much in 1628 as in the 1590s.[41] In other words, after the difficulties of the 1580s and 1590s—for a brief period both churches were unable to maintain their poor[42]—by the 1620s the stranger community was diminishing in size, but growing in wealth.

My final theme is the relationship between the strangers and the natives. The strangers are often portrayed as victims, but many were "betterment" migrants, and they often failed to honor the agreements under which they had been allowed to settle.[43] When English craftsmen cried foul and complained that the strangers were taking away their livelihood, they were not necessarily being unreasonable or expressing "native envy of an industrious minority."[44] Tudor Englishmen did not share the faith of late twentieth-century economists in market forces, but believed trade and industry needed to be regulated, for the good of both producer and consumer. Town governments tried to ensure that the strangers played a circumscribed economic role, which would complement (but not compete with) that of the natives. At Norwich the Walloons—always seen as the more amenable[45]—were prepared to accept this; the Dutch were reluctant. In time, they too largely fell into line because they had far more to gain than to lose from cooperation with the municipality, which possessed the legal, coercive power needed to back up the church's spiritual sanctions. Both had an interest in scrutinizing newcomers, to exclude those who might cause scandals or disorders or become a burden on the poor-rate. Both had an interest in maintaining economic and moral order and tried to suppress drunkenness, sexual misconduct, swearing, gambling, and Sabbath-breaking. Both had an interest in quality control: Norwich insisted that English workers' cloths should be inspected and sealed at the Walloon Hall, in order to raise standards and reassure consumers. Only on the question of limiting the strangers' economic activities did their interests diverge, but with so much in common, this issue bulked less large than it might have done.[46] Indeed, many regulations imposed on the strangers at Norwich had been requested by the Stranger churches.[47]

The relations between the strangers and their fellow-craftsmen were sometimes strained. An abortive rising in Norwich in 1570 was ostensibly directed against the strangers; however, the mayor blamed "divers professing papistry," and the conspiracy was linked to partisans of the recently disgraced Duke of Norfolk.[48] In 1613, there were "disturbances" after the Dutch procured a royal charter allowing them to practice any trade they chose; the city—supported by the French church—got the charter revoked.[49] In 1682, Onias Philippo brought some Huguenots from Ipswich and set them to work. A crowd attacked them, mortally wounding a woman; they left the house that night, but seem to have remained in the city. In March 1683, after a public execution, the "rabble" attacked those who had dealings with the Huguenots and those who had come from Ipswich. The militia restored order and was called out again in July to deal with a riot "when the French Protestants came to town."[50]

Such incidents reflect English hostility to foreigners in general and the French in particular.[51] However, anti-alien violence was far more verbal than physical and was often rhetorical, part of a process of bargaining. Town governments, almost in the same breath, complained of the strangers' unfair trading practices and praised their orderly lives and economic usefulness.[52] In Norwich, but not in Canterbury, this was recognized in 1598 when strangers were allowed to become freemen.[53] Indeed, the longer they remained in England, the more likely they were to build up social and business links with the natives.[54] Stranger churches tried hard to keep control over marriages, to prevent members from marrying out.[55] Even so, the churches suffered constant losses: the

Church of England—and later the Nonconformist churches—offered a Protestant alternative.

The exodus was accelerated by the issue of the poor rate. When the strangers settled in Norwich and Canterbury, the town government had insisted that they maintain their own poor. At Norwich it was stipulated that they pay "church dues"—towards the maintenance of the parish minister, but perhaps also for the relief of the poor—at the rate of one penny in the shilling on their house rents. They also paid a rate, assessed on their personal property, to provide for their own poor and the maintenance of their pastors. Payment of parish dues fell into disuse but was revived as the result of a dispute in 1612, and the strangers found themselves being pressed to pay both sets of rates. Some (of the second or third generation) denied that they were members of the Stranger churches and refused to pay or to serve as elders or deacons. Fearing that if they lost their wealthier members they would be unable to survive, both the Walloons and the Dutch appealed to the city for help; the city appealed to the Privy Council and secured orders that those identified as members should be compelled to remain so and to contribute to church funds.[56] Even so, some individuals, notably from the Castel and Decelé families, were consistently in arrears with their payments—even though they served as elders and deacons.[57]

At Canterbury, the initial agreement made no mention of paying parish rates, but in the seventeenth century overseers of the poor began to demand payment, and in 1647 the court of sessions decreed that the strangers should pay, as at Norwich, in respect of their real but not their personal property. The strangers fought this and similar rulings for more than thirty years, but meanwhile the overseers, backed by the mayor, continued to tax them.[58]

Apart from the financial incentives to leave the Stranger churches, their foreignness could seem an embarrassment. In 1684, the Norwich consistory urged all members of the church to behave like "des réformés, des persecutés et des frères de Jésus Christ"; if not, they risked provoking "la colère de Dieu et l'aversion de nos concitoyens."[59] It is questionable how far some "member" of the Walloon church saw themselves as French: an agreement with Isaac Decelé (about payment of dues) was entered into the *actes* in English.[60] The Norwich *actes* indeed tell a sad story of decline. Records were poorly kept: there are no entries between December 1663 and May 1664; between 1673 and 1683, the names of officers were recorded, but almost nothing else. In 1664, pastor Le Franc quit because he could not live on what he was paid. In 1669, it was noted that the church was desperately short of money because wealthy members refused to contribute. In 1686, Pastor Chauvin complained that the consistory was peevish and tyrannous, refused to pay what was due to him, and allowed Quakers into the congregation.[61] The Dutch church faced similar problems.[62] If the Norwich Walloon consistory's system of moral discipline was still functioning, there is little evidence of it in the *actes*. Even at Canterbury, much healthier in terms of numbers, the consistory often met with rude and defiant language.[63] In 1682, the consistory noted that "several" strangers had come without *témoignages*, attended church rarely (if at all), and committed scandals. It was resolved to exhort them to mend their ways or, failing that, to report them to the magistrate.[64] Simon Baudri roundly told the consistory that he appeared before it not because he regarded himself as a member of the church but because he had been summoned.[65] Meanwhile, cases of drunkenness, wife-beating, and sexual misconduct went on, with the consistories far more likely to forgive than to expel the offenders. They had little choice. Even in France, consistories had had to rely far more on persuasion than on coercion.[66] In England, other Protestant churches offered alternatives for the undisciplined or dissatisfied—especially as many increasingly saw themselves as English. Distinguished from their fellow-citizens only by their language, the assimilation of the strangers was only a matter of time.

Notes

1. See appendix.

2. Baron F. de Schickler, *Les Eglises du Refuge en Angleterre*, 3 vols. (Paris: Fischbacher, 1892), 1:313.

3. Norfolk Record Office (hereafter NRO), Case 17d, Book of Orders for Strangers (hereafter BOS), 1564–1643, transcript by F. Johnson, p. 21 gives 2,827. William J. C. Moens, *The Walloons and Their Church in Norwich: Their History and Registers, 1568–1832*, Huguenot Society Quarto Series (hereafter HQS) 1 (1887–88), part 1, p. 27 gives 2,866. The privy council later put the 1569 figure at 2,826: BOS, 127.

4. Francis Blomefield, *Essay towards a Topographical History of Norfolk*, 11 vols. (London, 1805–10), 3:290–91. The total at the end of the census is given as 3,993, although the ward-by-ward figures add up to 3,962. A separate count of men, women, and children gives a total of 3,925.

5. W. Hudson and J. C. Tingey, ed., *Records of the City of Norwich*, 2 vols. (London: Jarrold, for the Norwich City Council, 1910), 2:lxxxiii.

6. One thousand one hundred and thirty-two to 339 and 868 to 203 (men only): Schickler, *Les Eglises du Refuge en Angleterre*, 1:313; Blomefield, *Essay towards a Topographical History of Norfolk*, 3:291.

7. NRO, FC (French Church) 29/17, partially paginated, (entries under 1 April 1669, 29 Sept. and 3 Dec. 1685).

8. Ibid., (13 July 1684, 13 May 1688).

9. Blomefield, *Essay towards a Topographical History of Norfolk*, 3:291; Moens, *The Walloons*, 2:162–81, 184–87, 189–93. This last is more accurate than W. D. Cooper, ed., *Lists of Foreign Protestants and Aliens Resident in England, 1618–88* (Camden Society, 1862), 18–24.

10. Francis W. Cross, *History of the Walloon and Huguenot Church at Canterbury*, HQS 15 (1898), 107.

11. Anne M. Oakley, "The Canterbury Walloon Congregation from Elizabeth I to Laud," in *Huguenots in Britain and Their French Background, 1550–1800*, ed. Irene Scouloudi (London: Macmillan, 1987), 62; Cross, *History*, 36.

12. Cooper, *List of Foreign Protestants*, 7–10; Cross, *History*, 107 and n.

13. Canterbury Archives [hereafter CA], U47/H4, nos. 12 (printed Cross, *History of the Walloon*, 252), 24. (One source is hostile to the strangers; the other is friendly.)

14. Moens, *The Walloons*, 2:189–93; Cooper, *List of Foreign Protestants*, 7–10. Two denizens make up the 300. For the 1621 influx, see Cross, *History*, 89.

15. CA, Burghmote Minute Book [hereafter BMB] 4, fols. 163–64; Cross, *History*, 121.

16. Cross, *History*, 154–57.

17. Moens, *The Walloons*, 2:153–56.

18. Ibid., 2:207–16.

19. Cross, *History*, 24–25.

20. Ibid., 97, 121.

21. Ibid., 149, 153.

22. Robin Gwynn, *Huguenot Heritage: The History and Contribution of the Huguenots in Britain*, 2d edn. (Brighton: Sussex Academic Press, 2001), 37–40; Ronald Mayo, "The Bristol Huguenots, 1681–1791," *Proceedings of the Huguenot Society of Great Britain and Ireland* (hereafter *HSP*) 21 (1965–70): 438–40.

23. Cross, *History*, 145; CA, BMB 5. fol. 233.

24. For this paragraph and the next, see John Miller, "Town Governments and Protestant Strangers, 1560–1690," *HSP* 26 (1997): 577–89.

25. Moens, *The Walloons*, 2:207–16.

26. Ibid., 2:153–56.

27. M. F. Backhouse, "The Strangers at Work in Sandwich: Native Envy of an Industrious Minority, 1561–1603," *Immigrants and Minorities* 10, no. 3 (1991): 77–92; V. Morant, "The Settlement of Protestant Refugees at Maidstone in the Sixteenth Century," *Economic History Review*, 2d ser., 4 (1951–52): 212–14.

28. Moens, *The Walloons*, 2:189–93. Where two occupations are given, I have taken the first.

29. John F. Pound, "Government and Society in Tudor and Stuart Norwich, 1525–1675" (Ph.D. diss., Leicester University, 1975), 94.

30. Cross, *History*, 89–90, 141, 183–85, 191–203, 238, 252–53.

31. Ibid., 89, 141, 238; CA, BMB 5, fol. 233.

32. See M. J. Power, "East London Housing in the Seventeenth Century," *Crisis and Order in English Towns, 1500–1700*, ed. Peter Clark and Paul Slack (London: Routledge and Kegan Paul, 1972), 237–62. Some of the worst London slums were in Westminster: Norman Brett-James, *The Growth of Stuart London* (London: Allen and Unwin for London and Middlesex Archaeological Society, 1935), 143–44.

33. Blomefield, *Essay towards a Topographical History of Norfolk*, 3:290; Pound, "Government and Society," 28–29, 47–50; J. T. Evans, *Seventeenth Century Norwich* (Oxford: Oxford University Press, 1979), 34, 36–39.

34. Pound, "Government and Society," 9–10, 18–20; Blomefield, *Essay towards a Topographical History of Norfolk*, 3:294.

35. Figures based on Moens, *The Walloons*, 2:162–81, 184–87, 189–93.

36. Pound, "Government and Society," 51, 58–59, 77–83, 89–93, 97–98; idem, "The Social and Trade Structure of Norwich, 1525–75," *Past and Present* 34 (1966): 63–64; Evans, *Seventeenth Century Norwich*, 19–22; K. J. Allison, "The Norfolk Worsted Industry in the Sixteenth and Seventeenth Centuries, vol. 2, The New Draperies," *Yorkshire Bulletin of Economic and Social Research* 13 (1961): 63–65, 67–70, 72–74; C. W. Branford, "Powers of Association: Aspects of Social, Cultural and Political Life in Norwich, ca. 1680–ca. 1760" (Ph.D. diss., University of East Anglia, 1994), 136–51; Penelope J. Corfield, "A Provincial Capital in the Late Seventeenth Century: The Case of Norwich," in *Crisis and Order*, ed. Clark and Slack, 263–310.

37. Pound, "Government and Society," 45–47.

38. Brett-James, *The Growth of Stuart London*. ch. 2; P. Slack, *The Impact of Plague in Tudor and Stuart England*, (Oxford: Clarendon Press, 1990), 119–26, (on Bristol); Branford, "Power of Association," 30–31.

39. Pound, "Government and Society," 15–16.

40. Moens, *The Walloons*, 2:162–81, 184–87. I have omitted the small numbers from Carrow, Heigham, and Pokethorpe, outside the walls.

41. Conrad Russell, "Parliamentary History in Perspective, 1604–29," *History* 61 (1976): 12; Russell, *Parliaments and English Politics, 1621–29* (Oxford: Clarendon

Press, 1979), 49–53; Michael J. Braddick, *The Nerves of State: Taxation and the Financing of the English State, 1558–1714* (Manchester: Manchester University Press, 1996), 94–95.

42. Hudson and Tingey, *Records of the City of Norwich*, 2:195.

43. See Ian Archer, "Responses to alien migrants in London, ca. 1400–1650," in *Le Migrazioni in Europa secc. XIII–XVIII*, ed. S. Cavacchiochi (Florence: Le Monnier, 1994), 755–74; Miller, "Town Governments," 583–84

44. See Backhouse, "The Strangers at Work in Sandwich"

45. Hudson and Tingey, *Records of the City of Norwich*, 2:333; NRO, BOS, 141; Moens, *The Walloons* 1:31–32.

46. See Miller, "Town Governments"; Archer, "Responses."

47. NRO, BOS, 170–72, 200–202, 224, 231–33, 238–40, 252–53, 262–63, 266.

48. Ibid., 23; Blomefield, *Essay towards a Topographical History of Norfolk*, 3:284–85; Pound, "Government and Society," 345–49.

49. Blomefield, *Essay towards a Topographical History of Norfolk*, 3:364–65; Moens, *The Walloons*, 1:64.

50. Blomefield, *Essay towards a Topographical History of Norfolk*, 3:418; British Library, Microfilm M636/37, John Verney to Sir Ralph Verney, 24 March 1683; *Calendar of State Papers Domestic* (hereafter *CSPD*) *July–September 1683*, 363; NRO, Case 13b, no. 7, Lieutenancy Order Book, 1662–1704, fol. 83.

51. Gwynn, *Huguenot Heritage*, chap. 7; M. R. Thorp, "The Anti-Huguenot Undercurrent in late Seventeenth-century England," *HSP* 22 (1970–76): 569–80; Miller, "L'image de la France en Angleterre au XVIIe siècle" in *L'image de l'autre dans l'Europe du Nord-Ouest à travers l'histoire*, ed. Jean-Pierre Jessenne (Lille: Presses Universitaires de Lille, 1996), 217–24. In the early 1680s, an additional reason for the strangers' unpopularity (at least with Tories) was their association with Whiggery and Dissent: Joan Thirsk and J. P. Cooper, ed., *Seventeenth Century Economic Documents* (Oxford: Oxford University Press, 1972), 739–40; *CSPD Jan.–June 1683*, 103 (presentment of the Kent grand jury).

52. See Archer, "Responses"; Miller, "Town Governments."

53. C. M. Vane, "The Walloon Community in Norwich: the first hundred years," *HSP* 24 (1983–88): 133; P. Millican, ed., *The Register of the Freemen of Norwich, 1548–1713* (Norwich: Jarrold, 1934), and passim; CA, BMB 5, fols. 160, 233–35.

54. See Andrew Pettegree, "'Thirty Years On': Progress towards Assimilation among the Immigrant Population of Elizabethan London," in *English Rural Society, 1500–1800: Essays in Honour of Joan Thirsk*, ed. John Chartres and David Hey (Cambridge: Cambridge University Press, 1990), 297–312.

55. Cross, *History*, 59; Moens, *The Walloons*, 1:62.

56. Moens, *The Walloons*, 1:19, 55–56, 60–63, 67, 70; 2:285; *CSPD 1619–23*, 297; *CSPD 1629–31*, 419.

57. Moens, *The Walloons*, 1:55–57, 68, 82, 99, 107; Hudson and Tingey, *Records of the City of Norwich*, 2:149; William L. Sachse, ed., *Minutes of the Norwich Court of Mayoralty, 1630–31* (Norfolk Record Soc., 1942), 194; NRO, Case 16a, Mayor's Court Book (hereafter MCB) 24, fols. 127–28, 157, 167, 169, 231; MCB 25, fols. 49, 91; NRO, FC 29/17, p. 95 and under 7, 8, and 17 Feb., 4 Mar. 1669, 27 Apr. 1671, 1 Aug. 1672.

58. Cross, *History of the Walloon and Huguenot Church at Canterbury*, 28–29, 140–42; CA, BMB 5, fol. 82; CA, U47/H4, nos. 14, 24, 29.

59. NRO, FC 29/17 (5 Aug. 1684).

60. Ibid. (11 June 1671).

61. Ibid. (4 and 7 Dec. 1664, 20 Oct. 1669, and passim); Moens, *The Walloons*, 2:236–38. See also Gwynn, ed., *London Consistory Minutes*, 111, 116, 118.

62. See Moens, *The Walloons*, 1:57; Ole Peter Grell, "From Persecution to Integration: The Decline of the Anglo-Dutch Communities in England, 1648–1702," in *From Persecution to Toleration: The Glorious Revolution and Religion in England*, ed. Ole Peter Grell, Jonathan I. Israel, and Nicholas Tyacke (Oxford: Clarendon Press, 1991), 108.

63. Cross, *History*, 56–58, 90–91, 139, 224; CA, U47/A5C, 14 Nov. 1672, U47/A6, 110, 111, 121.

64. CA, U47/A6, 117.

65. Ibid., 111. He later proved more amenable, ibid., 118.

66. See J. Estèbe and B. Vogler, "La genèse d'une société protestante: étude comparée de quelques registres consistoriaux languedociens et palatins vers 1600," *Annales ESC* 31, no. 2 (1976): 362–88.

Appendix: Estimates of the Size of the Walloon Congregations at Norwich and Canterbury Based on Baptismal Registers

I have followed the method used by Robin Gwynn, "The Distribution of Huguenot Refugees in England," *HSP* 21 (1965–70): 404–36, except that he assumes a birthrate of 35 per thousand, whereas E. A. Wrigley and R. S. Schofield, *The Population History of England, 1541–71* (Cambridge: Cambridge University Press, 1989), 531–33 suggest an average crude birth rate of 31.84 per thousand for this period. I have accordingly used a multiplier of 31.4, which gives figures rather higher than Gwynn's. W. G. Hoskins, the doyen of local historians, suggested a multiplier of 30 (Pound, "Government and Society," 3*n*). In addition, Gwynn started in 1651; for the earlier period, I have used the entries in Moens, *The Walloons*, 2:1–113 and R. Hovenden, ed., *The Registers of the Walloon or Strangers' Church in Canterbury*, HQS 5 (1891), part 1. Like Gwynn, I have normally used five-year averages, which will even out the vagaries of particularly high or low yearly totals. There are also some problems of under-recording, which I shall indicate as appropriate.

Norwich

YEARS	BAPTISMS	AVERAGE	ESTIMATED CONGREG.
1596–1600	354	70.8	2223
1601–1605	321	64.2	2016
1606–1610	271	54.2	1702
1611–1615	215	43	1350
1616–1620	203	40.6	1275
1621–1625	160	32	1005
1626–1630	138	27.6	867
1631–1635	158	31.6	992
1636–1640	133	26.6	835
1641–1645	124	24.8	779
1646–1650	91	18.2	572
1651–1655	103	20.6	647
1656–1660	108	21.6	678
1661–1665	72	14.4	452
1666–1670	77	15.4	484
1671–1675	60	12	377
1676–1680	38	7.6	239
1681–1685	55	11	345
1686–1690	24	4.8	151

Norwich (*continued*)

1691–1695	23	4.6	144
1696–1700	18	3.6	113

Points to note:

1. The figures for the 1630s suggest that if, as it was alleged, 3,000 Protestants left Norwich in the 1630s, there were few Walloons among them: see Schickler, *Les Eglises du Refuge en Angleterre*, 2:43; Moens, *The Walloons*, 1:94, states that 140 families left Norwich for the Netherlands, besides those going to North America, but it is not stated that these families were strangers. In 1635, the synod claimed that there were 396 French (and 363 Dutch) communicants in Norwich: Moens, *The Walloons*, 1:90.

2. There is some evidence that record-keeping was disrupted in the late 1640s: only 5 baptisms are recorded for 1649, as against 17 in 1646, 29 in 1647, 14 in 1648, and 26 in 1650. This was anyway a time of severe divisions within the church: Schickler, *Les Eglises du Refuge en Angleterre*, 2:120–29.

Canterbury

YEARS	BAPTISMS	AVERAGE	ESTIMATED CONGREG.
1581–1584	226	75.3	2364
1591–1595	660	132	4145
1596–1600	476	95.2	2989
1601–1605	339	67.8	2129
1606–1610	351	70.2	2204
1611–1615	317	63.4	1991
1616–1620	347	69.4	2179
1621–1625	299	59.8	1878
1626–1630	443	88.6	2752
1631–1635	487	97.4	3058
1636–1640	459	91.8	2882
1641–Sept. 1644	354	95.4	2964
1647–1650	175	43.75	1374
1651–1655	196	39.2	1231
1656–1660	242	48.4	1520
1661–1665	273	54.6	1714
1666–1670	316	63.2	1984
1671–1675	371	74.2	2330
1676–1680	350	70	2198
1681–1685	378	75.6	2374
1686–1690	550	110	3454
1691–1695	513	102.6	3222
1696–1700	343	68.6	2154

Points to note:

1. For 1597, Cross (*History*, 36) gives a figure of 2,068 men, women, and children (based on the *actes* of the consistory).

2. There is clear evidence of disrupted record-keeping from the 1640s to the 1660s. In 1648, there were twenty baptisms recorded between 2 January and 5 March and then only fifteen between 2 April and 17 December; in 1654, there were only eleven between January and September and twenty-eight between October and December. In 1662, there are no entries between 6 April and 10 August (Hovenden, *Registers*, 211–12, 218–20, 239). As at Norwich, these years saw bitter divisions within the church: Schickler, *Les Eglises du Refuge en Angleterre*, 2:129–38, 183–86, 234–39; Cross, *History*, 121–38.

SEVEN

Uncertain Brotherhood

The Huguenots in the Dutch Republic

Willem Frijhoff

Before the Huguenot Refuge

When Louis XIV put his final ban on French Protestantism, the Huguenot refugees could have expected to find a strong sense of brotherhood in the Republic of the Seven United Provinces. Due to the welcome the Dutch had given other persecuted minorities—the Walloon Protestants, German Lutherans, Calvinists from the Palatinate, Anabaptists, Polish Socinians, English Puritans, and Quakers—the Huguenots looked forward to warm hospitality in the northern Netherlands and substantial help from the ecclesiastical and civil authorities, not to mention the inhabitants of that country themselves, regardless of their faith. Some decades earlier, even the partisans of the beheaded English king Charles I had found refuge in the Dutch Republic, despite its straightforward Protestant outlook and its republican constitution. Other factors stimulated a strong anti–Louis XIV state of mind which, in turn, benefited the Huguenots. The memory of the treacherous actions of the French king, his occupation of the country, the destruction of the countryside, and his financial exactions after the 1672 invasion, was fresh among the populace. His Inquisition-like, Jesuitic Catholicism that he had tried to impose upon the conquered provinces was hated. His absolutist style of governance was contrary to any tradition known in the Netherlands, and in particular to the civil liberties the Dutch had fought for during the eighty years of their war of independence. Finally, his arrogance towards the Dutch as—in his eyes—a newly bred nation of blunt and uncivilized traders, cheese mongers, and brokers, arisen from nowhere, was totally unacceptable to leaders and the people on the street of the Dutch provinces, who had a powerful sense of self-achieved identity.[1]

Being a republic with a ruling burgher aristocracy, the Dutch state structure was virtually perpendicular to that of France. The northern Netherlands was a horizontally organized country with a federal structure and a prevailing middle-class culture. In spite of its uniform outlook, it consisted of seven sovereign provinces, which struggled to achieve a minimal degree of unity, indispensable for common action abroad, or the harmony necessary on the front of foreign politics. The Dutch Republic was basically ruled by the representatives of semi-independent towns, with powerful councils and committees on every level of decision-making. France, on the contrary, was a monarchical, absolutist state, marked by hierarchical relations and a strong court culture, where the will and the whims of the man on the top were law. Hence, since the Huguenots brought their own culture with them, the seeds for future misunderstandings were inevitably sown at their arrival. Brotherhood was expected, but remained uncertain.

The Huguenots were not the first group of French-speaking refugees in the Netherlands. After the creation of the *Conseil des Troubles* (the so-called Council of Blood) in 1567 by the duke of Alba, the representative of King Philip II in the Netherlands, for the repression of Protestantism, a huge exodus of Protestants, mainly Calvinists, but also some Anabaptists and Lutherans, had started to move to foreign towns and regions. They went to England primarily, but also to Emden, Wesel, and Cologne on the eastern border, and to other safe places abroad.[2] After the beginning of the rebellion, consolidated by the rise of the northern economy, the Dutch towns themselves became safe havens for all kinds of religious minorities. Although the rebellion was first of all fought for political liberty (*libertatis ergo*), it was religious liberty that became for many its chief legitimation (*religionis ergo*). Yet, the Union of Utrecht, a treaty concluded on 23 January 1579 between the rebellious provinces, which would serve during two centuries as the basic constitution of the Dutch Republic, did not impose a single religion. It simply excluded the restoration of Catholicism as the sole religion of the state (article 2) but guaranteed at the same time to every inhabitant, including the Catholics themselves, full liberty of conscience (article 13) and left the regulation of confessional matters to the states of the different provinces. In fact, Calvinism—first mainly in its liberal expression, after the Synod of Dordrecht (Dort) of 1618–1619 in a more orthodox version—quickly became the only recognized public religion. It was the "ruling" or "privileged" church, the successor to Catholicism. It took over the use of the church buildings and of the church properties, was supposed to be the confession of the civil authorities, and determined henceforth all the public expressions of religion in the Dutch state. However, since civil authority in the Dutch Republic was not linked to any formally confessional structure of the state, theocracy never managed to impose itself upon the Dutch state or the Dutch society. Though Calvinist in outlook, the state remained fundamentally tolerant in practice.

Liberty of conscience was one of the main reasons why so many Protestants fled to the self-proclaimed state of the northern Netherlands after the fall of Antwerp in 1585. In spite of the prevailing historical image, recent research has made clear that many refugees of the so-called First Refuge were not militant Calvinists at all, but Lutherans, Mennonites, and even Catholics. Whatever their religion may have been, they followed the economic mainstream, the transfer of trade from Antwerp to Amsterdam, and the shift of industrial production from the southern to the northern Netherlands. They could do so the more easily as religious persecution was an explicit non-issue in the new Dutch Republic, and liberty of conscience remained guaranteed as long as non-Calvinist minorities did not practice their religion in public or strive for any form of political influence as a confessional group. Yet, in the long run many refugees adopted the new Calvinist faith, precisely because their confessional involvement had been rather weak. In religious matters too, they followed the mainstream. The declared Calvinists among the refugees, however, developed what Heinz Schilling has called a "theology of exile" (*Exulantentheologie*), in interaction with their intimate conviction to have been persecuted as God's chosen people by the Catholic powers of darkness. Together with the small but strong Calvinist minority in the North, they formed the nucleus of the future Calvinist majority, shaped its theology, developed its spirituality, and formulated a new identity for the society of the northern Netherlands: that of a "Dutch Israel," imbued by a sense of divine election, a missionary vocation, and a strong eschatological feeling.

The impact of the First Refuge on the northern Netherlands must have been tremendous, particularly in the coastal provinces, where the war was by then virtually over and where the economy flourished most.[3] Numbers vary according to different authors, but the lowest estimate suggests that there were about 100,000 refugees in the Dutch Republic alone. But numerous, detailed studies by Jan Briels plausibly argue that in reality about 150,000 refugees must have found their final refuge in the North, some of them in several stages, going first to the Rhineland (e.g., Wesel, Cologne) or to England, and from there to the Dutch Republic.[4] The city of Antwerp alone lost in a couple of years almost half of its inhabitants. On the other side of the balance, the overall population of the northern Netherlands must have increased by 10 percent, that of the coastal provinces Holland and Zeeland alone by 15 to 20 percent. The cities were the great beneficiaries of the stream of refugees. Some towns in the coastal provinces, like Haarlem and Middelburg, doubled their population in a few years due to the impact of the First Refuge. The population of Leiden, the principal center of textile manufacturing, increased by two thirds; it made Leiden for almost a century the second largest town in the Dutch Republic. Amsterdam, Rotterdam, and Gouda increased by one third, but even such smaller proportions (corresponding still to 35,000 refugees in the city of Amsterdam alone) could bring about a major change in the local economy and completely reorganize the social and cultural cityscape.

The French-speaking refugees from the south were called Walloons. Due to their language and their numbers, they managed in many places to maintain their own group identity, living together in distinct districts and organizing themselves in their own special way. Even their rather exuberant lifestyle remained characteristic of their southern origin, and was much criticized by the original Dutch population for its mannerism, its propensity to luxury, and its allegedly dissolute morality. Being outsiders in a well-organized society, the refugees, in particular the French-speaking part of them and those confessing a non-Calvinist faith, remained on the margins of political power and were not readily admitted in the town councils and other political or social institutions, but they were very much welcome for their skills, their fortunes, and their commercial networks. The first commercial monopolies, the East India Company (1602) and the West India Company (1621), benefited amply from their money, their energy, and their involvement in international trade. In all these aspects, the First Refuge of the Walloons prefigured the Second Refuge of the Huguenots, and secured the future of the latter.

The Walloon Congregations

Seen from the perspective of the Second Refuge, the most important achievement of the First Refuge was the elaboration of a stable network of institutions where French-speaking refugees could find appropriate help, shelter, and support: the local congregations of the Walloon church with their institutions of social support and charity, and on top of it the supervising authority of the Walloon Synod. They made the northern Netherlands from the outset an attractive place for the Huguenots.[5] The Protestants who fled from France to the northern Netherlands found there not only a society prone to accept them as brothers of the same faith, but also a fully developed system of assistance, accustomed to help persecuted co-religionists, and indeed an organized Reformed church using the same language and liturgy, and working with similar institutions as in their homeland. At first sight, the conditions were perfect. There was virtually no need for nostalgia.

In the 1680s, there still were Walloon congregations in many towns. The oldest French-speaking Reformed community in the northern Netherlands was that of Middelburg, the booming commercial capital of the province of Zeeland, located on the Scheldt River very close to Flanders, and a bishopric since 1559. Immediately after the conquest of the town by the army of the rebellious States-General in 1574, a Walloon community was founded there. Three years later, in 1577, the French-speaking Reformed refugees of Holland's first and oldest town, Dordrecht, requested the institution of a formal ecclesiastical community (realized in 1586), those of Amsterdam followed immediately after the Alteration (the change-over of the city to the Revolt and the Reformed creed) in 1578.[6] In 1589, the French-speaking Reformed community of Amsterdam was firmly established in its own church, the former conventual chapel of St. Paul's Brethren, and was served by three ministers. Many other Holland and Zeeland towns followed suit, as did some important garrison towns in the inner provinces, like Groningen, Maastricht, and Nijmegen. By 1640, there were twenty-five Walloon congregations with some thirty-five active ministers, some towns, like Amsterdam or Dordrecht, having more than one minister at their service. Of the thirty-two Walloon congregations which had been founded before 1661, there were still twenty-six left at the start of the Revocation process. It is true that ever since the second quarter of the seventeenth century, the

Walloon community slowly decreased in size, through the combined effects of fewer arrivals and an increasing integration. However, from the third quarter of the century, the swelling stream of Huguenot refugees began to fill up their places and finally took over their institutions.

Although the foundation of new parishes for the stream of the Walloon, and later of the French refugees, required some funding, those problems were not as important as they might seem at first sight. In many Dutch towns, the pre-Reformation ecclesiastical buildings, now void of canon and priests, monks and nuns, were still available for public use. Few had been demolished. Convents and monasteries, chapels and conventual churches had been converted into schools, workhouses, factories, guild-halls, orphanages, residences for church ministers or professors, and homes for other salaried officials of town and church. Since the Reformed church did not take over the old parish system but considered the whole town community as a single congregation, it needed fewer church buildings than the Catholics had formerly used. The chapels and churches still available largely outnumbered the needs. They were allocated to other ecclesiastical communities which had been formally recognized in communion with the Dutch Reformed church, like the English Presbyterians, the High German Calvinists, or the French-speaking Walloons. In Utrecht, for instance, the Walloon community obtained in 1656 the usage of St. Peter's Church, a beautiful eleventh-century collegiate church on a quiet place behind the cathedral, which it has conserved until today. In the 1680s, things had not sensibly changed: as often as a French religious community was founded, one of the existing chapels was given to their congregation.

On top of the Walloon church organization was the Walloon Synod. As early as 1578 the national Synod of Dordrecht (Dort)[7] allowed the rapidly growing number of French-speaking refugees from the southern Netherlands to organize for the regulation of their particular affairs their own synodal congregations at a provincial level. However, a national synod would remain the privilege of the whole undivided Calvinistic community of the northern Netherlands, since matters of doctrine, ceremonial, and ecclesiastical discipline could only be changed or regulated by common approval. After the fall of Antwerp (1585) and the departure of almost all the Calvinists from the South for the northern Netherlands, mainly the province of Holland, this autonomous Walloon Synod served in fact as a "national synod" for the refugees, its center of gravity being at Amsterdam.

One of its concerns was the intellectual formation of new Walloon ministers. The need for well-trained ministers brought about the creation of a *caisse des escoliers*, and finally of an educational institution closely linked to Leiden University, the Walloon College at Leiden.[8] This *Collegium Gallo-Belgicum*, called indifferently *Collège Français* after the language spoken and *Collège Wallon* after the destination and the origin of the first beneficiaries, was situated at the Groenhazengracht around the corner of the main university building on the Rapenburg. It was a formal institution of an ecclesiastical character, under the administration of the Walloon Synod. Founded in 1606 for eight stipendiaries, it received until its suppression in 1699 some fifty second- or third-generation refugee beneficiaries. This somewhat lethargic institution got a new infusion after the Revocation. On 26 January 1686, the states of Holland, guided by the curators of Leiden University, had stipulated an annual sum of 25,000 guilders to be reserved for the refugee ministers from France. Each married minister would receive 400 florins, each single one 250 florins. Freecoming money, or money available after the departure or death of a minister, would be given to the stipendiaries of the college. In November 1688, the refugee minister Pierre de Villemandie, a former rector of Saumur Academy, was appointed regent of the college. However, there were probably never more than three French stipendiaries, the states being more and more unwilling to reserve the necessary money, as the refugee problems intensified. In 1699, the college was closed and sold to the benefit of the university.

The Second Refuge
The Huguenot Exodus

It is well known that the old estimates of the number of refugees, made in the heat of the persecution, in the face of fierce indignation and a sentiment of extreme cruelty, are much too high. As early as 13 November 1685, an impartial observer like the Dutch resident at Cologne, Hendrick van Bilderbeeck, contested the number of half a million refugees mentioned by the refugee ministers passing through his office.[9] In the 1950s, the French Protestant historian Samuel Mours made a global estimate of 160,000 to 180,000 refugees, perhaps 200,000 including the eighteenth-century refugees, a rough number that since then has been revised downward but not seriously challenged.[10] For the Republic of the United Provinces, several numbers have been brought forward, with more or less precision. Mours provided for the Dutch Republic an estimated number of 50,000 or 60,000 refugees, which made this country with England the largest recipient, truly *"la grande arche des fugitifs"* as Pierre Bayle, the Rotterdam philosopher and a refugee himself, has called the Dutch Republic.

It is unnecessary to recall here in detail the many problems and pitfalls which lie in wait for whoever tries to make a global calculation of the number of Huguenot refugees. Does one count only the Huguenots established for long in a certain place, or all the Huguenots passing by? And how to distinguish between them? Many Huguenots had been repeatedly registered in several towns, provinces, and even countries in succession. Sometimes they were registered with, other times without, their families. Still more confusing is the distinction, within the Walloon congregations themselves, between newly arrived Huguenot refugees and old Walloon families, settled for generations in the town. In the town registers, French names do not always refer to refugees of both Refuges, but may as well point to people of Swiss origin, or to other economic migrants from France, the southern Netherlands, Burgundy, or Savoy, and quite a lot of them may not have been Calvinists at all. After all, there really were tacitly tolerated French-speaking Roman Catholic parishes in towns like Amsterdam, Leiden, and The Hague, with their own priests of French or Walloon origin. Since the second half of the seventeenth century, the development of commercial relations with the French colonies in America brought new French-speaking people into the commercial metropolis of Amsterdam and the expanding harbor of Rotterdam. There are problems with names, too. Sometimes the French form is used, sometimes they are Dutchified, like Le Blanc > De Wit, Le Beau > Schoone, or Renard > De Vos. The spelling of other names may be simply adapted to the Dutch pronunciation, like Blanchard > Blansjaar. The same holds for the Christian names, even when French preferences in name-giving are preserved. Berber (Barbe), Casper (Gaspard), and Reynier (Rainier), though being used in a Dutch spelling, testify nevertheless to French names. But how to be sure?

Traditionally, a number of some 50,000 to 75,000 Huguenot refugees had been adopted for the Dutch Republic; the detailed local research of the latter decades, combined with new demographic methods, has given some plausibility to Hubert Nusteling's estimate that the total number of Huguenot refugees settling long-term in the Dutch Republic did in fact not exceed 35,000. Many others migrated through the Republic—like the 4,000 *émigrés* who in 1693 came from Germany down the Rhine to sail to Ireland. That is less than 2 percent of the population of the country, estimated at roughly two million inhabitants around the turn of the seventeenth century. In comparison, the demographic impact of the First Refuge had amounted to at least 10 percent, but certainly much more in the coastal provinces.[11] At the same time, there is reason to believe that the initial influx of the Second Refuge was much better distributed over the country than that of the First, which took place in the heat of the war, when the inner provinces under the menace of the enemy were unattractive for refugees.

Apparently, most of the Huguenot refugees settled in the seven major cities of the Dutch Republic, all having more than 20,000 inhabitants: probably Amsterdam attracted slightly more than 5,000 refugees, roughly 2 or 2 1/2 percent of the city's population of more than 200,000. The Hague was second with about 2,750 refugees, at least 7 percent and perhaps even close to 10 percent of the local population, the highest rate of any city. Rotterdam, Leiden, Haarlem, and Delft, all in the province of Holland, and the city of Utrecht, came next in order. But the case of Leiden shows at the same time how tricky research into the Walloon congregations may be. Around 1650, the Walloon church of Leiden counted approximately 17,000 members (of a town population of 60,000 to 70,000). In 1680, the annual number of baptisms points to a community of not more than 5,000. The 150 baptisms of 1682 may correspond to a community of some 4,300 souls. In fact, the continuous reduction of the number of baptisms in this once-numerous community does not allow us to distinguish between the rhythm of decrease of the old Walloon group and the compensation brought by the influx of Huguenot refugees, the more so as Leiden was by that time on the verge of a deep economic crisis. It is quite probable that given this condition many refugees came to the second town of the Dutch Republic in order to try their luck, but that very few remained there after having experienced the malaise of the textile sector.[12] Anyway, if in the thirty largest towns the Huguenot immigration may have reached as much as 7 percent of the local population, the number of refugees fell rapidly after 1690, even if the French congregation continued to grow for a while, due to the relatively high birth rates in the group of refugees.

The Amsterdam citizenship books (*poorterboeken*) registered between October 1681 and October 1691 a total of 2,234 Huguenots coming into the town, among whom were only 214 women—which points probably to a striking underregistration of the female part of the refugees. This number seems to be that of the heads of households.[13] The peak year was, of course, 1686, with 721 new entries, the other years never exceeding 260. Of a group of 1,572 for whom the occupations are known, 40 percent worked in the productive sector, 60 percent in the services. Twenty-five percent were employed in the textile industry (the 120 silkworkers form the most frequently quoted occupation, the second being 85 tailors), 42 percent in commerce, trades, and shops, 7 percent in the health sector (76 surgeons), 4 percent as ministers (58), and 7 percent as seafaring men. Apparently, most of the refugees in Amsterdam belonged to the urban middle classes and made a living in producing luxury goods (silk, gold and silver, lace, and watches). Among the towns of origin, Rouen (240), Paris (214), Sedan (134), and La Rochelle (128) were the four most frequently quoted, but refugees really came from everywhere in France, including Montpellier (85), Bordeaux (55), Bergerac (48), and Nîmes (47).

Another measure of the importance and the variations of the influx is the number of baptisms in the Walloon church. Limiting ourselves again to Amsterdam, the evolution is quite striking. Around 1641–1645, when the city population amounted approximately to 150,000, the Walloon community of the town had reached its greatest extent, with an annual average of 274 baptisms, which might correspond to a community of probably close to 8,000 faithful, including the children. This made the Walloon community by then the fourth largest of the town, after the Dutch Calvinists (over 110,000 souls, but baptisms in the public Reformed churches may by then still have included many Catholics), the Catholics themselves (still very numerous, but numbers difficult to estimate due to the lack of many baptismal registers and unknown numbers baptized in the public churches), and the Lutherans (1,100 baptisms annually, i.e., about 30,000 faithful), but before the English Calvinists (a bit more than 1,000 souls) and the Arminians (slightly over 1,700). The assimilation process of the Walloon population brought the numbers down to 91 baptisms annually in the period 1676–1680, i.e., a Walloon congregation of 2,850 members in a city population slightly less than 200,000. But the influx of Huguenots brought about a sudden rise in the numbers; in 1686–1690 the annual number of baptisms rose to 227, in 1696–1700 even to 302, which might have corresponded again to a community of over 8,000.

In Amsterdam alone, some fifty *pasteurs* seem to have registered after 1685. A second Walloon church was built on one of the main canals, the Keizersgracht. The French deacons were said to be able to sustain in 1685 as many as 2,000 poor refugees. In 1705, the Walloon community, which as early as 1631 had organized its own social welfare by founding an orphanage, the *Walenweeshuis* on the Vijzelgracht (now the French cultural institute Maison Descartes), was obliged by the town council to accept the orphans of the French refugees. In fact, Amsterdam seems to have been the only Dutch town where the Huguenot refugees initially were not integrated into the old Walloon community but started in the newly built church a new Reformed community of French national origin. It was only after the dramatic decrease of the two communities that the two French-speaking parishes were united into a single Reformed congregation in 1715.[14] At the beginning of the nineteenth century, this community still remained the most important in the country and was still served by six ministers. Yet it will be clear that during a period of half a century from 1650 to 1700, the Amsterdam Walloon community went through a tremendous evolution: first a steep decline, then a still steeper rise, but at the same time a profound change in the nature of the community, from a predominantly Walloon congregation to one composed of French nationals. But quickly, the numbers started to decrease. In 1706–1710, only 223 baptisms were annually registered; in 1731–1735, not more than 147 per annum. By then, the French congregation had fallen to some 4,800 members, children included.[15]

Local research in other towns enables us to refine this picture. The town of Delft, for instance, counted around 1680 approximately 24,000 inhabitants in about 6,000 households. The 324 full members in the Delft Walloon church in 1685 may amount to 3 or 5 percent of the town's population, depending on the number of persons per household who were members of the church.[16] At Dordrecht, which was the first major town in Holland on the road to the North for people coming from the southern Netherlands and which counted by then about 20,000 inhabitants, the registers of Walloon church members mention between 1670 and 1740 a total of 352 newly arrived refugees who settled in the town, coming mostly from Picardy, Saintonge, Aunis, and Normandy, the main cities of departure being La Rochelle, Saint-Quentin, Sedan, and Saint-Jean-d'Angély. The Huguenots followed quite naturally the routes which were most readily available. Most refugees in the Netherlands came therefore from northern and western France, from Paris, Rouen and Ile-de-France, Aunis, Saintonge, and Poitou. Among the Dordrecht refugees were twenty-one ministers and forty-four "New Catholics," the others being mainly skilled craftsmen and middle-class merchants. The male cohort amounted to 59 percent, 41 percent being female. Many refugees seem to have been rather young and unmarried. About one-fifth of them had been registered in another foreign place, either in Holland, or in Germany, Switzerland, or England. Again, the rhythm of the arrivals is quite revealing. Before 1686 and after 1689, every year four or five new refugees were registered as members of the congregation; a first peak of refugees arrived in 1682, immediately after the beginning of the *drag-onnades*. During the years 1686–1688, the annual number of new refugees rose sharply to about eighty in 1686, and amounted to forty-five in 1687, and twenty-five in 1688. Apparently, the decline following the 1686 boom was as sharp as the increase had been, and after 1688 the numbers remained as uniformly low as before, until in 1733–1734 some thirty Vaudois refugees from Piémont arrived in the town. Even the smaller second wave of French refugees in 1693–1694 did not affect the town. In fact, many of the Huguenot refugees did not stay on in Dordrecht: within some years, one-quarter of them continued on to Rotterdam, The Hague, or Amsterdam, or to England or Germany. In fact, Dordrecht functioned mainly as a relay to another place of settlement. Mobility was at its zenith during the years 1686–1695. After 1695, the population stabilized. Those who remained in Dordrecht integrated into the local community after one or two generations, through intermarriage with Dutch-speaking citizens, as members of the guilds, or by the logic of their trade or occupation.[17]

The impact of the 1672 war with France is clearly visible in the diffusion of the Huguenot immigration over the country. Whereas from the 1580s to the 1620s the refugees to the southern Netherlands had mainly settled in the booming towns on the seaside, a century later the Huguenot refugees spread virtually over the whole country, including the towns of the inner provinces. Many of these towns, like Utrecht, Amersfoort, Kampen, Deventer, Zwolle, Zutphen, Arnhem, and Nijmegen, each with a population between 7,000 and 30,000 inhabitants, had badly suffered from the French and Munsterite occupation of the provinces of Gelderland, Overyssel, and Utrecht. They now competed with each other to attract refugees who would bring new skills, new money and new vitality. The same held for the city of Groningen and the maritime provinces of Friesland and Zeeland, which tried to improve their position through the influx of refugees. The States of Friesland, for example, voted in February 1686 to pay the salaries of ten refugee ministers willing to serve Huguenot congregations in the province.[18]

In fact, the twenty-five Walloon congregations still existing in the 1640s rose quickly after the start of the Revocation process in France and the arrival of the first wave of French refugees. The massive arrival of new ministers seems in many cases to have been decisive for the creation of new congregations. From 1684 to 1690, new French-speaking congregations, oddly still called "Walloon Churches," were founded in almost all the interior towns of some significance of the Dutch Republic, most towns with not more than a couple of thousand inhabitants: at Tiel, Harderwijk, Zaltbommel, and Doesburg in Gelderland; at Harlingen, Sneek, and Franeker in Friesland; at Veere and Tholen in Zeeland; even in the village of Dwingelo in rural Drenthe. The last congregation was founded in 1703 at Deventer, a major town of Overijssel with a small semi-university, the Athenaeum. Before that date, refugees had probably been integrated into the Dutch Reformed community, which held a reputation of inflexible orthodoxy. Other towns tried to find different solutions for the surplus of ministers. Thus, the states of the district of Zutphen tried in 1686 to benefit from the Huguenot influx for the foundation of the long-desired Illustrious School by presenting a professorship to minister Samuel Basnage de Flottemanville. All in all, between 1682 and 1703 the Huguenot Refuge created 37 new congregations, partly to sustain the 363 refugee ministers. Many of these local congregations remained small to very small: twenty, thirty families at most. They obtained the use of a chapel or a large town church, which they could barely maintain, and collapsed quickly under the financial burden within the congregation.[19]

Compared to the enormous influx of refugees from the southern Netherlands after the beginning of the Revolt, and to the steady immigration, much less spectacular but nonetheless quite numerous, into the Dutch Republic from the German and Scandinavian territories, the Huguenot migration was much smaller in number. Yet it struck public opinion much more and left a durable mark in on the nation's memory. Contemporary observers were obviously quite able to distinguish between the huge flow of refugees and the much smaller number of Huguenot settlers in the Dutch Republic. The converted Italian writer Gregorio Leti (1630–1701), burgher of Amsterdam since 1683 and official historiographer of the city, spoke in his description of the Netherlands *Teatro Belgico* (Amsterdam, 1690) of 1,200 Huguenot families settled in Amsterdam of a total number of 4,000 Huguenot families having fled to the Dutch Republic.[20] Such a striking underestimation suggests that the difference between the real numbers and the symbolic meaning of the Refuge may have been observed from the very beginning.

Beside the obvious dimension of inter-Protestant solidarity, some other factors may explain the immense symbolic weight of the Second Refuge. There was first of all the hostile relationship of the Dutch Republic with the king of France, who had attacked the country so treacherously a dozen years before, in 1672, under the false pretext of the defense and restoration of Roman Catholicism. The Huguenots could now appear as the domestic victims of the king, in a remarkable parallel to the king's foreign enemies, the Dutch themselves. Obviously they had the very same interests. Although France had been for a long time the principal political ally of the Dutch Republic, in 1667 the image of the French king suddenly changed in the Dutch opinion.[21] Henceforth, fury, cruelty, and arrogance were the king's distinguishing marks. After the Revocation, the king's image deteriorated still more; in broadsides and on popular prints, he was considered as "the plague of Christianity" and depicted as "the beast of the Apocalypse."[22]

One of the political actors who benefited most of this reversal was the stadtholder William of Orange, who had risen to power and prominence in the war against Louis XIV. By exploiting politically the Huguenot exodus, both inside the Dutch Republic and during his English expedition, and by destabilizing the network of political alliances and commercial supports that had been patiently woven by the ministers of the French kings during the past decades, William, with the help of the Orangist propaganda machinery, obviously used the Protestant passions for his own designs.[23] His genius was his ability to persuade the councils of even those towns which had everything to lose in a war against France, like Amsterdam, to resist actively the policy of the king of France. Seen from this angle of vision, the Huguenot refugees were just pawns on the chessboard of international commerce and politics, and an alibi for protectionism.

The second factor is still more ambiguous. The Huguenot migration was first of all a migration of literate people: the people of the book. Beside the ordinary Calvinist craftsmen, able to read and to write, and ready to defend their religion symbolized by the Bible, many of them were intellectuals: a few merchants, some noble families, but above all several hundreds of ministers, school teachers, printers, booksellers, and other literate people. Out of the 600 ministers who fled from France, at least 363 came to the Netherlands. At the Walloon Synod of April 1686 in Rotterdam, more than 200 ministers were registered who had during the previous year given proof of their refugee condition. The surplus of ministers was an embarrassing side effect of the Refuge. On the one hand, ministers could not be treated as ordinary craftsmen, since they were figureheads of the repression; on the other hand, they were far too numerous to serve in the existing or newly created local communities. On top of that, they were normally poor and came without any capital. The States of the different provinces created special funds for their sustenance. The States of Holland, for instance, funded in the years 1685 and 1686, 25,000 guilders for the subsistence of 70 ministers. But ministers, even poor ones, were masters of the word, and they could write. Together with other intellectuals, they started immediately a public debate about the king's crimes and reinforced the anti-French trend of Dutch public opinion in foreign policy. But in a few years, they not only had formed a strong bulwark against the politics of the French king, but also revived the strength of the French culture abroad, and they had added significantly to the Dutch Republic of Letters. In the Huguenot refugee community, religion, politics, and letters came together to form a true communicative society that was able to play efficiently with the public opinion of their new country.

Refugee Recruitment and Economic Policy

Informed by the swelling stream of refugees, and urged on by their needs and demands, several state assemblies and town councils took almost at the same time appropriate measures for the benefit of the refugees.[24] Announcements in the French gazettes and in the *Amsterdamsche Courant* tried to convince Huguenots of the liberty and the benefits they would enjoy when settling in the Dutch Republic. The first tangible measure was taken by the States of Friesland on 7 May 1681: all Reformed families of foreign origin who settled in the province would enjoy the same rights and privileges as the ordinary citizens. In the light of Friesland's structural economic problems, this measure was far from disinterested and not really generous. It simply abolished the distinction between citizens and non-citizens (inhabitants). But it was the first in a series of similar offers and proposals taken by other provinces and towns. From the outset, however, the economic goals of those ordinances were quite clear. Implicitly, and sometimes even explicitly, they aimed at the recruitment of highly skilled craftsmen, who were considered essential for the key sectors of the Dutch economy, and at the influx of solvent merchants. The authorities were much less, if at all, interested in peasants and unskilled workers.

The States of the province of Holland and West-Friesland took their first measure in favor of the refugees on 25 September 1681, when they granted full exemption from all the extraordinary provincial taxes for a period of twelve years to all persons of the Reformed religion who had had to leave their country for reasons of religion and wanted to establish themselves in the province of Holland. Struck by this apparent generosity, Friesland added a similar exemption on 16 October 1681, but since the first French refugees to enter the province were poor peasants, not the expected craftsmen, the province of Friesland decided in 1683 to give them some fallow land and to organize a collection for helping them to set up their farms. The province of Groningen followed with tax exemptions in September 1681 and October 1682, especially for textile manufacturing, and Holland voted other exemptions in 1688. When in 1686 the influx of refugees grew beyond expectations, the states of several provinces ordered to organize a collection for the refugees and renewed for long periods their generous offer of a special refugee status.

Local measures soon followed and completed provincial legislation. They were roughly of two kinds: the first was of an inclusive nature, the second of an exceptional kind. Free citizenship and free entrance into the guilds were granted on the one hand, while exemption from taxes and free exercise of commerce and craftsmanship outside the guilds were granted on the other. In the long run, the first model favored integration into the local community much more than the second one, which, though initially perhaps more generous and permitting a quicker start, put the refugees in an isolated position.[25] The first three towns to take action were Groningen, Amsterdam, and Leiden. At Groningen, the idea of supporting poor persecuted co-religionists was clearly enhanced by the wish to gain a new economic impetus: for the benefit of commerce and industry, refugees who were skilled workers, in particular in the textile business, were in September 1681 presented with free citizenship and free entrance into the guilds and corporations; the provincial states added immediately some further immunities and exemptions. Leiden, where the former prosperity of the textile industry had long since passed, took similar measures on 13 October 1681, adding exemption from municipal taxation. Haarlem, another important center of the textile industry, followed in 1683. It was only after the Revocation (17 October 1685) that the majority of the other towns took similar measures and came to a real competition for attracting the most interesting group of refugees. Exemption from taxation was normally granted for a limited period of time: three years, six, ten, sometimes twelve. A particular measure, proposed in Groningen, Leiden, and elsewhere, stipulated that the army henceforth would only use clothes of Dutch fabrication. By this measure, the authorities tried to revive, in a period of war and of military expansion, the local textile industry with the help of the refugee workers and to secure them at the same time a steady market for their crafts.

Of course, the regency of the major towns had traditionally close links with French partners, not only in the field of commerce, but also through family networks and cultural relations. The French Calvinists were not the only ones to flee from France; Dutch Calvinist merchants established in the major French commercial centers, like Rouen, La Rochelle, Nantes, or Bordeaux, and even Paris, had to return, and sometimes flee, back home too.[26] In the years leading up to the Revocation, the town councilors were therefore well aware of what happened in France. Some magistrates were particularly involved in the fate of the refugees, like the Amsterdam councilors Nicolaes Witsen and his uncle and protector Johannes Hudde, who were two of the four burgomasters of Amsterdam in 1685. Johannes Hudde was a well-known mathematician who corresponded with the leading scholars in Europe and was strongly interested in applied technology. He had been appointed burgomaster after the French invasion of 1672 and held from 1680 the so-called *magnificat*, i.e., the direction of the municipal policy, as first burgomaster. Witsen, who had extensively traveled in France and written a standard work on naval technology, was very much interested in the contributions the refugees could make to industrial development, in particular to the silk industry. The stadtholder was the main anti-French political force in the Dutch Republic and a strong supporter of the French protestants. As soon as the stream of Huguenots started in the early 1680s, the Amsterdam council decreed exemption from taxes for the refugees who would settle with their trade or crafts in the town. On the request of five refugee craftsmen, presented to the council on 12 September 1681, privileges were granted on 23 September and 7 October 1681 to all the refugees: free citizenship (compulsory for the exercise of a city function or the admission to a corporation), freedom from city taxes for three years, and the right to exercise their crafts outside the guilds.[27] The poor-relief boards and the deacons of the Reformed church were to provide poor refugees with some financial support, loans, or credit for setting up their craft or trade. These general measures reflect two preoccupations of the Amsterdam town council: first, to attract into the city subjects who would bring in their skills and their capital, in particular in some key sectors that were better developed in France than in the Netherlands. Secondly, to show a generosity towards the refugees that would be at least equal to that of other towns. The city council went so far as to order all merchants of the town to acquaint their partners in France with these attractive conditions and to persuade them to move to Holland.

Smaller towns acted in the same way. At Dordrecht, for instance, the city council decided on 6 December 1681 to grant to the Reformed refugees the free citizenship of the town, and during twelve years freedom from all the municipal taxes and from participation in the civic militia and the night watch. Four years later, on 14 November 1685, the guilds, which had a powerful position in Dordrecht and cherished their monopolies, became freely accessible to the refugees, under the conditions of verifiable residence in the town and a proof of mastership.[28]

Virtually all of these measures addressed merchants and craftsmen. In fact, the Huguenot influx into the Netherlands was of a very diverse social quality. Many nobles and intellectuals came together with the poorest among the unskilled workers, soldiers, and peasants. Many peasants settled in Zeeland, or in the section of Flanders that was under the authority of the States-General (*Staats-Vlaanderen*), around Aardenburg, Groede, Cadzand, or Oostburg. Frequent inundations and repeated plagues had partly depopulated this region, which threatened to fall into even worse condition. The influx of Huguenot peasants was therefore a gift from heaven. Agricultural success was guaranteed since they really did not come from far away. Virtually all of the 516 Huguenot peasants who in January 1686 settled around Sluis came from the area surrounding Calais, just beyond the other extremity of Flanders; they knew that kind of land and what was needed to make it fertile.[29]

The Dutch army recruited refugees too. Many refugees had been employed by the king of France, either as soldiers or as officers, especially many noblemen. Between 1686 and 1689, 530 officers were registered as refugees in the Netherlands. On a proposal of the stadtholder, in 1685 the states of Holland voted a supplementary credit of 100,000 guilders (later raised by another 50,000 guilders) for the creation of new military companies for the refugees. The States of Groningen did the same for two other companies. Ironically, quite a lot of the refugees may have been employed in the regiments which in 1672 had invaded the Netherlands for the restoration of Catholicism. Many Huguenot refugees entered the service of the stadtholder, like Isaac Dumont de Bostaquet (1632–1709), a Normandy nobleman who took part in the expeditions of William III of Orange in England and Ireland, one among the 736 Huguenot officers who accompanied the king.[30] But William proved to be as unreliable as his French counterpart. Whereas the Huguenots hoped for his intervention in France, the king-stadtholder adopted other political priorities, and with the Peace of Ryswick (1697) every hope of an armed intervention vanished.

Notwithstanding the employment facilities offered to peasants and soldiers, many refugees were highly skilled craftsmen indeed. Since they were in great demand in the Netherlands, the question must be asked—

though a satisfactory answer seems for the moment impossible—whether all the skilled refugees were really Huguenots, since it is quite evident by now that quite a lot of refugees of the First Refuge came to Holland for economic reasons and were not Protestants at all. The same might hold for the Protestant towns of France. Once the most active young Protestants had gone, Catholics were well advised to follow. Jonathan Israel has rightly argued that the arrival of the Huguenots in the northern Netherlands coincided with a very favorable conjuncture for precisely that group of skilled craftsmen: commerce and industry were recovering from the setback of the 1672–1677 war, the population had not yet fully recovered to the 1672 level, the commercial and industrial competition with the French enemy had regained much intensity, and a wave of mercantilist thinking favored the integration of highly skilled workers able to introduce industries which could be made profitable both within and outside the Republic. Combined with the effects of the vast urban extension projects of the 1660s, all this made housing relatively cheap, and both accommodation and work rather easy to find.[31]

Moreover, the arrival of highly skilled Huguenots coincided with and contributed to the acceleration and the recovery of the "rich trades" and the rise of the industry of luxury products in the years 1685–1689—two important assets of the Republic's commercial reputation and prosperity. Some towns overtly recruited skilled workers to enhance their own prosperity in competition with others, such as Amsterdam in 1681, where the city council tried to attract French workers for the manufacture of silk, camlet, and lace. Many Huguenot silkworkers from Lyon, Tours, and Nîmes strengthened the Dutch silk industry at Haarlem, where Abraham Legrand got a tax exemption for his factory. They increased the range, output, and quality of Holland's silk production and made the Dutch Republic one of the leading silk-producing nations of Europe. Huguenot shopkeepers opened fashionable boutiques in Amsterdam, The Hague, and other towns. Goldthread workers from Aurillac and elsewhere brought their skill to Amsterdam. Huguenot dressmakers, hatters, wigmakers, gold and silversmiths, and watchmakers, predominant in the Amsterdam influx and probably also at The Hague, introduced new standards of elegance and taste.

Yet, though the Huguenots dominated the fashion industry for a time, they did not manage, in spite of their particular skills, to have much impact on the bulk of the Dutch economy, and especially not on those industries in which the Dutch themselves were already operating successfully, such as the paper industry in the mill district on the river Zaan, north of Amsterdam, and on the Veluwe (Gelderland), and the glass industry. After the first fresh impetus by Huguenot papermakers from the Angoumois region, the Dutch paper industry mainly expanded by reducing the competition from the French.[32] Similarly, Huguenots were called by several town councils to set up glass factories, especially in low-wages towns outside Holland like Zwolle and Zutphen, but in spite of the 1688 import ban on French glass, most of them failed.[33]

Authors from France, such as Bishop of Avranches, Pierre-Daniel Huet, who was greatly interested in the sources of Dutch prosperity, lamented the economic losses that in their opinion the Refuge caused to the French nation. They deplored the departure of many highly skilled craftsmen or, like Jacques Le Moine de L'Espine, tended to blame the Huguenot Refuge for the new rise of export-orientated industrial activity in the Dutch Republic.[34] Yet, economically, the Second Refuge had not very much in common with the First. Whereas at the end of the sixteenth century the refugees contributed massively to the very foundation of the new economy of the Netherlands, both in matters of commerce and in industry, the Second Refuge apparently was successful only in a handful of specialized crafts. At best, it reinforced newly flourishing industries or existing trade networks. Even the new Huguenot capital did not play the primary role some had expected. Figures about the capital imported into the Dutch Republic vary greatly. They range from the one million guilders deposited in the Bank of Amsterdam according to ambassador Claude d'Avaux's estimates in 1683, to the huge influx of Huguenot millions which in 1687 obliged the bank to lower its discount rate. But after the crash of the Amsterdam Exchange in 1688, which affected, of course, the Huguenot investments as much as those of the Dutch themselves, and the slow degradation of the climate in favor of the refugees, many well-to-do Huguenot refugees seem to have left the Netherlands for England, where the king-stadtholder William III through his Glorious Revolution had in the meantime created, or restored, a better climate for the union of Calvinism, capitalism, and prosperity.[35]

It is remarkable, and still difficult to explain, why virtually all the business ventures of the refugees failed. A case in point is the factory of

Pierre Baille. Before his arrival at Amsterdam, he had been director-general of the royal manufactory of Clermont-de-Lodève in Languedoc. The city of Amsterdam granted him an interest-free loan of 50,000 guilders and during the first year the virtually free use of very young orphan children for starting his manufactory of 400 jobs. Notwithstanding these exceptional conditions, his business failed in March 1684, was taken over by the city but had finally to be closed in 1695, leaving a huge debt. Was over-production to blame? A clash between two national cultures of production and administration? Or between styles of *gestion* and authority? The question must remain open until further comparative research has been done into the historical business cultures of the European countries.

Solidarity was not expressed at the level of public administration alone. As early as 1681, the Walloon Synod pressed the States-General for the organization of a public collection in favor of the refugees. Not all of the Huguenots were skilled, literate, or rich; in fact, most were quite poor, or at least they arrived without means. As early as 1684, the Dutch Reformed church created a special committee for the support of the refugees, and in 1685, a new committee created at Amsterdam brought the Walloon consistory and town representatives together for the relief of the poor refugees. The compassion of the Dutch burghers sometimes outmatched the self-interest shown by the town councils. On several occasions, collections were held by parishes, towns, districts, and provinces, with a remarkable result: 10,000 guilders in Amsterdam in 1683, 8,000 at Haarlem in 1686, 8,000 in the Veluwe district of Gelderland. In 1695 at Amsterdam, and in later years in other cities, lotteries were organized for the refugees—a classic instrument of securing money for social welfare of which the Dutch were particularly fond. The money collected was handed over to the deacons of the local Walloon church, who could spend it for the refugees. In Amsterdam alone, until 1700 every year 50,000 guilders on average was collected and redistributed along these informal ways.[36] Yet something had changed by then. Within the towns, Dutch guild members, citizens, and other indigenous inhabitants were less ready to sustain long-established refugees with exceptional measures they would like to see applied to their own declining business.

Neither was the competition between the towns finally very profitable for the refugees. Apart from the growing resistance by the local workers' organizations, guilds, and corporations, the refugees were not really asked to integrate. With the help of the Walloon poor-relief boards, the revenue of the public collections and other particular funds, many refugees moved from town to town in order to get the best advantages and to make an easy new start elsewhere as soon as their businesses collapsed. Quite aware of the fact that Holland's commercial metropolis Amsterdam, with its high level of freedom in almost every aspect of public life and its rather generous social funding system, was deemed to be the final destination of every refugee with some common sense, the Amsterdam town council tried to prevent a massive influx into the city and stipulated in 1690 that only those refugees who arrived directly from France would henceforth benefit from the 1681 exemptions; others would be treated like ordinary inhabitants of the city. At that moment, the French refugees were themselves subject to some competition from other Reformed refugees: those who had to flee the devastated Palatinate and its atrocities—new victims of the Sun King and his war secretary Louvois. Other towns were equally tempted to restrict their former generosity. Groningen, for instance, made a distinction between ordinary refugees and soldiers. The latter had henceforth to rely upon the provincial subsidies alone.

Given the long terms of the granted immunities and exceptions—often up to twelve years—many refugees must have forgotten that their privileges would one day come to an end. In fact, from the beginning provinces and towns aimed at a quick assimilation of the refugees as persons, the exceptional measures being only allowed for economic, charitable, or political reasons. As soon as these conditions had disappeared, the measures were diminished or abolished. The process of assimilation was, therefore, accompanied by legislation at all levels. After 1700, gradually all the former privileges were abolished. Subsidies were limited to first-generation refugees. Between 1709 and 1715, the states of several provinces—and on 21 October 1715 the States-General themselves—decreed the naturalization of the refugees, thus depriving them not only of their (mostly virtual) relations with France and their relatives in that country, but also of their economic and political status of exception.[37] They became ordinary citizens, but barred from public offices. At the same time, however, their French possessions were secured. In fact, it was the Walloon Synod itself that in October 1710 had asked for the naturalization of the refugees in the territories administered by the States-General (Flanders, Brabant, Maastricht) in order to protect their right to inherit from their families in France.

Social Integration

Integration, or assimilation, was not the problem of the Huguenots alone. There were no general rules in the Dutch Republic. As a federal state, it had an essentially centrifugal structure. Sovereignty was not vested in the States-General, which were not more than the central executive for affairs of general interest, essentially war, peace, and diplomacy. Outside the Netherlands, the States-General were therefore the most visible institution of the country, but for the Dutch people themselves, the institutions that really mattered were the States of their province, and still more the town council, the burgomasters and the aldermen. The "nation" could be as well the city, the province, or the "fatherland," a notion that tended to cover the whole Dutch Republic.[38] Sovereignty was, in fact, vested in the provincial States, and more particularly in the deputies of the nobility and the towns who in every province composed the States. For the Dutch, the unity of reference, both juridically and socially, was therefore smaller than the Republic. Hence, integration was a problem common to all Dutch people moving around the country. Laws were different from province to province, and bylaws could vary considerably from town to town. A burgher of Delft was not allowed to take office nor to receive charity in the neighboring town of Rotterdam, ten miles away, pertaining to the same province and the same district, since he was considered a "foreigner" there. It was precisely for that reason that many towns distinguished between a "small" citizenship, easy to secure, and an expensive, "great" citizenship, much more difficult to obtain. The latter remained reserved to well-to-do people whom the ruling elite wished to live with, and to adopt as its neighbors, into its society, or even into its family. In fact, the Dutch authorities, and indeed the whole Dutch political system, were not in favor of xenocracy. Political power had to be reserved to the truly indigenous subjects enjoying full citizenship, pertaining to the same network of families, and sharing the same social strata.

One of the main problems for the integration of the refugees was therefore the political and institutional notion of the "foreigner."[39] A foreigner could succeed his social and economic assimilation without being able to achieve full political integration. This was all the less so as the civil authorities had during the past decades won with some difficulty the battle against Reformed theocracy. They mistrusted refugees who, like the Huguenots, were suspected of sympathy for a theocratic form of government. They would therefore not admit the Huguenot refugees to plain citizenship at the risk of the restoration of a theocracy long overcome. But this was precisely what many refugees were looking for: the Calvinist state that the French king had denied them. The Dutch state, however, was not a Calvinist state; it only looked so. Calvinism was its only public religion, but inside their homes the Dutch were free to practice the religion they wanted. The state asked a Calvinist confession for being admissible to public office, but that was all. Some Huguenot refugees, like the exiles of the First Refuge, wanted to go further; society itself had to be moral, godly, and Protestant. Obviously they quickly provoked some irritation, be it for their moral claims, for their eschatological view of political reality, or simply for poverty, which presented a challenge to Dutch society. In the eyes of the Dutch, the true stranger was he who did not recognize the primacy of the country's civil power but desired instead to promote that of the ecclesiastical authorities (Geneva, Dordrecht, the Walloon Synod). That was precisely what some Huguenots dreamed of creating.

Compassion could be one instrument of brotherhood, and hence of integration. Many stories were told, written, and published about the horrible fate of the French Protestants, not only that of the remaining faithful, like schoolmaster Jean Migault, but still more the fate of the refugees who were caught and sent to the galleys, like Jean Richard de Tibante, or the vicissitudes of a François Leguat, who after his unsuccessful attempt to found a Huguenot colony on the Mascarene Islands, fled in 1693 to the then Dutch island of Mauritius, and hence to Batavia where he was involved in a lawsuit.[40] In the eighteenth century, the Walloon Synod created the *Fonds des Galériens* in order to redeem Huguenots condemned to the galleys. Under the pressure of the persecution in France, Elie Benoist (1640–1728), refugee minister at Delft, wrote his commissioned *Histoire de l'Edict de Nantes*. It was published in French at Delft in 1695, with engravings by the Mennonite engraver Jan Luiken showing horrible scenes of persecution, and translated into Dutch in

1696. Other prints, notably by the influential engraver Romeyn de Hooghe, who a decade earlier had depicted the atrocities committed by the king's army in the Holland villages of Bodegraven and Zwammerdam, visualized in a pictorial language of utmost physical cruelty the terrible tyranny exerted by Louis XIV during his *dragonnades*.[41] No wonder that Louis was equated with the Beast of the Apocalypse.

Besides working together, as suggested above, integration could take many other forms. Local studies seem to suggest that the social integration of the second wave of Huguenot refugees was much quicker than that of the First Refuge. The Huguenots were, of course, less numerous, and many of their congregations were small. In the Walloon congregation at Dordrecht, for instance, intermarriage (*connubium*) was rather rare among the refugees. Only one fifth of them married other refugees; the others integrated into the local population. At Groningen and Bois-le-Duc, only half of the first generation refugees married within the Huguenot community.[42]

The main obstacle to a full integration of the refugees was at the same time their main asset, the French language. The Huguenots participated actively in the intellectual life of the Republic of Letters and promoted the advanced position of the Dutch in the international scientific community.[43] French was by the 1680s the status language of the Dutch upper classes. It replaced Latin as the international language of learned communication. The existing infrastructure of the Republic of Letters in the Dutch Republic (the great publishing firms, the book trade, centers of learning, libraries, private collections, illustrious schools and universities) acquired a powerful new impetus from the arrival of many learned Huguenots. Whereas, like Pierre Bayle, they managed to use the existing Dutch cultural infrastructure for the benefit of their own scholarship and to obtain a firm position in the international scholarly community, the Dutch learned community faced in turn new challenges and new chances.

Ever since the First Refuge, the Dutch had been the cultural brokers of Europe, translating, printing, teaching, and communicating whatever lived anywhere in somebody's mind. The Second Refuge reinforced this cultural infrastructure. The Huguenot Refuge attracted many printers, booksellers, writers, and journalists, precisely in those sectors which were already flourishing. They now received a new stimulus. The Refuge made the Dutch printing sector "le magasin de l'univers"—it is Voltaire's expression—the center of the European book trade.[44] At least one-third of the booksellers and printers working in Amsterdam between 1680 and 1725 were members of the Huguenot refugee community.

The Huguenot intellectuals invented new forms of communication. They started learned journals and made the book review one of the main instruments of criticism and of the diffusion of thought. The international role of Dutch periodicals for the diffusion of the book was invaluable: to start with, Pierre Bayle, *Nouvelles de la République des Lettres* (1684–1687), continued by Jean Bernard (1699–1718), the *Bibliothèque universelle et historique* (1686–1693), the *Bibliothèque choisie* (1703–1713), and the *Bibliothèque ancienne et moderne* de Jean Le Clerc (1657–1736), the *Histoire des Ouvrages des Savans* (1687–1709) by Henri Basnage de Beauval (1656–1710), and several others, those learned journals with their dense network of correspondents made the great printing towns of the Republic—Amsterdam in the first place, but also Rotterdam, Leiden, The Hague, Utrecht—the coherent center of literate Europe.[45] But until the second half of the eighteenth century, the influence of the Dutch book trade depended largely on the French-speaking production, such as the gazettes, among which above all the *Gazette de Leyde* de Jean Luzac, and the book trade represented by an international publisher like Marc-Michel Rey, or by the establishment at Amsterdam of renowned printers of music.

According to the periodization proposed by Van Eeghen, the international character of the Dutch book production was reinforced during the period 1572–1680, whereas the period 1680–1725 was characterized by a shift towards the production of books in French at the expense of books in Latin.[46] Of course, the emergence of French as the *lingua franca* of the European cultural elites and as the conversational language of the Republic of Letters played an important role here, but the massive immigration of French intellectuals was similarly a strong asset.[47] Around 1680, a new generation of booksellers arose in Holland who benefited strongly from the Huguenot impetus. Henry Desbordes, who in 1682 fled from Lyon, and the Huguetan brothers, who after the Revocation came from Paris, were among the foremost publishers of Amsterdam. The Huguetan brothers in particular made Amsterdam the center of the European book trade.[48] But young booksellers elsewhere benefited likewise from the Revocation. In Rotterdam, thirty-eight of ninety first editions, i.e., nearly half of the original book production printed by Reinier Leers (1654–1714), were due to Huguenots, among them Pierre Bayle (eight titles), Henri, Jacques and Samuel Basnage (together five titles), Jacques Abbadie (three), Pierre Jurieu (two), and Elie Benoist (one).[49] It has to be underscored that the Huguenot printings by a printer like Leers matched his publications of reputedly heterodox French Catholic authors who could not be published in their own country; the French Oratorians Nicolas Malebranche and Richard Simon, or the Jansenists Antoine Arnauld and Pasquier Quesnel. Yet, Leers remained cautious. The most violent anti-royalist books and pamphlets were published either under a pseudonym or in small shops destitute of recognizable forms of international networking and where the publishers could be trusted.

Whereas it remains doubtful whether the Dutch economy was significantly affected by the Huguenot Refuge, there is no doubt about its impact on the cultural sector of the Dutch society, its reading culture, universities, and academic life. Yet, as Jonathan Israel has noticed, "Bayle and the other Huguenot writers and intellectuals in Holland who did so much to promote new modes of thinking in Europe found it difficult to come to grips with the late Cartesian and Cocceian movements in the Republic."[50] One of the reasons was their poor mastery of the Dutch language—Bayle never really learned it, nor did he make much effort to do so—on the contrary, he lamented his French being degenerated by the surrounding Dutch. Inner-Dutch debates and controversies of the early Enlightenment—for example the tremendous debate around *De Betooverde Wereld* (*Le Monde enchanté*) of minister Balthasar Bekker (1691), though translated into French as early as 1694 but despised by Bayle, were barely taken up by the Huguenot intellectuals living in the Netherlands.

In a certain sense, Huguenot thinking developed along a particular line, which did not always cross inner-Dutch debates. Pierre Bayle, Jacques Basnage (1653–1723), and Prosper Marchand (1678–1756) were leading figures of the international intellectual scene, but they followed their own interests in the established Huguenot *internationale*. Some decades later, radical Huguenot thinkers, though, like Jean Rousset de Missy (1686–1762) and Jean-Frédéric Bernard (1683–1744) were involved in a radical critique of revealed religion, to which the Dutch on the whole remained rather refractory. What linked the Huguenots with the inner-Dutch intellectuals was probably their common rejection of Spinoza, his circle and his followers.[51] The Huguenot network linked the Republic stronger than before with the new French-speaking intellectual community, but it did not replace the old inner-Dutch Latin-speaking network of philologists, polyhistorians, law students, physicians, and above all theologians. In that sense, the integration of the Huguenots remained certainly rather partial.

Coexistence, Survival, and Identity

As Andrew Pettegree has put it, in the case of Holland the newcomers "were absorbed relatively painlessly, since the Republic had both considerable experience of welcoming Protestant religious exiles, and the social ethos to accommodate them."[52] Yet, problems of coexistence with the local population could arise.[53] The civil authorities of the Dutch Republic carefully maintained inside the Republic a balance of neutrality, always hesitating between favoring the public church and admitting competing Protestant communities, even conniving at a more or less clandestine exercise of the Catholic religion inside private buildings—yet the Reformed character of the Dutch state was one of its trademarks in the international arena. As the prime defender of Calvinism in Europe, it had to react against the Revocation.

Inside the Republic, some measures of retaliation were taken against the Catholics. Apparently these measures emanated more often from the local communities than from the authorities themselves. The higher those in power, the more cautious they were; public concord and harmony being the main public virtue in the Netherlands, as a warrant for civic peace. The correspondence of the internuncio with Rome mentions some "persecutions" of Catholics in towns like Rotterdam, Utrecht, and Arnhem, and in the provinces of Friesland, Groningen, and Gelderland, where Calvinism traditionally had a much more aggressive tone than in Holland, and one spokesman reported that the brother of a priest had been mistakenly stoned to death in Groningen—but the provincial authorities advised moderation, and the stadtholder himself, though a strong defender of the Calvinist cause, tried to prevent the provinces from taking retaliatory measures against Catholics.[54]

Much more important than those local interconfessional skirmishes was the problem of Huguenot survival itself. How did the Huguenots create and maintain their community of faith? Diaspora situations, where survival is a vital problem, always create conflicts and discussions about the best way to follow—which tends to be presented as the only possible and definite way for the survival of the group. After the Revocation, the huge numbers of intellectuals present in the Dutch Republic made these discussions more acute than before. As intellectuals, the refugee ministers cherished their own opinions in theological matters. A typical problem of exile is the tension between the divergence of interpretations and the need for internal cohesion. Some refugee theologians seemed to incline towards the Arminian positions of the Saumur Academy, and indeed to ideas close to Socinianism. In the northern Netherlands, the preexisting Walloon Synod was able to play the role of a recognized arbiter. Confronted with this dilemma, it opted for the orthodox interpretations and decided in 1686 to follow strictly the doctrine of the Synod of Dordrecht.

Although they were all Calvinists, the refugees did not agree among themselves on the political strategy with respect to France. Basically two attitudes prevailed. On the one hand, one faction held a traditional attitude of loyalty to the king as absolute monarch, and of political support for the fundamental laws, which implied a particular form of moral accommodation with the misfortune of the Huguenots, being in the minority and tolerated, and some support for a political foundation of that toleration. On the other hand, some refugees adopted a more challenging attitude of plain revolt against the treacherous king, who, though still respected as an absolute monarch, transgressed the divine and human laws that had set limits to his absolute power. Hence the king became a symbol of the excesses that announced the end of times, the Antichrist himself, in their eschatology. In the Dutch situation, the drama rose from the fact that the protagonists of these two profoundly antagonistic attitudes, the *frères ennemis* Pierre Bayle (1647–1706) and Pierre Jurieu (1637–1713), knew each other well as former professors at Sedan Academy, from where they both fled in 1681 to the same town and finished working in the same school, the first being appointed professor of philosophy and history at the small Illustrious School of Rotterdam, the other becoming a minister and professor of theology at the same institution.[55]

By October 1693, the quarrel had taken such a dangerous political turn that Bayle lost his job as a town professor because of his decidedly anti-Orangist attitude. In his eyes, William of Orange was a usurper of legal power. Jurieu, in his turn, suffered for his persecuted co-religionists and struggled for his brothers in the Desert. He defended the Reformed faith against the attacks of the French Catholics, and searched for signs from heaven predicting a speedy return of the fate. In his *Lettres pastorales* (1686–1694) he developed a particular idea of popular sovereignty. He overtly summoned his co-religionists in France to rebel against their treacherous and diabolical king, who had forfeited his kingship, and to flee out of the country. His eschatological feelings brought him to a sense of fulfillment of the biblical prophecies. He exulted at the Glorious Revolution as the victory of the Reformed faith, and saw in William of Orange the champion of international Calvinism.[56] Indeed, many refugee soldiers and officers fought in William's army.

Bayle, for his part, argued in his *Critique générale de l'histoire du Calvinisme* (1682) and his *Commentaire philosophique* (1686) for a partition of the political and the religious order, and ultimately of reason and faith. In his comments on the maxim *Compelle intrare* (Luke 14:23), Bayle proposed a formal distinction between religious and civil toleration, and made civil toleration the foundation and the warrant of religious pluralism and the main instrument for the neutralization of ecclesiastical intolerance. Whereas he advocated political submission to the sovereign, he asked at the same time for a civil toleration of the religious diversity that would overcome the present confusions. Jurieu, of course, was more popular among the persecuted crowd. Yet, Bayle's great idea of civil toleration, rooted in his philosophy, had won the future, perhaps because it could draw on a long practice of religious coexistence and pragmatic tolerance in the Dutch Republic. Whereas the Walloon Synod, inspired by minister Jurieu, condemned this idea as late as 1691, it was soon to become a major guideline for the regulation of religious affairs in the civil space, and hence for the secularization of the civil order, not only in the Netherlands, but in France too.[57] During the eighteenth century, the debate on toleration was continued with great seriousness and over a long period, in all the learned periodicals of the Republic of Letters. From Pierre Bayle to Étienne Luzac, it was typical of a certain form of liberal Protestantism, essentially of Huguenot origin.[58]

Incidentally, the question of survival got a new impetus when the French-speaking Vaudois, refugees from Piémont, came to the Netherlands in November 1733 and November 1734 and were admitted into the

Walloon churches. These refugees, however, were not free to settle anywhere. The States of Holland and West-Friesland assembled all the
refugees, 402 in total, and dispatched them among 14 Walloon communities of the province. In Dordrecht, for instance, 30 Vaudois arrived,
mostly craftsmen. Just like the Huguenots half a century before, they
received from the local authorities and the French community help for
lodging, work, and subsistence.[59]

The most important asset for the survival of the Huguenot community was not religion, however, but language. The social prestige attrib-
uted to the mastery of the French language was high. As early as the
sixteenth century, French had been taught in the Dutch-speaking
Netherlands (roughly the present-day Netherlands and Flanders, including Brussels) as a commercial language, whereas the process of state formation and the growing importance of the Burgundian court at Brussels
had introduced French as the language of the court. Since then, French
had become the major foreign language in the Dutch-speaking Netherlands. Next to the Dutch-speaking elementary schools a growing network
of so-called French schools arose, where pupils learned practical matters
and were taught in French.[60] The predominant Francophilia in the
Netherlands provided an opportunity for the refugees. Literate burghers
sought French friends or teachers, French servants were employed for the
domestic acculturation to French culture, and the French poor were
regarded as people to help not only because of their faith and poverty but
also as the persecuted victims of a higher culture. When after the Peace
of Ryswick the hope for a restoration of the Protestant religion in France
vanished, and at the same time the generosity of the recipient Dutch
declined, the Huguenots had to settle and to find stable jobs. They had
to take advantage of their main quality: their French-ness.

The Frenchification of the Dutch elites was in fact very much stimulated by the massive arrival of Calvinist refugees of good breeding and
excellent manners.[61] Just like one century earlier, Calvinism was for the
ordinary faithful not yet the austere religion that forbade all refinery of
manners. The French refugees were for many a cultural attraction. The
process of Frenchification of the Dutch elite is difficult to analyze, the
more so as after the end of the physical *grand tour* through France in the
1680s, French culture was appropriated in a different way: through education, books, and engravings much more than through visual experience.
In the eyes of public opinion, France as a political nation and the French

culture went henceforth separate ways, yet French culture was essentially
an aristocratic culture, a court culture, which was elaborated at the court
of the French king. The French language, though not being the language
of France alone, was formed and transformed through the narratives of
French writers and the social codes of French institutions.

Yet something changed with the arrival of the Huguenots. They
imported their way of life, a basic segment of the French everyday culture, and made it available to large sectors of Dutch society, whereas the
grand tour previously had only influenced the elite. However, the status of
French culture transferred into Dutch society was forcibly modified:
it remained an external element. The problem was that some French
refugees were quite convinced of the superiority of their culture. French
arrogance was a recurrent theme among the Dutch, even before the
breakdown of the diplomatic friendship. In his *Fraternal Letters* written in
1686–1687 the French minister Jean Tirel described of the dangers to
which his fellow refugees could be exposed abroad and warned them to
not behave as arrogant Frenchmen.[62] About 1725, the climate started
indeed to change gradually. A profound cleavage developed in Dutch
society between the aristocracy and the bourgeoisie. The Dutch bourgeoisie took the French manners and culture for a scapegoat in its fight
against the upper classes and the excesses of the ruling oligarchies. The
appreciation of French culture, formerly praised for its politeness, elegance, and courteousness, reached a turning point. Henceforth, its merits seemed to be the very causes of the Dutch decline. Cultivated French
people were henceforth seen as ridiculous, mannered, and precious.
Their morals and behavior were said to be the principal cause of Dutch
decadence; the ancient virtues of the antique Batavians had been cor-
rupted by the depravity of the French aristocrats, who exalted their honor
but—as Elie Luzac put in his analysis of the economic decline of Holland
(*Hollands rijkdom*, 4 vols., 1780–83)—despised the very foundations of
Dutch society: trade and the sound search for profit.[63]

The upper classes themselves invested heavily in French culture. The
prestige of the French language, together with the liberal outlook of the
majority of the Walloon congregations and the less dogmatic attitude of
the Walloon Synod, made the Walloon church the ideal alternative for
Dutch patricians and upper middle-class merchants, industrials and intellectuals who wanted to distinguish themselves from the official Dutch

Reformed church with its dogmatic and orthodox preachers and its grass-roots pietism. Ever since the beginning of the eighteenth century, the Walloon church functioned locally more and more as the aristocratic alternative for the popular, public, Dutch-speaking Reformed church. In Dordrecht, for instance, between 1670 and 1738, forty-four faithful of Dutch origin were confirmed in the Walloon church. Since there was full communion between the Dutch and the Walloon Reformed churches, and even with the English, Scots, and German Reformed communities in the major towns of Holland, people who wanted something special went sometimes to celebrate their marriage in the smaller non-Dutch churches.

By and by, the membership of Walloon congregations, in particular the smaller towns, lost its refugee outlook. They recruited an increasing number of Dutch citizens from local elites able to speak, or at least to understand French, and eager to distinguish themselves from the ordinary Dutch-speaking Reformed congregations. French, as the language of holy service, was henceforth the true distinguishing mark of the Walloon congregations, not a refugee origin or a French birthplace. After the decline in Huguenot arrivals at the beginning of the eighteenth century and the integration into the Dutch society of the second- and third-generation Huguenots, membership of the Walloon churches was therefore naturally limited to that part of the population that was able to understand or to speak French. According to the oldest reliable figures, not more than 6 or 7 percent of the Dutch youth, boys and girls together, but mostly in the upper classes, followed some form of French teaching in 1811.[64] Still, this figure reflects the situation as it was during the annexation of the Netherlands to the French Empire. In normal times, not more than one upon every twenty inhabitants must have been able to communicate fluently in French. That was the upper limit of the Walloon congregations after the assimilation of the French refugees into Dutch society.

Epilogue

What is left at present of the Huguenot communities in the Netherlands? First of all, some Walloons and Huguenots founded new colonies over-seas; the Walloons in New Netherland (present-day New York), the Huguenots in the Cape Colony, to which, in 1687–1688, the East India

Company sent 150 Huguenots and where in 1806 17 percent of the population was of Huguenot origin.[65] In Surinam the prospects were even better; as early as 1683, 300 Huguenot refugees came to reinforce the plantation economy of this West India Company colony.[66]

Within the Netherlands, the harvest is nevertheless rather poor. After the First Refuge, thirty-two Walloon communities had been founded prior to 1661. Between 1682 and 1703, the Huguenot Refuge added thirty-seven new congregations. A century later, however, few of them were left. At the end of the nineteenth century, seventeen congregations still existed; one century later, fourteen survived, all in the major towns of the country, assembling probably a bit more than three thousand members.

At the census of 1809, the first to include religious affiliation, in the whole city of Amsterdam only 1,093 Walloon Reformed members were listed, i.e., not more than 1 percent of the local Reformed community, and only a half percent of the town's population. The Walloon congregation had become by then the smallest denomination in the city.[67] The decline of the numbers is not easy to document, as the Walloon Reformed are often counted along with the Dutch Reformed. Yet the recruitment of ministers for the Walloon churches confirms this trend. Its evolution is quite striking. From 1575 to 1699, the number of Walloon ministers grew continuously to reach 144 newly ordained ministers in 1675–1699, whereas it declined slowly after 1700, and broke down after 1800. Both periods of Refuge saw a huge influx of foreign ministers: 80 percent of the newly ordained ministers in 1575–1599 and in 1675–1699, and their offspring were responsible for a new surplus some thirty years later. Soon, however, the local renewal of pastors, or pastors recruited locally, became predominant; after 1725, more than 75 percent of the newly ordained ministers were born in the Netherlands, and the accelerating decrease after 1750 shows that the Walloon church had lost its attractiveness even for the Dutch.[68]

Yet, during the eighteenth century, the Walloon congregations developed into regular parishes and lost their refugee character. One of the most evident signs of this normalization is the creation of institutions of charity, in particular schools for the poor children of the Walloon congregation, educated at the orphanage or instructed at the deacons' expense like those founded at Rotterdam and The Hague (both founded in 1739) and at Amsterdam (founded around 1780). At the turn of the eighteenth century there were probably more than 200 pupils at Amsterdam, more than 130 at The Hague, and 60 at Rotterdam aged between six and fourteen. The Amsterdam school was suppressed in 1942; at The Hague, the closure took place in 1964.[69]

The "General Regulation for the Administration of the Reformed Church," introduced by King William I in 1816 into his new realm of the (greater) Netherlands, absorbed the former Walloon synod. The fusion became effective in 1818. The new General Reformed synod included ten provincial representatives of the Dutch Reformed churches and one minister on behalf of the Walloon congregations. Since 1951, the fourteen Walloon congregations form a particular class on the national level within the Reformed church.

Some elements of Huguenot memory survive, including the French language, of course, and French family names, and also some church buildings. Many have been abandoned, and the parishes suppressed. The Amsterdam community has let out on lease its New Church for more than fifty years. In 1974, the community of Dordrecht sold its church, the late medieval *Gasthuiskapel* (hospital chapel) in the main commercial street of the town; it is now a sports shop. But the Huguenot cross, displayed in public buildings of the Walloon communities, has become the main instrument of Huguenot memory, and a visible symbol of group identity. Besides, the memory of Pierre Bayle is still fostered in Rotterdam, as a trademark of this city of toleration. As the "other" famous intellectual of the town, Pierre Bayle disputes his fame with Erasmus. Commemorative tablets have been fixed in the wall of the Walloon church: for Bayle as "defender of religious toleration" in 1961, for Jurieu as "the theologian of Rotterdam" in 1968; both were renewed in 1998.[70] The city of Rotterdam has established a Pierre Bayle lecture for intellectual achievement, and important Pierre Bayle prizes for art critics are granted every year by the Rotterdam Art Council. In the Huguenot tomb at the Crooswijk cemetery of Rotterdam, Bayle and Jurieu are buried brotherly together under one single stone, as a proof that their Huguenot condition restores the fundamental unity that their intellectual divisions had broken.

Notes

1. Basic studies on the culture and politics of the Dutch Republic: Willem Frijhoff and Marijke Spies, *1650: Hard-Won Unity*, trans. Mary Scholz (Assen:

Willem Frijhoff

Van Gorcum, 2003); Jonathan Israel, *The Dutch Republic. Its Rise, Greatness, and Fall, 1477–1806* (Oxford: Clarendon Press, 1995); Simon Schama, *The Embarrassment of Riches: An Interpretation of Dutch Culture in the Golden Age* (New York: Alfred A. Knopf, 1987).

2. Heinz Schilling, *Niederländische Exulanten im 16. Jahrhundert. Ihre Stellung im Sozialgefüge und im religiösen Leben deutscher und englischer Städte* (Gütersloh: Gütersloher, 1972); Bernard Cottret, *Terre d'exil: L'Angleterre et ses réfugiés français et wallons, de la Réforme à la Révocation de l'Édit de Nantes, 1550–1700* (Paris: Aubier, 1985); Andrew Pettegree, *Foreign Protestant Communities in Sixteenth-Century London* (Oxford: Clarendon Press, 1986); William J. C. Moens, *The Walloons and their Church at Norwich. Their history and registers, 1565–1832*, 2 vols. (Lymington: Huguenot Society of London, 1887–88); Douglas L. Rickwood, "The Norwich Strangers 1565–1643: A Problem of Control," *Proceedings of the Huguenot Society of Great Britain and Ireland* 24 (1983–88): 119–28; Ole Peter Grell, *Dutch Calvinists in Early Stuart London. The Dutch Church in Austin Friars, 1603–1642* (Leiden and New York: E. J. Brill, 1989); Andrew Pettegree, *Emden and the Dutch Revolt. Exile and the Development of Reformed Protestantism* (Oxford: Clarendon Press, 1992); Raingard Eßer, *Niederländische Exulanten im England des 16. und frühen 17. Jahrhunderts* (Berlin: Duncker and Humblot, 1996).

3. Paul Dibon, "Le refuge wallon, précurseur du refuge huguenot," *Dix-septième Siècle* 76/77 (1967): 53–74; Willem Frijhoff, "Migrations religieuses dans les Provinces-Unies avant le Second Refuge," *Revue du Nord* 80 (July-December 1998): 573–98 (with further references); J. Briels, "De Zuidnederlandse immigratie, 1572–1630," *Tijdschrift voor geschiedenis*, 100 (1987): 331–55; Oscar Gelderblom, *Zuidnederlandse kooplieden en de opkomst van de Amsterdamse stapelmarkt (1578–1630)* (Hilversum: Verloren, 2000).

4. See, for instance: Ilja M. Veldman, "Keulen als toevluchtsoord voor Nederlandse kunstenaars (1567–1612)," *Oud-Holland* 107 (1993): 34–58, for artists at Cologne; and Willem Frijhoff, *Wegen van Evert Willemsz, 1607–1647. Een Hollands weeskind op zoek naar zichzelf* (Nijmegen: SUN, 1995): 159–80, for a Flemish refugee who brought Puritan pietism from England to the northern Netherlands.

5. General overviews of the relations between the Huguenots and the northern Netherlands: W. E. J. Berg, *De réfugiés in de Nederlanden, na de herroeping van het Edict van Nantes. Eerste deel: Handel en nijverheid* (Amsterdam: Johannes Muller, 1845); H. J. Koenen, *Geschiedenis van de vestiging en den invloed der Fransche vluchtelingen in Nederland* (Leiden: Luchtmans, 1846); D. F. Poujol, *Histoire et influence des Églises wallonnes dans les Pays-Bas* (Paris: Fischbacher, 1902); Marc Jospin et al., *Les Églises wallonnes des Pays-Bas* (Amsterdam: Éditions de l'Écho des Églises wallonneses, 1963); H. H. Bolhuis, "La Hollande et les deux Refuges," *Bulletin de la Société d'histoire du protestantisme français* 115 (1969): 407–48; H. Bots,

G. H. M. Posthumus Meyjes, and F. Wieringa, *Vlucht naar de vrijheid: de Hugenoten en de Nederlanden* (Amsterdam and Dieren: De Bataafsche Leeuw, 1985); Christiane Berkvens-Stevelinck, "De Hugenoten," in *La France aux Pays-Bas. Invloeden in het verleden*, ed. Paul Blom et al. (Vianen: Kwadraat, 1985), 13–49; Cees Cruson, "De hugenoten als réfugiés," *De Gids* 148 (1985): 225–31; J. A. H. Bots and G. H. M. Posthumus Meyjes, ed., *La Révocation de l'édit de Nantes et les Provinces-Unies, 1685* (The Revocation of the Edict of Nantes and the Dutch Republic, 1685) (Amsterdam and Maarssen: APA-Holland University Press, 1986); A. T. van Deursen, F. R. J. Knetsch, S. B. J. Zilverberg, and G. J. Schutte, *De herroeping van het Edict van Nantes (1685) in de Franse en Nederlandse geschied-schrijving* (Amsterdam: VU Uitgeverij, 1987); Hans Bots, "Le Refuge dans les Provinces-Unies," in *La Diaspora des Huguenots. Les réfugiés protestants de France et leur dispersion dans le monde (XVIe–XVIIIe siècles)*, ed. Eckart Birnstiel and Chrystel Bernat (Paris: Honoré Champion, 2001), 63–74; Bots, "Le Refuge huguenot dans les Provinces-Unies. Orientation bibliographique," in *Conflits politiques, controverses religieuses. Essais d'histoire européienne aux 16e–18e siècles*, ed. Ouzi Elyada and Jacques Le Brun (Paris: Éditions de l'École des Hautes Études en Sciences Sociales, 2002), 101–17.

6. E. H. Cossée, "De Walen en hun gemeente te Dordrecht," *Kwartaal & Teken* 8, no. 1 (1982): 1–8; Delphine Boulenger, "L'Église wallonne de Dordrecht et la Révocation de l'Édit de Nantes (1670–1740)" (master's thesis, Université de Paris X–Nanterre, 1993); Fred van Lieburg, "Geloven op vele manieren," in *Geschiedenis van Dordrecht van 1572 tot 1813*, ed. Willem Frijhoff, Hubert Nustel-ing, and Marijke Spies (Hilversum: Verloren, 1998), 288–89.

7. This was the first synod of Dordrecht, not to be confused with the famous Synod of Dort of 1618–1619, which established Calvinist orthodoxy.

8. G. H. M. Posthumus Meyjes, *Geschiedenis van het Waalse college te Leiden, 1606–1699, tevens een bijdrage tot de vroegste geschiedenis van het Fonds Hallet* (Leiden: Universitaire Pers Leiden, 1975); Posthumus Meyjes, "Le Collège Wallon," in *Leiden University in the Seventeenth Century. An Exchange of Learning*, ed. Th. H. Lunsingh Scheurleer and G. H. M. Posthumus Meyjes (Leiden: Universitaire Pers Leiden and E. J. Brill, 1975), 111–35.

9. Bots, "L'écho du refuge huguenot dans quelques villes allemandes. La correspondance diplomatique des résidents néerlandais à Francfort, Cologne et Ratisbonne (1685–1687)," in *Grenzgänge. Literatur und Kunst im Kontext*, ed. Guillaume van Gemert and Hans Ester (Amsterdam: Rodopi, 1990), 429–30.

10. Samuel Mours, *Les Églises réformées de France* (Paris: La Librairie Protes-tante, 1958), 168–78; Philip Benedict, "The Huguenot Population of France, 1600–1685: The Demographic Fate and Customs of a Religious Minority," *Transactions of the American Philosophical Society* 81, no. 5 (1991).

11. On the numbers of Huguenot refugees, see H. P. H. Nusteling, "The Netherlands and the Huguenot émigrés," in Bots & Posthumus Meyjes, *La Révocation*, 17–34; Nusteling, *Welvaart en werkgelegenheid in Amsterdam, 1540–1860* (Amsterdam: De Bataafsche Leeuw, 1985), 262; E. Buning, P. Overbeek, and J. Vermeer, "De huisgenoten des geloofs: de immigratie van de hugenoten," *Tijdschrift voor geschiedenis* 100 (1987): 356–73; Israel, *The Dutch Republic*, 627–30; Hans Bots, "La migration huguenote dans les Provinces-Unies, 1680–1715. Un nouveau bilan," in *In dubiis libertas. Mélanges d'histoire offerts au professeur Rémy Scheurer*, ed. Philippe Henry and Maurice de Tribolet (Hauterive: Gilles Attinger, 1999), 271–81.

12. Bots, "La migration huguenote," 274.

13. Cees Cruson, "Huguenot Refugees in Seventeenth-Century Amsterdam" (paper presented at the Social Science History Meeting, Toronto, 24–28 October 1984).

14. M. G. Schenk, *Amsterdam stad der vroomheid* (Bussum: Kroonder, s.a. [after 1945]), 232–34.

15. Nusteling, "The Netherlands," 22, table 1; Nusteling, *Welvaart en werkgelegenheid*, 237.

16. Ingrid van der Vlis, *Leven in armoede. Delftse bedeelden in de zeventiende eeuw* (Amsterdam: Prometheus/Bert Bakker, 2001), 234–36.

17. Boulenger, "L'Église wallonne."

18. Israel, *The Dutch Republic*, 628.

19. For examples of local histories, see A. Wiegers, "De Réfugiés in Gaasterland," *Nederlands archief voor kerkgeschiedenis* 58, no. 2 (1978): 205–36; J. van der Spek, "Réfugiés pour la religion: de hugenoten in Utrecht," *Jaarboek Oud-Utrecht* (1999): 35–74; Huub van Heiningen, "Tolerantie met een dubbele bodem: Hogenoten en katholieken in Tiel," *Tijdschrift voor Nederlandse kerkgeschiedenis* 3, no. 2 (2000): 39–44.

20. Gregorio Leti, *Teatro Belgico, o vero retratti historici, chronologici, politici e geografici, delle Sette Provincie Unite*, 2 vols. (Amsterdam: G de Jonge, 1690), 2:146.

21. P. J. W. van Malssen, *Louis XIV d'après les pamphlets répandus en Hollande* (Amsterdam: H. J. Paris, 1936); Hans Bots, "L'image de la France dans les Provinces-Unies," in *L'État classique. Regards sur la pensée politique de la France dans le second XVIIe siècle*, ed. H. Méchoulan and Joël Cornette (Paris: J. Vrin, 1996), 341–53.

22. Bots, "L'écho de la Révocation de l'Édit de Nantes dans les Provinces-Unies à travers les gazettes et les pamphlets," in *La Révocation de l'Édit de Nantes et le protestantisme français en 1685*, ed. Roger Zuber and Laurent Theis (Paris: Société de l'Histoire du Protestantisme Français, 1986), 291.

23. Jacques Solé, "L'exploitation de la Révocation de l'édit de Nantes par le prince d'Orange," in *La Révocation de l'édit de Nantes et l'extérieur du royaume*, ed.

Michel Péronnet (Montpellier: Presses de l'Université Paul Valéry, 1985), 147–48.

24. P. L. Nève, "Le statut juridique des réfugiés français huguenots: quelques remarques comparatives," in *La condition juridique de l'étranger, hier et aujourd'hui.* Actes du Colloque organisé à Nimègue les 9–11 mai 1988 par les Facultés de droit et de Poitiers de Nimègue (Nijmegen: Faculteit der Rechtsgeleerdheid, Katholieke Universiteit, 1988), 223–46, with a list of ordinances published by the provincial States. For Groningen, see M. Bakker, et al. *Hugenoten in Groningen. Franse vluchtelingen tussen 1680 en 1720* (Groningen: Wolters-Noordhoff and Bouma's Boekhuis, 1985).

25. On the rights of citizenship and for admission into the Dutch guilds and corporations, see Piet Lourens and Jan Lucassen, "'Zunftlandschaften' in den Niederlanden und im benachbarten Deutschland," in *Zunftlandschaften in Deutschland und den Niederlanden im Vergleich,* ed. Wilfried Reininghaus (Münster in Westfalen: Aschendorff, 2000), 11–43.

26. Jules Mathorez, *Les étrangers en France sous l'Ancien Régime,* vol. 2 (Paris: Champion, 1921); E. Lesens, "La colonie protestante hollandaise, les Flamands, Hambourgeois et habitants des pays circonvoisins, à Rouen au XVIIe siècle," *Bulletin de la Commission d'histoire des Églises wallonnes* 5 (1892): 205–24; Jules Mathorez, "Notes sur la colonie hollandaise de Nantes," *Revue du Nord* 4 (1913): 1–46; A. Leroux, *La colonie germanique de Bordeaux,* vol. 1 (Bordeaux: Féret, 1918).

27. Leonie van Nierop, "Stukken betreffende de nijverheid der réfugiés te Amsterdam," *Economisch-historisch jaarboek* 7 (1921): 147–95, and 9 (1923), 157–213; van Nierop, "Amsterdam's vroedschap en de nijverheid der réfugiés," *De Economist* (1916): 821–37.

28. Boulenger, "L'Église wallonne," 1:92–94.

29. P. J. van Cruyningen, *Behoudend maar buigzaam. Boeren in West-Zeeuws-Vlaanderen, 1650–1850* (Wageningen: AAG-Bijdragen, 2000), 26–27.

30. *Mémoires d'Isaac Dumont de Bostaquet, gentilhomme normand, sur les temps qui ont précédé et suivi la Révocation de l'Édit de Nantes, sur le Refuge et les expéditions de Guillaume III en Angleterre et Irlande,* ed. Michel Richard (Paris: Mercure de France, 1968).

31. Israel, *The Dutch Republic,* 628–29; idem, *Dutch Primacy in World Trade, 1585–1740* (Oxford: Clarendon Press, 1989), 348–53.

32. J. W. Enschedé, "Papier en papierhandel in Noord-Nederland gedurende de zeventiende eeuw," *Tijdschrift voor boek- en bibliotheekwezen* 7 (1909): 97–188, 205–231.

33. P. W. Klein, 'Nederlandse glasmakerijen in de zeventiende en achttiende eeuw,' *Economisch-historisch Jaarboek* 44 (1982): 31–43.

34. Pierre-Daniel Huet, *Mémoires sur le commerce des Hollandois dans tous les états et empires du monde,* (Amsterdam: P. Brunel, 1718), 49–50; and Jacques Le Moine

de L'Espine, *Le négoce d'Amsterdam* (Amsterdam: P. Brunel, 1694), 41; both quoted by Israel, *Dutch Primacy*, 348.

35. Israel, *The Dutch Republic*, 630.

36. Hans Bots and René Bastiaanse, "Die Hugenotten und die niederländischen Generalstaaten," in *Die Hugenotten, 1685–1985*, ed. Rudolf von Thadden and Michelle Magdelaine (Munich: Beck, 1985), 58–59; French version: "Le Refuge huguenot et les Provinces-Unies, une esquisse sommaire," in *Le Refuge huguenot*, ed. Rudolf von Thadden and Michelle Magdelaine (Paris: A. Colin, 1985).

37. Nève, "Le statut juridique," 239–42.

38. N. C. F. van Sas, ed., *Vaderland. Een geschiedenis vanaf de vijftiende eeuw tot 1940* (Amsterdam: Amsterdam University Press, 1999).

39. Catherine Secrétan, "L'étranger dans les Pays-Bas au siècle d'or," in *De l'Humanisme aux Lumières. Bayle et le protestantisme. Mélanges en l'honneur d'Élisabeth Labrousse*, ed. Michelle Magdelaine et al. (Paris: Universitas and Oxford: Voltaire Foundation, 1996), 245–53.

40. G. H. M. Posthumus Meyjes, ed., *Verdrukking, vlucht en toevlucht: het dagboek van Jean Migault over de geloofsvervolging onder Lodewijk XIV* (original edition in French; Paris, 1910; reprint, Kampen: Kok, 1985); C. Koeman, "Brieven van Jean Richard de Tibante, een Hollands hugenoot op de galeien in Marseille, 1692–1705," *Tijdschrift voor zeegeschiedenis* 8 (1989): 25–44; Marcel Ducasse, "Le voyage de François Leguat dans l'Océan Indien (1690–1698)," *Revue historique des armées* 23, no. 1 (1996): 12–20.

41. Wolfgang Cilleßen, ed., *Krieg der Bilder. Druckgraphik als Medium politischer Auseinandersetzung im Europa des Absolutismus* (Berlin: Deutsches Historisches Museum, 1997): 216–27; F. Muller, *De Nederlandsche geschiedenis in platen*, vol. 1 (Amsterdam: Frederik Muller, 1863), 405–6, nos. 2672–78.

42. Bots, "La migration huguenote," 276.

43. G. C. Gibbs, "The Role of the Dutch Republic as the Intellectual Entrepôt of Europe in the Seventeenth and Eighteenth Centuries," *Bijdragen en mededelingen betreffende de geschiedenis der Nederlanden* 86 (1971): 323–49; Gibbs, "Some intellectual and political influences of the Huguenot émigrés in the United Provinces," ibid. 90 (1975): 255–87.

44. C. Berkvens-Stevelinck et al., ed., *Le Magasin de l'Univers. The Dutch Republic as the Centre of the European Book Trade* (Leiden and New York: E. J. Brill, 1992); Paul Hoftijzer and Otto S. Lankhorst, "Book History in the Netherlands. A Survey of Studies of the Early Modern Period," in *Histoires du livre. Nouvelles orientations*, ed. Hans Erich Bödeker (Paris: IMEC/Editions de la MSH, 1995), 139–96.

45. Hubert Bost, *Un "intellectuel" avant la lettre: le journaliste Pierre Bayle (1647–1706)* (Amsterdam and Maarssen: APA-Holland University Press, 1994);

Bots, ed., *Henri Basnage de Beauval (1656–1710) en de "Histoire des Ouvrages des Savans," 1687–1709*, 2 vols. (Amsterdam and Maarssen: APA-Holland University Press, 1976); Bots et al., ed., *De "Bibliothèque Universelle et Historique," 1686–1693. Een periodiek als trefpunt van geletterd Europa* (Amsterdam and Maarssen: APA-Holland University Press, 1981); Bots, ed. *La Diffusion et la lecture des journaux de langue française sous l'Ancien Régime/Circulation and reception of periodicals in the French language in the 17th and 18th centuries. Colloque/Congress, Nijmegen 1987* (Amsterdam and Maarssen: APA-Holland University Press, 1988); G. N. M. Wijngaards, *De "Bibliothèque Choisie" van Jean Le Clerc (1657–1736). Een Amsterdams geleerdentijdschrift* (Amsterdam and Maarssen: APA-Holland University Press, 1986).

46. I. H. van Eeghen, *De Amsterdamse boekhandel, 1680–1725*, 5 vols., (Amsterdam: Stadsdrukkerij, 1960–78).

47. Hans Bots and Françoise Waquet, *La République des Lettres* (Paris: Belin-De Boeck, 1997).

48. van Eeghen, "Europese 'libraires': de gebroeders Huguetan in Amsterdam (1686–1705)," *Documentatieblad Werkgroep 18c Eeuw* no. 53/54 (1982): 1–19.

49. Otto S. Lankhorst, *Reinier Leers (1654–1714), uitgever en boekverkoper te Rotterdam* (Amsterdam and Maarssen: APA-Holland University Press, 1983), 47–49.

50. Israel, *The Dutch Republic*, 931.

51. Ibid., 1038–41.

52. Andrew Pettegree, "Protestant Migration during the Early Modern Period," in *Le migrazioni in Europa, secc. XIII–XVIII*, ed. Simonetta Cavaciocchi (Florence: Le Monnier, 1994), 441–58, (quotation, 455).

53. Lenie van Lieshout, "Beleden, beschreven, beleefd, begrensd. Theorie en praktijk van tolerantie rond hugenoten in Nederland, 1680–1715," in *Grensverkenningen. Over groepsvorming, minderheden en tolerantie*, ed. Fons Strijbosch and Paul van Tongeren (Nijmegen: Katholieke Universiteit, Faculteit der Rechtsgeleerdheid, 1994), 31–44.

54. Jean Orcibal, *Louis XIV et les protestants* (Paris: Vrin, 1951), 150.

55. Elisabeth Labrousse, "Le Refuge hollandais: Bayle et Jurieu," *XVIIe siècle* 76–77 (1967): 75–93; Labrousse, *Conscience et conviction. Études sur le XVIIe siècle* (Paris: Universitas and Oxford: Voltaire Foundation, 1996), 135–237; F. R. J. Knetsch, *Pierre Jurieu, theoloog en politicus der Refuge* (Kampen: Kok, 1967); Elisabeth Israels Perry, *From Theology to History: French Religious Controversy and the Revocation of the Edict of Nantes* (The Hague: Nijhoff, 1973); Gerald Cerny, *Theology, politics, and letters at the crossroad of European civilization: Jacques Basnage and the Baylean Huguenot refugees in the Dutch Republic* (Dordrecht: Nijhoff, 1987).

56. Knetsch, "Pierre Jurieu and the Glorious Revolution according to his 'Lettres pastorales,'" in *Church, Change, and Revolution*, ed. J. H. van den Berg et al. (Leiden and New York: E. J. Brill, 1991), 145–66.

57. Geoffrey Adams, *The Huguenots and French Opinion, 1685–1787: The Enlightenment Debate on Toleration* (Waterloo, Ont.: Wilfried Laurier University Press, 1991).

58. Antonio Rotondò, *Europe et les Pays-Bas. Évolution, élaboration et diffusion de la tolérance aux XVIIe et XVIIIe siècles* (Florence: Università degli Studi, Dipartimento di storia, 1992); C. Berkvens-Stevelinck, J. Israel, and G. H. M. Posthumus Meyjes, ed., *The emergence of tolerance in the Dutch Republic* (Leiden and New York: E. J. Brill, 1997); Willem Frijhoff, "La tolérance sans édit: la situation dans les Provinces-Unies," in *L'acceptation de l'autre de l'édit de Nantes à nos jours*, ed. Jean Delumeau (Paris: Fayard, 2000), 86–107; J. Schillings, *Het tolerantiedebat in de Franstalige geleerdentijdschriften uitgegeven in de Republiek der Verenigde Provinciën in de periode 1684–1753* (Amsterdam and Maarssen: APA-Holland University Press, 1997).

59. Boulenger, "L'Église wallonne," 1:128–34; Van Lieburg, "Geloven op vele manieren," 288–89.

60. On the French school system, see Willem Frijhoff, "Université et marché de l'emploi dans la République des Provinces-Unies," in *Les universités européennes du XVIe au XVIIIe siècles. Histoire sociale des populations étudiantes*, ed. Dominique Julia, Jacques Revel, and Roger Chartier, vol. 1 (Paris: EHESS, 1986), 222–24; Frijhoff, "Le français et son usage dans les Pays-Bas septentrionaux," *Documents pour l'histoire du français langue étrangère ou seconde* 3 (June 1989): 108. A somewhat outdated but still valuable study of the diffusion of French in the Netherlands is the synthesis by K.-J. Riemens, *Esquisse historique de l'enseignement du français en Hollande du XVIe au XIXe siècle* (Leiden: Sijthoff, 1919).

61. Willem Frijhoff, "Verfransing? Franse taal en Nederlandse cultuur tot in de Revolutietijd," *Bijdragen en mededelingen betreffende de geschiedenis der Nederlanden* 104, no. 4 (1989): 592–609.

62. Jean Tirel, *Lettres fraternelles*, ed. Eva Avigdor (Paris: Nizet, 1984).

63. Willem Frijhoff, "Modèles éducatifs et circulation des hommes: les ambiguïtés du second Refuge," in *La Révocation de l'édit de Nantes et les Provinces-Unies*, 51–75, especially 72–74.

64. Frijhoff, "Université et marché de l'emploi," 222–24.

65. R. H. Du Pré, "Hercules Des Prez and Cecilia d'Athis: Founders of the Du Preez Family in South Africa," *Historia* (South Africa) 41, no. 1 (1996): 1–16; Israel, *The Dutch Republic*, 627.

66. Jean-Louis Poulalion, "Les Français dans l'histoire du Surinam," *Mondes et cultures* 46, no. 4 (1986): 775–89.

67. J. A. de Kok, *Nederland op de breuklijn Rome-Reformatie* (Assen: Van Gorcum, 1964), 325.

68. F. H. Gagnebin, "Liste des Églises wallonnes des Pays-Bas et des pasteurs qui les ont desservies," *Bulletin de la Commission pour l'histoire des Églises wallonnes,* 3 (1888): 25–64, 97–120, 209–40, 313–46; Gagnebin, "Pasteurs de France réfugiés en Hollande," ibid. 1 (1885): 97–151, and 4 (1890) 209–40; Willem Frijhoff, *La société néerlandaise et ses gradués, 1575–1814: une recherche sérielle sur le statut des intellectuels* (Amsterdam and Maarssen: APA-Holland University Press, 1981), 268–71. An updated biographical list of 404 refugee ministers has been published by Hans Bots, "Liste des pasteurs et proposants réfugiés dans les Provinces-Unies," in *La vie intellectuelle aux Refuges protestants,* ed. Jens Häseler and Antony McKenna (Paris: Champion, 1999), 19–68.

69. Françoise-Muriel Ratier, "Les écoles diaconales de l'Église Wallonne des Pays-Bas" (D.E.A. thesis, Université de Lille III, 1984).

70. V. H. de Villeneuve, *400 jaar Waalse Hervormde Kerk in Rotterdam,* (Rotterdam: Waalse Hervormde Kerk, 1999). At present, the archives and the library of the Walloon communities, known as the "Bibliothèque Wallonne" are at the University Library of Leiden.

EIGHT

Family Bonds across the Refuge

Carolyn Lougee Chappell

In November 1776, the Baron de Saint-Surin, residing in Celle in Lower Saxony, drew up his will. His chrysoprase ring, his round Dresden china box, and his gold medal of Prince Henry of Prussia he bequeathed to his "dear goddaughter" and niece Henriette de Champagné. To her father, his first cousin, he left, "as a mark of my esteem," portraits of himself and of his late brother the Prussian general La Motte-Fouqué, along with diverse portraits given to him by his patrons the Prussian princes.[1]

These testamentary choices had a certain significance, for by them Saint-Surin was leaving family treasures not to his nearest kin, residing in Germany as he was, but to more distant relations in Ireland whom he had never met. As he explained in his will, "Although I have never had the satisfaction, so desired, of seeing my cousin Monsieur de Champagné in Ireland, the ties of blood and epistolary commerce have nonetheless always united us in a sincere friendship." The Irish heir and the German testator were both second-generation "refugees," born and bred in their respective homelands well after the father of one and mother of the other —siblings—had escaped from La Rochelle in 1687. Eighty-nine years later, how was it that Saint-Surin was still cognizant of and intent upon honoring his Huguenot family bonds—to the benefit of an unknown cousin 700 miles away with whom he shared neither language nor nationality nor name?

Sixty years of the family's correspondence, along with three generations' account books,[2] suggest an answer and permit us to examine the experience of this one kinship network in the Refuge—or we might even say this familial diaspora—its tenor, its origins, and what it might tell us about Huguenot experience more generally.

The "sincere friendship" between the Irish cousin—whom I shall call the Dean, since he was an Anglican clergyman, Dean of Clonmacnoise and chaplain of the English Church at Portarlington in Ireland—and the Baron in Germany had been nurtured through private correspondence that extended, with some regularity, from mid-century down into the 1770s.[3] Its tenor was personal: long, warm, friendly letters on both sides expressed affection and solicitude for the well-being of family members. The Dean professed his "respectful attachment" and "implicit faith": "I am convinced that you have a true friendship for us." The Baron was good enough to say that he found the Dean's sermons, sent along by the Irish cousin, "very edifying." And he marveled at the news that the Dean's wife, already the mother of eleven children, was pregnant once again: "I would guess that this will be her last pregnancy: she has already so well acquitted herself of her duty to reproduce that she can without fear of reproach rest on her laurels and enjoy the pleasure of having so assiduously labored for restoration of the human race that war has so powerfully diminished."

The fiction, often repeated, that the Baron might some day visit Ireland served, perhaps, to mitigate the pervasive awareness of the distance between the worlds the two writers inhabited and the inadequacy of their vehicles for exchange. The Baron begged the Dean to "have the goodness to write to me in French in the future, to spare me the unpleasantness of receiving letters that I cannot understand" and that he could find no one to translate—chiding him, perhaps, without saying so, for so soon losing an ability to speak in his family's tongue. The Dean, lamenting the "few opportunities our people have to converse familiarly in French," took "recourse to an obliging friend to translate this letter, which means you will receive it much more politely dressed than the original." And the issue of unshared language resurfaced in his exchanges with Saint-Surin's brother, the Prussian general La Motte-Fouqué, who wrote to him in German. The Dean confessed his "mortification not to understand one word of it" ("I wish his secretary would write in French") and his fear that "I shall not easily meet with a person [even by sending to Dublin] who understands that language."

At least as perplexing and inhibiting to the amiable correspondence as unshared language was the disjunction in a second vehicle for exchange: currency. The Dean's bankers in England were unfamiliar with the Baron's money (Rixdollars), there being, it appeared, no "settled exchange" with pounds sterling. And that, even more than language, made it difficult for the two cousins to be sure they were being entirely fair with one another. For the family bonds they were attempting to create through the vehicle of their letters rested upon family bonds of another sort: shared financial instruments. The cousins were co-heirs to a portfolio of investments that resided (as neither of them did) in England and that they held in common—somewhat reluctantly—through the decade of the 1760s.

Those financial bonds originated with the Refuge, in the very aftermath of the Revocation, in the way their grandmother, Marie de La Rochefoucauld, dame de Champagné, rebuilt and then distributed the family's patrimony after their escape from France in 1687. And so the portfolio the distanced cousins inherited—the continuing link between them—rested ultimately upon the judgments she made and on her ability to adapt—alone—to the unprecedented circumstances of persecution and exile in which, among other losses, family bonds of the personal sort had been badly broken. So let us look at the Champagné family's beginnings in exile, Marie's adaptation at the head of her family to unprecedented situations—economic and personal—and then ask how this case does more than expose what Lawrence Stone called "the quirky eccentricity" of one family[4]—what it might suggest about experience in the diaspora.

The Champagné had been modest provincial nobility.[5] Marie and her husband Josias Robillard, seigneur de Champagné, each held as lineage properties seigneuries in Saintonge and Aunis[6] that both customary law on *propres* and recent edicts against sales of assets by Protestants prevented them from converting into cash that they could transfer out of the realm. Their experience with the cash transfers they did attempt—in principle rather easy to effect[7]—was, as their own accounts record, a series of anguishing and impoverishing setbacks.[8] Only seventeen years after emigrating would Marie at last collect from another refugee, Isaq Guion, an old debt of 35 livres that had until then eluded her because she had with her in Holland no written proof of the obligation. Only slightly less tardily would she succeed in recouping some of the 3,431 livres that Josias had left with another Protestant, Mr. Lardeau in La Rochelle, "on his good faith, having nothing written on it." (This sum alone represented about one-fifth of the value of Josias' real estate in Aunis.) "The money I have received came at different times and in various ways"; however, more than 40 percent of it had been lost, not through any dishonesty on Lardeau's part, but because "his wife was obliged to throw away all the papers that could betray it when he was taken prisoner . . . so there is nothing more to hope for here nor to complain about, but it is a loss that hurt."[9]

Even more damaging—and more revealing of persecution's fraying of bonds—was the loss of 800 livres confided to the seigneur de Brassac, a *nouveau converti*[10] with whose family the Champagné family tree was intertwined, in what a nineteenth-century descendant would label "a very sad transaction deeply tinged with premeditated swindling."[11] During Holy Week 1688, just days before his departure into exile, Josias left with Brassac a sum of cash he could not carry with him plus a gray brood mare to be sold. "I left him all that on his good faith, and we exchanged a thousand assurances of friendship, and I left to go to Paris."[12] Brassac never deposited the funds with the banker from whom Josias in exile could retrieve them. "There is what came of the grand offers of service he made me. . . . This is the pure truth of the matter. . . . May God pardon him the wrong he has done to a fugitive family in a strange country that was not able to sell a single inch of land before departing."

Brassac's perfidy was but a token of the family disintegration that often preceded the move into exile, as the persecution accompanying the Revocation increasingly took aim at the heart of families. Conflict between Protestant, Catholic, and *nouveau converti* kin had begun tearing apart the Champagné family well before the Revocation and would continue after it. The brother-in-law into whose hands the Champagné confided the infant daughter they left behind would be pursued in court by Marie's Catholic aunt until at last Marie's lineage lands spilled into the hands of her *nouvelles converties* sisters.[13] If family solidarities could transcend religious divisions in ordinary times,[14] they—like the community bonds that were also unraveling[15]—were susceptible to disintegration under pressure. The Champagné went into exile, then, already weakened—their fortune impaired and their family network truncated. Their attempt to keep the family together in exile began on the defensive. Could the family, in dispersion, rebuild its bonds?

The responsibility for doing so Marie de La Rochefoucauld quite consciously assumed when, only two years after taking her children into exile, she was widowed. In both the autobiographical escape memoir that served as a preface to her financial accounts and in her subsequent notes of transactions, she conveyed a sense of vocation as matriarch, as re-founder and head of the family: she represented herself preserving the family and its social identity by stewarding the family patrimony, securing patronage, setting up the children, winning pensions, collecting payments.[16] By using as contacts her former neighbors and distant kin, as well as her husband's military service for William of Orange, she placed her sons in the British army, the Dutch navy, and the military household of Anhalt-Dessau. She placed one daughter in the Society of Harlem[17]; two other daughters she married to refugee noblemen.[18] One of these, when widowed, moved—again, through contacts initially made among the Huguenot nobility of Poitou-Charente—to the household of madame von Bülow in Celle, from which vantage point she in turn placed her own three sons in the military households of Anhalt-Dessau and Prussia. The familial diaspora in which Marie, from her new home in The Hague, placed her children stretched, then, the breadth of Northern Europe.

In her ledger Marie recorded for her children's sake the patrimony that, as she conceived it, belonged to those children together: "For my purpose is to leave to my children all the instruction I can and that I believe necessary for their property and to make them see the use I shall make of it." That is, from the outset of her stewardship she shared the orientation toward future generations that Natalie Zemon Davis has called the "new sense . . . of the arrow of family fortunes in historical time,"[19] crafting her accounts and the transactions themselves with the day in mind when her children would take their own. In so doing, she left us not merely a record of her actions but a portrait of an ordinary investor at the turn of the eighteenth century. Not a titan like Adrienne-Marguerite Huguetan, daughter of the Huguenot financier in Holland Pierre Huguetan, a woman who in 1733 had capital totaling 338,084 florins, with 4,000 shares of the English East India Company and 3,000 new annuities of the South Sea Company.[20] But someone ordinary in the smallness of her stake, closer to "Everyman,"[21] the small investors who in very large numbers were more important as sources for the stream of cash that made the financial markets work than the few big rich investors who have gotten most attention because their records, too, are rich. In her case it is also the portfolio overall that we can see, not merely investments piecemeal as they appear on separate company listings. And perhaps we can infer both from the way she tracked what she always considered her children's inheritance and from her investment pattern something of her personality, mentality, and values. If so, we can "clothe in the firm flesh of human society"[22] the story of the by now rather well-known economic phenomenon of the Protestant International that is usually told in quantities.

Three patterns are discernible in the way Marie de La Rochefoucauld managed the Champagné patrimony between 1690 and 1717.[23] First, all the holdings of this formerly landed noble family came to rest in movables. The Champagné veered in exile, then, in the opposite direction from the typical French trajectory by which liquid income tended to get invested in land.[24] Marie had many reasons for investing exclusively in movables: her resources in exile were too meager to permit for acquiring landed property, she may also have developed a "migrant preference for semi-liquidity,"[25] and she was probably already familiar with bonds, since French noble families typically owned *rentes* in addition to their real property.[26] But the novelty that now *all* her fortune was intangible on occasion elicited from Marie the anxiety that intangible wealth no doubt deserves: "Dieu veille bénir la chose."

Second, Marie, though continuing to reside in Holland, came to concentrate her investments in England. Before her husband died, both he and Marie had lent small sums in England. Passing through Exeter en route from La Rochelle to Rotterdam, she left £100 (quite informally) with the local Huguenot pastor, Jacques Sanxay, to place as a personal loan to a parishioner. Josias did something similar as he passed through London with William's army in 1689, confiding 200 francs to Mr. Layout "sous sa bonne foi." Still, their portfolio was Dutch. Just days before he left The Hague in October 1688, Josias and Marie together lent to the Estates of Holland 5,000 florins at 4 percent. And when Marie first began managing the patrimony alone, all the funds she invested she placed in Holland.

All investments from 1695 on, however, she placed in England, moving to England, then, virtually at the first moment of the "English financial revolution." In this she was one of the thousands of Huguenots whose personal fortunes bankrolled the public Funds underwriting the stability of the English Crown and arguably effecting the success in the eighteenth century of that previously economically backward country, including its decisive advance ahead of France.[27] Her first purchase in England in 1695 was also made at the peak of sharply fluctuating exchange rates between guilders and pounds sterling: the guilder in Amsterdam gained 15 percent on the pound sterling between January of 1694 and August of 1695.[28] More particularly, the effect of this investment pattern was that Marie took on a new cosmopolitanism of economic interests that her family had not had before. This in turn involved her in ongoing trans-national exchanges of funds and reliance on networks of international dealers and bankers: a fact of her life came to be the notarized powers of attorney, letters of change, and conversion fees that such exchanges entailed.

More than this, and a sign of her capacity to adapt to new circumstances, Marie became, in time, something of a petty banker herself. It was unusual for women to handle other women's monies, though Huguenot women did commonly handle their own investments.[29] Nor would she have acted so in France; this new activity was, rather, a response to the fact that both her contacts and the capital markets in which she was involved were now cosmopolitan. Marie collected pensions and dividends from England for mesdames de La Primaudaye, de Vernillon, de Pardaillan, and Des Roches, as well as pensions from Holland for madame de Villars, who in 1708 had on deposit with Marie "382 livres that I promised to pay her when it pleases her." In 1711, Louis Royrand Des Clouseaux, her agent in London, was holding in Marie's account ten tickets on the lottery, of which four belonged to her own family, two to madame de Villars, and two to madame von Bülow. She exchanged money in Holland from several Huguenot women for money in her own London account. Money passed through her hands from monsieur de Lilleferme in Bordeaux to his son in London. From 1708 until at least 1712, madame de Guiran deposited a 2,000–florin Holland government bond with Marie, who collected the interest and forwarded payments to Guiran's creditors. In a sense, then, Marie acted, informally, as a kind of early women's bank; all her agents were men, all her "clients" but two were women.

The third pattern in Marie's investments is the degree of speculation. For the most part she was quite conservative and in this seemed typical of "the Huguenot community's investing habits."[30] She favored cautious assets; the Old Indies, bonds on the Estates of Holland and the King of Spain, and notably the English public debt Funds were secure forms of investment. She drew dividends and interest by holding for longer terms rather than trading for capital gains. And she selected and traded with an eye to yield, for example in 1699 selling the bonds on the Estates of Holland that she and her husband had bought because the yield was too low: "we have always had war and often I have not had half of the 4%." She sold her 6 percent bond on the King of Spain to move her funds to 8 percent English tallies.

But she was not entirely un-adventuresome. Tallies on English taxes,[31] tickets on state lotteries,[32] tontines on her daughters' lives[33]: all these were instruments for the investor avid for the up-side risk. In 1711, she reacted to a rumor that the English government was going to float a new lottery by sending a buy order to her dealer in London, who had to disabuse her of her imagined lottery. And she encumbered her largest single holding, her Dutch Indies shares, for cash which she invested elsewhere in an operation that amounted to extended-term margin investing.

Having scattered her children and her investments widely across the Refuge, Marie then divided the patrimony in a way that both dispersed it through the Refuge and made of it as strong a continuing family bond as possible. What is interesting about Marie is that—sitting in Holland, cut off from her old home in France, with her investments and children *un peu partout*—she distributed her patrimony as if it and they were still in Aunis-Saintonge and as if it were still *propres* rather than movables. Apart from one interlude of pique when she disinherited her spendthrift eldest son, she adhered in her successive wills to the constraints upon *succession noble* in the Aunis and Saintonge *coutumes*, which were not legally binding on her, and declined to partake of the testamentary freedom those same *coutumes* offered for disposition of a fortune, like hers now, consisting of movables. By the letter of the Aunis and Saintonge *coutumes* she was free to dispose of all her property (since it was all movables) in any way she chose, both during her lifetime in any *inter vivos* gifts she might choose to give and by her will.[34] Instead, she kept track of sums each child received as loans or for placements (dowries, purchase of military commissions) in her book of accounts, with the express notation that these sums were to be subtracted from the legacy each child would eventually receive. She gave her eldest son a preference legacy (*préciput*) of one-fifth, and she divided the remainder equally among her six surviving children.[35]

She might, alternatively, in the family's changed circumstances, have used her testamentary discretion, in the interest of future generations, to leave the patrimony all to one child as a way of helping at least one branch of the family to maintain some status—a strategy perhaps appropriate to a downwardly mobile family. Or perhaps have limited the inheritance to those with progeny. Instead, she adhered to the egalitarian spirit of the *coutumes*, so unusually generous to younger children. Perhaps by treating her children in the portions (though of a smaller pie) that they would have had in France, she hoped to smooth over the rupture of emigration. Perhaps she deemed this the best way to avoid friction in a family that had escaped from conflict and had since been subject to its own internal tensions, each in its own way exacerbated by emigration: between husband and wife about whether to emigrate, between daughter and mother over who deserved credit for the successful escape,[36] between mother and eldest son over his wasteful spending. Be that as it may, she expressed in her decision her own fundamental conviction about what equity was for her family as a whole. And the means by which the children received their portion expressed, too, her disinclination to make choices among them. For in 1722, the children met in The Hague and received their equal portions of the patrimony by drawing straws.[37] It was in this way that investments in Holland and England got dispersed, in varied lots, to heirs living in the far-flung locales of Germany and Ireland. The correspondence of the Baron de Saint-Surin, the Dean Champagné, and the general La Motte-Fouqué took place because the investments dispersed in 1722 eventually reconcentrated in them as the only living grandchildren of Marie de La Rochefoucauld.

To return to that correspondence—nearly fifty years after division of the patrimony re-crafted by Marie de La Rochefoucauld, the cousins transacted business in their letters, but they did not limit themselves to business matters. What they added to the business is significant for the meaning, persistence, and eventual disintegration of this familial diaspora. As mentioned earlier, they expressed sentiments of familial affection. But notable in addition is the way they defined themselves to each other, especially the way each situated himself in a patronage network and the attempts they made, ultimately without success, to make family bonds connect their two worlds.

In their letters to each other, neither portrayed himself as part of the Refuge, whether understood as a religion or as a community of expatriates, though both were living in Huguenot towns. Neither spoke of France, their forebears, or any shared identity from their familial past.

Each instead talked about himself in the terms most different from those the other used, as if defining himself by the contrast. Both, that is to say, spoke in culturally specific voices. The Dean situated himself in the English kin network that his father's fortunate marriage accrued: with Lord and Lady Forbes, Lord Granard, Lord and Lady Paget. The Baron, for his part, placed himself in a courtly network, emphasizing his brother's favor with Frederick the Great (enumerating at some length the gifts with which the monarch showered him) and his own friendship with Prince Henry. When recounting his sojourns at the court at Rheinsberg (boasting of his roles in the theatricals: "soit dit sans vanité, I made the spectators weep"), he assumed that he was instructing his cousin the clergyman about "la politesse ordinaire des cours" and hoped the pastor would not be scandalized by the courtly pleasures and amusements that were "fort à la mode dans ce pais."

Still, differentiated as they were, they made two interesting attempts at founding between them, in a sense, a family joint venture. Saint-Surin offered to sponsor the Dean's sons for positions as pages with either Frederick or Henry: "my brother and I will gladly use our credit to this end." When the Dean welcomed the opportunity to place his sons "under the protection and care of a respectful and affectionate relation," Saint-Surin suggested the Dean send the sons who promised to become the tallest, for the prejudice of the late Prussian king "for human colossuses" lingered on. But repeated attempts on Saint-Surin's part could not make good on his offer, for reasons of nationality. The prince had to give all court places to native nobility: "he has already committed his word to several families of this country, for these are posts destined to nationals virtually without exceptions. I am extremely mortified that this project has not met with success." The Dean understood: "it would be rather ungracious to introduce a Foreigner into an Imployment that is so much sought after by natives."

For his part, the Dean initiated an attempt at cosmopolitan patronage when he asked his German cousins to help him get a lucrative benefice in the Irish Church, suggesting their king and prince send "a letter of recommendation in my favor for the Court of England" and asking the General to speak to the English ambassador in Berlin "recommending me to him as having the honor of being among your relations." This initiative failed because the networks of influence turned out not to overlap: the

German cousins knew no one who was in contact with the ambassador, and the princes would decline to recommend anyone not known to them personally.

With the failure of the patronage projects and the sale of the jointly held bonds by 1770, the record of the "epistolary commerce" ceases, and perhaps the commerce itself did as well. What has it netted us? I will not argue the issue of typicality, subscribing as I do to the position that a case need not be replicable in order to be authentically historical and that "particulars, especially perhaps peculiar instances testify to the 'normality' of contingent combinations or mutations."[38] But suppose, instead, we pursue Emmanuel Le Roy Ladurie's binary typology of historians as either "truffle-hunters" who dig into a limited terrain up close and personal or "parachutists" who see the whole from afar.[39] Where in the parachutist's field of vision would the truffle I have just exhumed show up? And how might more such finds improve the parachutist's view?

First, this truffle would show up, for the parachutist, in the forward arrow of family fortunes in historical time. The case of the Champagné/Saint-Surin/La Motte-Fouqué family illustrates how refugees sometimes crafted, from the resources available in their new localities, new forms of patrimony to substitute for those they lost upon emigration, in so doing providing a new basis for the solidarity of the family line across the distances of the diaspora. In France, kinship had had a material basis in property: the land or workshop or perhaps venal office that moved through inheritance down the family line. On these, kin had some claim —whether near or remote—and hence a reason to stay in touch with their relations and apprised of their situation. When this material basis for family solidarity was lost upon emigration, for how many did family solidarity itself also disappear? How commonly (and through what means) did the first-generation refugees (no doubt, all important for the long-term survival of the family) assemble new sets of immovables or movables around which the kin group could revolve?

Marie de La Rochefoucauld made a future for the Champagné by implementing a family strategy of alliances/placements and investments that used new financial instruments in a new location in the service of old familial values.[40] She implemented a family discipline in the interest of maintaining the same inheritance strategy that would have been applied if they were still landed. As a widow, head of the family, abstracted from her kin context, she was free from any constraints except her own values as she picked and chose among the resources the new locale offered. The cosmopolitan cast she gave to the reconstructed patrimony tied family branches across the distances of the diaspora, without replicating the kind of inter-lineal antagonisms that had perhaps helped drive them out of France at the Revocation.

Second, this truffle would show up for the parachutist in the panorama of the "Huguenot International." The Huguenot diaspora needs to be conceptualized—not as a mere dispersion—but as layers of superimposed networks that cut across local and national boundaries to lend cohesion to the Refuge. The most famous of these were the interchanges of finance and trade that have been dubbed the "Protestant International."[41] But other networks ran from congregation to congregation, between pastors, among intellectuals, through the readership of publications[42]—and, among the nobility, between kin and from client to patron. This last, the nobles' "plane" of the diaspora, rested upon long-standing cosmopolitan patronage networks that predated the Revocation, having long circulated military men[43] and marriageable women through what were just beginning to become more and more *im*permeable national frontiers.[44]

The Champagné used that preexisting patronage network—now infused with newly arrived Huguenot expatriates in both client and patron roles—to resettle their first and second generations in diaspora.[45] We would understand the Refuge better if study of numerous families' diaries, letters, account books, patronage practices, and genealogies[46] could bring this "plane" of the diaspora to the fore as an "international," in particular identifying the part that women played as agents of family fortunes and patronage and keepers of kin links—a part that is certain to have been far greater in this "plane" than in the financial or trade international.[47]

Finally, this truffle would show up for the parachutist in the patchwork of more and more sharply contrasting cultures that harbored the refugees. The Baron and the Dean could not make the cosmopolitan patronage network operate trans-nationally for the third generation as it had for the first—in part because the network itself had splintered as nationality came to take precedence over religion or kinship or caste— the native sons were now the pages—and in part because they, the first exile-born generation, as Samuel Romilly testified, "desired nothing less than [they desired] to preserve the memory of their origin."[48] The cousins' correspondence itself, a discourse of contact between a German and a Briton, already incorporated the forces for losing contact: even as the structure of capital markets worked to bring them together, increasingly strong national fidelities made them speak different languages, both literally and figuratively. Marie de La Rochefoucauld lived out her life (d. 1730) as a refugee, a French woman abroad. Her daughter Suzanne, who had emigrated at age nineteen, did the same, never learning German though she lived nearly forty years in Celle. Her son Saint-Surin probably spoke French as a courtier rather than as a Huguenot, and his brother the general was (as Saint-Surin said) "prussien à brûler." By the late eighteenth century, can we in fact still speak of a Huguenot diaspora, given that the refugees' children were part of their native lands?[49]

It was within their respective national contexts—rather than in the cosmopolitan Refuge—that both lines of the Champagné descendants emerged fully as a history-making family. The two sons of the Dean who could not become Prussian pages became British generals, defeated in America, victorious at Waterloo. The Dean's grandson was the marquess of Anglesey, a prominent Tory and one of the richest peers in England, who was dubbed "The Waterloo Marquess" because he commanded the English cavalry at the decisive battle over France.[50] On the German side, the General La Motte-Fouqué's grandson was the esteemed romantic poet, author of *Ondine*. Both lines, then, in their new nations became far more distinguished than they had been in France—a remarkable long-term success effected by the same combination of military profession, patronage, patrimony, and family solidarity through which the Champagné had managed to maintain their place in the risky but all-important Revocation generation.

Appendix: Marie de La Rochefoucauld's Investments after 1687

Assets Mentioned in the Account Books:

Date	Investment	Price
1687	Loan through Jacques Sanxay	£100
1688–1699	Loan to the Estates of Holland	5000 florins
1690	Shares in East India Co. (Holland)	13,357 florins
By 1691	Tontine on her three daughters	(no value mentioned)
1691	Loan to the King of Spain	2000 florins
1692	Loan to the King of Spain	2000 florins
1692	Tontine on daughter Suzanne	734 florins 81 ½ p.
1695	Tallies	£100
1695	Lottery Tickets	£56 4s.
1699–1704	Salt Tax Tallies	£600
1699	Tallies	£102 17s. 3d.
1699	Tallies	£500
1699	Tallies on Coal and Leather	£500
1699	Tallies on Coal and Leather	£300
1703	Tally on Coal	£100
1704	5 Shares of Old Indies Co.	£591 5s.
1707	Annuities	(no value specified)
1711	Lottery Tickets	£20

Inventory of What Des Clouseaux Held for Her, 1709

Annuities @ £20
Annuities @ £30
5 Shares Old Indies Company (no value specified)
3 Tallies on Leather and Coal (£300, £100, £30)

Her Son Josias' Inventory of Her Holdings, 1722[51]

£500	Stock in the Indies Company (England) @140% £700
	interest due on them £35:2s:11d
£1175:6s:9d	Stock in South Sea Company @90%[52] £1057:5s:9d
	interest due on them £35:2s:11d

[3 contracts on Indies Co. (Amsterdam)]

TOTAL £1827:11s:3d

Notes

1. Testament (extract) and Deposition of François Baron de Saint-Surin, Champagné Papers B18–B19. The cousins' aunt Marianne, also residing in Celle, had previously done something similar, bequeathing to the same Irish nephew her two portraits of her brother the Saxon Lieutenant-General François-Auguste de Champagné and of his wife Marie de Polentz (Champagné Papers B19).

2. I am deeply grateful to Leila Philippa Scott, the current holder of the Champagné family papers and a seventh-generation direct descendant of Marie de La Rochefoucauld and José de Robitland, seigneur de Champagné. Words cannot express my gratitude to her for generously, and always graciously, welcoming me to her home to study the papers. Petra Coffey, who has worked on Champagné history because her family are their descendants, was the key to my finding the current holder; I am indebted to her for her kind assistance and friendship.

3. These latters are in the Champagné Papers, C3. That the earliest extant letter between the Dean and Saint-Surin, dated 31 October 1760, is not the first they exchanged is clear from the text. Perhaps only those letters were preserved that had a financial component in them and hence potential utility as legal documentation.

4. Lawrence Stone, *Family and Fortune: Studies in Aristocratic Finance in the Sixteenth and Seventeenth Centuries* (Oxford: Clarendon Press, 1973), xvii.

5. The modesty as well as the venerability of their standing is apparent by contrast with, for example, their contemporaries in the Depont family of La Rochelle *négociants:* see Robert Forster, *Merchants, Landlords, Magistrates: The Depont Family in Eighteenth-Century France* (Baltimore: Johns Hopkins University Press, 1980).

6. The real property Josias left behind in Aunis was evaluated in 1689 at 17,635 livres (*Extrait de l'Estat de liquidation des biens delaissez par ceux de la religion RPR de La Rochelle et pays d'Aunis. Evalués par l'intendant Begon. 1689*, Archives Nationales T T232 xix [5]). Marie's property was much more substantial, but no

overall figure appears for it in the inventory at the moment of seizure (Champagné Papers A39a) or in the records of its subsequent management by the Régie des biens des religionnaires (Archives Nationales TT17).

7. Solange Deyon, "Les Relations de famille et d'affaires de Jean Claude d'après sa correspondance à la veille de la Révocation (1683–85)," *Bulletin de la Société de l'Histoire du Protestantisme Français* 116 (1970): 152–77; Paul Bert, *Histoire de la Révocation de l 'Edit de Nantes à Bordeaux et dans le Bordelais (diocèse de Bordeaux), 1653–1715* (Geneva: Megariotis, 1977), 91–100.

8. It has sometimes been said that the ease with which funds could be transferred from France to the Refuge made it not much of a sacrifice to leave. Certainly this was the intendant's perception (see the intendant of La Rochelle Pierre Arnoul in Bibliothèque Nationale MSS fr. n.a. 21331–35). There surely were cases in which a smoothly functioning division of labor funneled money from the old homestead to the exiles. The pastor Tirel's denunciation of the concerted strategy by which families left certain of their members in France to conserve and transmit the patrimony suggests that such a strategy was put in practice. [Jean Tirel,] "*Lettres fraternelles d'un prisonnier à ses freres fugitifs et dispersez dans les divers pays de Suisse, d'Allemagne, Hollande, Dannemarck, Suede, Pologne, Angleterre, etc.,*" British Library Harley MS 70248. A fuller documentation on such an effort to collect French debts while in exile is contained in Winifred Turner, ed., *The Aufrère Papers: Calendar and Selections* (London: Butler and Tanner, 1940), 41–56. The refugee Antoine Aufrère, who fled to Holland in August 1687, tried to collect, from exile, a debt owed to him by the marquise de La Muce, sister of the comte de La Suze. Before emigrating, he transferred ownership to a Paris banker so the latter could collect it for him—a legal fiction. The matter occupied the heirs of all three parties as well as friends of Aufrère back in France and was only settled in 1730, with a much shrunken principal eventually being paid to Aufrère's nieces.

9. Archives Nationales TT435 i reports destruction of the house of the sieur Lardeau de Chaumont for holding RPR services therein, and TT418 ii (3) details the confiscation of the property of Lardeau de La Sarpaudie in the parish of Villefagnan.

10. Charles Prévost de Touchimbert, seigneur de Brassac, abjured 1 October 1685. When, later that month, his brother Casimir was imprisoned in the Bastille, Brassac was allowed to visit him because the authorities thought he would be helpful in converting the prisoner (Bibliothèque de l'Arsenal, Archives de la Bastille 12474, fols. 439–41). Brassac worked hard to convert his own wife and daughters (Archives départementales de la Vienne C52 #12: Estat des filles nouvelles converties qui peuvent payer pension dans les communautéz des nouvelles catholiques dans la paroisse de St. Hilaire Fontenay, 28.6.1698).

11. Sir Erasmus Dixon Borrowes, *Manuscript History of the Champagné Family*, Champagné Papers B1, 16–17.

12. Memo by Josias Robillard de Champagné, Voorburg, 3 October 1688, Champagné Papers A51.

13. That brother-in-law was Casimir Prévost de Touchimbert, brother of Brassac. Casimir's own family was dissolved by the Revocation: his son fled to Holland, his daughters were taken away to convents (Bibliothèque Nationale MS fr. 7051, fol. 16; Archives Nationales O'33, fols. 231–32; Nicolas-Joseph Foucault, *Mémoires*, ed. Frédéric Baudry [Paris: Imprimerie Impériale, 1862], 528). Champagné papers A52 is a manuscript copy of the judgment rendered by the Parlement of Bordeaux on the custody dispute between Casimir Prévost de Touchimbert and Magdeleine de Saulière, Marie's aunt. The original proceedings are recorded in Archives départementales de la Gironde (Bordeaux), *Arrêts*, liasse 1021 (11–31 August 1691).

14. Elisabeth Labrousse, "Conversion dans les deux sens," in *La Conversion au xviie siècle. Actes du xiie colloque de Marseille (janvier 1982)*, ed. Roger Duchêne (Marseille: Centre Méridional de Recontres sur le XVIIè siècle, 1983), 161–77; Robert Sauzet, *Contre-Réforme et réforme catholique en Bas-Languedoc: le diocèse de Nîmes au xviie siècle* (Paris: Diffusion Vander-Oyez, 1979).

15. Keith P. Luria, "Rituals of Conversion: Catholics and Protestants in Seventeenth-Century Poitou," in *Culture and Identity in Early Modern Europe (1500–1800): Essays in Honor of Natalie Zemon Davis*, ed. Barbara B. Diefendorf and Carla Hesse (Ann Arbor: University of Michigan Press, 1993), 65–81. For other illustrations of the loss of cohesion in the Huguenot family ("la moralité baissait"), see Orentin Douen, *La Révocation de l'Édit de Nantes à Paris, d'après des documents inédits*, 3 vols. (Paris: Fischbacher, 1894) 2:494ff. By contrast, among the Lacger of Castres, "religious divisions were simply not permitted to shatter family solidarity. . . . The bonds of family affection overcame confessional rifts": see Raymond A. Mentzer Jr., *Blood and Belief: Family Survival and Confessional Identity among the Provincial Huguenot Nobility* (West Lafayette, Ind.: Purdue University Press, 1994), 157. Yves Krumenacker recounts cases in which trans-confessional solidarity in Poitevin communities continued to operate during the persecutions: "'Un de mes amis, catholique romain. . . ,' catholiques et protestants au temps des dragonnades," in *De l'Humanisme aux Lumières, Bayle et le protestantisme: mélanges en l'honneur d'Elisabeth Labrousse*, ed. Michelle Magdelaine et al. (Paris: Universitas, 1996), 67–75. Gregory Hanlon finds confessional coexistence "structurally plausible and widespread" in his fine study *Confession and Community in Seventeenth-Century France: Catholic and Protestant Coexistence in Aquitaine* (Philadelphia: University of Pennsylvania Press, 1993). A significant research project would investigate comparative cases in order to identify the role of family

discipline (the extent to which the extended family maintained or lost its ability to mediate and resolve disputes) in differentiating those families who emigrated and those who stayed at the Revocation.

16. See my "'The Pains I Took to Save My/His Family': Escape Accounts by A Huguenot Mother and Daughter after the Revocation of the Edict of Nantes," *French Historical Studies* 22 (1999): 5–67.

17. The Société des dames françaises de Harlem, founded in 1683 by the marquis de Venours in premises provided by the magistrates of Harlem and with financial help from the Princess of Orange, was designed as an asylum for thirty noble French widows and *demoiselles* "sans famille et parfois sans ressources." See D. Allégret, "Société des dames françaises de Harlem," *Bulletin de la Société de l'Histoire du Protestantisme Français* 27 (1878): 315–22, 518–24, 557–63.

18. Suzanne married Charles de La Motte-Fouqué, baron de Thonnai-Boutonne, 12 December 1692 at The Hague (Champagné Papers B14 and Gemeente Archief, The Hague; Notarielle Protocollen 739:629–32); Henriette Silvie de Robillard de Champagné married Charles Bonnart, seigneur Du Marest d'Antoigny, 31 December 1712 at The Hague (Leiden Collection).

19. Natalie Zemon Davis, "Ghosts, Kin, and Progeny: Some Features of Family Life in Early Modern France," *Daedalus* 106 (1977): 92.

20. Eduard Van Biema, *Les Huguetan de Mercier et de Vrijhoeven: Histoire d'une famille de financiers huguenots de la fin du xviie jusqu'à la moitié du xviiie siècle* (The Hague: M. Nijhoff, 1918), 37–38.

21. Alice Clare Carter, "The Huguenot Contribution to the Early Years of the Funded Debt, 1694–1714," in *Getting, Spending, and Investing in Early Modern Times: Essays on Dutch, English, and Huguenot Economic History* (Assen: Van Gorcum, 1975), 80–82. The small investor was more usual in Holland than in England (where average holdings were higher): Alice Clare Carter, "Financial Activities of the Huguenots in London and Amsterdam in the Mid-Eighteenth Century," in *Getting, Spending, and Investing*, 103.

22. A. G. Dickens, "Preface" to *The Anglo-Dutch Contribution to the Civilization of Early Modern Society* (Oxford: Oxford Univeristy Press, 1976), 9.

23. See the appendix for lists of her investments. Documentary sources used to track her investments while she lived in Holland include, in addition to her own account book and her son Josias' two account books, the notarial documents in the Gemeente Archief, The Hague; Notarielle Protocollen/Periode 1670–1811, 668:343, 669:139, 670:109, 672:421, 674:195, 675:427, 676:135–36, 676:139–40, 676:323, 681:199, 682:249, 739:629–32, 743:329, 749:452–55.

24. Alice Clare Carter notes that preference for and persistence in urban, movable investments were typical of Huguenots and attributes this in large part to "their ingrained earlier experience in France." See "The Family and Business of

Belesaigne, Amsterdam, 1689–1809," in *Getting, Spending, and Investing*, 107–22. But Carter's assumption that Huguenots in France were urban and commercial is only partially accurate, for it ignores the prominence of nobles among the refugees. The Champagné exception to Carter's assumption comes to light from precisely the kind of family history Carter calls for ("detailed genealogical research"). A helpful list of sources that discuss the emigration of noble Huguenots is in Suzanne Hoyez and André Ruffelard, *Les Migrations protestantes sous le règne de Louis XIV: essai sur l'état de la question*, 2 vols. (Paris: typescript, 1978) 1:223.

25. Carter, "Belesaigne," 122.

26. She was almost certainly, however, not one of the experienced investors whose financial acumen, whose "skill that can make money breed money," was so essential a contribution to the economic advance of the lands of refuge (Carter, "Financial Activities," 91). "The Huguenots brought from France, where *rentes* were well established, a technical skill which acted on our financial developments as their industrial skills acted on our trade" (Carter, "Huguenot Contribution," 77).

27. P. G. M. Dickson, *The Financial Revolution in England: A Study in the Development of Public Credit, 1688–1756* (New York: St. Martin's Press, 1967); Carter, "Huguenot Contribution," 76–90; Charles Wilson, "The Anglo-Dutch Establishment in Eighteenth Century England," in *Anglo-Dutch Contribution*, 11–32.

28. Dickson, *Financial Revolution*, 357.

29. Carter, "Financial Activities," 98.

30. Ibid., 92.

31. Tallies were *short-term* loans to the exchequer against future tax receipts. They often needed to be discounted from face value since the date of repayment was uncertain. Depending upon the discount from face value (which raised the actual rate of return), they could be very lucrative. For example, Salt Tax tallies until 1700 traded at 6 percent to 36 percent below par; after 1700 they more often traded at par. So in the period when Marie bought them they had a windfall yield. See Dickson, *Financial Revolution*, 344–64.

32. Lotteries were a form of government loan in which one bought a ticket and received interest on it for a stated period of time on the chance of winning annuities of various values. "The unrealistic generosity of the terms offered made the lotteries highly popular. . . . [They] tapped the general rage for gambling. . . . In the harsh and uncertain conditions of eighteenth-century life the state lottery was a perennial way of escape into wealth and leisure—if only in the imagination." Lottery annuities were converted to 5 percent South Sea stock after 1717 (Dickson, *Financial Revolution*, 54, 74, 84–89).

33. Tontines were long-term survivorship loans according to which subscribers continued to receive a pro rata share of earnings only so long as their nominee

was alive. Pro rata shares increased as nominees died until one subscriber (or a specified small number of subscribers) would, in a windfall, receive all the capital. First practiced from the 1670s in the United Provinces by both municipalities and private syndicates as a speculative form of annuity, their advantage over regular annuities was the possibility that the annual payout would increase over time, but like all *rentes viagères* they were also vulnerable to total loss for those whose nominees died. In the early years, tontines were not always calibrated to the age of nominees, so they would have been an especially attractive "bet" for young adult nominees. Marie's children were past childhood when she nominated them, and this investment in fact paid off well for the Champagné patrimony. Josias noted in his account book about 1737 that the capital (originally 15,435 florins) was now 24,900 florins and the family's share (originally 735 florins) now 3,000. So while the capital had increased in value by 61 percent, the family's share had more than quadrupled in forty-five years. And at that point if Susanne were to survive just five more of her co-nominees, the family would receive a capital payout of 8,000 florins (a return on investment of nearly 11:1).

34. René-Josué Valin, *Nouveau commentaire sur la coutume de La Rochelle et du pays d'Aunis*, 3 vols. (La Rochelle: Chez R-J. Desbordes, 1756), 3:119.

35. Gemeente Archief, The Hague; Notarielle Protocollen 749:452–55 and Testament of Marie de La Rochefoucauld, 22 November 1701, in The Hague, Champagné Papers A53. "Gisante au lit malade," she annuls her 1693 Amsterdam will "conformément aux intentions de feu son espoux que Josias de Robillard son fils ainé prene par préciput et avantage la 5e partie de tous les deniers et autres effets mobiliers qui se trouveront après mon décès soit en nature ou obligations ou autrement." As it turned out, Josias, the eldest son, received very little at the 1722 division since he had already received in positions and loans nearly his entire inheritance. As he explained in a letter to his brother François-Auguste: "J'ai mangé mon blé en herbe" (Champagné Papers B10).

36. See my "The Pains I Took to Save My/His Family."

37. Joint Agreement signed at The Hague, 24 April 1722, Champagné Papers B7.

38. Randolph Starn, "Introduction: 'The New Erudition,'" *Representations* 56 (1996): 1–7.

39. Cited by Robert Forster, "Family Biography," in *Biographie und Geschichtswissenschaft: Wiener Beiträge zur Geschichte der Neuzeit* 6 (1979): 126.

40. Recent migration studies have emphasized migrants' creative responses to changed circumstances that enabled them to perpetuate earlier cultural patterns and premigration values in new surroundings. For a review of recent approaches in migration studies, see Hans Christian Buechler and Judith-Maria Buechler, ed., *Migrants in Europe: The Role of Family, Labor, and Politics* (New York: Greenwood Press, 1987), especially the introductory overview, 1–7, and Leslie Page Moch,

Moving Europeans: Migration in Western Europe since 1650 (Bloomington: Indiana University Press, 1992).

41. Herbert Lüthy, *La Banque protestante en France, de la Révocation de l'Édit de Nantes à la Révolution*, 2 vols. (Paris: S.E.V.P.E.N., 1959, 1961); John F. Bosher, "Huguenot Merchants and the Protestant International in the Seventeenth Century," *William and Mary Quarterly* 52 (1995): 77–102.

42. Anne Goldgar, *Impolite Learning: Conduct and Community in the Republic of Letters, 1680–1750* (New Haven: Yale University Press, 1995); John Christian Laursen, ed., *New Essays on the Political Thought of the Huguenots of the Refuge* (New York: E. J. Brill, 1995).

43. Derek A. Watts, "La Notion de patrie chez les mémorialistes d'avant la Fronde: Le problème de la trahison," in *Les Valeurs chez les mémorialistes français du xviie siècle avant la Fronde*, ed. Noémi Hepp and Jacques Hennequin (Paris: Klincksieck, 1979), 195–209; Henri Sée, "Les Idées politiques à l'époque de la Fronde," *Revue d'Histoire Moderne et Contemporaine* 3 (1901–02): 713–38; V. L. Tapié, "Comment les Français du xviie siècle voyaient la patrie," in *Comment les Français voyaient la France au xviie siècle*, ed. Roland Mousnier (Paris: C.N.R.S., 1955), 37–58. My sense is that the existence of this traditional cosmopolitan network eased the movement of noble Huguenots into exile, serving as a vehicle they could continue to use, but not for long.

44. Similarly, the "Huguenot International" as a network of trade and finance blossomed after the Revocation from preexisting overseas networks of financial relations and commercial activities: see Bosher, "Huguenot Merchants" and L. M. Cullen, "The Huguenots from the Perspective of the Merchant Networks of W. Europe (1680–1790): the Example of the Brandy Trade," in *The Huguenots and Ireland: Anatomy of an Emigration*, ed. C. E. J. Caldicott, H. Gough, and J.-P. Pittion (Dun Laoghaire: Glendale Press, 1987), 129–50.

45. Nobles like the Champagné were more numerous among refugees than has sometimes been recognized. Twenty-five percent of Dublin Huguenots (though only 2 percent of the French population) were nobility. Galway's emigration "was neither more nor less than a total switch of personal allegiance from Louis XIV to William III and could almost be compared to a great noble bringing along his vassals in his train to serve a new master." See Raymond Pierre Hylton, "Dublin's Huguenot Communities: Trials, Development, and Triumph, 1662–1701," *Proceedings of the Huguenot Society of Great Britain and Ireland* 24 (1985): 221–31.

46. Bosher, "Huguenot Merchants," 100: "The serious use of genealogy . . . is a tool that may prove to be as useful in its way for discovering the social movements of early modern times as statistical analysis has already been."

47. I have in mind on a cosmopolitan scale something like what Sharon Kettering's work has done for patronage networks within France: see, for example, her "Patronage and Kinship in Early Modern France," *French Historical Studies* 16

(1989): 408–35. This would also be very like what John Bosher has done for the financial International in his "Huguenot Merchants."

48. Samuel Romilly, *Memoirs*, 3 vols. (London: J. Murray, 1840) 1:335.

49. Too often historians have measured "assimilation" (a term I have avoided, in favor of the concept of loss of cosmopolitan identities and bonds) in terms of passage of time rather than turnover of generations. See, for example, Jon Butler, *The Huguenots in America: A Refugee People in New World Society* (Cambridge, Mass.: Harvard University Press, 1983).

50. The marquess of Anglesey, *One-Leg: The Life and Letters of Henry William Paget, First Marquess of Anglesey, K.G., 1768–1854* (London: Jonathan Cape, 1961), 19–22.

51. Marie took her share in South Sea Stock and sold all of it in May 1724 (British Library, MS 15945). François-Auguste was even quicker to dispose of his, selling it in January 1723 (British Library, MS 15945). On the other hand, the £233.6s.8d of Old South Sea Annuities that the Reverend George Champagné, son of the Dean and Canon of St. George's Chapel, Windsor, bequeathed to the Chapel in 1822 to endow prizes for the boys and girls in the National School at Windsor may have been a long-term holding from this same family heritage (*Report of the Charity Commission on the Parish of New Windsor*, 1911). This last information I owe to Randolph Vigne through Petra Coffey.

52. On the involvement of Huguenots residing in Holland in the South Sea speculation of 1720, see Charles Wilson, *Anglo-Dutch Commerce and Finance in the Eighteenth Century* (Cambridge: Cambridge University Press, 1941), 103–8.

NINE

The Huguenots and the American Immigrant Experience

Jon Butler

The Huguenot immigrant experience in American history is both fascinating and perplexing. It is fascinating because so much of the Huguenot experience remains a mystery. Despite substantial scholarship on the subject, the timing of the Huguenot immigration to America in the 1680s and 1690s, so early in the history of both New York and South Carolina, means that it occurred in decades for which many documents simply have not survived. As a result, we remain ignorant about many of its most crucial and fascinating details. And it is perplexing because the combination of what we do know plus the mystery of what we do not know leaves us puzzled about many important issues.

For example, we know far more about the Huguenot immigrant experience in late-seventeenth- and early-eighteenth-century America than we do about the Huguenot refugee experience in much of Europe. This has been true since Charles Washington Baird published his *History of the Huguenot Emigration to America* in 1885, the first substantial book on the Huguenot emigration after 1685 ever to appear and still a classic and important study.[1]

Most serious, the Huguenot experience in eighteenth-century Britain remains without deep systematic study. When George Rudé wrote his well- known book *The Crowd in History: A Study of Popular Disturbances in France and England, 1730–1848*, which rehearsed London's famous "Spitalfields Riots" of the 1770s, he described the French weavers who constituted many of the participants without mentioning or discussing their overwhelmingly Huguenot background. Actually, it would have been difficult for Rudé to do so. Historians have been far more interested in the very small numbers of Huguenots who arrived in England in the six-teenth and early seventeenth centuries than in the more important Huguenot refugees who crowded into Britain after 1680 and who were the forebears of the Spitalfields rioters.[2]

Moreover, what we do know about the Huguenot immigration to America often defies both expectations and seemingly settled historical truths. How do we explain the Huguenot migration to the British colonies in America? Did the immigrants come for material or spiritual opportunities? How do we explain their experience in America? Why did men and women known for specialized occupations overwhelmingly become farmers and planters? How do we explain the turn to slavehold-ing among a people exiled for religious persecution? How do we explain the Huguenots' astonishingly rapid marriage assimilation in the British mainland colonies? Why did refugee support for independent Huguenot congregations decline after 1720, not merely in the small Huguenot set-tlements in America but in the large refugee centers in Europe, such as London?

Contrary to many myths about early modern Europe, migration was a surprisingly common feature of early modern European life in the six-teenth and seventeenth centuries. Scots, for example, were a remarkably immigrating people. In the sixteenth and seventeenth centuries, Scots immigrated to England, Ireland, Scandinavia, and the Netherlands. Indeed, by 1620 almost 30,000 Scots were living in what is now modern Poland. Germans from Prussia and other German-speaking states regu-larly immigrated to eastern Europe in search of both land and safety.[3]

The European exploration of America in the middle and late six-teenth century was part of this broader European pattern of immigration, although initially only a very small and insignificant part. It does, at the same time, account for why so much early immigration to America and exploration was private, not public. In the twilight of the early modern era, the state—whether in Britain, France, or Spain—often simply could not finance New World expeditions on its own. As a result, English, French, and Spanish authorities offered private inducements to the men and women willing to risk New World exploration and settlement.[4]

French Protestants were active both as explorers and as emigrants. The astonishing discovery by Chester DePratter, of the University of South Carolina, of Charlesfort, the Huguenot outpost built by Jean Ribaut on

Parris Island, South Carolina, in 1562, reveals how close that exploration and emigration really was to a major center of Huguenot settlement more than a century later, even if it already was lost in the local memory, only to be raised by archaeologists and historians in the 1990s. In fact, Huguenots were active in substantial French exploration and settlement of the New World. This occurred most notably in Brazil, but later in what is modern Florida and also in what now is modern South Carolina, as the discovery of Charlesfort indicates.[5]

Here, Huguenots found themselves driven to New World exploration and settlement for three primary reasons. First, they were servants of the pre-Revocation French state. In the Edict of Nantes, the state promised crucial if limited religious freedom and was willing and even eager to use French Protestant merchants, navigators, and sailors in the service of New World exploration. Second, Huguenots were inquiring intellectuals fascinated by New World exploration, much as were their Catholic counterparts. Third, they were Protestants intent on demonstrating the validity and vigor of their faith. They competed eagerly with Catholicism and with Catholics. And they were reluctant to take a back seat in New World exploration for fear that their hard-won advantages on both sides of the Atlantic would be lost and their privileges removed. For these reasons, it is scarcely surprising that the New World interested French Protestants at the center of sixteenth- and seventeenth-century European intellectual, political, and spiritual life.[6]

The Revocation of the Edict of Nantes in 1685 drastically upset vigorous French Protestant participation in sixteenth- and early-seventeenth-century French life and culture. The background of the Revocation of the Edict of Nantes in 1685 is too complex to discuss here. Whatever its origins, its effects were devastating. The Revocation was one of early modern Europe's most effective demonstrations of the rising power of the modern state. Ominously, it occurred at a very early stage in the evolution of the modern state. Hundreds of thousands of French Protestants were forced to recant their faith and commitment. Louis XIV's technique of repression became a textbook example of ways to alter both public and private behavior, techniques that even the darkest reading of Machiavelli's *The Prince* might not have suggested (Machiavelli was, after all, deeply committed to republican government). The Revocation forced French Protestantism into a permanently minor role in French politics and

French culture. Thus, the Revocation achieved Louis XIV's principal objectives even if it did not expunge Protestantism from France completely, although that had been Louis XIV's aim.[7]

The Revocation created the Huguenot diaspora—the Refuge—the forced flight of several hundred thousand Protestants from France between 1680 and 1700. The Huguenot flight constituted the largest single population movement and forced religious change in early modern Europe except for the expulsion and forced conversion of Jews in Spain a century earlier. In social terms, it displayed what historians sometimes euphemistically call "non-selective" emigration characteristics. The exile cut across lines of class, gender, and age. Rich and poor, old and young, men and women all left France in the Huguenot exodus of 1680–1700.[8]

The Huguenot flight was different than the voluntary population movements of early modern Europe among Scots and Germans, for example. One sign centered on gender. Women and children could be found throughout the Huguenot flight from France in enormous numbers. In addition, the Huguenot Refuge also attracted the old, although voluntary migrations usually drew their clientele from among young men between fifteen and thirty years of age. Class and wealth probably were important but not necessarily in stereotypical terms. Few exiled Huguenots were wealthy. But if they were poor in their cities of exile, and indeed they were, that was because they left assets behind in France, not because they had none before the Revocation.

In fact, Huguenot exiles from France often resembled Scottish immigrants to Poland, Scandinavia, England, or Ireland more than we might realize. Huguenot exiles often came from families of at least modest means. They were skilled workers and small farmers who not only possessed training and some money but the knowledge, confidence, and "wherewithal" that come with it. Even if forced to leave France, they represented the familiar background of modest success, drive, acquisitiveness, and determination that frequently characterized voluntary immigrants to other European countries and to America.[9]

The experience of the Huguenots in America was both similar to and remarkably different from the experience of subsequent voyagers to America. Theirs was a "second-stage" emigration. French language recruitment pamphlets from colonial entrepreneurs, such as William Penn and the South Carolina proprietors, indeed circulated in France before and after the Revocation of the Edict of Nantes, and Bertrand Van Ruymbeke has discovered several late-seventeenth-century pamphlets describing the British colonies, including South Carolina, in French depositories. But few Protestants left France with America in mind. Rather, America came into mind as their first places of exile turned sour.[10]

Huguenots were strongly affected by the dismal conditions in places like London and Rotterdam and by negative European reaction to the refugees. The London committees established to aid French Protestants provided money to settle refugees in New York and South Carolina largely to remove them from England, much like American colonization societies aimed to ship free African Americans to Liberia in the antebellum era. The aid records reveal desperate poverty on the part of the refugees. Men and women who departed for America frequently had applied for shoes, beds, and clothing in London, for example. America thus became—out of force and out of choice—a new place of refuge that many French Protestants had never imagined.[11]

And what was their experience in America? Frankly, it was overwhelmingly positive. Yes, Boston Puritans complained about the French Protestant practice of celebrating Christmas, and yes, English residents of South Carolina complained about French Protestant voters and, for a while, attempted to restrict the franchise among Huguenots in South Carolina. But everywhere else, and in many ways astonishing even for the late seventeenth and early eighteenth centuries, the experience of the Huguenots in America was far better than even the emigration literature promised. Indeed, it could fairly be said that Huguenot emigrants enjoyed benefits that the colonization literature itself did not always anticipate. This was true in four ways.[12]

First, French Protestant settlers in America discovered almost no legal prohibitions against their full participation in colonial British society. The 1697 South Carolina Naturalization Act was only the most official statement of a broad practice in which British imperial officials and colonial authorities allowed French Protestants full British liberties in the mainland colonies. Everywhere, French Protestants quickly owned land, voted, and held public office at a rapid pace probably unequaled by any other immigrant group in American history.[13]

Second, the French Protestant refugees arrived at the point that the colonies were poised for massive economic expansion and cultural transformation. Their skills and adaptability fitted a society about to undergo

remarkable growth in both domestic and external trade. In South Carolina, Nicholas de Longuemare served a pressing demand for his repair of
watches, his silver and gold production, and his engraving skills, as well
as his hog farming, all of which is documented in the marvelous journal
that de Longuemare kept in South Carolina between 1700 and 1710.[14]

Huguenot refugee settlement in America in the 1680s and 1690s
coincided with a vast expansion in colonial landholding based on cheap
government land prices. This was true for Huguenots everywhere in
Massachusetts and Rhode Island, New York, and especially in South
Carolina. Huguenot refugees bought land in vast quantities at extremely
cheap rates. As a consequence, Huguenots also rather quickly shifted
occupations and, in doing so, predicted a major pattern for immigrants in
America down to the beginning of the twenty-first century. Huguenots
who had been tradesmen and skilled laborers in France and in exile in
London became farmers in America. Not all subsequent immigrants followed the same progression, but many changed occupations as a matter
of course in America. Indeed, some German Jewish immigrants of the
antebellum era, for example, likewise followed the old Huguenot pattern,
merchants and tradesmen becoming farmers in the old west east of the
Mississippi River.[15]

Third, in both South Carolina and New York, Huguenots became
slaveholders, a pattern that would mark the Huguenot refugees and those
they enslaved in all the unfolding centuries of American history.
Huguenots forwarded the commitment and enthusiasm for slavery
demonstrated by South Carolina's British proprietors. To some extent,
this was surprising. There had been at least some criticism of slavery as
inhumane by seventeenth-century French Protestant authorities. In addition, the Huguenots' own experience of repression and coercion in the
era of the Revocation might have militated against engaging in New
World slaveholding. Finally, Huguenot exiles bitterly criticized Louis
XIV's slave-like use of Protestant prisoners in the infamous French galleys in the 1690s and early 1700s. Yet in America, Huguenots turned to
slavery with considerable force, eagerly using enslaved Africans not only
in South Carolina but also in the agricultural settlement of New Rochelle
in New York as well.[16]

Fourth, Huguenots quickly won acceptance into British colonial society. This acceptance was most visible in the astonishing Huguenot rates of
marriage to English settlers throughout the colonies and to Dutch settlers

in New York. Huguenot intermarriage approached 50 per cent of all Huguenot marriages as early as 1700, and for both men and women, scarcely a decade after their arrival in the colonies. True, the Huguenot liking for non-Huguenot spouses could be interpreted as a way to escape a Huguenot culture disliked by English and Dutch colonists. But little evidence supports such an interpretation. Instead, it signified English and Dutch willingness to take Huguenot spouses. All these colonists— English, Dutch, and French—were nominally Protestant and white, and in this regard, they predicted a later pattern within larger Protestant, Catholic, or Jewish circles. In the nineteenth and twentieth centuries, national identities gave way to larger religious identities. A broader, generic Protestantism, Catholicism, or Judaism supplanted national and ethnic identities within these major religious universes, the pattern that the sociologist Will Herberg described for the mid-twentieth century brilliantly in his *Protestant-Catholic-Jew* published in 1955.[17]

Huguenots also came to colonial politics early and often. In their three major places of settlement—Massachusetts, New York, and South Carolina—Huguenots rather quickly voted and held political office. Boston voters elected several Huguenots as constables and tithing men by 1710. New York authorities made Huguenots freemen in the 1680s, allowed them to vote in city and provincial elections, and elected them to the New York City Council as early as 1700. It was vigorous Huguenot voting in South Carolina Assembly elections in the 1690s that produced a backlash against Huguenots in the colony. This slowly waned, and by the 1720s Huguenots were being elected regularly to the Assembly. In all three colonies, Huguenots again ushered in a pattern common to the nineteenth-century immigrant experience in America: politics signaled both acceptance in America and a way to achieve it if the dominant society was reluctant.[18]

Huguenots helped achieve religious pluralism in America as well. We may remain puzzled by the Huguenot departure from the old independent Huguenot congregations. By the 1720s, these congregations in Boston, New York, and Charleston saw many Huguenot descendants join English and Dutch Protestant congregations—Anglican, Presbyterian, Baptist, even Quaker. Were these refugees rejecting their Huguenot heritage? Or, were they choosing an American future—a future that would witness the growth of an amazing religious pluralism across the whole of American society. In America, there would be a religion for every person and a person for every religion. The individual, not the state, made spiritual choices. And the individual might create a religion when no acceptable alternative seemed available.[19]

This turn toward religious pluralism among Huguenot refugees in America helps explain one of the most difficult episodes in Huguenot history, South Carolina's Dutartre affair of 1723–1724. The Dutartre family had probably earlier embraced the religious radicalism of London's so-called "French Prophets," who were refugees from the so-called "Cévennes War" of the early 1700s. Their London-published tracts circulated in South Carolina and described their prophecies and their attempts to raise the dead. Unhappy with South Carolina Huguenot congregations in the rural countryside and in Charleston, the Dutartres created a spiritual world of their own. They took others' spouses for their own, refused to pay taxes, and ultimately resisted the government, resulting in bloodshed and death, for which they would pay with their own execution by the South Carolina government in 1724.[20]

The Dutartres, as well as Huguenots who became Anglicans, Presbyterians, Congregationalists, Baptists, Quakers, all exhibited a turn toward the pluralism and eclecticism that typified America from the 1730s into the nineteenth and twentieth centuries. It was a pattern that demonstrated how thoroughly American religion even in the colonial era was not Puritanism writ large. Indeed, it could be said that the capacity of American religion for assimilation, pluralism, and experimentation followed the history of colonial Huguenots writ large, from their movement into other Protestant congregations to experimentation of dubious and certainly dangerous character.[21]

Ultimately, Huguenots found powerful ways to shape an American identity through marriage, land purchases, and both personal success and failure in Britain's mainland colonies. Later, in the nineteenth century, long after the last independent French Protestant Church had closed during the turmoil of the American Revolution, descendants of these Huguenot refugees reestablished a group identity that fissured in the colonial era through the cultivation of genealogy, ultimately in organizations such as the Huguenot Society of South Carolina that traced ancestors back into the late seventeenth century and to France itself.[22]

The Huguenots, especially in South Carolina, also would have a fascinating parallel in the postbellum period. After the Civil War, hundreds of Africans freed from slavery took new surnames that included many

Huguenot names, such as Manigault, Mazyck, and Horry. These names still denote the identities of thousands of African Americans across the United States. African Americans earned these names in the crucible of slavery, just as Huguenots of the 1680s and 1690s earned their freedom—and defined and redefined their identities—in the crucible of European religious repression. Taking Huguenot names did not necessarily bespeak some special relationship of African Americans to Huguenots as a group. As the historian Leon Litwack has observed, it customarily meant that these African Americans took the names of men and women with whom their lives were inextricably bound and with whom they had shaped communal as well as individual meaning, even if that meaning was strained, reluctant, and difficult. In claiming Huguenot names, African Americans claimed a process of struggle that Huguenots themselves knew well and on which they could claim experience but no patent. It was identity itself and the root of human experience.[23]

In all, then, Huguenots were shaped by and became shapers of the American immigrant and migrant experience itself in the broadest context. This became true whether in the north or the south, whether among the modestly or adamantly religious or even the irreligious, and whether among the poor or the rich. Huguenots became part of the American dream, a dream they could scarcely envision when they arrived, but a dream they made and shaped not only through the future but the past.

In recent decades, many Americans have voiced dark challenges to that dream—more challenges than French Protestant refugees faced in British America in the 1680s and 1690s. Many Americans now discuss immigrants and immigration in mean and vindictive terms, advocating restrictions on a wide range of public services, from education to legal aid and welfare, among legal and illegal immigrants alike, treating immigrants as though they were suspects to be watched, dangers to the American future. This new suspiciousness and vindictiveness is unworthy of the American past. And it is specifically unworthy of the Huguenot heritage, an experience of overwhelming openness, engagement, and participation in a society where French-speaking strangers quickly exercised power and influence far beyond anything they might have dreamed of, much less achieved, in France under the impress of Louis XIV's anti-Protestant decrees or in London amidst unimaginable refugee poverty.

This dream has not always been perfect. But it was and is worthy nonetheless. And few authors better described it than did F. Scott Fitzgerald in the final page of *The Great Gatsby*, published in 1925.

And as I sat there brooding on the old, unknown world, I thought of Gatsby's wonder when he first picked out the green light at the end of Daisy's dock. He had come a long way to this blue lawn, and his dream must have seemed so close that he could hardly fail to grasp it. He did not know that it was already behind him, somewhere back in that vast obscurity beyond the city, where the dark fields of the republic rolled on under the night.

Gatsby believed in the green light, the orgiastic future that year by year recedes before us. It eluded us then, but that's no matter—tomorrow we will run faster, stretch out our arms farther. . . . And one fine morning—

So we beat on, boats against the current, borne back ceaselessly into the past.

Fitzgerald's evocation of that dream was indeed modern. But it was not a description that seventeenth-century French Protestants, recently arrived in Charleston, New York, or Boston, would have found uncongenial. The reason is simple. Rather than being utopian and filled with descriptions of unimaginable and frankly impossible riches, Fitzgerald admitted men's and women's frailties as well as their strengths; he acknowledged and embraced struggle and failure as often as he embraced achievement and success.

Huguenots experienced all of those capacities in their American immigration. And the descendants of Huguenots, like all other immigrant Americans, would well honor their long engagement with the American immigrant experience, an experience that at the start of the twenty-first century remains vibrant through the modern refugees who still seek America, as Huguenots did three centuries ago.

Notes

1. Charles Washington Baird, *History of the Huguenot Emigration to America* (New York: Dodd and Mead, 1885). Also see Arthur Henry Hirsch, *The Huguenots of Colonial South Carolina* (Durham, N.C.: Duke University Press, 1928).

2. George F. E. Rudé, *The Crowd in History: A Study of Popular Disturbances in France and England, 1730–1848* (New York: Wiley: 1964), 47–78. On Huguenots in seventeenth-century Britain, see Bernard Cottret, *Huguenots in England: Immigration and Settlement, c. 1550–1700* (Cambridge: Cambridge University Press, 1991); Margaret Cox, "The Huguenots of Spitalfields: The Evidence from the Christ Church Project," *Proceedings of the Huguenot Society of Great Britain and Ireland* 25 (1989): 21–38; A. V. B. Gibson, "Huguenot Weavers' Houses in Spitalfields," *East London Papers* 1 (1958); Christopher Hartop, *The Huguenot Legacy: English Silver 1680–1760, from the Alan and Simone Hartman Collection* (London: Thomas Heneage, 1996); Anne J. Kershen, *London, the Promised Land?: The Migrant Experience in a Capital City* (Aldershot: Avebury, 1997); Irene Scouloudi, "Alien Immigration and Alien Communities in London, 1558–1640" (Master's thesis, University of London, 1936); Alicia St. Leger, *Silver, Sails, and Silk: Huguenots in Cork, 1685–1850* (Cork: Cork Civic Trust, 1991)

3. See Nicholas Canny, ed., *Europeans on the Move: Studies on European Migration, 1500–1800* (Oxford: Clarendon Press, 1994); Peter Clark, "Migration in England during the Late Seventeenth and Early Eighteenth Centuries," *Past and Present* 83 (1979): 57–90; David Souden, "'East, West—Home's Best'? Regional Patterns in Migration in Early Modern England," in Peter Clark and David Souden, ed., *Migration and Society in Early Modern England* (London: Hutchinson, 1987), 292–332.

4. The variety of English efforts to colonize America in the seventeenth century can be traced in Nicholas Canny, ed., *The Origins of Empire: British Overseas Enterprise to the Close of the Seventeenth Century*, vol. 1 of *The Oxford History of the British Empire* (New York: Oxford University Press, 1998).

5. John Noble Wilford, "A French Fort, Long Lost, Is Found in South Carolina," *New York Times*, 6 June 1996.

6. Thomas Cogswell, "Foreign Policy and Parliament: The Case of La Rochelle, 1625–1626," *English Historical Review* 99 (1984): 241–67; Robert Mandrou, *Histoire des Protestants en France* (Toulouse: Privat, 1977); Nancy Lyman Roelker, *One King, One Faith: The Parlement of Paris and the Religious Reformations of the Sixteenth Century* (Berkeley: University of California Press, 1996).

7. Elisabeth Labrousse, *"Une fois, une loi, un roi?" Essai sur la Révocation de l'Édit de Nantes* (Geneva: Labor et Fides, 1985); Bernard Cottret, *L'Édit de Nantes: 1598: pour en finir avec les guerres de religion* (Paris: Perrin, 1997); Jacques Solé, *Les origines intellectuelles de la Révocation de l'Édit de Nantes* (Saint-Etienne: Publications de l'Université de Saint-Etienne, 1997); *Saumur, capitale européenne du protestantisme au XVIIe siècle* (Fontevrault-l'Abbaye: Centre culturel de l'ouest, 1991); Jon Butler, *The Huguenots in America: A Refugee People in New World Society* (Cambridge, Mass.: Harvard University Press, 1983), 13–40.

8. The best synoptic treatment is Myriam Yardeni, *Le Refuge Protestant* (Paris: Presses Universitaires de France, 1985). Also see Yardeni, "Conversions et Reconversions dans le Refuge Huguenot," *Dimensioni e problemi della ricerca storica* (1996): 239–46; Marie-Jeanne Ducommun, *Le Refuge Protestant dans le Pays de Vaud: Fin XVIIe-début XVIIIe s., aspects d'une migration* (Geneva: Droz, 1991). Anne Goldgar, *Impolite Learning: Conduct and Community in the Republic of Letters, 1680–1750* (New Haven: Yale University Press, 1995), and Gerald Cerny, *Theology, Politics and Letters at the Crossroads of European Civilization: Jacques Basnage and the Baylean Huguenot Refugees in the Dutch Republic* (Dordrecht: Martinus Nijhoff, 1987) describe the late-seventeenth- and early-eighteenth-century international intellectual world in which refugee Huguenots figured prominently.

9. Butler, *The Huguenots in America*, 41–68; M. Philippe Chareyre, "Les Protestants de Saumur au XVIIème siècle, Religion et Société," in *Saumur, capitale européenne du protestantisme au XVIIe siècle*, 27–70; Margaret M. Escott, "Profiles of Relief: Royal Bounty Grants to Huguenot Refugees, 1686–1709," *Proceedings of the Huguenot Society of Great Britain and Ireland* 25 (1991): 257–78; Didier Poton, "Les Protestants de Saumur au XVIIème siècle, Étude démographique," in *Saumur, capitale européenne du protestantisme au XVIIIe siècle*, 11–26.

10. Bertrand Van Ruymbeke, "L'émigration huguenote en Caroline du Sud sous le régime des Seigneurs Propriétaires: Étude d'une communauté du Refuge dans une province britannique d'Amérique du Nord (1680–1720)" (Ph.D. diss., University de la Sorbonne-Nouvelle Paris III, 1995), 184–281; Van Ruymbeke, "A 'Best Poor Huguenot's Country'? The Carolina Proprietors and the Recruitment of French Protestants" (paper presented at the International Seminar of Atlantic Studies, Harvard University, Cambridge, Mass., Sept. 1996).

11. A. P. Hands and Irene Scouloudi, ed., *French Protestant Refugees Relieved through the Threadneedle Street Church, London, 1681–1687*, vol. 49 of *Publications, Huguenot Society of Great Britain and Ireland* (London, 1971), 17–18, 223, 227; Butler, *The Huguenots in America*, 33–34, 59–60.

12. Butler, *The Huguenots in America*, 78–79, 101–6; M. Eugene Sirmans, *Colonial South Carolina: A Political History, 1663–1763* (Chapel Hill: University of North Carolina Press, for the Institute of American History and Culture, 1966), 61–62.

13. Butler, *The Huguenots in America*, 85–87, 92–93, 95–99, 123–27, 131–32, 149–54, 174–83.

14. John J. McCusker and Menard Russell R., *The Economy of British America, 1607–1789* (Chapel Hill: University of North Carolina Press, for the Institute of American History and Culture, 1985); Jon Butler, *The First American Revolution: Transforming Britain's Colonies Before 1776* (Cambridge, Mass.: Harvard University Press, 2000), chap. 2; Samuel G. Stoney, "Nicholas de Longemare, Huguenot

Goldsmith and Silk Dealer in Colonial South Carolina," *Transactions of the Huguenot Society of South Carolina* 55 (1950): 38–69.

15. For a later pattern involving Catholic immigrants to Quebec see Leslie Choquette, *Frenchmen into Peasants: Modernity and Tradition in the Peopling of French Canada* (Cambridge, Mass.: Harvard University Press, 1997). On Jewish farmers see Gabriel Davidson, *Our Jewish Farmers and the Story of the Jewish Agricultural Society* (New York: L. B. Fischer, 1943); Jonathan D. Sarna, *Jacksonian Jew: The Two Worlds of Mordecai Noah* (New York: Holmes and Meier, 1981), chap. 4; and Ellen Eisenberg, *Jewish Agricultural Colonies in New Jersey* (Syracuse: Syracuse University Press, 1995).

16. On Huguenot slaveholding see Butler, *The Huguenots in America*, 100–101, 122–23, 150–51, 174–76.

17. On later patterns in intermarriage in the United States see Richard Bernard, *The Melting Pot and the Altar: Marital Assimilation in Early Twentieth Century Wisconsin* (Minneapolis: University of Minnesota Press, 1980); Will Herberg, *Protestant-Catholic-Jew: An Essay in American Religious Sociology* (Garden City, N.J.: Doubleday, 1955). On Huguenot intermarriage see Butler, *The Huguenots in America*, 80–84, 107, 132–34, 159–60, 186–89.

18. On Huguenot political participation in America, see Butler, *The Huguenots in America*, 80, 84, 102–5, 127–31, 147–49, 154–56, 184–86, and Van Ruymbeke, "Crossing the Rubicon: The South Carolina Huguenots and the Issue of Naturalization" (paper presented at the conference "Out of New Babylon. The Huguenots and their Diaspora," Charleston, 1997), which offers a more muted picture.

19. The history of religious pluralism in the eighteenth-century colonies is described in Jon Butler, *Awash in a Sea of Faith: Christianizing the American People* (Cambridge, Mass.: Harvard University Press, 1990), chap. 6.

20. Among the eighteenth-century tracts at the library of the Huguenot Society of South Carolina in the mid-1970s were *An Account of the French Prophets and their Pretended Inspirations* (London, 1708), which attacked the French Prophets, and *Plainte, & Censure des Colomnieuses Accusations Publiées Par le Sr Claude Grosteste de la Mote* (London, 1708), which defended them, as well as several London tracts by John Lacy supporting the French Prophets. See Butler, *The Huguenots in America*, 117–20, on the Dutartre affair, and Hillel Schwartz, *The French Prophets: The History of a Millenarian Group in Eighteenth-Century England* (Berkeley: University of California Press, 1980), for the French Prophet movement in Britain and Europe.

21. The importance of pluralism in colonial religion can be seen in a remarkable eighteenth-century source, Charles Woodmason: Richard J. Hooker, ed., *The Carolina Backcountry on the Eve of the American Revolution: The Journal and*

Other Writings of Charles Woodmason, Anglican Itinerant (Chapel Hill: University of North Carolina Press, for the Institute of Early American History and Culture, 1953).

22. There is, as yet, no history of the formation of groups such as the Huguenot Society of South Carolina or, for that matter, of the rise of genealogy in nineteenth-century American culture, but for a beginning on the general topic see Robert M. Taylor Jr. and Ralph J. Crandall, ed., *Generations and Change: Genealogical Perspectives in Social History* (Macon, Ga.: Mercer University Press, 1986).

23. Leon F. Litwack, *Been in the Storm So Long: The Aftermath of Slavery* (New York: Alfred A. Knopf, 1979), 228, 248–51, 454.

TEN

Huguenot Merchants and the Development of South Carolina's Slave-Plantation and Atlantic Trading Economy, 1680–1775[1]

R. C. Nash

In the late seventeenth century, Louis XIV's persecution of French Protestants, or Huguenots, culminating in the Revocation of the Edict of Nantes of 1685, led to a massive flight of Huguenots from France and their diaspora amongst a number of neighboring countries, including Holland, Prussia, Switzerland, and England. The vast majority of the 50,000 Huguenots who went to England settled permanently in the country, but about 2,000 of them moved on to British America in the late seventeenth and early eighteenth centuries.[2] These transatlantic migrants established substantial communities in three colonies—South Carolina, Massachusetts, and New York—but it was in South Carolina that they had their greatest effect on the economic and social evolution of British America. The great majority of migrants to South Carolina arrived in the years 1680–1695, shortly after "Carolina" was founded in 1670. Most of the Huguenots who fled from France to England in the late seventeenth century were middle-aged or elderly, but the migrants to South Carolina were predominantly young, single or married adults, as older refugees were not generally prepared to suffer the hardships involved in crossing the Atlantic and settling in a new colony.[3] By circa 1700, there were 400–500 migrants in the colony and perhaps 100 children born to Huguenot parents in America, making up some 15 percent of South Carolina's white population of 3,250.[4]

Jon Butler has provided the most compelling thesis on the character of the Huguenot migration to South Carolina and on its impact on the colony's economic and social development. Butler argues that the Huguenot migrants to America were generally poor and that many had spent several years in England living wholly or partly on charity before migrating to America. He also shows, however, that the migrants were rich in human capital, bringing with them a wide range of artisanal and industrial skills, but that in practice these skills were of scant value in a frontier colony like South Carolina, where the population's small size and limited wealth produced little demand for specialized craftsmen. Besides, the future of the colony lay not in sericulture, linen weaving, or the dozens of other crafts practiced by the Huguenots, but in the slave-plantation production of naval stores, rice, and indigo, the export staples which dominated South Carolina's economy from 1700 to the Revolution. Butler argues that the principal theme of the history of the South Carolina Huguenots is the success that they displayed in integrating themselves into the mainstream of South Carolina's evolving agricultural economy and in shaping its evolution. The majority of the migrants settled in a small number of compact agricultural settlements and, taking advantage of the generous land grants made by the South Carolina proprietors to migrants, channeled their energies and ambitions into slave-plantation agriculture. Indeed, until the 1750s, their accumulation of land and slaves outpaced that of non-Huguenot colonists, although thereafter the Huguenots' lead over other colonists evaporated. Butler further argues that the Huguenots' successful assimilation into South Carolina's economic life was matched by their social assimilation, by their absorption into the mainstream of the colony's religious, political, and cultural life. The Huguenot churches, first in the rural areas and then in Charleston, conformed to Anglican practices or ceased to exist. The Huguenots intermarried with non-French colonists to the point where, by the mid-eighteenth century, marriages purely between individuals of French descent were a rare event. Finally, in South Carolinian politics, the Huguenots acted not as the delegates of French-populated areas, but as non-partisan representatives of the wider population. The conclusion to Butler's powerfully argued thesis is that the Huguenots arrived in the late seventeenth century as French-speaking, Calvinist exiles, but that by 1750 they had become simply South Carolinians. They had French surnames, but in every other way, "they were indistinguishable from all other settlers in the colony, except of course slaves."[5]

Butler's thesis has been challenged in some respects by John F. Bosher's work on Huguenot merchants in Boston and New York and Bertrand Van Ruymbeke's dissertation and other studies on the

Huguenot migration to South Carolina. Bosher argues that research on the Huguenot immigration to America has neglected the fact that the Huguenot diaspora strengthened and extended the international trading networks that Huguenots had formed since the late sixteenth century. The great success of the Huguenot merchants in America is explained not by their rapid and complete assimilation into local societies but by the opposite, by their continuing membership of a distinctive, separatist and international trading culture, which was organized through family-based Huguenot trading networks. The considerable achievements of Huguenot merchants in America are partly explained by their adaptation to local economic conditions, but mainly by their exploitation of their transatlantic mercantile connections. Van Ruymbeke's exhaustive study of the first generation of Huguenots in South Carolina also emphasizes that the Huguenots' success as agriculturists should not overshadow the powerful contribution they made to Charleston's early urban and mercantile development.[6]

This paper takes up Bosher and Van Ruymbeke's theme and considers the South Carolina Huguenots in the colonial period not, in Butler's terms, as planters and slaveowners but rather as merchants and traders. The paper is divided into three sections. Section I asks two questions. First, what contribution did the South Carolina Huguenots make to the development of the colony's mercantile economy and how did this contribution compare with their impact on slave-plantation agriculture? Second, to what extent was the success of Huguenot merchants in South Carolina based on their connections to prominent circles of European-based Huguenot merchants, in the way suggested by Bosher. Section II focuses on the Huguenot merchants' social behavior in Charleston and asks if the merchants sustained their position in South Carolina's commercial economy through a high degree of mutuality and collaboration based on their common ethnic background. Section III concludes by asking what light does the study of South Carolina's Huguenot merchants throw on recent debates about the Huguenots in British America?

I

From the late 1680s to 1775, three generations of Huguenot merchants traded in South Carolina. The first, the immigrant group, was active in trade from circa 1680 to circa 1720 and included eighteen Huguenot migrants who became major merchants in Charleston (table 1). This is not a complete listing of Huguenot merchants of the first generation but does include all the leading merchants who were active in trade for ten or more years. There were also forty English migrants who were merchants for ten years or more, indicating that Huguenots made up about 30 percent of the first generation of major South Carolina merchants. For the second and third generations of merchants, those who traded from 1720 to 1775, I have focused on two sets of sample years—1738–1743 (second generation) and 1762–1767 (third generation.) There were twenty-four Huguenots who were leading Charleston merchants in the years 1738–1743, who made up 23 percent of a Charleston merchant community which numbered 104 merchants in these years (table 2). The third generation, identified here as those active in trade from 1762–1767, consisted of 37 merchants, 22 percent of a Charleston merchant community of 170 merchants.[7] The share of trade controlled by Huguenot merchants was more or less equivalent to their proportion of the merchant population as a whole. For example, 22 percent of the import trade in slaves in 1735–1775, and 21 percent of the import trade in general merchandise in 1735–1765, was handled by Huguenot merchants or by mercantile firms which included Huguenot partners.[8]

Huguenot merchants thus played a major part in South Carolina's commercial economy in the colonial period. Indeed, they made a greater relative contribution in this sphere than in slave-plantation agriculture. Butler has shown that Huguenots and their descendants made up 6 to 10 percent of slave-holders in colonial South Carolina in the years 1736–1765; the evidence presented here indicates that they provided a much higher proportion (22 to 30 percent) of Charleston's merchant community in the same period.[9] Of course, the great majority of successful Huguenot merchants, like their English counterparts, went on to acquire land and slaves, but their fortunes were founded in trade and shipping not in agriculture.[10]

Given that the Huguenots and their descendants represented only a small and declining proportion of South Carolina's population, how can we account for their central and sustained role in South Carolina's commercial economy?[11] To a large extent, the Huguenots' success in business reflected the fact that they arrived in South Carolina very soon after its foundation in 1670, at a time when the colony's trading and commercial system was taking shape. In the late seventeenth century, four significant groups of Huguenot immigrants were established in the colony. The first large group of Huguenots arrived in South Carolina under the leadership of René Petit and Jacob Guérard in 1680. They formed a French agricultural colony in the area which became known as the Orange Quarter, which in 1700 had a French population of about a hundred. In the next fifteen years, 300 or so more Huguenot migrants settled in three locations. By 1690, a number of families had settled on the Santee, about sixty miles north of Charleston, which in 1700 had a French population of about 110. A small group settled in Goose Creek, close to Charleston, which numbered about 30 in 1700. Finally, Huguenots settled in Charleston, which had a French population of 200 in 1700, that is, about a quarter of Charleston's white population.[12] Thus, although the Huguenot agricultural communities have attracted the greatest attention from historians, the main Huguenot migration was to Charleston.

These migrants reached Charleston at a critical point in its development. Charleston was only relocated from its original site—Old Charles Town on the Ashley River—to its present location in 1680. In the 1680s and early 1690s, Charleston was a village surrounded by a wilderness, a point of entry for immigrants rather than a trading port. South Carolina had almost no exports other than a few deerskins and some provisions, and these minor trades were run by planter-merchants from their plantations as a professional merchant class had not materialized in the port.[13] In the next twenty-five years, Charleston, with the rise of its export trades in deer skins, rice, and naval stores, became a significant commercial and shipping center in the English transatlantic trading system.[14] The Huguenots fortuitously reached Charleston at exactly the right time: at the point when the city was undergoing rapid development, yet lacked an established merchant community, thus allowing the newly arrived to have their greatest impact. The Huguenots were present at the birth of Charleston's commercial economy, and they played a major part in shaping the city's subsequent economic evolution.

The Huguenot migrants took such good advantage of commercial opportunities in South Carolina because they were very largely of an urban origin, many of them coming from a bourgeois and trading culture. Van Ruymbeke has shown that more than 65 percent of the migrants came from French towns and cities, with nearly a third coming from La

TABLE 1: *Huguenot Migrants to South Carolina Who Became Leading First-Generation Merchants*

Pierre Buretel	Pierre Manigault
Benj. de La Conseillere**	Issac Mazyck I
James Du Poids D'Or	John A. Motte**
Paul Douxsaint**	Lewis Pasquereau
Benjamin Godin**	Pierre Pasquereau
John Guerard I	Henry Peronneau I
John LaRoche	Pierre St. Julien
Francis LeBrasseur	Abraham Satur
Jacques LeSerrurier	Jacob Satur

** arrived after 1700. The others arrived before 1700, or at a time which is unknown. Merchants listed traded in South Carolina for ten years or more in the period 1685–1730.

Sources: South Carolina Department of Archives and History, Records of the Secretary of the Province, 21 vols., 1675–1731; Records of the South Carolina Court of Common Pleas, Judgment Rolls, 1703–1730; Court of Chancery, Oversize, 1736–1760, no. 3, Samuel Wragg versus Joseph Wragg, 4 June 1749; Records in the British Public Record Office Relating to South Carolina, 1663–1782, (Microcopy), vols. 1–16; PRO., Colonial Office, 5/509, Naval Office, Port Charles Town, 1717–1724; Guildhall Library, London, Account Book of Alexander Baily and Nathanial Lewis, MSS 11,096, 1711–1712; Alexander S. Salley, *Journal of the Commons House of Assembly of South Carolina, 1692–1735*, 22 vols. (Columbia, S.C., 1907–47); Stuart O. Stumpf, "The Merchants of Colonial Charleston, 1680–1756" (Ph.D. diss, Michigan State University, 1971), 6–7, 18–20; Anne K. Gregorie, ed., *Records of the Court of Chancery of South Carolina, 1671–1779* (Washington, D.C.: American Historical Association, 1950); William L. McDowell, ed., *Journals of the Commissioners of the Indian Trade, 1710–1718* (Columbia: The South Carolina Department of Archives and History, 1955); bibliographical essays and notes in *Transactions of the Huguenot Society of South Carolina*, cited below in notes 37, 46; Caroline T. Moore, *Records of the Secretary of the Province, 1692–1721* (Columbia: University of South Carolina Press, 1978); Caroline T. Moore and Agatha A. Simmons, *Abstracts of the Wills of the State of South Carolina, 1670–1740* (Charlotte, N.C.: The Observer Printing House Company, 1960); Walter B. Edgar and N. Louise Bailey, *Biographical Directory of the South Carolina House of Representatives*, vol. 2. *The Commons House of Assembly, 1692–1775* (Columbia: University of South Carolina Press, 1977); R. C. Nash, "Trade and Business in Eighteenth-Century South Carolina: The Career of John Guerard, Merchant and Planter," *South Carolina Historical Magazine* 96 (1995); Van Ruymbeke, "L'émigration huguenote," vol. 1.

TABLE 2: *Second-Generation Major Huguenot Merchants, Active in Trade 1738–1742*

Peter Benoist [A]	Gabriel Manigault [M]
David Dalbiac [P]	Issac Mazyck II [M]
Peter Delemestre [I]	Samuel Montaigut [P]
Paul Douxsaint** [M]	Jacob Motte [M]
Benj. Godin** [M]	John Mayrant [P]
John Guerard II [M]	John Neufville I [P]
Gab Guignard [I]	Henry Peronneau II [M]
Benj. D'Harriette [I]	Arthur Peronneau [M]
Peter Horry I [P]	Samuel Peronneau I [M]
Paul Labilliere [P]	Samuel Prioleau [P]
William Lasserre [I]	Philip Prioleau [P]
Peter Leger [A]	Matthew Roche [I]
	John Royer [M]

** A merchant of the first generation who continued to trade in the second generation.

Social origins of merchants indicated by:
[I] = Immigrant [M] = Merchant [P] = Planter [A] = Artisan.
[I] = 5 (20%) [M] = 10 (40%) [P] = 8 (32%) [A] = 2 (8%)

TABLE 3: *Third-Generation Major Huguenot Merchants, Active in Trade, 1762–1767*

Peter Bacot [P]	John Guerard** [M]
Peter Bochet [P]	Theodore Gaillard [P]
Anthony Bonneau [P]	William Guerin [P]
Daniel Bourdeau [P]	Peter Horry II [M]
Issac Bourdeau [P]	Henry Laurens** [A]
Samuel Chollet [I]	James Laurens [A]
Alex Chovin [P]	Peter Leger** [A]
Paul Douxsaint II [M]	Daniel Legare [A]
Gideon Dupont [P]	Samuel Legare [A]
John Fabre [A]	Thomas Legare [A]
John Lewis Gervais [I]	Gabriel Manigault** [M]

TABLE 3 (*continued*)

Peter Manigault [M]	Arthur Peronneau** [M]
Jacob Motte [M]	Henry Peronneau III [M]
Peter Mazyck [M]	Samuel Peronneau II [M]
Edward Neufville [M]	Samuel Prioleau** [M]
John Neufville II [M]	Philip Prioleau** [M]
John Perdriau [A]	Edward Simons [P]
James Poyas [M]	Maurice Simons [P]
John Poyas [M]	Peter Villepontoux [P]

** A merchant of the second generation who continued to trade in the third generation.

[I] = 2 (5%) [M] = 16 (42%) [P] = 12 (32%) [A] = 8 (21%)

Sources: Merchants in Tables II and III have been identified from:

(a) Lists of importers and exporters in: W. Robert Higgins, "Charles Town Merchants and Factors Dealing in the External Slave Trade, 1735–1775," *South Carolina Historical Magazine* 65 (1964): 205–17; Stumpf, "South Carolina Importers of General Merchandize, 1735–1765," ibid. 84 (1983): 1–10; W. O. Moore Jr., "The Largest Exporters of Deerskins from Charles Town, 1735–1775," ibid. 74 (1973): 144–50; J. A. Calhoun, M. A. Zierdan, and E. A. Paysinger, "The Geographic Spread of Charleston's Merchant Community, 1732–1767," ibid. 86 (1985): 207–20.

(b) Lists of owners of ships clearing Charleston, 1738–1739 and 1762–1767; ships manifests showing consignors of rice and indigo on ships bound from Charleston, January to April 1764. It is assumed that owners of ships making two or more voyages carrying rice and indigo were traders in those commodities, PRO., Colonial Office, 5/509, 511, Naval Office, Port Charles Town, 1738–1739, 1762–1767.

(c) Business accounts and papers: Charleston Museum Archives, Charleston, Merchant's Day Book [James Poyas], 1761–1764; South Carolina Historical Society, Charleston, 34–325, Merchant's Day Book [James Poyas], 1764–1766; South Carolina Department of Archives and History; Inventories of Estates, 1736–1776; Records of the South Carolina Court of Common Pleas, Judgment Rolls, 1731–1775; Records of the Secretary of State, Miscellaneous Records, 1732–1776; New York Public Library, Transcripts of the Commission of Enquiry into Losses of American Loyalists Amongst the Audit Office Records, vol. 52, 505–17, vol. 54, 266–74, vol. 56, 576–95; PRO., Treasury Office Papers, 79, American Loyalist Claims Commission, vols. 5, 15, 36, 42.

Rochelle and the lesser ports in its vicinity. A high percentage of the male migrants (a quarter) were merchants, and another 11 percent were drawn from the ranks of the minor gentry or *écuyers* of western France, a class which had close links with the urban bourgeoisie. The proportion of merchants amongst the French migrants was much higher than amongst the English migrants to South Carolina or, indeed, than was found in the French Protestant migrations to the Caribbean and to Canada.[15] It is not, therefore, surprising that many of the French migrants to South Carolina became merchants, retailers, and shipowners in Charleston. We can trace the origins of sixteen of the eighteen first-generation Huguenot merchants (table 1). Of these, twelve were descended from merchant families of towns in western France, principally Bordeaux, La Rochelle, Rouen, and Tours, two were the sons of Normandy noblemen, and two were the sons of a Calvinist minister.[16] To give examples, Isaac Chardon was descended from a family which had been important Protestant merchants of Tours for several generations. Louis Pasquereau Sr., a merchant in Tours who originated from an Angers merchant family, migrated to South Carolina with his wife Madeleine Chardon, Isaac Chardon's cousin, and their two sons, Louis and Pierre Pasquereau, who both became first-generation merchants in Charleston.[17]

However, while we can establish the impeccable merchant pedigree of the majority of Charleston's first-generation Huguenot merchants, can we show that their success in Charleston was founded on the exploitation of their international trading connections, in the manner suggested by Bosher? Certainly, it is possible that those migrants who arrived before 1700, and who were descendants of mercantile families of western France (the Pasquereaus, Pierre Buretel, Jacques LeSerrurier, Pierre Manigault, Henry Péronneau, etc.) succeeded in transferring merchant capital from France to England and then to South Carolina. However, we have almost no evidence to prove this, and the frequent claims made by historians about the supposed funds brought by Huguenot merchants to America are highly speculative.[18] Indeed, the fact that many Huguenots who arrived before 1700 only became merchants after some years in the colony, that is after having tried their hands at non-mercantile occupations, suggests very strongly that they lacked the trading capital and the European connections which would have given them a ready entry into foreign trade. For example, John Guérard Sr., the son of the Normandy nobleman Jacob Guérard, who co-founded the Petit-Guérard colony, occupied himself for nearly a decade as a weaver and planter before entering trade. Similarly, Pierre Manigault, who was of a La Rochelle mercantile family, was for some time a planter and then rum distiller, and only began trading with the West Indies many years after his arrival in South

Carolina.[19] Moreover, while the evidence about the trading operations of these early Huguenot merchants is meager, it suggests that their trading connections in England were mainly, although not exclusively, with merchants of English rather than of Huguenot descent.[20]

For the merchants who arrived after 1700, we find more concrete evidence that the success of Huguenot merchants in South Carolina was based on their connections to prominent networks of European-based Huguenot merchants. The Revocation of the Edict of Nantes strengthened Huguenot economic power by dispersing Huguenot merchants amongst the leading trading centers of Europe. The Huguenots were the most important element in the massive influx of foreign merchants into England (including also Dutch and German Protestants and Portuguese Jews) which itself was the most important change experienced in the organization of English foreign trade in the late seventeenth and eighteenth centuries. Huguenot merchants had traded in London from the late sixteenth century, but the first major wave of Huguenot merchant-migrants to England came in the post-Revocation period, mainly from western France, from the ports and inland trading towns which had prospered in the seventeenth-century expansion of the Atlantic economy and which were dominated by Protestant merchants. These refugee merchants traded principally with northern Europe and the Mediterranean.[21] Insofar as they had colonial interests, these were focused on the established trades to the West Indies and to Boston and New York; before 1700, these merchants took little interest in the insignificant Anglo-Carolinian trade.[22]

However, in the early eighteenth century, Charleston's growing importance as a trading port began to attract the attention of two sorts of Huguenot merchant firms in London. First, and most importantly, a number of Huguenot firms which originated in western France established family members in Charleston as resident agents in the Anglo-South Carolinian trade. For example, David Godin, a rich Rouen merchant, had been naturalized in London in 1693, where he traded in partnership with his elder son Stephen. In about 1700, his younger son Benjamin was dispatched to South Carolina, where he formed what was probably, after the business of Joseph and Samuel Wragg, Charleston's most important merchant-firm of the early eighteenth century. Alongside the Godins there were a number of other prominent London-domiciled Huguenot mercantile families with representatives in Charleston in the early eighteenth century—including the Belins, Douxsaints, LeSerruriers, and Saturs (table 1).[23] Second, a number of recently arrived London Huguenot merchants traded with South Carolina's Huguenot merchants even though they lacked family connections in the colony. These included René Baudouin and Pierre Renew, formerly merchants of Tours and Bordeaux respectively, who traded mainly with Europe but who had subsidiary interests in the South Carolina trade.[24] However, despite this increased involvement of London Huguenot merchants in the Anglo-South Carolinian trade, the bulk of the commerce at the English end in the early eighteenth century was organized by English merchants. Thus, in 1719, the sole year in the eighteenth century for which we have detailed data, 24 percent of rice imports and 17 percent of naval stores imports into London from South Carolina were handled by the Huguenot merchants of London; the remaining imports were dealt with by London merchants of English extraction. Similarly, in the years 1717–1720, of the 160 London-based individuals listed as owners of ships in the Charleston trade, only 22 (14 percent) were London Huguenots.[25]

Nevertheless, the early eighteenth century marked the high-water mark of the involvement of London firms of Huguenot origins in the South Carolina trade, and thereafter the dominance of London firms of English extraction became more or less a complete one. First, the prominent, family-based connections between Huguenots in London and Charleston established in the early eighteenth century did not survive after 1720, as merchant families in South Carolina became planters or died out and as merchants in England of Huguenot origins turned to other trades and interests. For example, Benjamin Godin in Charleston withdrew from trade and became a major planter and slave owner, as did his sons, while the London Godins withdrew from the South Carolina trade and concentrated their interests in the commerce with northern Europe, Russia, and the Mediterranean.[26] The family connections exemplified by the Godins had provided the main trading links between Huguenot merchants in Europe and South Carolina in the early eighteenth century. When, after 1720, such links disappeared, the involvement of European Huguenots in the South Carolina trade depended on the extent to which the London Huguenot merchant community as a whole participated in the trade. This community grew in size and wealth in the middle decades of the eighteenth century, but its character was changing in a way which tended to decrease rather than enhance any links between London and Charleston Huguenot merchants. The first major wave of Huguenot merchant-migrants to England had come largely from western France, a region whose economy was based on Atlantic trade, and a few of these merchants, as we have seen, became important traders to South Carolina. However, the second major wave of Huguenot merchants, which arrived in England from the 1720s, came mainly from Languedoc and Switzerland. These Anglo-Swiss and Anglo-Languedocian firms had vast commercial and financial interests, but they specialized in the major European and Mediterranean trades, and they were as deeply or more involved in international banking and finance as in commodity trade. Insofar as they had colonial interests, these were in the Virginia and the West Indies trades, and the great majority of these firms had no connections with South Carolina.[27]

There were, of course exceptions to this rule, comprising a small number of leading London Huguenot firms who continued to trade to South Carolina as a subsidiary line of business. For example, Joseph and Henry Guinand, brothers born in Lunel in Languedoc, formed one of the dozen most important firms of Languedoc merchant-bankers in London. Their main interests were in the financing of the Asian and Languedoc trades and in British government stocks. Circa 1750, however, the elder Guinands sent their younger brother Peter to Charleston, where he formed a firm with his fellow Huguenot Andrew Fesch, which, backed by the London Guinands, established a substantial trade in dry goods and slaves. Peter Guinand and Fesch moved into planting, again with London backing, but their deaths in South Carolina in the early 1760s left the firm heavily in debt to the London Guinands, who then took over and managed the Carolina estates. Another example is Peter Simond, born in the Huguenot settlement at the Cape of Good Hope in 1690, who received his commercial education in Amsterdam before moving to London in 1715, where he formed, with his brother, a leading firm trading to the West Indies. In the late 1720s and 1730s, Simond developed major interests in the southern mainland colonies. He was the London commercial agent for the trustees of the new colony of Georgia, managed several ships in the South Carolina trade, specializing in the rice trade from Charleston and virtually monopolized the naval stores trade from Georgetown in the 1730s, and he acquired extensive lands in the Purrysburgh area. From 1740, however, Simond withdrew from the South Carolina trade, concentrating instead on the West Indies trade, British government stocks, and supplying the French tobacco monopoly.[28]

These post-1720 connections between Huguenots in England and South Carolina are of interest in themselves, but they were only minor threads in the organization of a trade that was dominated by English, not Huguenot, merchants. In the decades before the American Revolution there were two main groups of London merchants trading to South Carolina. The most important group consisted of British merchants who had traded for long periods in Charleston and who then returned to London to set themselves up as "Carolina" merchants.[29] The second group, London merchants who traded to South Carolina but who had never resided there, were more varied. They included a number of English merchants with major interests in the slave and West Indies trade, but who also had connections with South Carolina, along with a wide circle of London wholesalers (linen drapers, ironmongers, etc.), types of businessmen who played a very significant part in financing the export trades to British America.[30] Charleston Huguenots wishing to enter international trade were required to forge connections with these English merchant groups rather than with London Huguenot merchants. For example, when the young Huguenot merchant Henry Laurens (tables 3, 4) began trading in Charleston in the late 1740s, he did so by ordering goods from wholesalers and merchants in London and a number of provincial ports, establishing his creditworthiness on the basis of his close connection with the Scot James Crokatt, the leading Carolina merchant in London at that time. None of the merchants he dealt with were Huguenots. Indeed, a close reading of his vast commercial correspondence for the period 1747–1775 reveals that Laurens seldom dealt with English-based Huguenot merchants and that such contacts were always incidental to his main business connections with English firms in London, Bristol, and elsewhere.[31] The central nature of the connections between Charleston's Huguenot merchants and the core of *non-Huguenot* London merchants who controlled the South Carolina trade is shown in table 4, which lists the English agents and bankers for a large sample of Charleston Huguenot merchants in the period 1755–1775.

In every case but one, the Charleston Huguenot merchants dealt with one or other of the elite London firms of English extraction which dominated the wider financial and commercial relations between London and

South Carolina.[32] To sum up: the majority of the migrants who made up the first generation of Huguenot merchants in South Carolina were descended from merchant families in western France. However, with the exception of a few prominent individuals who arrived after 1700, it appears that these merchants did not establish themselves in Charleston on the basis of their connections to international networks of Huguenot merchants. In any case, from circa 1720 the influence of English-based Huguenot merchants in the Anglo-Carolina trade diminished. What then does explain the important and above all the sustained role that the South Carolina Huguenot merchants played in Charleston's trade from circa 1720 to the American Revolution?

II

In other colonial cities, the replenishing and expansion of merchant communities was based to a large degree on migration. For example, Gary B. Nash has shown that in colonial Philadelphia there were 143 merchants in the city's second generation of merchants from 1711–1740, of whom 50 percent were migrants, only 20 percent were the sons of first-generation Philadelphia merchants, and 30 percent were the sons of artisans, farmers, etc. Reviewing the evidence for Philadelphia and other colonial cities, he concluded that the economic and political power of first-generation merchants in new colonies rapidly disintegrated:

> The building of economic dynasties . . . proved to be unusually difficult in the seaport towns of colonial America. Commercial centres were growth centres, always characterised by the arrival of new men on the make.[33]

Migration was also of great significance to the renewing and expansion of the English merchant community of Charleston. In the period 1750–1775, for example, between one-third and one-half of the merchants who sat as representatives in South Carolina's Commons House of Assembly were recent arrivals.[34] However, there was relatively little Huguenot migration to South Carolina after 1700, with the exception of the settlements at Purrysburgh in the 1730s and at New Bordeaux in the early 1760s, neither of which made much impact on the Charleston business community: only five (20 percent) of the second generation of South Carolina Huguenot merchants and only two (5 percent) of the third generation were migrants.[35]

TABLE 4: *South Carolina Huguenot Merchants, 1750–1775: Trading Activities and English Commercial and Financial Connections.*

| | IMPORT TRADES | | | EXPORT TRADES | | STATUS OF TRADE* | BRITISH AGENTS-BANKERS-CREDITORS |
	Dry	Slave	General	Rice/Indigo	Deerskins		
South-Carolina Born Merchants							
Gideon Dupont		*				CA	John Nutt[a]
John Guerard	*	*	*	*	*	I	William Jolliffe[b]
William Guerin	*	*	*	*	*	CA	Greenwood & Higginson[c]
Henry Laurens	*	*	*	*	*	CA	Richard Oswald[d], John Nutt
Peter Leger Gabriel	*	*	*	*	*	I	Greenwood & Higginson
Manigault	*	*	*	*	*	CA	Neufville & Rolleston[e]
Samuel & Arthur Peronneau	*		*	*	*	I	John Beswicke & Co.[c]; Sarah Nickleson[f]
James Poyas	*		*	*		I CF	John Beswicke & Co.; Greenwood & Higginson
Maurice & Edward Simons	*	*	*	*	*	CF	Greenwood & Higginson; Davis, Strachan & Co.[g]
[John Wagner] & Peter Bochet	*			*	*	I	Greenwood & Higginson

TABLE 4 (*continued*)

Immigrant Merchants

| Sam Chollett & | * | * | CA | Bourdieu & Chollett;[h] |
| John L. Gervais | | | | Richard Oswald |

* "Status of trade" refers to types of entrepreneurial activities carried on by Charleston merchants.

CA = Commission Agent, indicating that the merchant concerned mainly bought and sold slaves, dry goods, and rice on commission for English and other principals.

I = Independent Trader, indicating that the merchant acted as an independent entrepreneur: that is, he traded on his own account and risk.

CF = Country Factor. Country factors acted for the South Carolina planters, rather than British merchants, selling the planters' rice and other crops on commission in Charleston. The factors also imported dry goods and other commodities on their own accounts, which they sold on a retail and wholesale basis. The numbers of independent traders and country factors grew rapidly in the period from circa 1740 to the Revolution.

Notes on British Firms

[a]JOHN NUTT. The major merchant firm in the trade in the 1760s and 1770s after Greenwood and Higginson, see below. Had close connections to the Scot, James Crokatt (the preeminent British merchant in Charleston in the 1720s and 1730s, and who from 1737 was London's leading Carolina merchant and the colony's agent). Nutt's interests in South Carolina were handled by his brother Joseph, a merchant in Charleston in the 1750s and 1760s.

[b]WILLIAM JOLLIFFE. Major merchant of Poole, Dorset, with mercantile and shipowning interests in South Carolina from circa 1720 to circa 1760. John Guerard's partner from 1748–1760.

[c]JOHN BESWICKE; GREENWOOD & HIGGINSON. London firms trading to South Carolina. Original firm founded in London by John Beswicke, a major merchant in Charleston in the 1730s and 1740s, his nephew William Higginson, and William Greenwood. Beswicke died in 1764. Greenwood's son,

TABLE 4 (*continued*)

also William, was then sent to Charleston, where he formed a partnership with the Huguenot-descended Peter Leger, see tables 2 and 3. Greenwood and Higginson was by far the leading London-Carolina firm on the eve of the Revolution.

[d]RICHARD OSWALD. A Scot who became a London merchant of great wealth and vast interests, with particular concerns in the West Indies and slave trades, although he also had important connections with South Carolina and with the colonization of Georgia and Florida. Close associate of Henry Laurens.

[e]NEUFVILLE & ROLLESTON. The Huguenot John Neufville and his sons John and Edward Neufville were Charleston merchants active in trade from the mid-1740s to the mid-1760s. Edward then moved to England, where he traded in partnership with the English merchant Christopher Rolleston, first in Bristol and then in London.

[f] SARAH NICKLESON. John Nickleson and Thomas and Richard Shubrick had migrated from England to Charleston, where they established a major trading firm in the 1730s and early 1740s. Nickleson married the Shubricks' sister, Sarah. In the early 1740s, Richard Shubrick and Nickleson moved to London, where they set up major and separate houses in the Carolina trade. After Nickleson's death, circa 1760, his widow, Sarah, carried on the business for some years.

[g]DAVIS, STRACHAN & Co. Major firm in trade from circa 1769.

[h]BOURDIEU & CHOLLET. See endnote 32.

The later generations of Charleston Huguenot merchants therefore emerged from within South Carolina society itself. First, while many successful British merchants in Charleston returned to England, Huguenot merchants did not regard England as "home," and few of them returned to England to retire or to set themselves up as merchants. Consequently, the Huguenot merchant community did not suffer a serious loss of talent and capital in a reverse flow of migration to England. This meant that Huguenot merchants, unlike their English counterparts, created a number of trading dynasties in Charleston. This was all the more remarkable given that South Carolina's very high levels of mortality led to a high proportion of families dying out in the male line.[36] Thus, of the eighteen first-generation Huguenot merchants for whom information survives, only twelve had surviving sons, while six had only daughters or no surviving children. But of the twelve, eight had one or more sons who followed them in trade, while three had sons who became planters, and one had a son who resided in the West Indies.[37] As late as the 1760s, nine (25 percent) of the major Huguenot merchants of Charleston were the sons or grandsons of first-generation merchants. In contrast, only one of the 100 or so English merchants active in trade in the 1760s was descended in the male line from the first generation of Charleston merchants.[38] Second, the great success of the Huguenots as planters meant that they were well positioned to place themselves, and especially their sons, in trade in Charleston so that planters or their descendants made up eight (33 percent) of the second and twelve (32 percent) of the third generation of merchants. Finally, Huguenots always made up a significant proportion of Charleston's artisan population, an occupational group which made a useful contribution to the formation of Charleston's merchant community, providing two (8 percent) of the second and eight (21 percent) of the third generation of Huguenot merchants.

Given that the Huguenot merchant community in Charleston was replenished from within colonial society rather than by further migration from Europe, is it the case that Huguenots sustained their strong position in South Carolina's mercantile economy through a high degree of reciprocity and cooperation based on their common ethnic background? There were three main ways by which such "ethnic association" could have promoted economic success: shared religious and cultural activities, business partnerships, and marriage alliances.[39] The highest incidence of ethnic association is found, as one might expect, between the Huguenot merchants of the first generation. The French church in Charleston remained a strong center of Huguenot religious practice from its foundation in the early 1680s to 1719, and during this period many of its most prominent members and benefactors were leading Charleston merchants. For example, in 1693, three of the five elders of the church were important traders.[40] With respect to marriage practices, we have information about a total of nineteen first and second marriages contracted by first-generation Huguenot merchants; fifteen of these marriages were with French women and four with English women, although three of the English marriages were with second wives and took place after the French merchants in question had been in America for many years. The first-generation merchants also formed twelve business partnerships: ten of these involved solely French merchants, of which seven firms brought together partners who were closely related by blood or marriage. Two partnerships were formed between French and English merchants.[41] The "sociale endogamie" of the first-generation took a number of forms. For example, three of the daughters of first-generation merchant Jacques LeSerrurier married French merchants, including LeSerrurier's principal business associates, Issac Mazyck and Pierre de St. Julien (table 1). An example of a different kind is provided by Elizabeth Buretel, the widow of the merchant Pierre Buretel. From her husband's death in 1703 to her own death in 1727, Madame Buretel lived on the interest drawn from loans she made to 110 South Carolina planters, merchants, and artisans. Her debtors were mainly Huguenots, including a number of the merchants listed in table 1, as well as other less prominent Huguenot merchants.[42]

However, amongst the second and third generations of merchants, there was a sharp decline in the high degree of religious, economic, and marital cohesiveness which characterized the first generation of Huguenot migrants. Charleston's French church was irretrievably damaged in 1719 by the departure for England of its long-serving pastor, Paul L'Escot, and subsequently the great majority of Huguenot merchants worshiped at the city's English churches or ceased to engage in regular religious practice. Aside from the French church, there were no other French institutions in Charleston, and consequently the full part that Huguenot merchants played in the city's eighteenth-century social and cultural life was achieved through membership of prestigious clubs and societies which were dominated by English members and officers.[43] After

1720, then, there is little evidence that Huguenot merchants participated in religious and cultural activities of a distinctively French character. With respect to business alliances, the great majority of Huguenot merchants of the second and third generations operated in partnerships for most of their careers in order to ease the problems of raising trading capital.[44] For the period 1740–1775, we have information about sixty-two mercantile partnerships entered into by fifty-four Huguenot merchants: twenty-two (35 percent) of these partnerships involved solely French merchants, of which twelve involved fathers and sons, brothers, or other close family relations. The other forty partnerships (65 percent) were formed between French and non-French merchants. The pattern of trading partnerships, therefore, does show evidence of cooperation between Huguenots, but, as in the first generation, these partnerships were based as much on family connections as on a common ethnic background.[45] For marriages, we have information about sixty-two first and subsequent marriages contracted by fifty-one Huguenot merchants of the second and third generations: nineteen (30 percent) of these marriages were with French-descended women and forty-three (70 percent) with English women or those descended from other nationalities. Obviously, the stock of potential marriage partners was much larger than that of business partners and much less Huguenot in composition, as Huguenots made up about 25 percent of the merchant community but only about 3 percent of the population. Huguenot merchants therefore showed a clear but far from overwhelming preference for French wives.[46]

The generally exogamous nature of the marriages undertaken by Huguenot merchants of the second and third generations provides some support for Butler's view that Huguenots so frequently intermarried with non-Huguenots that, by the 1760s, marriages between people of French descent were uncommon. But this is not surprising since Butler's main evidence is drawn from St. Philip's Parish in Charleston, the city's main Anglican Church, where many Charleston merchants were married.[47] However, the marriage practices of Huguenot merchants differed from those of the Huguenots in the agricultural settlements who, as Friedlander shows, were much more likely to marry French spouses and to live out their lives in French neighborhoods. Friedlander analyzed a large, colony-wide sample of 740 marriages involving one or two French partners. The majority of marriages were endogenous ones through the 1760s, and even for the fourth generation, 40 percent of marriages were endogenous. For the rural population, the consciousness of a common ethnic origin remained an important factor in the choice of a marriage partner throughout the colonial period.[48] By contrast, for the Huguenot merchants of Charleston, at least after the first generation, the ethnic origin of marriage partners was less important than their occupational status and wealth. Thus, of the sixty-two merchant marriages discussed above, twenty (32 percent) were with women from mercantile families, while the great majority of the rest were with women from established planting families. In the major decisions about their careers, that is in decisions about the choice of business and marriage partners, Huguenot merchants acted as members of a close-knit and cosmopolitan English and French business community, with its distinctive "mercantile" patterns of marriage and business cooperation, rather than as members of an ethnic minority.[49]

Indeed, most Huguenot merchants of the second and third generations moved flexibly between the French and English groups within the wider Charleston business community, although Huguenot merchants did demonstrate a significant tendency to reaffirm their Huguenot connections in their later careers, as is shown by the following examples. First, Jacob Motte, the son of the migrant merchant John Motte, was apprenticed in 1711 to a prominent Huguenot merchant of the first generation, Francis LeBrasseur. On the completion of his apprenticeship in 1720, Jacob Motte went into business with the English migrant Charles Hill, his father's former partner, and then in 1725 struck out on his own, becoming one of the major merchants in Charleston. At about the same time he married an English wife, Elizabeth Martin. In later years, however, Motte returned to his Huguenot roots. In the 1750s, he formed a business partnership with James Laurens, Henry Laurens's brother and a major second-generation Huguenot merchant, and in 1763 he married Anne LeBrasseur, the daughter of the Huguenot merchant to whom Motte had been apprenticed exactly fifty years before! Similarly, John Guerard II, began his trading career in 1730 when he entered into a partnership with Benjamin Godin, his father's former partner. In 1735, he formed a major trading partnership with Richard Hill, Charles Hill's son, and he married Richard's sister, Elizabeth. When Hill died in 1746, Guerard formed a twenty-year partnership with the English merchant William Jolliffe. In this last phase of his career, however, Guerard rediscovered his Huguenot connections. First, he was linked in business with the planter David Godin, Benjamin Godin's son. Second, following the death of his first wife in 1744, he married Marrianne Godin, Benjamin Godin's daughter and his own cousin.[50] A final example is Henry Laurens, who married an English wife and whose partners were the English immigrants George Austin and George Appleby, and who mainly traded with English merchants. Yet from the 1760s, as Laurens moved from being a loyal British citizen to become one of South Carolina's leading patriots, we see the reemergence of his Huguenot identity. First, Laurens gave a helping hand to a number of Huguenot migrants to America, including the young, poor Huguenot migrant John Lewis Gervais (tables 3, 4), in whose plight Laurens clearly detected strong echoes of his own family's history. Second, in the early 1770s he traveled in Britain and on the continent of Europe. He was highly critical of many aspects of English and French life, although he did try to trace his ancestors in La Rochelle, and he showed a far greater respect for Geneva, that "wonderful republic." As he wrote in Geneva in August 1774:

> If the oppressions of America continue, and her efforts to get rid of them prove ineffectual, I shall not hesitate about settling in this part of the world. There are no nobility, no standing army, no taxes, no custom-house officers, and, above all, no King—the support of whose pride, pomp, and intolerable vanity by courtiers, called *necessary expenses*, inevitably produces these, and a thousand other grievances.[51]

These examples show that important Huguenot merchants of the second and third generation, no matter how Anglicized they were in their business partnerships and choice of wives, retained a strong if latent sense of their Huguenot origins.

III

How does the evidence presented here reflect on recent debates on the Huguenots in South Carolina? First, while Butler and others have placed great emphasis on the Huguenots' contributions to the development of slave-plantation agriculture, this paper has shown that Huguenots throughout the colonial period played a very significant and hitherto unappreciated role in South Carolina's commercial economy. The Huguenots represented only a small and declining fraction of the colony's population, but from the 1680s to the 1770s they comprised an important component of the Charleston merchant community. Their decision to become merchants in late seventeenth-century Charleston was shaped by the experience and knowledge gained in the culture from which they fled, the commercial and bourgeois world of the French Atlantic ports. Nevertheless, Bosher's argument that the success of Huguenot merchants in America was based on their connections with prominent Huguenot merchants in Europe has only a limited application to the Charleston Huguenots. A few leading Huguenot firms in England did have interests in South Carolina, but none of them established major connections with Charleston Huguenots, other than with members of their own families. Huguenot merchants in England, insofar as they had colonial interests, participated far more in the trades to the West Indies and to the other mainland colonies than in the trade to Charleston. The success of the Huguenot merchants of Charleston was underpinned, as was that of the English merchants of Charleston, by their connections with the non-Huguenot circles of London and provincial merchants who controlled the Anglo-South Carolinian trade.

Second, Huguenot success was boosted by the cohesive economic and social behavior of the first-generation Huguenot merchants, whose families were linked by numerous religious, business, and marriage connections. But this ethnic cooperation declined amongst the merchants of the second and third generations, who did not engage in a distinctively French religious and cultural life and who were more likely to take business partners from the English, rather than the Huguenot, merchant community and to marry English rather than French spouses. This appears to confirm Butler's view that "refugee cohesion had suffered serious erosion as early as 1710 and had then thoroughly shattered by 1750," but we need to make three qualifications to Butler's argument.[52] First, there was a very high degree of ethnic association between the Huguenot merchants of the first generation until circa 1720. Second, the awareness of a common French heritage and ethnicity did not disappear amongst the Charleston Huguenot merchants of the second and third generations, a number of whom rekindled their Huguenot connections in their later lives. Third, Butler fails to distinguish clearly between the behavior of the Huguenots in the agricultural communities and those in Charleston. Amongst the rural Huguenots, French neighborhood communities and endogenous marriage patterns survived far into the colonial period and beyond. The urban Huguenots, on the other hand, maintained a distinct identity, but as part of a cosmopolitan, Protestant trading community held together by innumerable business and marriage connections, connections which were based more on a communal sense of vocation or occupation, than on an awareness of shared ethnicity and origins.

Finally, were the Huguenot merchants integrated and absorbed into South Carolina culture and society, as Butler has suggested, or should we heed Bosher's argument that Huguenot merchants in America maintained a distinctive, commercial culture based on their links to international, Huguenot trading networks? The universal decision of South Carolina Huguenots to become naturalized English subjects shows that they had no desire, or at least expectation, of returning to their mother country. Nevertheless, the Huguenot merchants did not transfer their allegiance from France to England, nor did they focus their loyalties, as did refugee Huguenots in other societies, on their family ties to international clans of Huguenot merchants. Rather their allegiance appears to have been to South Carolina. Certainly, they assimilated themselves far more thoroughly into colonial society than did the British merchants, many of whom harbored, and indeed implemented, long-term plans to return to Britain. This became clear at the Revolution, when numerous South Carolina merchants and storekeepers of British descent declared themselves Loyalists, whereas the overwhelming majority of merchants of French origins were ardent supporters of the Revolutionary cause.

Notes

1. The research in South Carolina, upon which this paper is partly based, was made possible by a grant from the Economic and Social Research Council, England, and from the University of Manchester. I would also like to thank my colleague Steve Rigby and my good friend Hilary Wood for their excellent comments on earlier drafts of this paper.

2. Robin D. Gwynn, *Huguenot Heritage: The History and Contribution of the Huguenots in Britain* (London: Routledge, Kegan and Paul, 1985), 35–6; Jon Butler, *The Huguenots in America: A Refugee People in New World Society* (Cambridge, Mass.: Harvard University Press, 1983), 27–28, 47–49.

3. The rigors faced by migrants are described in the celebrated letter by Judith Giton, who migrated to South Carolina in 1685, aged about twenty; see, Slann Legare Simmons, "Early Manigault Records," *Transactions of the Huguenot Society of South Carolina* (hereafter *THSSC*) 59 (1954): 25–27.

4. Butler, *Huguenots in America*, 27–20, 50–52, 56–60; Butler, "The Revocation of the Edict of Nantes and Huguenot Migration to South Carolina," in R. M. Golden, ed., *The Huguenot Connection: The Edict of Nantes, Its Revocation, and Early French Migration to South Carolina* (Dordrecht: Kluwer Academic Publications, 1988), 64–67; Amy E. Friedlander, "Carolina Huguenots: A Study in Cultural Pluralism in the Low Country, 1679–1768" (Ph.D. diss., Emory University, 1979), 86–102; Bertrand Van Ruymbeke, "L'émigration huguenote en Caroline du Sud sous le régime des Seigneurs Propriétaires: Etude d'une communauté du Refuge dans une province britannique d'Amérique du Nord (1680–1720)" 2 vols. (Ph.D. diss., Université de la Sorbonne-Nouvelle, Paris III, 1995), 1:357–58; idem, "The Huguenots of Proprietary South Carolina: Patterns of Migration and Integration," in Jack P. Greene, Rosemary Brana-Shute, and Randy J. Sparks, ed., *Money, Trade, and Power: The Evolution of Colonial South Carolina's Plantation Society* (Columbia: University of South Carolina Press, 2001), 27–29. For population estimates for South Carolina see, Peter A. Coclanis, *The Shadow of a Dream: Economic Life and Death in the South Carolina Low Country, 1670–1920* (New York: Oxford University Press, 1989), 64–66.

5. Butler, *Huguenots in America*, 91–143; the quotation is from 92. Friedlander, "The Huguenots and the Historians," *THSSC*, 94 (1989): 5, also stresses the Huguenots' preoccupation with agriculture: ". . . many of the skilled artisans must have come to terms with the economic reality of the colony, namely, that acquisition of land was the name of the game." For an earlier view that the Huguenots assimilated rapidly see, Arthur H. Hirsch, *The Huguenots of Colonial South Carolina* (Durham, N.C.: Duke University Press, 1928), 90–102, 165–95.

6. John F. Bosher, "Huguenot Merchants and the Protestant International in the Seventeenth Century," *William and Mary Quarterly* 52 (1995): 77–102; Bosher, "The Imperial Environment of French Trade with Canada, 1660–1685," *English Historical Review* 108 (1993): 50–82; Van Ruymbeke, "L'émigration huguenote," 2; idem, "The Huguenots of Proprietary South Carolina," 32–37.

7. Data on Charleston merchants are taken from my wider research project on the Charleston business community. See R. C. Nash, "Urbanization in the Colonial South: Charleston, South Carolina, as a Case Study," *Journal of Urban History* 19 (1992): 12, 19–23; Nash, "The Organization of Trade and Finance in the Atlantic Economy: Britain and South Carolina, 1670–1775," in Greene, Brana-Shute, and Sparks, ed., *Money, Trade, and Power*, 74–107. Huguenot merchants had an even more prominent role in the trade of South Carolina's second and third ports, Georgetown and Beaufort. This, in part, reflected the nearness of the ports to areas of French settlement, such as Purrysburgh and the Santee. See Records of the South Carolina Court of Common Pleas, Judgment Rolls, 1773, 26A, South Carolina Department of Archives and History (hereafter SCDAH);

Lawrence S. Rowland, "The Purrysburg Swiss in the Beaufort District," *THSSC* 98 (1993): 20–26; Philip M. Hamer et al., ed., *The Papers of Henry Laurens*, vols. 1–12 (Columbia, S.C., 1968–90) 6:434*n*; George C. Rogers Jr., *The History of George Town County, South Carolina* (Columbia: University of South Carolina Press, 1970), 47–52.

8. Data based on firms paying £500 or more in import duties on slaves and £200 or more in import duties on general merchandise; see W. Robert Higgins, "Charles Town Merchants and Factors Dealing in the External Slave Trade, 1735–1775," *South Carolina Historical Magazine* (hereafter *SCHM)* 65 (1964): 205–17; Stuart O. Stumpf, "South Carolina Importers of General Merchandize, 1735–1765," *SCHM* 84 (1983): 1–10.

9. See Butler, *Huguenots in America*, 123–24, tables 1–3, for data on slave-holding by Huguenots and non-Huguenots.

10. See Nash, "Organization of Trade and Finance."

11. Huguenots made up about 15 percent of the white population in circa 1700 but only 3 percent in circa 1770; see Friedlander, "Carolina Huguenots," 5.

12. Memorandum of Peter Girard, 14 March 1699, Records in the British Public Record Office Relating to South Carolina, 1663–1782, 36 vols. (Micro-copy), vol. 4, 1698–1700, SCDAH; Hirsch, *Huguenots of Colonial South Carolina*, 14–26; Van Ruymbeke, "L'émigration huguenote," 2:663–64.

13. See SCDAH, Records in the British Public Record Office Relating to South Carolina, 1663–1782, 36 vols. (Microcopy), Vol. 2, 199, 218–20; Vol. 4, 88; Vol. 5, 150–55; Verner W. Crane, *The Southern Frontier, 1670–1732* (Durham, N.C.: Duke University Press, 1929), 108–36; Stumpf, "The Merchants of Colo-nial Charleston, 1680–1756" (Ph.D. diss., Michigan State University, 1971), 6–7, 18–20; Carville V. Earle, "The First English Towns of North America," *Geo-graphical Review* 67 (1977): 41–44.

14. Nash, "Urbanization in the Colonial South," 3–6.

15. Van Ruymbeke, "L'émigration huguenote," 1:296–310, 323–24; idem, "The Huguenots of Proprietary South Carolina," 32–34.

16. Information on the origins of first-generation Huguenot merchants comes mainly from: Records of the Secretary of the Province, 21 vols., 1675–1731, SCDAH; Records in the British Public Record Office Relating to South Caro-lina, 1663–1782, 36 vols. (Microcopy), SCDAH; Van Ruymbeke, "L'émigration huguenote"; idem, "The Huguenots of Proprietary South Carolina"; Edgar and Bailey, *Biographical Directory*; Hirsch, *Huguenots of Colonial South Carolina*; Butler, *Huguenots in America*; Louis Manigault, "The Manigault Family of South Caro-lina," *THSSC* 4 (1897): 48–57; Katharine B. Mazyck, "Notes on the Mazyck Family," *THSSC* 3 (1932): 43–53; Myrta J. Hutson, "Early Generations of the Motte Family of South Carolina," *THSSC* 56 (1951): 57–63; Virginia Gourdin,

"Madeleine Chardon, of Tours, Touraine and Her Family," *THSSC* 91 (1986): 64–104.

17. Gourdin, "Madeleine Chardon," 68–73; Van Ruymbeke, "L'émigration huguenote," 1:95–96, 334; idem, "The Huguenots of Proprietary South Carolina," 37–39.

18. For examples of such speculation see Manigault, "The Manigault Family," 54; Hirsch, *Huguenots of Colonial South Carolina*, 229, 232; Gourdin, "Madeleine Chardon," 67, 74; Van Ruymbeke, "L'émigration huguenote," 1:308–9.

19. Manigault, "The Manigault Family," 52–55; Simmons, "Early Manigault Records," *THSSC* 59 (1954): 32–33; Stumpf, "Merchants of Colonial Charleston," 25, 42, 49–50; Friedlander, "Carolina Huguenots," 110; Maurice A. Crouse, "Gabriel Manigault: Charleston Merchant," *SCHM* 68 (1967): 221; Nash, "Trade and Business," 8–9; Van Ruymbeke, "L'émigration huguenote," 1:355, 2:584, 662; idem, "The Huguenots of Proprietary South Carolina," 34–35.

20. See Records of the Secretary of the Province, 1694–1705, 253; 1714–1717, 65; 1711–1717, 8, SCDAH; Account Book of Alexander Baily and Nathaniel Lewis, 1711–1712, (which shows a number of accounts between Charleston Huguenot and Bristol merchants), MSS 11,096, Guildhall Library, London; "Will of Peter Pasquereaux," *THSSC* 13 (1906): 15–17; "Will of Isaac Chardon," *THSSC* 45 (1940): 69–71; "Will of Francis LeBrasseur," *THSSC* 48 (1943): 50–53.

21. Charles Wilson, *Anglo-Dutch Commerce and Finance in the Eighteenth Century* (Cambridge, Mass.: Harvard University Press, 1941), 138–39, 160, 203; Herbert Luthy, *La banque protestante en France de la Révocation de l'Édit de Nantes à la Révolution*, 2 vols. (Paris: S.E.V.P.E.N., 1959–61), 1:78–84, 2:81–83; Guy Chaussinand-Nogaret, *Les Financiers de Languedoc au XVIIIe Siècle* (Paris: S.E.V.P.E.N., 1970), 161–213; Jacob M. Price, *France and the Chesapeake: A History of the French Tobacco Monopoly, 1674–1791, and of Its Relationship to the British and American Tobacco Trades*, 2 vols. (Ann Arbor: University of Michigan Press, 1973); Alice C. Carter, *Getting, Spending and Investment in Early Modern Times: Essays on Dutch, English and Huguenot Economic History* (Assen: Van Gorcum, 1975); D. W. Jones, *War and Economy in the Age of William III and Marlborough* (Oxford: Blackwells, 1988), 253–60; François Crouzet, "Walloons, Huguenots and the Bank of England," *Proceedings of the Huguenot Society of Great Britain and Ireland* 25 (1990): 167–78; Stanley Chapman, *Merchant Enterprise in Britain From the Industrial Revolution to World War I* (Cambridge: Cambridge University Press, 1992), 29–35; David Ormrod, "The Atlantic Economy and the 'Protestant Capitalist International,' 1651–1775," *Historical Research* 66 (1993): 197–208; Bosher, *Business and Religion in the Age of New France, 1600–1760: Twenty-Two Studies* (Toronto: Canadian Scholars' Press, 1994), for example, 211–13.

22. The rise of the Huguenot merchants of New York, for example, was very rapid: by 1703, there were thirty-one Huguenot merchants in the city compared with twenty-nine English and thirty-six Dutch merchants, Butler, *Huguenots in America*, 85–87, 150–54; Bosher, "Huguenot Merchants and the Protestant International." On the other hand, almost no Huguenot merchants went to Philadelphia, founded in 1680, and which was as commercially undeveloped at the time of the Huguenot migration as Charleston; see Gary B. Nash, "The Early Merchants of Philadelphia: The Formation and Disintegration of a Founding Elite," in Richard S. Dunn and Mary M. Dunn, ed., *The World of William Penn* (Philadelphia: University of Pennsylvania Press, 1986), 354–62. For the minor late-seventeenth-century trade organized by Huguenot refugees of western France from Plymouth, England, to South Carolina see Alison Grant, "By Sea: Huguenot Maritime Links with Seventeenth-Century Devon," *Proceedings of the Huguenot Society of Great Britain and Ireland* 25 (1993): 451–63.

23. Samuel Wragg versus Joseph Wragg, 4 June 1749, Court of Chancery, Oversize, 1736–1760, no. 3, SCDAH; Records of the Secretary of the Province, 1711–1717, 42–46; vol. B, 1722–1724, 176–77; vol. F, 1727–1729, 74–5, SCDAH; Records of the South Carolina Court of Common Pleas, Judgment Rolls, 1720, 71A-1, SCDAH; Records in the British Public Record Office Relating to South Carolina, 1663–1782, 36 vols. (Microcopy), vol. 9, 141; vol. 10, 91; vol. 11, 111, 225–26, 235, SCDAH; London Port Book, Christmas 1718–Christmas 1719, Newby Hall MSS, NH 2440, Archives Dept., Leeds City Library (Sheepscar Branch), England; Caroline T. Moore, *Records of the Secretary of South Carolina, 1692–1721*, (Charleston: n.p., 1978), 227; "Peter Pasquereaux," 15–17; Edgar and Bailey, *Biographical Directory*, 2:283–84, 403, 591–92; Nash, "Trade and Business," 8–9; Gourdin, "Madeleine Chardon," 101–3; Van Ruymbeke, "L'émigration huguenote," 2:592, 669; idem, "The Huguenots of Proprietary South Carolina," 32–35.

24. The main sources for identifying London Huguenot merchants trading to South Carolina in the early eighteenth century are: signed petitions, memorandums, etc. submitted by London merchants to the Lords of Trade and other agencies recorded in Records in the British Public Record Office Relating to South Carolina, 1663–1782, vols. 1–17 (Microcopy), SCDAH; Records of the Secretary of the Province, 21 vols., 1675–1731, SCDAH; Records of the South Carolina Court of Common Pleas, Judgment Rolls, 1703–1720, SCDAH; lists of owners of ships in the Charleston trade, PRO., Colonial Office, 5/509, Naval Office, Port Charles Town, 1717–1732, SCDAH. For Baudouin and Renew see, in addition, Records of the Secretary of the Province, 1694–1705, 229–30, SCDAH; Jones, *War and Economy*, 254–56; Gourdin, "Madeleine Chardon," 76; Armand Mauzey, "On to Glory," *THSSC* 82 (1977), 119–23.

25. London Port Book, Christmas 1718–Christmas 1719, Newby Hall MSS, NH 2440, Archives Dept., Leeds City Library (Sheepscar Branch), England; the Port Book is incomplete: see Price and Paul G.E. Clemens, "A Revolution of Scale in Overseas Trade: British Firms in the Chesapeake Trade, 1675–1775," *Journal of Economic History* 47 (1987): 18–20. For ship ownership see, PRO., Colonial Office, 5/509, Naval Office, Port Charles Town, 1717–1720. In the early eighteenth century there was a close coincidence between the shipowning and trading groups; hence, the distribution of ship ownership is a useful guide to the pattern of trade organization.

26. Amongst other Anglo-South Carolinian families: the Belins ceased to trade in South Carolina; the LeSerruriers who had been engaged in trade left the colony, while the Saturs died out in the male line; the Douxsaints continued in trade in Charleston, although their contacts with the London Douxsaints ceased. On these families see Records of the Secretary of the Province, vol. F, 1727–1729, 74–75, SCDAH; Records of the Secretary of the State, Miscellaneous Records, Main Series (hereafter Miscellaneous Records), vol. KK, 1754–1758, 110–11, SCDAH; Moore, *Records of the Secretary*, 227; Wilson, *Anglo-Dutch Trade*, 113–14; Price, *France and the Chesapeake*, 1:394, 625; Edgar and Bailey, *Biographical Directory*, 2:283–85, 403; Van Ruymbeke, "L'émigration huguenote," 1:352–54; Gourdin, "Madeleine Chardon," 101–3; "Belin," *THSSC* 89 (1984), 153–54.

27. See the sources cited in note 21. See also William A. Shaw, ed., *Letters of Denization and Acts of Naturalization for Aliens in England and Ireland, 1701–1800, Publications of the Huguenot Society of Great Britain and Ireland*, Quarto Series, 27 (1923), which gives the origins of most London Huguenot merchants.

28. Other notable London Huguenot merchants with minor interests in the South Carolina trade, circa 1720 to circa 1770, include James Blaquiere, James Bourdieu and Samuel Chollet (see below, note 32), Pierre Cabibel, James Chalie, Charles, Elias and Noah de La Fontaine, Charles Noiray, Ciprieu Rondeau and Matthew Testas. For these merchants and the Guinands and Simonds see William Ancrum Account Book, 11163, 1757–1758, 1776–1782 (containing some accounts of Guinand and Fesch), South Carolina Library, Columbia, South Carolina; Miscellaneous Records, Vol. BB, 1732–33, 27–38, October 1732 Claims Against James Le Chantre; PRO., Colonial Office, 5/511, Naval Office, Port Charles Town, 1762–1767, SCDAH; London Port Book, Christmas 1718–Christmas 1719, Newby Hall MSS, NH 2440, Archives Dept., Leeds City Library (Sheepscar Branch), England; Price, *France and the Chesapeake*, 1:540, 543, 564; 2:687–99, 738–41, 1018–19; Luthy, *La banque protestante*, 1:66, 231–32; 2:240 351; Chaussinand-Nogaret, *Les financiers du Languedoc*, 182–83, 188; Harriette Leiding, "Purrysburg, A Swiss-French Settlement of South Carolina, on the Savannah River," *THSSC* 39 (1934): 31; Philip M. Hamer et al., ed., *The*

Papers of Henry Laurens, for example, 2:155; 3:2–3, 49, 51, 81*n*, 120–22, 218, 229, 412, 492; 4:47–49, 60–63; 7:204, 392*n*; 8:437, 673–74; J. A. Lefroy, "The British Factory at Leghorn: Some Huguenot Associations," *Proceedings of the Huguenot Society of Great Britain and Ireland* 22 (1971–72): 81–89; Randolph Vigne, "The Killing of Jean Calas: Voltaire's First Huguenot Cause," ibid., 23 (1981–82): 280–82.

29. These London firms included two with Huguenot partners, James Poyas and Co. and Neufville and Rolleston, firms founded by Carolina-born Huguenots who moved to London, not by established London Huguenot houses which had spawned connections in Charleston. On the whole, however, Charleston Huguenot merchants were much less likely to move to England than Charleston merchants of English extraction, see below p. 25.

30. See Nash, "Organization of Trade and Finance," 85–92 and notes to table 4.

31. Hamer, *Papers of Henry Laurens*, see especially citations in note 28; for Laurens's early career see ibid., 1:8–28, 56–58, 182–85, 200–212, 230–32.

32. The exception to this rule, in table 4, was the short-lived Charleston firm of Chollet and Gervais, a migrant firm of recent creation, which drew on the credit of their London backers, the Anglo-Swiss Huguenot firm Bourdieu and Chollet and the Scot Richard Oswald. James Bourdieu was born in England of Huguenot parents and was a London merchant from the 1740s, first on his own account and then from 1769 in partnership with the Swiss-born Huguenot immigrant Samuel Chollet. The firm had vast trading and financial interests, especially with France. In the 1750s and 1760s, the firm developed a small import trade in South Carolina indigo, and then circa 1770 Chollet's son, Samuel Chollet Jr., was sent to Charleston to establish a "very capital house in the Carolina trade." Backed by the London firm, Chollet, in partnership with another Huguenot migrant John Lewis Gervais, a protégé of Henry Laurens, traded in slaves and dry goods in the early 1770s, but he failed to establish a stable partnership with Gervais, and in 1774 he returned to London. Price, *France and the Chesapeake*, 2:687–99, 738–41; Luthy, *La banque protestante*, 2:240, 382–87; Hamer, *Papers of Henry Laurens*, 8:496–98, 517, 546, 636–38; 9:127–28, 167, 324–25. For Oswald, see table 4, notes.

33. Nash, "Early Merchants of Philadelphia," 340–41, 350, 359–62. The quotation is from p. 350. Nash was unable to identify the origins of 41 of the 143 second-generation merchants. I have assumed that two-thirds of these unidentified merchants were migrants, given that it is much more difficult to trace the origins of migrants than of individuals born in America. Thomas M. Doerflinger, *A Vigorous Spirit of Enterprise: Merchants and Economic Development in Revolutionary Philadelphia* (Chapel Hill: University of North Carolina Press, 1986), 55–56,

analyzes a sample of 91 Philadelphia merchants for the colonial period as a whole, over one-third of whom were immigrants.

34. Richard Waterhouse, *A New World Gentry: The Making of a Merchant and Planter Class in South Carolina, 1670–1770* (New York: Garland Publishing, 1989), 169–71.

35. See tables 2 and 3. Only two Charleston merchants, James and John Poyas, were descended from a Purrysburgh settler, John Lewis Poyas.

36. On mortality rates see, Coclanis, *Shadow of a Dream*, 42–43; Van Ruymbeke, "L'émigration huguenote," 1:93–95.

37. See notes to table 1 and Manigault, "Manigault Family," 48–57; Simmons, "Early Manigault Records"; Mazyck, "Mazyck Family," 43–53; Hutson, "Motte Family," 57–63; Gourdin, "Madeleine Chardon," 64–104; [Notes on Will of Issac Mazyck], *THSSC* 14 (1907): 39–41; Hutson, "Peronneau of South Carolina," 49–58; "Will of Isaac Chardon," *THSSC* 45 (1940): 69–71; "Will of Francis LeBrasseur," 50–53; "Francis LeBrasseur," *THSSC* 59 (1954): 39–42; Nash, "Trade and Business"; Van Ruymbeke, "L'émigration huguenote." Gary Nash has shown that 40 percent of the first generation of Philadelphia merchants "either had no sons or lost their sons before they reached adulthood," see his "Early Merchants of Philadelphia," 342–43.

38. The most prolific Huguenot family was that of Peronneau, who produced at least eight leading merchants in the colonial period; see tables 1–4; Records of the Secretary of the Province, C, 1722–1724, 11–12, SCDAH; Hutson, "Peronneau of South Carolina," *THSSC* 89 (1984): 49–58.

39. One could add a fourth way, the residential clustering of French merchants in Charleston's business districts. However, the only substantial study of the spatial distribution of Charleston's merchants does not suggest that Huguenot merchants gathered together in a distinctive quarter; see, J. A. Calhoun, M. A. Zierdan, E. A. Paysinger, "The Geographic Spread of Charleston's Merchant Community, 1732–1767," *SCHM* 86 (1985): 207–20.

40. On Charleston's French church, see Hirsch, *Huguenots of Colonial South Carolina*, 50–60; Van Ruymbeke, "L'émigration Huguenote," 2:372–95, 421–23, 450–60; idem, "The Huguenots of Proprietary South Carolina," 39–40; Butler, *Huguenots in America*, 107–20, 134–43.

41. See above, note 37.

42. Inventory of Elizabeth Buretel, 1727, Records of the Secretary of the Province, Vol. F., 1727–29, 94–95, SCDAH; Elizabeth M. Pruden, "Investing Widows: Autonomy in a Nascent Capitalist Society," in Greene, Brana-Shute, and Sparks, *Money, Trade, and Power*, 347–49; [Notes on Will of Isaac Mazyck]; Van Ruymbeke, "L'émigration huguenote," 1:352–54, 365; idem, "The Huguenots of Proprietary South Carolina," 26–27; Pruden shows that the Widow

Buretel was not unique; over a third of her sample of women who lived off money-lending in the period 1720–1770 were "affiliated with the French Huguenot community."

43. For example, the Charles Town Library Society, founded in 1748, had 125 members in 1750, of whom 10 were French, including 8 merchants; see Hirsch, *Huguenots of Colonial South Carolina*, 161, 164.

44. On partnerships see, Nash, "Trade and Business," 9–11.

45. Trading partnerships have been identified mainly from Records of the South Carolina Court of Common Pleas, Judgment Rolls, 1730–1775, SCDAH, in which the most frequent litigants by far were merchant firms suing for the recovery of debts; see also miscellaneous business papers cited in table 3, n. (c); Hamer, *Papers of Henry Laurens*; Edgar and Bailey, *Biographical Directory*, vol. 2. In the 1760s, if Charleston Huguenot merchants had chosen their business partners randomly from amongst the merchant community, then 25 percent of their selections would have been fellow Huguenots.

46. Marriages have been traced mainly through: Robert Wilson, "Prioleau Family," *THSSC* 6 (1899): 24–27; "Will of Gabriel Guignard," *THSSC* 38 (1933): 89–100; W. Allan Moore Jr., "The Bonneau Family," *THSSC* 52 (1947): 38–39; Martha Burns, "Vincent Guerin of St. Thomas and St. Denis," *THSSC* 69 (1964): 37–43; "Bacot Records," *THSSC* 77 (1972): 93–103; Edward Gaillard, "A Brief Outline of My Family Background," *THSSC* 82 (1977): 85–93; Mazyck, "Notes on the Mazyck Family"; "Early Generations of the Legare Family in South Carolina," *THSSC* 46 (1941): 72–81; "Perdriau," *THSSC* 68 (1963): 72–85; Hutson, "Peronneau of South Carolina," 49–58; Robert F. Clute, ed., *The Annals and Parish Register of St. Thomas and St. Dennis Parish in South Carolina, from 1680–1884* (Baltimore: Clearfield Company Reprints and Remainders, 1974); Alexander S. Salley Jr., ed., *Register of St. Philip's Parish, 1720–1758* (Columbia: University of South Carolina Press, 1971); D. E. Huger Smith and Salley, ed., *Register of St. Philip's Parish, 1754–1810* (Columbia: University of South Carolina Press, 1971); A. S. Salley Jr., ed., *Marriage Notices in the South-Carolina Gazette and Its Successors (1732–1801)*, (Albany, N.Y., 1902); Moore and Simmons, *Abstracts of the Wills, 1670–1740*; Moore, ed., *Abstracts of the Wills of the State of South Carolina*; Vol. 2 1740–60; Vol. 3, 1760–1784 (Columbia, S.C.: R. L. Bryan Company, 1964, 1969).

47. Butler, *Huguenots in America*, 132–34. His other evidence is taken from the Register of St. Thomas and St. Denis Parish, records which were kept by British ministers and which "probably exclude marriages performed by the French ministers at St. Denis"; the quotation is from ibid., 133, table 5, note b.

48. Friedlander, "Carolina Huguenots," 252–66, 278–81. See also Van Ruymbeke, "The Huguenots of Proprietary South Carolina," 39–40.

49. Of course, while the urban and rural Huguenots had different social and marital patterns, there were very important connections between the two groups. Many Huguenot merchants married planters' daughters or shifted from trade to the ownership of plantations and slaves, while the rural planters provided many recruits for the Charleston merchant community in the second and third generations.

50. Hutson, "Early Generations of the Motte Family," 57–63; Edgar and Bailey, *Biographical Directory*, 2:478–80; Hamer, *Papers of Henry Laurens*, 2:285, 4, 122n; Nash, "Trade and Business," 6–29.

51. Hamer, *Papers of Henry Laurens*, 4:331–38; 5:33–34; 8:316, 496–98, 503, 517, 528, 546, 636–37; 9:51–52, 56–57, 127–28, 294–95, 308–12, 324–25, 377–79, 540–41 (from which the quotation is taken).

52. Butler, *Huguenots in America*, 92.

ELEVEN

The Huguenots of Colonial New York City

A Demographic Profile

Joyce D. Goodfriend

On 29 November 1773, the *New York Gazette and the Weekly Mercury* published a notice that Mr. Bontecou, a French gentleman, for many years an inhabitant of New York City, had died a few days before at the age of ninety-two.[1] Daniel Bontecou was a member of the Huguenot community that flourished in the city at the turn of the century.[2] Born in La Rochelle, he had arrived in New York by way of England in 1689 as a boy, accompanied by his father, Pierre Bontecou, and other family members.[3] Except for a youthful voyage to the Spanish Main, he had lived in the city all his life.

Bontecou had prospered, first running a tavern where meetings of the Common Council were held in the 1720s, and then becoming a shopkeeper.[4] When he made his will in 1772, he called himself a gentleman.[5] An active participant in civic life, he voted in the elections of 1761, 1768, and 1769, and was elected tax collector for the North Ward in 1724.[6] Over the years, he was a mainstay of the French church, serving the congregation as elder and as treasurer.[7] In the mid 1760s, when he was well over eighty, he played a major role in the bitter dispute that sundered the congregation and left it on the brink of dissolution.[8]

At the time of his death in 1773, Bontecou quite possibly was the last survivor of the group of refugees who had settled in New York City in the final years of the seventeenth century. His longevity clearly marks him as exceptional. Also unusual was his lifelong devotion to the French church, since the majority of his peers had withdrawn from the congregation by the end of the 1720s. But Bontecou's personal history does exemplify two key elements of the Huguenot experience in New York City that have not been subjected to systematic analysis—the demographic failure of many refugee families after the first generation and the high incidence of migration among first- and second- generation New York Huguenots. It also underlines the impressive record of persisting families in carving out a niche for themselves in urban society. Examining Daniel Bontecou's life in a broader context provides not only a demographic foundation for the story of the disintegration of New York's Huguenot community, but suggests a parallel story of successful adaptation to a new environment.

When Daniel Bontecou made his will in 1772, he had no survivors. Without members of his immediate family to whom to leave his property, he chose to divide his estate between his brother's son and Mary Bassett, the wife of pewterer Francis Bassett.[9] He bequeathed £100 to his nephew, Timothy Bontecou Jr., of New Haven, a silversmith like his father. The remainder of his estate was given to Mary Bassett, whose husband Francis, a third-generation Huguenot, had stood with Bontecou during the strife in the French congregation. The Bassetts obviously were Bontecou's closest friends, and it is not difficult to imagine that Mary Bassett had cared for Bontecou toward the end of his life. The trusted Francis Basset was appointed sole executor.

Daniel Bontecou typified a number of New York Huguenots in his failure to perpetuate his family in the city. He and his wife Marie Machet's only son, Daniel (Jr.), baptized in 1713, is reputed to have married a much older Huguenot woman, but there is no evidence of the marriage or even that the boy lived to maturity.[10] Daniel Bontecou's experience was not uncommon. Of a sample of 128 male immigrants, 56 (44 percent) apparently did not have second-generation family members who survived to adulthood.[11] Such widespread demographic failure seems implausible, but the timing and severity of the 1702 yellow fever epidemic in New York City, in which approximately 570 people died, may have been optimum for wreaking havoc in the Huguenot community.[12] The paucity of death records for the French church makes impossible any accurate estimate of how many Huguenot families suffered losses at this time.

Compounding the problem of inadequate death records is the dearth of information on many immigrant families. To assume that all families who left no further traces in New York records died out (or even died out in the male line) is unreasonable. Given the Huguenot propensity for migration, it is probable that some relocated. Until authoritative genealogies are assembled for these immigrant families, we are forced to rely on wills and documents concerning estate administration to prove that an individual died unmarried or that a couple had no surviving children.

Claude Brueys, a merchant, most likely was single when he died, since he mentioned neither a wife nor children in the will he made in 1702 on the eve of his death.[13] Other refugees had married, but may not have produced any offspring. Francois Hulin left his entire estate to his wife Susanna, except for a donation of £10 to the poor of the French congregation.[14] However, the majority of male refugees who died without leaving second-generation successors had been parents.

In a few instances, there is clear-cut evidence that children predeceased their parents. By the time he wrote his will in 1722, sixty-year-old Elias Neau, a merchant who became celebrated for his work as the Anglican catechist of blacks in New York City, had lost his wife, Susanne Paré, as well as the daughter baptized in the French church in 1692.[15] Although Neau had many legatees, the only family members he designated as beneficiaries were nieces and nephews.

In most cases, it is the lack of any subsequent mention in local records that compels us to infer that sons and daughters died before reaching adulthood. Mariner Jacob Rattier had married Jael Arnaut in Rhode Island in 1689, and his son Jacob was born there in 1690.[16] The will he made in 1702 in New York, soon after settling there, mentions his son Jacob and his wife's two children from a previous marriage.[17] In May 1704, the New York Common Council granted the widow Jael Rattier "Liberty to follow any Lawfull Trade or Imployment . . . for the better Obtaining A livelyhood for her and her family."[18] But there is no later reference to Jacob Jr., who most likely died young.

Even refugee families known to have had numerous offspring apparently left no successors in the second generation. André Stuckey, a prominent merchant, and his wife Marie Brossard had nine children baptized in New York's French church between 1702 and 1710.[19] Though Stuckey was still living in the city in 1724, there is no record of any of his children reaching maturity there.[20] The case of mariner Bartholomew Feurt, is even more puzzling. When Feurt wrote his will in 1712, he named three sons and two daughters as his heirs.[21] However, there is no mention of these children in other city documents.

Many of New York's Huguenot immigrants, like Daniel Bontecou, probably watched their children die young. But casting a wider genealogical net most likely would reveal that some untraced individuals moved out of New York City and therefore should be classified as migrants. As of now, twenty-five Huguenots from the immigrant generation are known to have left the city, in most cases taking their sons and daughters with them. Members of the second generation, once grown, also moved out of the city. At least twenty have been identified to date, but surely there were more.

Most of the first-generation refugees who left the city sought new homes in settlements where Huguenots had already established a presence. The most popular destinations for New York's Huguenots were two rural settlements in the vicinity of the city where French Protestants had concentrated—New Rochelle in Westchester county and Staten Island, or Richmond county.[22] In essence, these were satellite communities of Huguenots, and there was human traffic back and forth between them and the city. At least nine French Protestant refugees who initially settled in New York City opted to move to New Rochelle within a decade or so of their arrival in the city. Zacharie Angevin, a tailor, first appeared in New York in 1690, when he married Marie Naudin in the French church.[23] He had moved his family to New Rochelle by 1705, when he was chosen as town constable.[24] In 1710, when a census of the town was taken, Angevin, then forty-six, and his wife and children were enumerated.[25] Though Zacharie Angevin could not write—he signed the church register with a mark when he married—by the time he made his will in 1739 he had acquired a considerable amount of property, including a house and homestead of fourteen acres, two acres of meadow, and three slaves.[26] Jean Coutant's family also appeared on the 1710 census.[27] By 1717, yeoman Jean Coutant was dead, but his widow was able to complete the purchase of a house and land in New Rochelle.[28]

The opportunity to acquire land as well as the existence of a nucleus of French Protestants on Staten Island served as a lure for other New York Huguenot immigrants. Several former residents of the city were listed on the 1706 Staten Island census, among them members of the Mercereau and Rezeau clans and Salomon Latanier, whose sole appearance in the New York records was as a voter in the 1701 municipal election.[29] A few immigrants struck out independently for places outside New York. Daniel Jouet settled in Elizabethtown, New Jersey, and André Laurent journeyed to another major area of Huguenot settlement, Charleston, South Carolina.[30]

Those first-generation immigrants who chose to leave New York City were, in most cases, young enough to still shape their futures in a new direction. One exception was James Ballereau, a shipwright, who married in the French church in 1702 and was made a Freeman of New York City in 1709. Ballereau was still living in the city in 1731, when he was elected collector for Montgomerie Ward.[31] His exodus from the city occurred at the end of his working life. When he wrote his will in 1733, he identified himself as "now of the town of Rye."[32]

Daniel Bontecou's brother, Timothy, did not follow in the footsteps of these migrants. Bontecou family tradition relates that Timothy, who was born in New York City in 1693, traveled to France to learn the trade of silversmith and married there before returning to America.[33] He was living in New Haven by 1735, the date his wife Mary was buried there, but he may have attempted to set up shop in New York City before then, since he was elected constable of the North Ward in 1730.[34] Timothy Bontecou's odyssey was atypical of New York's Huguenots, but the fact that he chose to leave the city was not.

Huguenot refugees in other parts of the world exhibited a pattern of multiple migrations, and so it is not surprising that New York's Huguenots were mobile as well. Not only did the original immigrants leave the city, but their children did too. Among those second-generation New York Huguenots who embraced the tradition of migration were the children of merchants Elie Boudinot Jr., Benjamin Faneuil, and Benjamin D'Harriette. Elie Boudinot Jr. had arrived in New York City with his father, also a merchant, about 1688. In 1699, he married Marie Catherine Carre, the daughter of merchant Louis Carre. When their son, Elias III, finished his apprenticeship to silversmith Simeon Soumain in 1728, he clearly was not ready to put down roots. He first traveled to Antigua, where the widow and children of his father's stepbrother lived, married there twice, and had a son. In 1736, the peripatetic Boudinot opened a shop in Philadelphia, but by the early 1750s he had transplanted his family to Princeton, New Jersey. Later, he moved to Elizabethtown, New Jersey, where he died in 1770.[35]

Elias Boudinot III left New York after his father had died. So too did the children of merchant Benjamin Faneuil. Following the elder Faneuil's death in 1719, the entire Faneuil family, consisting of his widow Anne, two sons, and four daughters, removed to Boston, where Benjamin's brother André was a highly successful merchant. Peter Faneuil ultimately inherited the fortune of his uncle, who had never married. His brother Benjamin and his sisters all married people from the Boston area.[36]

A Huguenot son's migration was not always contingent on the death of his father. Merchant Benjamin D'Harriette's son and namesake moved to Charleston in the 1720s and soon became a wealthy merchant and a large landholder.[37] Benjamin Jr., who was an only child, may have convinced his father of the opportunities to be found in Charleston, for the father briefly transplanted himself and his wife to Charleston in 1737.[38] But by 1739, Benjamin Sr. was back in New York, where he died in 1741, leaving the bulk of his estate to his only son, who remained in Charleston until his death in 1756.[39]

Immigrants' daughters as well as sons left New York for new homes, but their migration was likely to have been precipitated by the wishes of their husbands. The three daughters of Auguste (August) Grasset, collector of the weigh house, who was slain in New York City's 1712 slave rebellion, all resided outside the city. Both Hester, the wife of Louis DuBois, and Marianne, the wife of Henry de Money, lived on Staten Island, while Martha and her husband Joseph Oldfield lived in Jamaica, Long Island.[40] Samuel, the only surviving son of Auguste Grasset, initially settled on Staten Island near his two sisters, but later moved to Charleston.[41]

Migration, along with demographic failure, greatly depleted New York's Huguenot population. If the number of known migrants is combined with the number of men who did not reproduce or whose children are untraceable in city records, then it becomes evident that nearly two-thirds (82; or 64 percent) of the 128 original Huguenot families did not persist in New York City in the male line. Determining how many of these families were perpetuated in the female line is complicated by the fact that daughters ceased to carry the family surname. Merchant Pierre Morin had three sons and five daughters baptized in New York's French church. But only three daughters are known to have grown to adulthood and married in the city, Marie and Esther Morin, who both wed merchant Andre Fresneau, and Marie Anne Morin, who married merchant John Scott.[42] Though the surname Morin died out in New York City, it was preserved as the middle name of two well-known early Americans, revolutionary leader John Morin Scott (Pierre Morin's grandson) and poet Philip Morin Freneau (Pierre Morin's great-grandson).

Documenting the female lines of the Morin family is relatively simple because of the celebrity of their descendants, but in other cases the task of tracing women can be daunting, especially given the high incidence of marriages to non-Huguenots among French New Yorkers. Even though the difficulties associated with tracing females are bound to lead to an underestimate of the number of persisting families, it is safe to say that only a minority of the original refugee families had second- or third-generation members who carried on in New York City.

In the mid-eighteenth century, only forty-six (36 percent) of the original families had second-generation members living in New York City. Not all of these families would persist into the third generation. Take the Pouttreau family, for example. Three of the six children born to Daniel Pouttreau, a leather dresser, and his wife Marie Cousson between 1689 and 1701 lived in New York City as young adults. Marie Pouttreau (born 1691) married Jacques (James) You, a perriwigmaker, and had nine children baptized in the French church between 1710/11 and 1728. Her younger brother Daniel (Jr.) (born 1698) quite possibly was apprenticed to You, since he listed his occupation as wigmaker when he became a Freeman of New York City in 1721. Abraham (born 1701), the youngest member of this refugee family, was termed a goldsmith when he took an apprentice in 1727. Abraham had been married to Maria Vreelant in the Dutch Reformed church in 1726, and his children were baptized there. The Dutch Reformed churchyard was the site of the burial of two of his infants in 1727 and 1731, and he himself was buried there in 1744.[43] What happened to his brother Daniel and to his sister Marie and her children? As far as we know, the three second-generation members of the Pouttreau family disappeared from New York City without leaving any descendants in the third generation.

Only 25 (20 percent) of the original 128 families persisted into the third generation in the male and/or female lines. Family continuity could never be taken for granted, even if several of one's children survived to adulthood. The case of Elie Pelletreau, a tallow chandler and shopkeeper, is instructive. Of Pelletreau's six sons and one daughter, four sons reached marriageable age. But Jean and Elie both had died by the time their father made his will in 1728 and though, between them, they had had six children, only Jean's two daughters remained alive in 1728. The third son, François, had moved to Southampton on Long Island before he married in 1721.[44] Paul Pelletreau, a tallow chandler like his father, alone carried on the family name in New York City through his son Elie.

A more successful persisting family was the Bassetts, the family to which Daniel Bontecou's friend Francis Bassett belonged. Francis was the grandson of Huguenot refugee Francis Basset, a sailor who settled in New York City prior to 1689 and had died by 1700. In 1707, the sailor's widow, Marie Magdalen Bassett, apprenticed her son Francis Bassett (Jr.), then fifteen years old, to pewterer William Horsewell for seven years. Her other son John undoubtedly served a similar apprenticeship, because he too became a pewterer. John Bassett, the father of Daniel Bontecou's friend Francis, had three sons and two daughters, all of whom were living in 1760. Francis and Frederick both followed in their father's footsteps as pewterers, while their brother John became a mariner, like his grandfather. Mary's husband was Samuel Waldron, a blacksmith who in 1766 acquired the right to operate the Ferry from Manhattan to Brooklyn. Marguerite Bassett married John Young late in life.

What distinguished families like the Bassetts, who perpetuated their lines over three generations? First and foremost, it was their good fortune in having survived in a medically perilous environment. New York's population was decimated not only by the 1702 yellow fever epidemic but also by a virulent outbreak of smallpox that raged in the city in 1731, causing over 500 deaths.[45] Many Huguenots must have succumbed to these diseases.

By opting to remain in New York City over the generations, persisting families made clear that they considered their prospects for material rewards greatest in an urban center. Merchant dynasties like the De Lanceys, Crommelins, Desbrosseses, and Jays depended on the seaport's trade for their profits. Their commercially derived wealth quickly gained them access to political power. The well-to-do denizens of the city constituted a desirable pool of potential clients for attorneys John Morin Scott and John Jay and physician James Jay and potential customers for skilled artisans such as the Bassetts (pewterers), the Le Rouxs (silversmiths) and the Tillous and Isaac Garnier Jr. (chairmakers). Small traders and practitioners of lesser crafts—examples are shopkeeper Peter Vergereau (Jr.), saddlers Samuel Bourdet (III) and Louis Thibou, cordwainer John Targé, tailor John Laboyteaux, and tallow chandler Paul Pelletreau —also stood to reap substantial benefits in a growing urban economy. For these Huguenots, prosperity hinged on the rate at which goods and services were bought and sold.

Migrants, by contrast, viewed economic security as linked to the acquisition of land. Those of the immigrant generation who turned their backs on the city and planted their families in New Rochelle or Staten Island may have valued stability as much as prosperity. Memories of past persecution as well as a yearning for a communal life with other French refugees induced them to cluster among compatriots.

Huguenots who maintained their residence in New York manifested an affinity not only for the competitiveness of the urban sphere but also for its cultural complexity. For French Protestant merchants, as John F. Bosher has argued, national identity became superfluous in a religious world that excluded Catholics.[46] Artisans also placed little weight on ethnic purity, judging from their willingness to intermarry with Dutch and English New Yorkers. Not surprisingly, the high rates of intermarriage among New York's Huguenots coincided with the weakening of their ties to the city's French church.

As the colonial era ended, only some Bassetts, Garniers, and Pelletreaus —and the aged Daniel Bontecou[47]—remained in the French church that had meant so much to the original immigrants. In the wake of the violent turmoil in the congregation in the mid-1760s, goldsmith John Hastier and merchant Jacques Desbrosses had transferred their allegiance to Anglican Trinity Church, where a number of other Huguenot descendants—primarily De Lanceys, Jays, Crommelins, and Desbrosseses, but also Tillous and Le Rouxs—already spent the Sabbath, while Peter Vergereau became a communicant of the Presbyterian Church, joining John Targe and John Laboyteaux. Samuel Bourdet,[48] Louis Thibou, and some Tillous attended the Dutch Reformed church, while Joseph Tillou united with the Baptist congregation. Elizabeth Ayrault, the granddaughter of a refugee tailor named Daniel Mesnard became a Moravian.[49] She had been baptized in New York's French church, but when her mother, Judith Mesnard Ayrault, took as her second husband Lawrence Kilburn, a Danish-born portrait painter who was a Moravian, Judith joined this congregation and raised her daughter in this faith. The young woman married a Moravian and, with her family, moved to Bethlehem, Pennsylvania, at the outbreak of the Revolution.

The exodus of all but a handful of refugee family members from the French church by the late 1760s and their dispersion among a variety of denominations suggests the supple quality of Huguenot identity in colonial New York. Unfettered by loyalty to the French nation and eager to capitalize on the economic opportunities present in their new surroundings, the city's Huguenots took whatever steps were necessary to promote their interests in British America. Forging business and political alliances with a diverse array of individuals, worshipping in the Anglican, Dutch Reformed, and Presbyterian Churches, and choosing mates from dissimilar backgrounds were effective means of securing their place in a cosmopolitan city. If one consequence of this strategy was the collapse of the cohesive French Protestant community that Daniel Bontecou had known in his youth, another was the advancement of the persisting families. The secret of their success may have been their ability to blur but not efface their identity.

Notes

1. *New York Gazette and the Weekly Mercury*, November 29, 1773.

2. On the New York City Huguenot community, see Jon Butler, *The Huguenots in America: A Refugee People in New World Society* (1983) and Joyce D. Goodfriend, *Before the Melting Pot: Society and Culture in Colonial New York City, 1664–1730* (Princeton: Princeton University Press, 1992). Background information on Huguenots who settled in New York can be found in Charles W. Baird, *History of the Huguenot Emigation to America*, 2 vols. (New York: Dodd and Mead, 1885).

3. John E. Morris, *The Bontecou Genealogy. A Record of the Descendants of Pierre Bontecou, A Huguenot Refugee from France, In the Lines of His Sons* (Hartford, Conn., 1885). Unless otherwise indicated, all information on Daniel Bontecou's life comes from this source.

4. Herbert L. Osgood, ed., *Minutes of the Common Council of the City of New York, 1675–1776*, 8 vols. (New York: Dodd and Mead, 1905), 3:281, 314, 431; *Collections of the New-York Historical Society*, 1895, 462.

5. *Collections of the New-York Historical Society*, 1899, 144.

6. *A Copy of the Poll List, of the Election For Representatives for the City and County of New-York . . . MDCCLXI* (New York, 1880); *A Copy of the Poll List, of the Election For Representatives for the City and County of New-York . . . MDCCLXVIII* (New York, 1880); *A Copy of the Poll List, of the Election For Representatives for the City and County of New-York . . . MDCCLXIX* (New York, 1880); *Minutes of the Common Council*, 3:354.

7. John A. F. Maynard, *The Huguenot Church of New York: A History of the French Church of Saint Esprit* (New York: French Church of Saint Esprit, 1938).

8. Ibid.

9. For an abstract of Daniel Bontecou's will, see *Collections of the New-York Historical Society*, 1899, 144. The entire will is printed in Morris, *The Bontecou Genealogy*.

10. The baptism of Daniel Bontecou (Jr.) is recorded in Alfred V. Wittmeyer, ed., "Registers of the births, marriages and deaths of the 'Eglise Françoise à la Nouvelle York.' from 1688 to 1804" in *Collections of the Huguenot Society of America*, vol. 1 (New York: Douglas Taylor, 1886), 127. The family tradition regarding Daniel Bontecou Jr.'s marriage is found in Morris, *The Bontecou Genealogy*.

11. In *Before the Melting Pot*, I identified 128 male Huguenot refugees present in New York City at the turn of the eighteenth century, using the city's 1695 and 1699 tax lists, the 1701 list of voters, and the 1703 census. For this paper, I have attempted to trace these 128 men and their families over three generations, using local and regional records.

12. For a discussion of the 1702 yellow fever epidemic, see Goodfriend, *Before the Melting Pot*, 133–34.

13. *Collections of the New-York Historical Society*, 1892, 343–44.

14. Ibid.

15. For Neau's will, see *Collections of the New-York Historical Society*, 1893, 254–55. For the baptism of his daughter Suzanne in 1692, see Wittmeyer, ed., "Registers of the births, marriages and deaths of the 'Eglise Françoise à la Nouvelle York,'" 22. On Neau's life, see Sheldon S. Cohen, "Elias Neau, Instructor to New York's Slaves," *New-York Historical Society Quarterly* 55 (1971): 7–27, and Butler, *The Huguenots in America*, 161–65, 167–69.

16. "Records of the French Church at Narragansett, 1686–1691," *New York Genealogical and Biographical Record* 70 (1939): 236–41, 359–65; 71 (1940): 51–61.

17. *Collections of the New-York Historical Society*, 1892, 354.

18. *Minutes of the Common Council*, vol. 2, 264.

19. On Stuckey's family and trade, see John F. Bosher, "Huguenot Merchants and the Protestant International in the Seventeenth Century," *William and Mary Quarterly* 3d ser., 52 (1995): 81–83. For the baptisms of Stuckey's children, see Wittmeyer, ed., "Registers of the births, marriages and deaths of the 'Eglise Françoise à la Nouvelle York.'"

20. For Stuckey's presence in New York City in 1724, see Wittmeyer, ed., "Registers of the births, marriages and deaths of the 'Eglise Françoise à la Nouvelle York,'" 364.

21. *Collections of the New-York Historical Society*, 1893, 113.

22. On the Huguenot communities in New Rochelle and Staten Island, see Butler, *The Huguenots in America*. For biographical information on the Huguenots

of New Rochelle, see also Morgan H. Seacord, *Biographical Sketches and Index of the Huguenot Settlers of New Rochelle, 1687–1776* (New Rochelle, N.Y.: Huguenot Historical Association of New Rochelle, 1941).

23. The record of Angevin's marriage is in Wittmeyer, ed., "Registers of the births, marriages and deaths of the 'Eglise Françoise à la Nouvelle York,'" 9.

24. Jeanne A. Forbes, ed., *Records of the Town of New Rochelle, 1699–1828* (New Rochelle: Paragraph Press, 1916), 53. Angevin purchased property in New Rochelle in 1702. Ibid., 32–39.

25. "The List of the Towne of New Rochelle & c. XBR [December] 9th, 1710," *The Documentary History of the State of New-York*, 4 vols., ed. E. B. O'Callaghan (Albany, N.Y.: Weed, Parsons, and Co., 1850–51), 3:571–72. New Rochelle's Huguenot families can be traced over the eighteenth century through the 1710 census, the 1767 town tax list, the 1771 census and the 1790 census. On these sources, see Robert V. Wells, "While Rip Napped: Social Change in Late Eighteenth-Century New York," *New York History* 71 (1990): 14–18. I am grateful to Professor Wells for providing me with copies of these documents.

26. *Collections of the New-York Historical Society*, 1894, 283–84.

27. See note 25.

28. Forbes, ed., *Records of the Town of New Rochelle*, 155–57.

29. The Staten Island census of 1706 is in John E. Stillwell, *Historical and Genealogical Miscellany; Data relating to the Settlement and Settlers of New York and New Jersey*, 5 vols. (New York, 1903–32), 1:149–56.

30. An abstract of the 1711 will of Daniel Jouet, of Elizabeth Town, New Jersey, (proved in 1721) is printed in *Documents Relating to the Colonial History of New Jersey, XXIII. Calendar of New Jersey Wills, vol. 1, 1670–1730*, New Jersey Archives, First Series (Paterson, N. J., 1901), 269. On Laurent, see David Duncan Wallace, *The Life of Henry Laurens* (New York: G. P. Putman's Sons, 1915).

31. *Minutes of the Common Council*, 4:44.

32. *Collections of the New-York Historical Society*, 1894, 130.

33. Morris, *The Bontecou Genealogy*.

34. Ibid.; *Minutes of the Common Council*, 4:27, 30.

35. On Elias Boudinot (III), see George Adams Boyd, *Elias Boudinot: Patriot and Statesman, 1740–1821* (Princeton: Princeton University Press, 1952) and Carla Mulford, ed., *Only for the Eye of a Friend: The Poems of Annis Boudinot Stockton* (Charlottesville: University Press of Virginia, 1995), 12.

36. On the Faneuils, see "Data Relative to the Faneuil Family," *New York Genealogical and Biographical Record* 47 (1916): 123–24; and Butler, *The Huguenots in America*, 87–88.

37. Arthur Henry Hirsch, *The Huguenots of Colonial South Carolina* (1928; reprint, Columbia: University of South Carolina Press, 1999), 221–23. On the

family and trade of Benjamin D'Harriette Sr. see Bosher, "Huguenot Merchants and the Protestant International," 83–85.

38. On 8 October 1737, it was noted in the membership records of New York City's Dutch Reformed church that Benjamin D'Harriette and his wife, Anna Outmans, had left the congregation, with an attestation, for the French church in Charleston. D'Harriette had become a communicant of the New York Dutch Reformed church on 25 May 1731, transferring his membership from the city's French church. On 19 November 1739, Benjamin D'Harriette Sr. was again received as a communicant of the New York City Dutch Reformed church with the notation that he had come from the French church in Charleston. "Records of the Reformed Dutch Church in the City of New York—Church Membership List," *New York Genealogical and Biographical Record* 60 (1929): 279, 346.

39. *Collections of the New-York Historical Society*, 1894, 331–32.

40. *Collections of the New-York Historical Society*, 1893, 86; Neil D. Thompson, "Auguste Grasset of La Rochelle, London, and New York City," *National Genealogical Society Quarterly* 66 (March 1978): 3–15. On Augustus Grasset's murder by a slave, see Kenneth Scott, "The Slave Insurrection in New York in 1712," *New-York Historical Society Quarterly* 45 (1961): 48. One of the slaves indicted as an accessory to the murder of Grasset belonged to André Stuckey. On New York Huguenots' predilection for slaveholding, see Butler, *The Huguenots in America*, 150, 175–76.

41. Thompson, "Auguste Grasset of La Rochelle, London, and New York City."

42. On the Morins and the Fresneaus, see Lewis Leary, *That Rascal Freneau: A Study in Literary Failure* (1941; reprint, New York: Octagon Books, 1964), 4–17. On the Morins and the Scotts, see *Dictionary of American Biography*, s.v. John Morin Scott.

43. "Record of Burials in the Dutch Church, New York," *Year Book of the Holland Society of New York*, 1899, 184.

44. On Francis Pelletreau, whose son Elias became a silversmith, see Dean F. Failey, *Long Island is My Nation: The Decorative Arts and Craftsmen, 1640–1830* (Setauket, N.Y.: The Society for the Preservation of Long Island Antiquities, 1976).

45. John Duffy, *A History of Public Health in New York City, 1625–1866* (New York: Russell Sage Foundation, 1968), 53–54.

46. Bosher, "Huguenot Merchants and the Protestant International."

47. Daniel Bontecou's loyalty to the French church may have wavered in his final years. On 12 January 1772, the "Wife of Daniel Bonticau" was buried in the Dutch Reformed churchyard. "Record of Burials in the Dutch Church, New York," *Year Book of the Holland Society of New York*, 1899, 148.

48. The religious identities of Huguenot descendants were not always clearcut. Samuel Bourdet, for example, had been baptized in the French church. On the evening of 14 April 1759, he was married to Sara van Vorst, a woman of Dutch descent, "in the presence of some members of the Bourdet family in the Chamber of the French pastor, Jean Carle." But when Samuel died prematurely in 1764, he was buried in the Dutch Reformed churchyard, where his mother, Judith Blagg Bourdet ("The Widow Bourdet") had been buried in 1759. The Dutch Reformed church was also the site of his sister Susanna's marriage to Johannes Louw and the baptisms of several of their children. Wittmeyer, ed., "Registers of the births, marriages and deaths of the 'Eglise Françoise à la Nouvelle York,'" 246; "Record of Burials in the Dutch Church, New York," *Year Book of the Holland Society of New York*, 1899, 149.

49. On Elizabeth Ayrault and her mother Judith Mesnard Ayrault Kilburn, see Howard S. F. Randolph, "Jacob Boelen, Goldsmith, of New York and His Family Circle," *New York Genealogical and Biographical Record* 72 (1941): 285*n*.

TWELVE

A Colony of "Native French Catholics"?

The Protestants of New France in the Seventeenth and Eighteenth Centuries

Leslie Choquette

I

Beginning in 1627, French law explicitly forbade Protestants to settle permanently in Canada. Early attempts at ecumenical colonization had raised a certain amount of havoc, particularly in Acadia, as described by Samuel de Champlain:

> I have seen the Minister and our Curé get into fist fights over the difference in religion. I do not know who was the most valiant, and who threw the best punch, but I know very well that the Minister complained sometimes to Sieur de Mons [the king's lieutenant-general, himself a Protestant] of having been beaten, and resolved the points of controversy in this fashion. I leave to you to think whether that was fair to see; the Savages were sometimes on one side, sometimes the other, and the French, mingled according to their diverse belief, said abominable things of both religions, although Sieur de Mons made peace as best he could.[1]

This particular dispute continued into the following year, 1605, when both clergymen were stricken with scurvy. They died within days of one another, and, according to Marc Lescarbot, the first chronicler of the colony, the sailors "put them both into the same grave, to see whether dead they would live in peace, since living they had never been able to agree."[2]

The charter of the Company of the Hundred Associates, promulgated by Cardinal Richelieu in 1627, stipulated in article II: "Without it being permitted, however, for the said associates and others to send any for-eigners to the said places, thus to people the said colony with native French Catholics, and those who command in New France shall be enjoined to see that the present article be executed exactly as written, not suffering it to be contravened for any reason or occasion, lest they answer for it personally."[3]

This exclusion of Protestants, which, it should be noted, applied only to those recruited to "people" the colony, remained in force throughout the French Regime.[4] Richelieu put it into effect for several reasons, not least among them the internal dissentions described above. He could not but have been aware of them. For over a decade, the Catholic hierarchy in New France had been carrying out an anti-Protestant campaign, com-plete with book burnings and vitriolic pamphlets. In 1626, for example, the Récollet Le Caron warned: "Those who say derisively that what our priests consecrate at the altar is a White John, that his Holiness is the Antichrist, that if they could get their hands on the God of the papists, they would strangle him, . . . [and] on the last monk, they would eat him, who say that the . . . antiphons we sing in honor of the Virgin Mary are hangman's songs, are not suited to execute such a design [to plant the Catholic, Apostolic, and Roman religion, plus to discover, people, build, clear, and maintain there all native Frenchmen who would like to live there]."[5]

Nonetheless, that Richelieu proved susceptible to this propaganda speaks less to his ideological commitment than to his political concerns. The charter of the Hundred Associates was drawn up on 6 May 1627, a time when the threat of Protestant treason weighed heavily on Richelieu's mind. Indeed, the final ratification took place outside of La Rochelle, preparatory to the yearlong siege that deprived the Protestants of the last fortified city granted to them by the Edict of Nantes.[6] In the case of North America, the proximity of the English compounded the potential danger of Protestant disloyalty. Religious ties had outweighed national allegiance more than once in recent memory, and Richelieu refused to risk either a defection of French Protestants to the Thirteen Colonies or an English takeover of New France with Protestant complicity. (Riche-lieu's fears were not unfounded. In 1628, the colony fell briefly to the English, assisted by a Huguenot traitor.)

Yet the charter of the Hundred Associates never succeeded in elimi-nating Protestants from Canada, owing partly to its own ambiguity and partly to lackadaisical enforcement. Father Lucien Campeau has shown that the years 1627–1663 witnessed the arrival of "a good many by the vessels of the company," although his qualification, "without them ever having been, to our knowledge, disturbed," is more dubious.[7] One thinks, for example, of the case of Daniel Vuil, the only immigrant executed for the crime of sorcery under the French Regime. Vuil was a Huguenot miller who arrived in Canada in 1659, the same year as Bishop Laval, and who abjured his religion to marry an adolescent girl he met during the voyage. The girl's parents, alleging his "bad morals," refused their consent, and shortly thereafter accused him of employing *maléfice* (evil spells) to torment their daughter with demons and specters. Bishop Laval took it upon himself to investigate, and the dossier he compiled contains a revelatory "permission to inform against Vuril [*sic*], who, relapsed into heresy, nonetheless abuses the sacraments."[8]

Vuil's execution notwithstanding, Protestants continued to arrive in the colony. In 1670, Bishop Laval addressed a memorandum to the king accusing them of holding "seductive discourses," distributing books, and assembling amongst themselves "to celebrate the religion." Six years later, the Superior Council of Quebec remained concerned enough about the situation to promulgate a law stipulating that "Protestants do not have the right to assemble for the exercise of their religion under pain of chastisement," but adding that "Protestants can come to the colony during the summer," and even spend the winter, provided they "live as Catholics without scandal."[9]

The Council's distinction between temporary and permanent migration and its willingness, however reluctant, to condone the former were implied by the original wording of the exclusion. This interpretation, moreover, prevailed for most of the French Regime. As late as the 1740s, Protestant merchants from Montauban, La Rochelle, and Rouen sojourned unmolested in the colony, some for a season, others for several, still others for many years. The French merchant house of Dugard, nominally Catholic itself, maintained two factors in Quebec, year-round, in the decades before the Conquest. Both of these men, François Havy and his cousin Jean Lefebvre, were Protestants from Normandy.[10] Protestants also figured among the crew members who laid anchor each season in the port of Quebec City.[11]

The only period during which de facto toleration of temporary Protestant migration did not exist was, predictably, 1685–1715. As historian

Marc-André Bédard has pointed out, though, the hostile religious climate was not the only reason for the almost total disappearance of Protestant merchants from the colony during these years. Economic difficulties, specifically, the disruption of commerce in the wake of virtually continuous warfare, also played a role.[12]

Protestant settlement, as mentioned above, was another matter altogether. After 1627, permanent residents of Quebec and Acadia were required to be Catholic. Nonetheless, Protestants did manage to settle in Canada during the French Regime. Marc-André Bédard's book, *Les Protestants en Nouvelle-France*, lists 477 Protestant settlers of Quebec, exclusive of 231 Protestant prisoners of whom little is known. Of the 477, some 233 were either Huguenots or else European Protestants (Swiss and Germans primarily) who arrived as soldiers of the French army. The rest apparently made their way to Canada, either voluntarily or under duress, from the Anglo-American colonies.

The immigrant sample that I assembled for my book, *Frenchmen into Peasants*, included 110 of the 233 European expatriates mentioned by Bédard, as well as 51 others.[13] Since these last, thirty-seven men and fourteen women, also, for the most part, settled in Quebec, I can estimate at about 300 the number of Protestant *habitants*, exclusive of the Anglo-Americans. This number is by no means insignificant, especially when one considers that it roughly equals the number of colonists from a northwestern French province such as Perche or Anjou.

Furthermore, this estimate is surely too low because the Canadian archives used by Bédard and myself are incomplete in their enumeration of Huguenots. The most recent study of Canada's first Protestants, Robert Larin's *Brève Histoire des protestants en Nouvelle-France et au Québec*, relies instead on French archives to advance "the hypothesis of a presence of Huguenot origin of around 5 to 6 percent within the [Quebec] population." To accept this hypothesis, Larin notes, is "simply to recognize that the migratory flow toward the colony was in the image of the whole population of the metropolis, which included a Protestant population of around 5 percent in the middle of the seventeenth century."[14]

Jesuit historian Lucien Campeau has dismissed the Protestant backgrounds of these settlers as irrelevant, arguing that as isolated individuals, "Like most of the Catholics, they surrendered after a while to the intense religious climate of the colony, whose common religion they adopted."[15] Yet if former Huguenots eventually resembled their Catholic neighbors as regards religious practice, in certain respects, the behavior of the two groups continued to differ. Mary Ann LaFleur's study of Notre-Dame-des-Anges, a Jesuit seigneurie near Quebec City, has revealed that over four generations, immigrants of Huguenot background had a 66 percent rate of persistence on the land, as opposed to only 25 percent for life-long Catholics.[16] In the Canadian diaspora, it appears, even converted Protestants remained distinct in some ways from the general population.[17] What then can be said of their French backgrounds?

II

First, the regional origins of Protestant immigrants to New France did not completely reflect the implantation of Protestantism in France. The Atlantic provinces dominated Protestant immigration as they did Catholic, and the eastern provinces sent few Protestants in spite of their strong reformed traditions. Only within the Atlantic provinces did the distribution of Protestant immigrants more or less resemble that of the religion (see table 1).

More than three-fifths of the Protestants I studied came from the central western provinces of Aunis, Saintonge, and Angoumois. Curiously, my sample did not include any Poitevins, although Protestantism was important in Lower Poitou, and even more so around Niort.[18] Poitou's Protestants did not, in principle, refrain from emigration. Of the twenty indentured servants who left Chef-Boutonne (Deux-Sèvres) for the Antilles between 1643 and 1714, three came from Protestant families, and two from families divided along religious lines. Marc-André Bédard, moreover, identified seven Protestants from Poitou in Canada, and Robert Larin eighteen more through research in French local archives. According to Larin, "A methodical study, aiming for exhaustivity and covering Upper and Lower Poitou, would certainly permit us to multiply by at least four or five the traditional number of seven Poitevins in the Huguenot profile in New France."[19]

This importance of the Center West, with or without Poitou, resulted from the role of La Rochelle in the Canadian trade, including the trade in immigrants. As soon as Richelieu died in 1642, merchants from the Company of the Hundred Associates began recruiting labor in the city. In the 1650s, they delegated this responsibility to merchants in La Rochelle, the most active of whom were the Protestants François Perron and

TABLE 1: *Provincial Origins of Protestants*

PROVINCE	CHOQUETTE	BÉDARD
Aunis	79	80
Normandy	16	15
Saintonge	11	16
Guyenne	9	13
Languedoc	7	5
Brittany	3	3
Alsace	2	3
Angoumois	2	5
Gascony	2	1
Ile-de-France	2	5
Béarn	1	0
Comtat	1	0
Dauphiny	1	0
Foix	1	0
Poitou	0	7
		[25, LARIN]
Provence	0	2
Touraine	0	1
TOTAL	137	156

Jacques Pépin. Canadian recruitment would remain a specialty of La Rochelle until the Conquest of the colony by the English.[20]

It is possible that there were even more Protestants among the immigrants recruited in La Rochelle than the documents attest. Although places of origin are at best an imprecise indicator of the religion of immigrants, they are of interest nonetheless. In the Diocese of La Rochelle, immigration to Canada was clearly higher in the more Protestant areas. This was especially the case with women, 8 percent of whom reached Canada from a region with few Protestants, 4.9 percent from a region of low Protestant density, 10.9 percent from a region of average Protestant density, and 83.3 percent from a region of high Protestant density. The comparable figures for men are, for regions with few Protestants, 1.4 percent, for regions of low Protestant density, 9.2 percent, for regions of average Protestant density, 17.2 percent, and for regions of high Protestant density, 72.1 percent.[21]

It is, at any rate, certain that the immigrants recruited in La Rochelle had a bad reputation in the colony. In 1684, for example, the intendant complained to the naval minister that "they have sent six more girls here to teach the savage girls . . . of Montreal to sew, weave, and make lace; they have taken from around La Rochelle six miserable servants who were found on the street, and whom one would wish to send back to France, not being of good reputation. . . . For these sorts of designs, prudish, aged, and very skilful women are required, and these are young, vicious, and very ignorant."[22] As for the bishop, he had already been complaining for twenty years that "the people taken from La Rochelle are, for the most part, of little conscience and almost without religion, lazy and very slack at work, and very poorly suited to settle [*habituer*] a country, deceivers, blasphemers."[23]

After the Center-west, Canada's Protestants came primarily from Normandy, Guyenne, and Languedoc. The parts of these provinces that were involved were noteworthy as Protestant strongholds, if not for their ties with Canada. Thus, in Guyenne, Périgord and Quercy were more important than the region of Bordeaux, and in Languedoc, five of seven immigrants came from Gard or Ardèche rather than Haute-Garonne. Generally speaking, the figures of Bédard are in agreement with my own. The central western provinces claimed an even greater share of the total in his sample than mine, but in neither did the Swiss and German border regions (as opposed to Switzerland and Germany proper) provide more than a token contribution.

The urban/rural distribution of Protestant immigrants was strikingly different from that of the French population, or even of French Protestants. Of the 139 people to whom I could attribute a community of origin, only 19 came from villages or *bourgs*, while fully 86 percent were urban. Furthermore, over three-quarters of the town dwellers had abandoned cities of more than 10,000 inhabitants, first and foremost La Rochelle. The French situation was virtually a mirror image of this one, with about 85 percent of French men and women living in communities of fewer than 2,000 inhabitants.

Protestant immigration was both concentrated and dispersed, with sixty-nine immigrants coming from La Rochelle[24] and one or two from most other communities. Only Rouen and Marennes (Saintonge) fell somewhere in between, with seven and five Protestants respectively.

The social origins of Protestant immigrants were also uncharacteristic. A social class could be ascribed to 102, or nearly two-thirds of the Protestants in my sample. Of these, there were nine nobles, thirty-three bourgeois, four peasants, twenty-one laborers, and thirty-five artisans. Canadian Protestants thus enjoyed a relatively elevated social status. Like their French counterparts, they were an economically privileged, if legally disadvantaged, population.

The occupational structure of this population was fairly clear, with information available for more than four-fifths of the immigrants.[25] The most important category, soldiers and officers, accounted for a similar percentage of Protestant as of overall immigration, just under a third. Historian André Corvisier's observation that in France "the proportion of Protestants in the army was much higher than what it was in the population" does not seem to apply to Canada.[26]

Other branches of activity peopled by Protestants included commerce, carpentry, the maritime trades, and the clothing industry. Commerce did not predominate over the other options, but it might have had my sample included temporary immigrants more consistently. Regardless of the prohibition against Protestant settlement, at least eleven Protestants arrived as indentured servants.[27]

The sex ratio within this immigrant group was quite unusual. One in every four Protestants was female, as opposed to one in every eight immigrants overall.[28] Most of these women immigrated as single *filles à marier,* with the intent of marrying in the colony, but there were also five married women, two domestic servants, and one child under the age of fifteen. The reasons for this enhanced female presence are not entirely clear. Perhaps, as Father Louis Pérouas has suggested, women were simply more amenable to conversion than men.[29] Immigrants must have been aware that residing in Canada would require outward conformity to Catholicism, at the very least, and such a prospect may have elicited different responses from the two sexes. A second possibility has been suggested by historian Nelson Dawson, who believes that French ecclesiastics intentionally dumped on the colony impoverished young women whom they had "saved" from Protestantism and placed in institutions. In shipping them to Canada, so the argument goes, they hoped to prevent these women from returning to their Protestant milieu, while at the same time freeing themselves from the obligation to support them.[30]

III

What can be concluded from this brief survey of Protestant immigration to Canada? First, that the status of religious minorities in French Canada was more ambiguous in practice than in principle. Protestants could reside in the colony for extended periods or even settle there, provided that they eschewed non-Catholic forms of worship. As temporary immigrants, they could, at most times, identify themselves religiously without risking deportation.

Protestant settlers were primarily scattered individuals from urban and Atlantic backgrounds. Some were noble, but most seem to have come from bourgeois or artisanal families. Curiously, on at least one Canadian seigneurie, they proved to be more committed farmers than their more rural Catholic counterparts.

Unlike the British colonies to the south, Canada never provided a hospitable haven to dissenters, and the few who ended up there were in no position to defy authority. Nonetheless, small numbers of non-Catholics succeeded in carving out a niche for themselves in the long or short term, and their very presence testifies to the impossibility of recruiting a completely homogeneous society from a multi-ethnic and multireligious metropolis.

Notes

1. Cited in Marcel Trudel, *Histoire de la Nouvelle-France*, 3 vols. (Montreal: Fides, 1963–83), 2:25.

2. Cited in Trudel, *Histoire de la Nouvelle-France*, 2:51.

3. Cited in Marc-André Bédard, *Les Protestants en Nouvelle-France, Cahiers d'histoire*, vol. 31 (Quebec City: Société historique de Québec, 1978), 20.

4. Jesuit historian Lucien Campeau provides an alternative reading of the charter of the Hundred Associates, based on the distinction between "the common and general law, which made the whole country under the authority of the king a Catholic country, and the exceptional law, which accorded liberty of conscience to the Huguenots on every territory under royal jurisdiction." According to this reading, "It is not true that New France was made off-limits to the Calvinists in

1627. It could not have been because they were free to live everywhere in French territory in conformity with their faith. When the charter of the Company of the Hundred Associates, fundamental law of New France, prescribed the establishment of a colony of Catholics, it was simply conforming to the laws of the realm; every dependency of the French Crown was by definition Catholic. Any exclusion of the Huguenots would have had to be explicit, for the Edict of Nantes would then have been abrogated on this point." Nonetheless, as Marcel Trudel has pointed out, de facto revocation is exactly what did take place, legal hairsplitting notwithstanding. See Lucien Campeau, *Monumenta Novae Franciae*, 8 vols. (Quebec City: Presses de l'Université Laval, 1967–94), 2:100–102, and Marcel Trudel, "Le Protestantisme s'établit au Canada," *Revue de l'Université Laval* 10 (1955): 3.

5. Cited in Campeau, *Monumenta*, 2:105.

6. Although the siege of La Rochelle did not begin until November 1627, Richelieu arrived outside the city the previous spring. See Louis Canet, *L'Aunis et la Saintonge de Henri IV à la Révolution* (La Rochelle: Pijollet, 1934), 24–32.

7. Campeau, *Monumenta*, 2:101.

8. Cited in Trudel, *Histoire de la Nouvelle-France*, vol. 3, pt. 1:318.

9. Cited in Bédard, *Les Protestants en Nouvelle-France*, 29–30.

10. Letter of Beauharnais and Hocquart to the minister, 18 September 1741, Archives des Colonies, Aix-en-Provence, France. C11A, 75: 14, and Dale Miquelon, *Dugard of Rouen: French Trade to Canada and the West Indies, 1729–1770* (Montreal: McGill-Queen's University Press, 1978), 18, 70, 72, 142.

11. Louis Pérouas, *Le Diocèse de La Rochelle de 1648 à 1724: sociologie et pastorale* (Paris: SEVPEN, 1964), 136.

12. Bédard, *Les Protestants en Nouvelle-France*, 32–35.

13. See Leslie Choquette, *Frenchmen into Peasants: Modernity and Tradition in the Peopling of French Canada* (Cambridge, Mass.: Harvard University Press, 1997), 129–36. The 123 Protestants named by Bédard whom I did not study were mostly soldiers or merchants.

14. See Robert Larin, *Brève Histoire des protestants en Nouvelle-France et au Québec (XVIe-XIXe siècles)* (Saint-Alphonse-de-Granby: Éditions de la Paix, 1998), 137.

15. Campeau, *Monumenta*, 2:101.

16. Mary Ann LaFleur, "Seventeenth-Century New England and New France in Comparative Perspective: Notre-Dame-des-Anges, A Case Study" (Ph.D. diss., University of New Hampshire, 1987). It is unclear why Protestants, who were more likely to come from urban backgrounds, were more stable agricultural settlers than Catholics on this Jesuit seigneurie. Perhaps it had to do with Jesuit Superior Paul Lejeune, himself a converted Huguenot.

17. For other examples of the persistence of Huguenot identity despite religious conformity, see John F. Bosher, *The Canada Merchants, 1713–1763* (Oxford: Oxford University Press, 1987), 43, 119, 161; Bernard Cottret, *The Huguenots in*

England: Immigration and Settlement, c. 1550–1700 (Cambridge, Mass.: Harvard University Press, 1991), 265; Patrice Higonnet, "French," in *Harvard Encyclopedia of American Ethnic Groups*, ed. Stephan Thernstrom (Cambridge, Mass.: Harvard University Press, 1980), 383–85; and Larin, *Brève histoire des protestants*, 111–12.

18. An estimated 7 percent of the population of Lower Poitou was Protestant in 1685. See François Baudry, *La Révocation de l'Édit de Nantes et le protestantisme en Bas-Poitou au XVIIIᵉ siècle* (Trévoux: Jeannin, 1922), 283–84.

19. See Gabriel Debien, *Les Engagés protestants de Chef-Boutonne ou les difficultés de l'histoire sociale* (Poitiers: Oudin, 1956), 8–9, and Larin, *Brève Histoire des protestants*, 133.

20. See Choquette, *Frenchmen into Peasants*, 257–61.

21. This division of the Diocese of La Rochelle into four zones is taken from Louis Pérouas and Nelson Dawson. See Pérouas, *Le Diocèse de La Rochelle*, and Nelson Dawson, "Les Filles à marier envoyées en Nouvelle-France (1632–1685): une émigration protestante?" *Revue d'Histoire de l'Église de France* 72 (1986): 265–89. Archival research carried out in La Rochelle by Pauline Therrien-Fortier lends further support to this hypothesis. Based on this research, up to a third of the immigrants who left La Rochelle for Canada between 1627 and 1700 were raised as Protestants. See Jacques Mathieu, "Mobilité et sédentarité: stratégies familiales en Nouvelle-France," *Recherches Sociographiques* 28 (1987): 216, and Larin, *Brève Histoire des protestants*, 136–37.

22. Letter of De Meulles to the naval minister, 1684, Archives Nationales de France, Archives des Colonies, Aix-en-Provence, France. C11A, 6:399.

23. Memorandum of Bishop Laval, cited in Archange Godbout, "Les Émigrants de 1664," *Mémoires de la Société Généalogique Canadienne-Française* 4 (1951): 224–25.

24. Or seventy-eight according to Bédard, *Les Protestants en Nouvelle-France*, 43.

25. Bédard's occupational sample is not directly comparable to mine because it includes the Anglo-American Protestants. Our conclusions are similar nonetheless. Among the most important categories in his table are the army, commerce, the maritime trades, and carpentry. See Bédard, *Les Protestants en Nouvelle-France*, 61.

26. André Corvisier, *L'Armée française de la fin du XVIIe siècle au ministère de Choiseul: le soldat*, 2 vols. (Paris: PUF, 1964), 1:288–91. According to Canadian documents, the percentage of Protestants in both the army and the population was around 1 percent. The Protestant presence in the army was, however, significantly higher in the aftermath of the Revocation. In 1686, the Canadian intendant counted ninety-nine Protestants in the Canadian troops, or around 8 percent. See Louise Dechêne, *Habitants et marchands de Montréal au XVIIe siècle* (Paris: Plon, 1974), 474–75; and Larin, *Brève Histoire des protestants*, 133.

27. Whereas merchants and sailors were clearly temporary emigrants, the status of indentured servants was more ambiguous. While technically recruited as

colonists, they could not be termed *habitants* prior to the expiration of their contracts, "hence the possibility for Huguenot indentured servants to spend several successive winters without being inconvenienced." See Trudel, *Histoire de la Nouvelle-France*, vol. 3, pt. 2:28–29.

28. Bédard cited only sixteen *filles à marier* for the entire French Regime, whereas my sample included forty-one women. The discrepancy may be a matter of definition, since I considered as Protestant some women who may have converted before their departure. See Bédard, *Les Protestants en Nouvelle-France*, 54–55.

29. For example, of the roughly 300 abjurations that occurred in La Rochelle in the three years following the siege, fully 80 percent concerned women. According to Pérouas, "the principal explanation of these conversions appears to be the jump in the birthrate, habitual in the aftermath of hecatombs, doubtless linked to the disappearance of numerous young Protestant men. Even supposing that the vital registers are not fully complete, we must admit that the movement toward conversion barely affected the Huguenot population as a whole." Similarly, among New England captives in New France, women were far more likely to convert to Catholicism than men. See Louis Pérouas, "Sur la démographie rochelaise," *Annales: Économies, Sociétés, Civilisations* 16 (1961): 1133–34, and John Demos, *The Unredeemed Captive: A Family Story from Early America* (New York: Knopf, 1994), 79.

30. Dawson, "Les Filles à marier envoyées en Nouvelle-France," 286–88. Dawson's hypothesis, while fascinating and plausible, nonetheless lacks conclusive proof.

THIRTEEN

The Protestants and the Colonization of the French West Indies

Gérard Lafleur and Lucien Abénon

National Origins of the Protestants

The Huguenots

The Huguenots played a crucial role in the French Antilles during the first years of colonization. Of diverse origins, they had a significant economic influence, notably during the beginning of the sugar industry, for which France was in great part indebted to the Dutch settlers from Brazil. Nonethless, the Huguenots in the French Islands had to face persecution by Louis XIV, who wished as much to eradicate Protestantism in the West Indies as in France.

When the first island, Saint-Christophe (St. Kitts) was officially conquered by Belain d'Esnambuc in the name of the French king, an independent Huguenot community was living on the island among small bands of Carib aborigines. The French settlers, all from Normandy, were headed by Le Vasseur. They cultivated tobacco, as did some English colonists and a few Caribs. Although the rules of the *Compagnie de Saint-Christophe*, which had just been chartered, officially prohibited the immigration of non-Catholic settlers, Huguenots made up the majority of the island's inhabitants. In 1640, Le Vasseur and a group of his coreligionists, with the material assistance of the Governor-General Poincy, attempted to found a Huguenot republic on the Island of Tortuga off the coast of Saint-Domingue (Haiti). Le Vasseur had barred all Catholics from the island and installed his own pastor. This experiment lasted twelve years and ended with the assassination of its leader.

The origins of the other settlers are quite difficult to trace because Huguenots who resided on the islands did not have their own church or probate records. These documents were kept by priests, and their appearance on a register necessarily implied a religious ceremony (christening, marriage, or burial). Therefore, historians have had to use other sources such as censuses or administrative and private correspondence in order to identify Huguenots among the population. The forced conversion that the Huguenots faced in 1687 also gives some details about those who did abjure and those who obstinately refused and chose to emigrate. The lists that were compiled during this period and the inventories of their property also provide information.

This research shows (table 1) that the great majority of the Huguenots who settled in the Antilles until 1687 came from La Rochelle, then from Dieppe, Bordeaux, and their hinterland. The others were from scattered areas throughout France. The first who settled came from Normandy and Brittany because it was in these areas that persecution, or at least limitations on their activities were first enforced. La Rochelle provided a large contingent of emigrants from the time Jean-Baptiste Colbert had chosen it as a supply base for the Caribbean colonies in the 1660s. The port's growth was well established by 1664 with the foundation of the *Compagnie des Indes Occidentales*, (West Indies Company) whose capital was supplied by bankers from La Rochelle. When Bordeaux and its hinterland, which converged with southern trade routes following the Garonne Valley, began to gain economic importance, increasing numbers of Huguenots from that area began settling the islands.

The Dutch Reformed

Although small in number in comparison with settlers from other nations, the Dutch also played an important role in the colonization of the French Antilles. The Dutch had a very large merchant fleet which allowed them to keep the area well supplied, despite the fact that the French monopoly prohibited them from purchasing these goods. They established themselves as merchants in major market towns such as Basse-Terre, Guadeloupe, Saint Pierre, Martinique, and on Saint-Christophe, maintaining ties to Amsterdam, Rotterdam, Middleburg, and Flessingen. In 1654, the situation changed radically as the Dutch who had settled in Brazil were driven out by the Portuguese.

Under the aegis of the Dutch West Indies Company, the Dutch had established their sovereignty over a vast territory comprising all of the

Brazilian "northeast." The Portuguese led a great offensive against the Dutch and defeated them. The Dutch surrender was signed in Taborda, near Recife on 25 January 1654, and allowed them to leave with their property and the manufacturing elements of their sugar plantations. Controlling the sugar trade to northwest Europe and the slave trade in Africa, the Dutch searched for land amenable to the cultivation of sugarcane.

Some of them landed in Martinique, but the governor, Jacques Dyel Du Parquet, who welcomed them at first, then turned them away under pressure by the Jesuits who reminded him of the laws that barred non-Catholics from the island. They made their way to Guadeloupe where they were warmly received by Governor Charles de Houël, who had tried unsuccessfully to grow sugarcane. About 1,200 Dutch refugees aboard 10 ships sailed into the harbor of Basse-Terre. Among the 900 who landed there were 300 Walloon and Flemish soldiers, 300 slaves, 200 women, and the rest *maîtres de case*, that is, sugar growers.[1] One thousand people out of a total island population of fifteen thousand represented a significant demographic shift. This radically changed the characteristics of the population with the introduction of many slaves who replaced the indentured servants. They created an economic system that endured until the nineteenth century.

The plantation owners turned to Africa for labor and looked to Europe to sell and ship their products from the colonies, introducing the French West Indies into the world economy. Furthermore, troops constituted a very significant addition to the population at the time when the wars with the Caribs had resumed. Grenada was so sparsely inhabited that it was all but abandoned when reinforcements of Dutch soldiers arrived and maintained it under French control.

The Dutch settled on all of the islands but were the most numerous in Guadeloupe. They purchased land cleared by poor white settlers (*petits blancs*) who were then immigrating to Saint-Domingue. Guadeloupe enjoyed a period of extraordinary prosperity which governors of the other islands envied, especially the governor of Martinique, Du Parquet, who had rebuffed them. However, when more Dutch settlers later arrived from Brazil, this time he received them graciously and offered them land in the Grand Cul de Sac, which became Fort-Royal and later, Fort-de-France. This settlement was raided and partially destroyed by Caribs. A few families, most of them Sephardic Jews, took refuge in the town of

Saint-Pierre where they formed a small community. The other settlers, all Calvinists, were scattered across the island.

The original West Indian Huguenot population was thus strengthened by Dutch settlers, also of the Reformed faith. In a Catholic environment, these Protestants, despite their diverse origins, formed a close-knit community through endogamous marriages and commercial alliances. This community was stronger in Guadeloupe than in Martinique and had more of a French influence on Saint-Christophe than on the other islands. It was less visible on the smaller islands such as Marie-Galante, Sainte-Croix, Saint-Martin, Saint-Barthélemy, and Sainte-Lucie.

The Economic Influence of the Protestants

Trade

From an economic standpoint, a distinction must be made between early colonization and the period after 1654, when sugarcane cultivation was introduced. From the beginning of colonization, the Dutch controlled trade without having settlements. Planters bought provisions from them and sold them their products. The Dutch went to France, however, to contract indentured servants for terms of three years. Incidentally, servant labor networks show that most servants hired to serve in the Antilles were Huguenots whereas most Catholics went to Canada.

Investments in the Antilles were usually made by groups of families who traditionally engaged in trade with Newfoundland and Morocco, and who began sending a few ships to the islands. Then, in order to insure their cargo, they would invest in a plantation (*habitation*), which would be managed by a member of the family. They hailed from Dieppe, Le Havre, Saint-Mâlo and increasingly, from La Rochelle, whose mercantile bourgeoisie was starting to take an interest in the Antilles. French ships were so small, however, that goods were not sufficiently protected during the voyage, and many shipowners instead specialized in transporting indentured servants.[2] An illustration of this phenomenon is Jacques Pépin, a La Rochelle merchant who participated in nine voyages between 1636 and 1655. He began with an eighty-five–ton ship, which he chartered with two other merchants. Every year he sent a frigate to the islands until his death in 1664. Nicolas Bonneau is another typical example. He began trading with the French Antilles in 1643, at a time when part of his trade was with Morocco. He was the principal member of a family association equipped both to fish in Newfoundland and trade with Spain and Morocco. This association first engaged a fifty-ton ship to the Caribbean trade, then later used larger vessels.[3] Over time, these associations developed an interest in buying property, especially after 1654, with the development of sugarcane cultivation. As with shipping, each partner would buy a share in order to reduce the risk.

In the 1660s, Colbert tried to eliminate Dutch traders from the islands by creating the *Compagnie des Indes Occidentales*, which had a monopoly on trade. In order to create this company, he approached Huguenot financiers. Despite his opposition, the edict that chartered this new entity prohibited the participation of non-Catholics, but this measure was generally ignored, as the company employed many Protestants. The first company *commis généraux* (principal agents) of Martinique and Guadeloupe, Du Buc and Rouvelet (or Rovelet) and later Pierre Le Royer of Saint-Christophe were Huguenots and experienced difficulties due to their religion. They had forged ties with the French and Dutch Calvinist merchants in market towns who were hostile to the new *Compagnie*. Minor posts were also held by Protestants already settled in the islands. In Guadeloupe, for example, sieur Thévenon was a weight-master for the West Indies Company in the town of Baillif, and Reck and Jean Le Royer held the same post in Basse-Terre.

Agriculture

The cultivation of sugarcane and the production of sugar expanded the trading role of the French and Dutch Protestants. Attempts to produce sugar on the French islands began early on, with the efforts of Dutchman Samuel Trézel, though with disappointing results. The Dutch who arrived from Brazil had brought a select type of cane and a technique for bleaching the sugar and manufacturing *formes*, porous clay containers for removing the molasses from the raw sugar.[4] Upon their arrival, they purchased high-priced, cleared land, but within a short time they not only recovered the cost of the land but also firmly established themselves as growers and producers of sugar. Eleven years later, the governor of Guadeloupe, Charles-François Du Lion wrote to the Seigneurs of the West Indies Company that "the majority of the beautiful plantations on the island were started with loans from these foreigners."[5]

Most of the sugar planters who succeeded in the French Antilles were in partnership with financiers based in Rotterdam, Flessingen, Leiden, and Hamburg who had also provided the funds to develop Dutch Brazil. Several examples show that these partnerships, which were contracted for trade with Brazil, continued in the French West Indies. This was the case of the Sweerts (Suers in the French documents) brothers, Paul, Jacob, and Jean. Together they owned a ship and operated a company in Brazil, to which one of their wives later made reference.[6] One of the brothers, Paul, a merchant in Amsterdam, was responsible for receiving goods shipped from the Antilles and sending supplies back. When they took refuge in Guadeloupe, they maintained the same system. Paul remained in Amsterdam, Jacob bought and managed a *habitation* near Basse-Terre, and Jean was in charge of the warehouse in Basse-Terre.[7] The financial syndicate consisted of a main company run by several members of the family, with several branches composed of each individual family member and their outside partnerships, which complemented and strengthened the parent company.[8] Trade relations of the French islands were essentially conducted with the Netherlands, at least until 1664 when the *Compagnie des Indes Occidentales* was chartered. French and Dutch Protestants came into contact in the Antilles, quickly found interests in common, and worked to preserve them.

The Huguenots used the same trade techniques as the Dutch. They formed family partnerships with the financial backing of their coreligionists. The occupations that they could legally practice, maritime trade and banking, led them to invest in colonial activities. When in 1664 Colbert founded the *Compagnie des Indes Occidentales*, he successfully requested their assistance. At the beginning, they were small investors who wished to diversify their commercial activities. In fact, those activities which had first been perceived as minor became more important. Sugar planting in the Antilles became their main occupation while the trade component ranked behind.[9] These investors, who were merchants and wealthy financiers accustomed to making large-scale investments, had close mutual ties. In the Antilles, they met fellow Dutch Calvinists with whom they felt united in the same cause. This rapprochement is at the origin of the formation of a unique social class made of Protestant "bourgeois" who owned land and sugar plantations.

In 1669, an account of annual sugar production was done for Guadeloupe.[10] This document gives the historian an idea of the Protestants' contribution, which was particularly important in Guadeloupe and Marie-Galante. For Guadeloupe, sugar production was estimated at 3,579,000 pounds of sugar for 101 sugar plantations. Protestants owned twenty-nine of these, with a production of 1,138,000 pounds (32 percent). For Marie-Galante, Protestant-controlled production amounted to 172,000 pounds out of 796,000 (21 percent), with three sugar plantations out of twelve. In 1671, a census and land survey were conducted for the larger islands.[11] In Guadeloupe, 104 sugar mills, 103 sugar plantations, and twenty-two vinegar distilleries were inventoried. Protestants owned thirty-four mills (33 percent), thirty-five sugar plantations (34 percent) and nine distilleries (41 percent). In Martinique, twenty-four of the 112 sugar plantations that were inventoried (21 percent) belonged to Huguenots. At that date, out of 7,793,000 pounds of sugar processed on the island, Huguenots produced 2,003,000 (26 percent). Thus, in the 1670s, Huguenots controlled between one-fourth and one-third of the value of sugar production for Guadeloupe, Martinique, and Marie-Galante, before measures were taken to first drive the Dutch settlers from the islands and then limit the freedom of the Protestant community in general.

The Religious Question until the Revocation of the Edict of Nantes

At first, there was true tolerance of the Protestants. Priests had no qualms about christening children of reformed parents in return for a vague promise of a future—and quite uncertain—conversion. Thus, for example, a priest at Capesterre, Guadeloupe, recorded: "On October 17, 1654, I christened Elisabeth aged 15 months, daughter of the Seigneur known as Flamore, a reformed Walloon who promised to raise her in our religion in which I was instructing him."[12] The priest just added the mention "heretic" next to the parents' names. This relative tolerance did not extend to all religious acts. In Guadeloupe, for example, Protestant marriages do not appear to have been performed openly. It seems that children were christened in the Catholic Church but that the Huguenots married off the French islands, either in France or on foreign-held islands, and accepted that funerals would not be religious in character.

Things changed quickly as the reign of Louis XIV reached its midpoint. As early as 1679, a memoir regarding Huguenots and Jews settled on the islands accused them "of having their christening, marriage, and funerary ceremonies in English churches."[13] This accusation was undoubtedly aimed at the reformed population of Saint-Christophe, who could easily attend Protestant services since all they had to do was to cross a poorly watched border to the English half of the island. Their problem, of course, was to have these acts recorded by French priests, who were the only French authority empowered to make them legal.

The Code Noir, promulgated a few months before the Edict of Fontainebleau (Edict of Revocation) in March 1685, declared all reformed marriages illegal, and therefore made it impossible for Huguenots to have legitimate offspring. This measure essentially placed all non-Catholic settlers outside the law. Huguenots could only submit or emigrate. Among those who remained, a few converted but with little sincerity. In 1698, the intendant François-Roger Robert explained that

> most of the Huguenots who own a *habitation* and Negroes are concerned enough to send their slaves to church on Sundays and holidays, but they, their wives and their children dispense themselves of the sacraments and of all the exercises of the Catholic religion and when some of them are about to pass away they usually die obstinate in their heresy refusing to see and hear a priest. If they want to marry, a few submit themselves to the rituals of the church and others seek men of religion easy to persuade or some ship chaplain who marry them with little difficulty, which nonetheless rarely occurs.[14]

Evidently such a situation was very unfavorable to the reformed population, which saw the relative tolerance that they had once enjoyed disappear.

The Edict of Fontainebleau and the Huguenots in the Antilles

Measures that restricted freedom of worship in France had few repercussions in the Antilles because no churches with a confirmed pastor had ever been officially organized. Huguenots had always worshipped in private and continued to do so without hindrance. Huguenots from France who had been sentenced to the galleys for refusing to abjure settled in the islands. They found refuge among their coreligionists, who quickly helped them to escape.[15] Louis XIV seems to have regarded the religious question in the colonies as a secondary problem to be addressed as a special case.

The Role of the Jesuits

The Jesuits' offensive against Protestantism became more extensive with the end of the Dutch War (1672–1678) and the death of the governor general, Jean-Charles de Baas, a Huguenot although officially converted to Catholicism. The new governor general, Charles de Courbon, Comte De Blénac, knew the policy that was followed in France regarding the Huguenots. The local context was favorable for the eradication of Protestantism.

In 1678, the Father Superior of Martinique, Reverend Father Farganel, accused the Huguenots of holding *assemblées* (conventicles).[16] The day after these accusations were made, on 1 September, Sieur Turpin, an administrative and criminal judge on Martinique, received instructions to "use all the rigor of the judicial system against all those who took part in the *assemblée*." The entire community was sentenced to a heavy fine. A month later, the Capuchin who was responsible for the Fort-Royal parish asked the governor of Martinique to "keep them from worshipping at the head of the ships in the careenage in hush tone." The governor discussed it with the intendant and turned down the request.[17]

In Saint-Christophe, the Catholic authorities tried to humiliate the Huguenots by "forcing them to decorate their front doors" on the day of the Blessed Sacrament, which they refused to do. They were sentenced, once again, to a heavy fine.[18] Despite threats that became more and more specific, private worship continued, albeit more discreetly. The local administrative authorities responded to the solicitations of the religious orders with so little enthusiasm that the latter went directly to the king.

In 1679, anti-Huguenot measures were advocated but never implemented. It seems that this was due to the influence of Colbert, who wished to maintain the prosperity of the islands. Memoirs such as "Remonstrance regarding the Jews on Martinique" (26 December 1681), which were meant to dissociate the Jewish problem from the Protestant, were sent to the governor general on 13 February 1683. This was not without consequence as twenty-four months later the order to expel the Jews was received in Martinique.[19]

With the Jewish "problem" solved and the death of Colbert (1683), a new memoir on the Huguenots in the Antilles left France in 1685.[20] It advocated the implementation of the same measures as those in France. This request was well heeded, as shown by the order later addressed to De Blénac and Gabriel Du Maitz de Goimpy on 30 September 1686 which forced local Huguenots to abjure.[21]

Implementation of the King's Orders

Upon receiving these orders, local authorities appear to have been dismayed. Living in the islands, they were cognizant of the socioeconomic effects of their implementation. On 6 March 1687, a memoir from De Blénac and the intendant Du Maitz acknowledging the receipt of these orders described the situation. They had acted with great moderation. They met with the superiors of the religious missions to adopt a concerted policy. A report on their discussions showing that "they had resolved to postpone for a few weeks the implementation of the royal order to slow down the rate of emigration" was sent to the king.[22] These orders had caused a lot of agitation and the fear of rebellion was great, especially on the islands where the Protestants were the more numerous, as in Guadeloupe and Saint-Christophe. The authorities had to reassure the population. De Blénac wrote to all the local governors instructing them to observe the Huguenots and prepare them to meet with the intendant.

The time came to implement the royal orders. The Huguenots of Martinique were gathered together on 17 March. The orders were read to them, and the island's military commander was instructed to register conversions while the governor general and the intendant were busy on the other islands.[23] These two officials went to Guadeloupe in order to assist that island's governor. They assembled the Huguenots in the fort in Basse-Terre on March 26 where they were given the orders without any comment and allowed to return home.[24] The governor-general sailed back to Martinique on 31 March while the intendant went to Saint-Christophe. There, the situation had deteriorated because the island's governor, the Chevalier de Saint-Laurens, had imposed restrictive measures since 1686, which had spread fear among most local Huguenots and prompted them to flee to the English side. When the intendant arrived, the governor summoned all remaining Huguenots and ordered them to abjure.

Abjurations

Conversion was the main objective of the royal policy, and local Huguenots had to be persuaded without being frightened so as to avoid an exodus. Due to the efforts of the religious orders, especially the Jesuits in Martinique, some Protestants had abjured before royal orders reached the islands. The others stood firm in their faith. Those who owned goods and property such as land and sugar plantations and who had not planned an escape were forced to convert, sincerely or nominally. Historians know how these abjurations took place in Capesterre, Guadeloupe, because conversion rolls (*registres de catholicité*) have been preserved. The main Huguenot heads of families were gathered in the fort of Saint-Charles de Basse-Terre on 26 March 1687. Easter celebrations being over, Governor Hinselin and the *lieutenant du roi*, De La Malmaison, started to work on obtaining the conversions of the most prominent Huguenots on the island.

On 10 April 1687, the main heads of families repaired to the Dominican convent in Capesterre, where they abjured "all sorts of heresies and especially Calvin's."[25] Among them was Jean Poyen, a sugar planter who held the rank of captain in the cavalry and who embodied the tie between the Huguenots and the Protestants of Dutch origins. Poyen hailed from Sainte-Affrique du Rouergue, Languedoc, whereas his wife, Lucresse Ganspoël, was born in Brazil, the daughter of Samuel Ganspoël and Pauline Vandevelde. Poyen was at the center of a familial and mercantile network and was both an influential settler and a Protestant symbol. He was accompanied by his brother, François, a prominent merchant who owned several shops in Guadeloupe, Saint-Christophe, and Bordeaux.[26]

Also among these first converts was Moyse Petit, from La Rochelle. He was married to the daughter of Nicolas Classen, who had entered in partnership with Charles Houël in 1654. Classen's estate was extensive and was being managed by his stepson, who served as his executor. Petit went to the convent with his brother-in-law Samuel Classen, aged 19.

Isaac Nicolas, also from La Rochelle, was a sugar planter with ties to the Parisian banking community. Others were not so eminent, such as Jean Duffaud from Saint-Affrique du Rouergue and Paul de Gennes, from a noble family in Brittany. De La Malmaison followed the group to serve as a witness, which shows the importance given to these conversions since these were to serve as examples. Afterwards, Dominican friars visited their homes to register the conversions of their wives and children, as well as that of Pierre Brozet, captain of an infantry company. Conversions continued until 12 July. Historians do not have the same type of records for the other Guadeloupe parishes, but it is quite likely that the procedure was nearly identical, as well as in Martinique, whose governor had received similar orders. Island officials thus could boast to the king that all Huguenots in the French Antilles had converted to Catholicism without violence or damage, which resulted in royal congratulations.[27]

On Saint-Christophe, the conversions did not take place with such apparent ease. The island was divided between the French and the English, and its governor lacked psychological and political acumen. His arbitrary measures frightened away a large number of Huguenots. Intendant Du Maitz went to the island and personally registered the conversions of eighteen or twenty remaining Huguenots. Among them was Mme. de Sallenave, the wife of the *lieutenant du roi*, who headed the Huguenot resistance and regularly attended Protestant services with a group of Huguenots on the English side of the island.[28]

At the end of May, in theory, most of the Huguenots in the French Antilles had converted and were thereafter referred to as *nouveaux convertis*. With the exception of Marie-Galante, where the governor announced the conversion of five people, smaller islands were purposefully ignored to avoid weakening an already tiny population.

Early escapes

Among the types of escape, the historian must distinguish between those that preceded forced conversions from other kinds. The islands remained a crossroads, and after a more or less lengthy stay, settlers often left for other colonies that held more opportunity for them, such as the Greater Antilles or the North American mainland. In this type of out-migration, no mention should be made of religion. Flight for religious reasons was regarded as such from 1685 when the Edict of Fontainebleau was implemented in the islands through the promulgation of the Code Noir, a "Royal edict regulating order on the islands of America."[29] The first articles of this edict prohibited Judaism and limited Protestantism. This law had no practical effect on the Huguenot community, as the chevalier de Saint-Laurens, governor of Saint-Christophe, confirmed and deplored.[30] As for the Jews, they had already been expelled. At that time only the less-affluent Huguenots had made a discreet departure and can be identified only in the archival records of their destinations.[31]

As we have seen, the first Huguenots to escape were from Saint-Christophe because of the governor's policy. They were merchants who sold their goods and then, towards the latter part of 1685, crossed to the English side, where they knew they would be welcomed and could find ships bound for North America. Then the movement swelled as sugar planters began to leave. In April 1686, "two entire families of the religion [Huguenot] reached the English quarter with their furniture, cattle and about 40 Negroes."[32] These families were from Basse-Terre, but on the other side of the island in Pointe-à-Sable, Ance Louvet, and Capesterre, other families were also fleeing, leaving behind their land if they could not sell it beforehand.[33] Many Huguenots escaped over a relatively short period of time. In Basse-Terre, for example, without counting the slaves that they had taken with them, the governor counted forty Huguenot departures.[34]

In Guadeloupe, a few families escaped preemptively but the movement was never as large as on Saint-Christophe. Two sugar planter families of Dutch origin (Corneille and Zuart) left the island with their goods for Surinam, where they had relatives. Another, a merchant by the name of Gombeau, left for New York. These early escapes enabled Huguenots to flee under relatively good conditions and relocate with their slaves without major difficulties. As a result, the king recommended "that the orders given in that respect be such as to make impossible for Huguenots to escape with their possessions and Negroes."[35]

With the exception of the governor of Saint-Christophe, most officials had resigned themselves to the fact that it was impossible to retain people who wanted to leave. They did not have the means to control both the English and Dutch islands and the coasts. Besides, French settlers were accustomed to smuggling with their foreign neighbors.

There seems to be a common denominator among these early escapes. They all occurred between April and July 1686. Most Huguenots regrouped on the English side of Saint-Christophe and chartered a ship to New York, where they arrived in November. This group was mostly composed of Huguenots from Saint-Christophe with a few Protestants from Guadeloupe and Martinique.[36] They quickly merged with the New York Huguenot community that had been present in the colony for many years.

Escapes Following Promulgation of the Royal Orders
As has been shown, the royal orders were received with mixed feelings, depending on local conditions. However, the requirement to abjure, attend mass, and especially to receive the sacraments forced the

Huguenots to take a stand. On Saint-Christophe, the Protestants reacted immediately, as those who remained knew that the governor was impatiently waiting for these orders and that they would be subject to many humiliating and arbitrary measures.

Therefore, when on 26 March 1687 the arrival of the governor-general and the intendant on Guadeloupe to obtain the conversions of the Protestant population became known, the Huguenots of Saint-Christophe began preparing their escape while waiting for confirmation that reached them a day later. In a few days, all the remaining Huguenots crossed the border to the English side, with the assistance of English officers.[37] On Saint-Martin, which was divided between France and the Netherlands, Huguenot refugees were helped by Dutch officers who sent ships for their rescue. The Chevalier de Saint-Laurens denounced this situation to the king, writing that "officers of the King of England and the governor of Saint-Eustache [Statia] encourage our soldiers and our indentured servants to desert and the Huguenots to flee on their ships from this island [Saint-Christophe] and Saint-Martin."[38] On the other islands, escapes were spread over several years. In these cases, Huguenots waited for the laws that prohibited them from selling their properties to fall into disuse. A family member would remain behind to maintain the estate while relatives settled on an English island or the North American mainland. As a consequence of this exodus, the Huguenot community on the island gradually decreased and the wealth of its remaining members increased.

The Post-Revocation Context

From a religious perspective, the Revocation had no immediate decisive impact. Some Huguenots left and others remained. Eventually, however, the islands became *toutes catholiques*. Remaining Huguenots converted first nominally while doing nothing that might shock Catholics, then with more sincerity. This evolution often stretched over several generations. While a father remained faithful to his faith, his son ceased to be a practicing Protestant, and the grandson became a true Catholic.

In Guadeloupe, a few families such as the Poyens, the Gressiers, and the Besnards resisted religious absorption for a longer period of time. They intermarried to secretly preserve their Protestantism but needed dispensations for their consanguineous marriages, which added to the basic problem of the illegality of Huguenot marriage. A case in point is the marriage between Hubert Gressier and his cousin Suzanne Poyen that took place in a Catholic Church after the bride and groom had done all they could to avoid conversion for several years.

The death of a Huguenot could lead to equally serious difficulties. When they were near death, Huguenots preferred to conceal their condition so as not to be interred in a Catholic cemetery. In 1734, the parish priest of Capesterre, Guadeloupe, noted in the church records: "Although everyone knows, it has just come to my knowledge that on July 9 of last year, demoiselle Poyen, widow of Sieur Jean Gressier, passed away. She was buried in her garden as a Calvinist despite my efforts to bring her to the bosom of the Church. She was 52 years old as indicated by her son-in-law Hubert Gressier."[39]

On Martinique, the Edict of Fontainebleau struck a decisive blow to Protestantism. A document from 1711 shows that the Huguenot community was more widely dispersed than on Guadeloupe, even if a few families remained in Case-Pilote, intermarrying among themselves.[40] For example, the Lecurieux, Doëns, and Volcart families seem to have experienced more difficulty in preserving their faith than those on Guadeloupe as shown by the fact that Jean Doëns, one of the key members of the Martinique Huguenot community, was buried in 1726 "under the pew of Monsieur Volcart after receiving the last rites."[41] This was also the case of his wife who died two years later.

Nonetheless, there do not seem to have been as many abjurations in Martinique as in Guadeloupe simply because fewer eighteenth-century conversion rolls have been preserved, with the exception of a few parishes. In 1715, however, the priest of Macouba interred Pierre Laujol, aged 25, who "after converting, died in the Catholic religion."[42] Protestantism would recede faster in Martinique than in Guadeloupe.

From the eighteenth century on, the Huguenot communities inhabiting the Lesser Antilles continued to decline until they disappeared completely. In 1789, they no longer appeared to exist except perhaps on Saint-Martin. It was only much later in the nineteenth century that these communities came to life again but with a very different social and religious framework. Some old Huguenot families who have survived and who belong to the Creole aristocracy hardly remember their religious roots.

Notes

This essay was translated from French by Bertrand and Meredith Van Ruymbeke. The translators wish to thank Philip Boucher for his comments.

1. Réverend Père Dutertre, *Histoire Générale des Antilles habitées par les Français*, 4 vols. (Paris, 1667–71; reprint, Fort de France, Martinique: Editions des horizons caraïbes, 1973), 1:438–39.

2. Ibid., 1:469.

3. Marcel Delafosse, "La Rochelle et les îles," *Revue d'Histoire des Colonies* 36 (1949): 267–68.

4. Poyen de Sainte-Marie, *De l'exploitation des sucreries*, (Point-à-Pitre: Year IX of the French Republic 1807), 87.

5. Du Lion to the minister, (8 April 1665). Centre des Archives d'Outre-Mer (hereafter C.A.O.M.), Aix-en-Provence, Colonies, C7A1 fol. 8.

6. Petition from Constance Van Ganspoël, 1673, C.A.O.M., Colonies, C7A2 fol. 290.

7. Roll of the inhabitants of Guadeloupe, 1664, C.A.O.M., G1 469.

8. Petition from de Loër to M. Du Lion, to the *Conseil Souverain*, 1673, C.A.O.M., C7A2, fol. 291.

9. For investments in the sugar plantations, see Delafosse, "La Rochelle et les îles," 261–62.

10. 26 Dec. 1669, C.A.O.M., C7A1.

11. C.A.O.M., G1 468 Guadeloupe, G1 Martinique (no extant census), G1 471 Saint-Christophe.

12. Archives départementales de la Guadeloupe, microfilm 5, Registres de Catholicité de Capesterre.

13. C.A.O.M., C8B1, Mémoire touchant les huguenots etles Juifs de l'Amérique, 1679.

14. De Robert à N. de Basville, C.A.O.M., Aix-en-Provence, B21 fol. 173 (27 August 1698).

15. Gérard Lafleur, *Les protestants aux Antilles françaises du Vent sous l'ancien régime* (Basse-Terre, Guadeloupe: Société d'Histoire de la Guadeloupe, 1988), 180–202.

16. Copy of the order given to Sieur Turpin, (1 Sept. 1678), C.A.O.M., C8A2, fol. 111.

17. De Blénac to the minister, (1 Oct. 1678), C.A.O.M., C8A2, fol. 87.

18. Memoir on the Jews and the Huguenots, 1679, C.A.O.M., C8B1.

19. Letter from the King to the Chevalier de Saint-Laurens and to [Intendant] Bégon, (24 Sept. 1683) C.A.O.M., B10, fol. 9. De Blénac was then absent from the colony.

20. Memoir on the Huguenots in America, ca. 1685 [?], C.A.O.M., C8B1.

21. Letter to De Blénac and Du Maitz, (30 Sept. 1686), C.A.O.M., B12, fol. 71.

22. Memoir from De Blénac to the King, (6 March 1687), C.A.O.M., C8A4, fol. 233.

23. Letter to De Blénac and Du Maitz in Guadeloupe, (28 March 1687), C.A.O.M., C7A3, fol. 117; Excerpts from letters written from the islands between 15 August 1686 and 6 May 1687, C.A.O.M., C8A4, fol. 249.

24. de Hinselin to the minister, (5 May 1687), C.A.O.M., C7A3, fol. 117 and fol. 143.

25. Church records of the parish of Capesterre, (10 April 1687), Archives Départementales de la Guadeloupe.

26. Memoir from the King to MM De Blénac and Du Maitz, 31 September 1686, C.A.O.M., B12, fol. 71,.

27. Memoir from the King, (25 August 1687), C.A.O.M., B13, f.64; From the minister to Blénac, (25 August 1687), B13, fol. 76.

28. Memoir for the Marquis de Seignelay, (25 May 1687), C.A.O.M., C10 B1, Box V.

29. *Le Code Noir ou recueil des réglements* [1685], (Basse-Terre: Société d'Histoire de la Guadeloupe; reprint, Fort-de-France: Société d'Histoire de la Martinique, 1980).

30. Memoir from De Saint-Laurens, (23 July 1686), C.A.O.M., C10B1, Box V.

31. See for example the records cited in Charles W. Baird, *History of the Huguenot Migration to America*, 2 vols. (New York: Dodd & Mead, 1885), 206, n. 2.

32. Memoir from Saint Laurens to the Marquis de Seignelay, (23 July 1686), C.A.O.M., C10 B1, Box V.

33. Lafleur, *Histoire des protestants*, 238.

34. Excerpt from "The estimates of Huguenots who have left this island", (24 May 1687), C.A.O.M., G1 498, fol. 103.

35. The King to M. Hinselin, (13 Jan. 1687), C.A.O.M, B13, fol. 5.

36. Baird, *History of the Huguenot*, 231n. 3, 232n. 1.

37. Memoir from de Saint-Laurens to the Marquis de Seignelay, (25 May 1687), C.A.O.M., C10B1.

38. Memoir from de Saint-Laurens to the King, (8 Nov. 1687), C.A.O.M., C8A4, F.370.

39. Church records of the parish of Capesterre, Guadeloupe, Archives Départementales de la Guadeloupe, microfilm, 5Mi.

40. List of Huguenots who are in the French Islands in America, C.A.O.M., C8A18, fol. 141.

41. Archives départementales de la Martinique (ADM), Registers de Catholicité.
42. Ibid.

TABLE 1: *Geographic Origins of the Huguenots Settled in the French Antilles*

Origine des protestants français

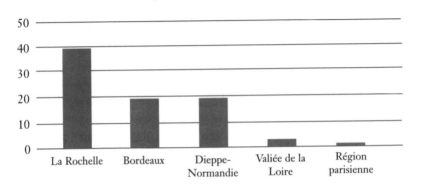

284

FOURTEEN

The Cape Huguenots and Their Legacy in Apartheid South Africa

Philippe Denis

On 31 December 1687, twenty-two French Protestants boarded the *Voorschoten*, a ship chartered by the Delft Chamber of Commerce, for the Cape. Their names—Marais, Fouché, Pinard, Malherbe, Le Roux, etc. —are borne today by thousands of Afrikaners. In the months that followed, six similar ships arrived at the Cape. In total, approximately 180 Huguenots immigrated to South Africa between 1687 and 1689. They played a decisive role in the development of the new colony. On account of an active policy of assimilation, they did not take long in integrating completely with the group of Dutch settlers. Their descendants contributed, for better and for worse, to the history of South Africa.

This paper intends to present the results of the South African research on the Huguenot refuge in the Cape. It will cover the period from the arrival of the first ships of refugees from Holland (1688) to the interruption of religious services in French in the colony (1726). The last section will consider the question of the long-term influence of the Huguenot immigration on South African society.[1]

The historiography of the Huguenot Refuge in South Africa presents two contradictory aspects. On one hand, it is over-abundant.[2] There are countless books and articles, in English, Afrikaans, or French, on the history of the South African Refuge, written particularly on the occasion of anniversaries. Huguenot history is part of the Afrikaner heritage. In a country isolated for a long time and subject to intense ideological pressures, all that could contribute to the exaltation of Afrikaner nationalism was welcome.

Yet, this abundant production is, on the whole, of mediocre quality. The study of Huguenot genealogy is flourishing,[3] but a rigorous demographic study of the Huguenot population is still lacking.[4] The economic aspects of the refuge were better studied,[5] but the works on this topic give an impression of amateurism. The areas best covered are the religious history[6] and the history of language and literature.[7] They are both located at the heart of the Afrikaner identity.

One has to note, finally, the scarcity of publication of the sources. The principal collection of documents relating to the Refuge's history, the work of Colin Graham Botha,[8] dates from 1919 and contains several errors and omissions. The correspondence of Pierre Simond, the first minister of the French Protestant community in the Cape Colony, deserves, without doubt, publication.[9] Furthermore, the catechism of the French refugees, which exists in a Dutch version, remains unpublished.[10] Several lists of Huguenots were compiled by modern authors.[11] They are very useful, but they do not replace the critical publication of the original documents.

The Huguenots in South Africa

The First French Protestants at the Cape

The planned immigration of Huguenots to South Africa began in 1687. But the French Protestant immigration movement had begun earlier. The first French Protestant at the Cape was none other than Marie de La Quellerie, the wife of Jan van Riebeeck, the founder and first commander of the colony. Van Riebeeck noted the following in his journal, on 13 June 1660:

> Today pastor Gerard Olckenburgh conducted the Lord's Supper and there were numerous French people in the church, amongst them captain Véron and several of his countrymen who participated in the communion.[12]

The increasing intensity of the persecution in France in 1660 and in the following years provoked the flight of several French Protestants to Holland. Some, such as François Villion and the brothers François and Guillaume Du Toit, then chose to immigrate to South Africa.

Another well-known refugee was Guillaume Chenu de Chalezac, lord of Aujardière. Aged fourteen, this native of Bordeaux left his home on 22

March 1686 with the aim of escaping religious persecution. Abandoned on the coast of the former Ciskei while his ship continued its journey to East India, he lost all his companions in a massacre before being adopted by a Xhosa tribe. He spent one year with the family of an African chief, hunting and waging war with the members of the tribe. He only returned to Holland on 24 October 1689. From there he went to Prussia, where he became an officer and civil servant until his unexpected death in 1731.[13]

The Invitation of the Dutch East India Company
The Cape Colony was governed by the Dutch East India Company (*Vereenigde Oostindische Companie*), a private company representing the interests of six Chambers of Commerce in the Netherlands. This situation lasted until the British occupation in 1795. The Dutch East India Company employed agents—545 of them in 1700—who, together with the free burghers, constituted the major part of the colony's population. The perils of the voyage and the fear of sickness made the recruitment of agents difficult. As a result, most agents were people of modest means, hailing from Holland, Germany, Scandinavia, and Switzerland.

The invitation made to the French Protestants who had settled in Holland in the aftermath of the Revocation of the Edict of Nantes is to be understood in this context. The Huguenots were also underprivileged, even if, before their exile, their living conditions were sometimes comfortable.

As early as October 1685, shortly before the decree revoking the Edict of Nantes, the Lords XVII had passed a resolution recommending the sending of French refugees to the Cape Colony:

> To encourage farming, which seems increasingly to be flourishing, and to reduce somewhat the heavy expenses incurred by the Company in connection with the upkeep of the garrison, a large number of colonists [shall] be sent out. These must include French refugees of the reformed religion, especially those understanding the cultivation of the vine, the making of vinegar and the distillation of brandy.[14]

A first group of refugees left Delfthaven on 31 December 1687 on board the *Voorschoten*. Six similar ships, the *Borsenburg*, the *Oosterland*, the

Schelde, the *Berg China*, the *Zuid-Beveland*, and the *Wapen van Alkmaar*, set sail between February and July 1688. The journey took five or six months in the best conditions. In total, some 180 French refugees—we will return to this figure—arrived in South Africa. Men outnumbered women two to one. About a third of the passengers were children. All the adult males, with the exception of a pastor, a hatter and a merchant, were husbandmen and vinedressers.

In a letter dated 16 November 1687, the Lords XVII asked the Commander of the colony, Simon van der Stel, to treat the refugees with kindness and to assure their subsistence until they became capable of supporting themselves.

"We have granted them a minister," they added, "so that they may enjoy the exercise of their religion." This minister, Pierre Simond, a native of Nyons, Dauphiny,[15] who was serving the Walloon church of Zierikzee before his departure, was the most educated of the refugees. It was he who acted as spokesman for the French in their increasingly difficult negotiations with the colonial authorities.

The welcome, at first, was excellent. The company procured food, livestock and money to the newcomers. A sum of 18,000 florins, originally destined for the evangelization of the island of Taiwan, was distributed amongst them. And above all, they received land, in a mountainous area recently opened to colonization, near the newly established towns of Stellenbosch and Drakenstein.

Forced assimilation

Before their departure, the Huguenots had taken an oath to observe the laws and orders of the Dutch East India Company.[16] This agreement turned out to be more difficult to keep than expected. It was based, in fact, on a misunderstanding. The Lords XVII and the Commander of the colony took it for granted that the French people would become integrated as soon as possible with the Dutch settlers. There was no question of giving them any autonomy. In the matter of ecclesiastical discipline, the colonial authorities expected total obedience from the churches. The refugees, and especially their minister, shared radically different views. They wanted to be given a special status, comparable to the one they had in France before the Revocation of the Edict of Nantes or to that of the Walloon church in the Netherlands, which was allowed a considerable degree of autonomy in practice and language while remaining part of the Dutch Reformed church.[17] The Huguenots saw themselves as a separate body within the Cape Colony with specific religious and economic rights.

Given this misunderstanding, confrontation was unavoidable. The conflict focused on two issues: the allocation of land and the use of the French language in church and at school. In a letter sent to the Lords XVII on 12 June 1690, Simon van der Stel unambiguously stated his policy. "It is our aim," he wrote, "that [the Huguenots] should become integrated with their fellow countrymen." With this objective in mind, he allocated to the Huguenots farming sites that were separated from each other. In this way, he thought, the French people would be forced to speak with their Dutch neighbors. For the Huguenots, this was unacceptable. They wanted the Commander to give them new sites so that they could stay together. Scattered as they were, they were unable to send their children to the same school. All social life was impossible. On the other hand, they wanted to have their own church in Drakenstein where they were in the majority, with a separate consistory and the divine service in French. They did not want to go to the Stellenbosch parish, which was mostly frequented by Dutch settlers.

On 15 June 1689, Pierre Simond argued his case in a long letter to the Lords XVII,[18] but he only gained small concessions. A few months later, he presented the Commander with a petition requesting a new allocation of land and the establishment of a consistory in Drakenstein. This time, Simon van der Stel reacted very negatively. These "supposed refugees," he reported to the Lords XVII, were just hypocrites. Instead of farming the land as they had promised to do, they led "indolent" lives and kept on making unreasonable requests. "They were of a mind to have their own Magistrate, Commander or Prince to be chosen from the people to whom they proposed transferring the obedience at present paid to the Honorable Company."[19] Despite this expression of anger, however, the Commander maintained a good relationship with the refugees, as is shown by the fact that he was a witness at the baptism of Pierre Simond's eldest daughter the following year. A settlement of the dispute, in any event, was in sight. At the end of 1690, the Lords XVII gave authorization, in a letter to the Commander, to establish a consistory and a school in Drakenstein. The schoolmaster would teach the children of French descent to read and understand the Dutch language "in order to unite our nations by all means." The use of the French language was thus maintained for the time being. On the other hand, the Lords XVII expressed their opposition to any redistribution of land. The Huguenots were to remain separated, so as to integrate themselves faster with the rest of the colony.[20]

The replacement, in 1699, of Simon van der Stel by his son, Wilhelm Adriaen van der Stel, as governor of the Cape Colony[21] contributed to the deepening of the conflict. Soon after his appointment, the Governor asked the Council to stop the immigration of French people to the Cape Colony. He kept complaining about them, saying that they did not behave well and that they had little understanding of farming. It was probably the deterioration of the political situation which caused Pierre Simond, the most determined defender of the Huguenots' autonomy, to abandon the struggle. Another reason was his wish to present his new translation of the Psalms to the synod of the Reformed Churches in Holland. He preached his last sermon in Drakenstein on 9 April 1702, just before sailing for Europe.

Simond's departure was used as an excuse by the Lords XVII to withdraw permission for the use of French at church services in Drakenstein. There was nothing, by that time, which could prevent the rapid assimilation of the French refugees into the Dutch settler population. The decision made by the Lords XVII to put an end to the immigration of French refugees to the Cape also contributed to the disappearance of a distinct French identity. Significantly, the new minister of the Drakenstein community, Henricus Beck, was a Dutchman. At the time of his appointment, the majority of the faithful could not follow his sermons in Dutch, so he was allowed to preach in French every second week. This measure, however, was only temporary. In 1718, the decision was made that the minister would preach in both languages, but at different times. The schoolmaster, Paul Roux, a passionate defender of the French language, died in 1723. In 1726, Jérémie Roux, his son and successor, was told that the use of French for religious services was no longer justifiable. By that time, there were only twenty-five persons left who could speak Calvin's language. Roux nevertheless continued to teach French to the children of Drakenstein until at least 1730.

In 1752, a French traveler, Nicolas Louis de La Caille, still found a few children who were able to speak French, but, he noted, the chances of survival of the French language in the Cape Colony were almost nil:

With respect to the refugees, they have preserved the French language, and have taught it to their children, but the latter, partly because they trade with the Dutch, and Germans who speak the Dutch language, and have married and become connected with them, have not taught French to their children. There are no longer any of the old refugees of 1680 and 1690 at the Cape, only their children remain who speak French, and they are very old.[22]

La Caille's predictions proved to be correct. In 1783, François Le Vaillant, another French traveler, only found one elderly person who could speak French.[23] He was the last witness of the French Huguenot community.

Aspects of the Immigration to South Africa

Demographic structure[24]

It is difficult to determine with precision how many French refugees arrived on board the various ships chartered by the Dutch East India company in 1687 and 1688 because several passenger lists are lost. But other documents give reasonably accurate numbers. On 1 April 1688, the Lords XVII put the number of Huguenots at 151. In a letter written to the Lords XVII on 12th June 1690, Simon van der Stel estimated that they were about 150, a figure which corresponds to the one above.

We must also take into account the refugees that subsequently arrived. Pieter Coertzen, who has compiled his own list on the strength of various documents, believes that 138 French refugees arrived in 1688, twenty in 1689, nine in 1690, and eleven in 1691. The end total is thus 178. This figure is not far from that of 171 which appears in the lists of the recipients of the funds originally destined for the poor of Taiwan in June 1691.

According to the *muster rolls*, the colony consisted of 856 free burghers in 1692. The French, taking into consideration the three refugees who arrived in 1692 and the twenty-odd people who were established before 1688, were about 200, that is, approximately 23 percent of the colony's free burghers.

In 1702, the Huguenots numbered 229. This figure does not include an indeterminate number of Dutch East India Company agents of French origin, whose religion and exact origin are unknown.[25] At that time, the Cape Colony numbered 1,334 free burghers and 545 company agents.[26]

At the beginning of the century, the French people thus represented 17 percent of the free burghers and at least 13 percent of the white population as a whole.

Maurice Boucher's study of the Cape Huguenots' European background provides information about the geographic origin of the French refugees. The regions supplying the largest contingent of Huguenots were Provence and Artois, followed by Normandy, Orléanais, Ile-de-France, and Languedoc. There were very few refugees originating from central and southwestern France.[27]

Anne Drabczuk notes that out of the 121 surnames borne by the seventeenth-century refugees, only thirty-eight are still in use today. The "disappearances" are due to two factors. Several Huguenots, like Louis Barre, Jean Lecheret, Pierre Lefevre, Louis François Migault, Pierre Sabatier, and Gilles Sollier, returned to Europe once their five-year contract with the Dutch East India Company had expired. Others, like Jacques de Savoye and Pierre Simond, left at a later stage. The second factor is, of course, the absence of male descendants in the second or subsequent generations.[28]

The families that stayed were characterized by a high birth rate, due to early marriages and frequent remarriages. Based on the study of the genealogical trees of sixty-six families, Anne Drabczuk estimates that from the second generation, the number of children per family was higher among the descendants of Huguenots than among their fellow citizens of Dutch origin. She also notes a high rate of endogamy among the former: 52 percent of marriages were celebrated between Huguenots of the first generation, 40 percent of the second generation, 41 percent of the third generation, and 37 percent of the fourth generation.[29]

Religious Life

The Dutch minister François Valentyn, who was in the Cape in 1714, was all but impressed by his visit to the local congregation:

> When I went to Holy Communion, I found that the church members totalled 40 men and 48 women only, including those in the return-fleet, of whom there were a number, and it was entirely surprising that among those who approached the Table there was no member of the Council of Policy, and apparently also none of them was a church member. In the interior, the situation is probably twice

as bad. From this it can be seen how little so many Preachers have gained in all these years by their toil among these inhabitants, due in no way to the faltering of their zeal but to the stupidity and insolence of the Burghers.[30]

This testimony is a corrective to the popular picture of a pious and austere Calvinist colony. But what about the Huguenots? As far as they are concerned clichés also require revision.[31] The dedication of the French refugees to the Reformed cause was far from being unanimously recognized. In November 1689, as we have seen, Simon van der Stel criticized in the strongest possible terms the "supposed French refugees" who dared question his authority:

Under the appearance of having left their King on account of religious oppression, [they] escaped from France to other countries and especially to Holland in order that, under the guise of zealous and staunch adherents of the Protestant religion, they might lead lazy and indolent lives.[32]

These accusations, it must be noted, were not directed at the whole group of refugees but only at "twelve or thirteen" of them who refused the sites allocated to them by the Commander. Van der Stel's declarations should not be accepted uncritically, of course. But it is interesting to note that he found it acceptable, in a report addressed to the Lords XVII, to cast suspicion on the refugees' religious fervor.

Pierre Simond, who tried to act as a mediator between the refugees and the colonial authorities, was not the target of van der Stel's accusation. But he also came under attack. While fulfilling the role of pastor, not without indulging, it seems, in some kind of authoritarianism, he was at the head of a prosperous farm. According to Randolph Vigne, Simond was the wealthiest of the fourteen Huguenot slave-owners present during those years.[33] This financial success seems to have created resentment amongst some of the refugees. His most vehement opponent was Jacques de Savoye, a man who, significantly, left South Africa some time later because of bankruptcy. During a dispute, he did not hesitate to call Simond a "false pastor, unworthy minister, hypocrite, Tartuffe, priest, Jesuit, Judas, Kaffir."[34]

This conflict poisoned the first years of Simond's ministry in South Africa. The French congregation of Drakenstein managed nevertheless to organize. A temporary building—"more a barn than a church," according to François Valentyn's description in 1705[35]—was used as a place of worship. It was replaced in 1718 by a proper church. On 8 November 1688, the Dutch East India Company appointed a schoolmaster, Paul Roux, who remained in charge until his death in 1723. It was he who undertook the writing of the catechism. Divided into eight parts, his work had no direct link to any existing catechism but conformed entirely to the Reformed orthodoxy.[36]

As mentioned earlier, a consistory was instituted at the end of 1691. Three elders and four deacons were elected. Apart from two cases of excommunication,[37] we know very little of its first years of operation since the existing registers only start in February 1715. By that time, the minister was Petrus Van Aken, a Dutchman like his predecessor Henricus Beck, and French was rapidly losing ground in favor of the Dutch. The consistory made various suggestions to encourage the involvement of the faithful. Spiritual literature was distributed and charitable work organized. The Lord's Supper was celebrated four times a year. Because of lack of means, the communion wine was drunk from beer glasses. The consistory's main task, according to the Reformed tradition, was to deal with disciplinary matters. In 1716, for instance, a certain Mrs Bruël appeared before the consistory in connection with rumors that "she was living with a wicked slave." She was instructed to sell the slave and to improve her life. As she was prepared to do so, she was barred from participating in the Lord's Supper until she had complied with the consistory's instructions. She did so at the end of the same year and she was reintegrated.[38]

Judging from a sermon which was later printed in Holland, the preaching was, in Simond's time, of good quality. Trained at the Dié Academy, Dauphiny, a Protestant school modeled on the Geneva Academy, the founder of the Drakenstein congregation was a qualified theologian. Published in Haarlem in 1707 under the title *La vraye Adoration et les Vrays Adorateurs, ou Sermon sur ces paroles du Chap. 4. de l'Evangile selon S. Jean v. 23 & 24*, this sermon was first delivered in Cape Town on 25 January 1699, then again in Amsterdam on 17 October 1706.[39] In the version we have, the text does not make any direct reference to the situation of the Huguenots in the Cape Colony. But it contains a violent attack against the Roman religion, an indication that the author had suffered persecution at the hands of the Pope's agents. In his sermon,

Simond argued that the external worship of ancient Israel, which combined internal devotion and external observances, had given way, since the coming of Jesus, to a worship "in spirit and truth" which corresponded fully to God's wishes for humankind. There was no way one could revert to the old style of worship. The Lord, who knew the "infirmity" of his people, had only recommended a limited number of ceremonies, namely, Baptism and the Holy Supper, which contained nothing "fleshly and laborious." All the ceremonies practiced in the Roman Church, such as the pilgrimages, the recitation of the Rosary, the veneration of relics, and the wearing of religious habits, were not only frivolous but pernicious. They were totally opposed to the will of God as expressed in the Gospel of St. John. The only worship that pleased the Lord was the worship in spirit and truth as instituted by the New Law.

Another proof of Simond's theological ability was the fact that he translated the Psalms into French while ministering to the Drakenstein congregation.[40] Since the time of the Reformation, the standard version of the Psalms was, in the French-speaking Reformed churches, the text established by Clément Marot and Théodore de Bèze in the sixteenth century. As time went on, however, this version came to be seen as obsolete, in view of the rapid evolution of the French language. More and more, the Catholic polemicists were making jokes of a religion which pretended to reach out to the people while using a language that nobody could understand any more. Eventually, the decision was made—at the church of Charenton outside Paris—to ask one of the local pastors, Valentin Conrart, to write a new translation of the Psalms. Conrart then moved to Geneva and died soon afterwards. Completed by another pastor, Marc Antoine La Bastide, the translation was printed in Geneva in 1679. It was officially adopted by the Genevan church in 1698. Yet, a number of French-speaking churches continued to use the old version of the Psalter. The Company of Pastors of Geneva was concerned with preserving the uniformity of liturgy among the Reformed churches of French language. It was to achieve this goal that, in January 1700, they took the unprecedented step of sending a circular letter to all the French-speaking churches, recommending that all of them adopted the Conrart-La Bastide version.

This initiative provoked a bitter controversy in the European Reformed community. The French theologian Pierre Jurieu, who had taken refuge in Holland after the Revocation of the Edict of Nantes, took the lead in the opposition to the Conrart-La Bastide translation. He argued that a new Psalter would upset the ordinary people in the churches. At his instigation, several churches, including the Threadneedle Street Church in London, chose to keep to the old version. The situation in Holland was more complicated. The Walloon Protestants, who had been in the country for more than a century and were not acquainted with the new way of speaking French, tended to be more conservative. Jurieu was fully on their side. But the Conrart-La Bastide version of the Psalter also had supporters, as is shown by the number of editions printed in Amsterdam after the Revocation.[41] The French church of Amsterdam, significantly, expressed support for the new version.[42] This variety of opinions explains why the synod of the Walloon churches in Holland opted, at a meeting held in September 1700 in Rotterdam, for a middle way. The delegates decided not to adopt the Conrart-La Bastide version, as the Church of Geneva had recommended, but instead to ask five of the member churches to work on a new translation of the Psalms.[43]

It was in this context that Simond set about writing a new translation of the Psalms in rhymes. In June 1699, he got news that the English king had authorized the Huguenot churches in England to use the new version of the Psalms. Finding the Conrart-La Bastide translation inappropriate, Simond decided to write his own metrical translation of the Psalms. He completed the work in three months without, he wrote in the preface of the book, neglecting any of his pastoral duties. The fact that such an important enterprise could have been carried out in Africa, he commented, was just another sign of God's grace:

> I want everybody to know that there is no desert, in Africa or elsewhere, dry or arid as it may be, where God does not spread out, as it pleases him, the waters of his grace, and that he performs his works with the help of the meanest instruments and those we find the most unexpected, so that glory may be rendered to, him.[44]

Meanwhile, the decision made at the Rotterdam synod to write a new translation of the Psalms for the use of the Walloon churches reinforced Simond's desire to return to the Netherlands. It was the Dutch East India Company's policy to allow its agents to go home after twelve years of service. Simond's application was sent to the Lords XVII at the beginning of 1701,[45] but because no successor could be found, it was not until April 1702 that he received permission to leave his post.

Simond's translation never received any official recognition. Much to his disappointment the synod of the Walloon churches, gathered in Utrecht on 3 May 1703, decided against adopting his metrical version of the Psalms. The reason given was that the matter had already been decided at the previous synod at The Hague.[46] Despite this rebuttal, however, Simond decided to go ahead with the publication of his translation. He chose to publish only the first part of the Psalter,[47] letting the reader judge whether it was worth pursuing the enterprise. The book appeared in Amsterdam in 1704, at the author's expense, under the title *Les Veilles afriquaines ou les Pseaumes de David, mis en vers François*.[48]

Relations with the Indigenous People

Most European travelers, whether French or not, were prejudiced by crass ignorance with regard to the African population. Thus Jean-Baptiste Tavernier wrote in 1679:

> Of all the people I have seen in my travels, I never found any more hideous nor more brutal than the Comouks of whom I have made mention in my accounts of Persia and those of the Cape of Good Hope who are called Kaffirs or Hottentots.[49]

Another example will reveal, by contrast, the surprising open-mindedness of Pierre Simond in his dealings with the indigenous peoples. Pierre Leguat, a Huguenot who visited the Huguenots in the Drakenstein mountains, revealed a veritable aversion for the Khoikhoi—the name by which the Hottentots are known today:

> The Hottentot Kaffirs are people with an ugly and unpleasant face,
> if one can give to such animals the name of men.

How, he wondered, "are these ugly people who live like pigs" capable of thinking about their way of being dressed? They band together and live in holes or under little thatched cottages. Even if they follow mysterious ceremonies, strictly speaking they have no religion. The important thing, he concluded, was to use them as domestic helpers, as the Huguenots tried to do.

With all the filth and foolishness of these people, one can make good use of them and for a piece of bread, or tobacco, one makes them work an entire day.[50]

Pierre Simond's attitude differed in its humaneness. While recognising that the KhoiKhoi did not lack "reason," he was looking at ways of "steering them to a more reasonable way of life." The first task, in his view, was to convince them of the necessity of dressing in European fashion. In any case, they were to be treated "with all possible humaneness." This policy, he concluded, would have the double advantage of submitting them to the Dutch East India Company's authority and of leading them to the Gospel.

One should not be mistaken. His paternalism was in no way different from the one, rightly condemned, of the missionaries of the subsequent centuries. But at least he considered the indigenous people to be capable of being converted. In the Cape Colony, such an apostolic concern was exceptional.

The missionary views of Pierre Simond were stated in his letter of 15 June 1689 to the Lords XVII. The passage relating to the KhoiKhoi deserves to be quoted extensively:

After having spoken to you of my flock, I beg permission, My Honorable Lords, to speak of the natives of the country, those whom we commonly call Ottentots. They come every day to my house, and I have recognised that they do not lack reason nor docility, which allows us to hope that, with a bit of care, we can steer them to a more reasonable way of life, which will serve to prepare the path to the Lord and, through their knowledge of Him, lead them to our way of life. I believe it will only suffice to let them taste the sweetness of it, and I have little doubt that they will soon prefer it to their way of life, which they themselves acknowledge to be very wretched. And for that there is no need to care for specific individuals among them who do not have the courage to renounce the ways of their nation, nor to scorn the mockery of their companions. I think it best to undertake the humanising of two or three troops from the same quarter, which could be, in total, 80 or 100 people. I am not of the opinion that we should estrange them, but rather that we send people to live among them, who can build some houses for them, and who can give them bread and other things to enthral them, and to cultivate the good land that exists in their quarter and to leave them the fruit of their work. I do not doubt that in this way they will soon get used to cultivating the land themselves once they have recognised the usefulness of it.

I also believe it would not be in vain to force them to abandon the skins with which they cover themselves. It seems to me that with their clothes, so different to ours, they must regard themselves as people of another species who must have nothing in common with us. We could make a lot of progress if we could make them dress like ourselves. I do not believe that one, two or three could be induced to dress differently from the others as they would be mocked by them. But I do not doubt at all that if one were to present clothes to an entire group, they would take them willingly, especially if we had prepared them nicely, and if we chose a cold period during which to do this, because their clothes leave them half naked and they are not unsensitive to the cold, as it would seem that they very much like to warm themselves.

On the whole, it would be necessary to treat them with all possible humaneness, and to give them all the attention they could possibly desire. If we succeed with some groups, their example would soon attract others, and there is every reason to believe that they will come from all sides to live under this form of life, and in the same way under the obedience of Your Noble Company, and then under that of the Gospel, which will be very glorious and very useful to Your Noble Company.[51]

The Huguenot Legacy

What is left of the Huguenots three hundred years after their arrival on South African soil? Their assimilation, as we have seen, was rapid and complete.[52] Nonconformist attitudes, such as the one adopted by Pierre Simond with respect to the KhoiKhoi, remained short-lived. The modest origin of the Huguenots and their lack of education prevented them from exercising any direct influence on the theological and literary culture of the colony.

At a deeper level, however, the Huguenots may have left a mark on the development of Dutch Reformed theology. In a recent book, Jonathan

Gerstner has argued that the French Reformed tradition of church discipline, which tended to work against the church-state tradition of the Netherlands, continued to play a role among the descendants of Huguenots long after the French language had ceased to be spoken. In the 1770s, an entire section of the Drakenstein farming community refused to acknowledge an elder who was allegedly guilty of misconduct. This led to a schism which only subsided after the retirement of the pastor.[53] This episode indicates a surprising degree of theological knowledge among the Drakenstein farmers. Their insistence that the church was to be made up only of confessing believers who gave evidence of a moral life worked against the tendency, common among the Dutch colonists, of identifying the entire European community as redeemed. Yet, even though these ideas resulted in the cutting off of some Europeans from God's people, the majority position of Dutch Reformed covenant theology —that the children of God's people were already holy from birth— remained unchallenged. The French Reformed emphasis on church discipline did not affect the "thousand generation covenant."

It is in place names that the Huguenots have left the most visible traces. According to Pieter Coertzen's survey, forty-three of the 107 farms originally occupied by the Huguenots in the Stellenbosch and Paarl areas have retained French names until the present day.[54] In the rest of the country, many small towns and villages preserve the memory of the Huguenots in their names.[55]

The most lasting contribution of the Huguenots to the South African nation was to consolidate Afrikaner identity. First of all, they contributed to the demographic expansion of the Afrikaner group. As mentioned at the beginning of this paper, their surnames are today among the most commonly borne among the Afrikaners. It has been noted that the names of nine of the thirty-six most important white families of the country— Nel, Du Plessis, Coertzen, Fourie, Du Toit, Le Roux, Viljoen, Marais, and Du Preez—are of French origin.[56] Christian names such as Pierre, Louis, or Jacques, also bear witness to the Huguenot roots of the South African population. According to a survey published in 1974, the proportion of descendants of Huguenots in the total Afrikaner population was 14.6 percent.[57]

Interestingly, although the percentage of descendants of German immigrants among the Afrikaner people is much higher. But the German legacy has never been properly recognized in South Africa.[58] By contrast, the Huguenot heritage has been, and still is, the object of real worship. Considering the bad relationship between the Huguenots and the Dutch East India Company in the years following their arrival in the Cape Colony and the fact that they were subjected to a policy of forced assimilation, this is rather ironic. But the real Huguenot history had long been forgotten. More important was the symbol—of Christian heroism— which the Huguenots represented.

For more than a century, the Afrikaner movement has made use of the Huguenot past as a constitutive element of the emerging national identity.[59] This is a case of "invented tradition," in the sense defined by Eric Hobsbawm. The term "invented tradition" includes both those traditions actually reinvented, constructed and formally instituted and those emerging in a less easily traceable manner within a brief and dateable period and establishing themselves with great rapidity. The peculiarity of "invented" traditions is that the continuity with the past is largely fictitious.[60]

The first attempt to erect a monument in Franschhoek to keep the memory of the Huguenots alive dates from 1824. The project only succeeded a century later, but in the meantime a number of monuments and institutions commemorating the Huguenots were erected. The first one was the *Sticht Simondium*, a school built in the vicinity of Franschhoek in 1851. The Huguenot College of Wellington, a seminary for girls opened in 1872 by the Reverend Andrew Murray, and the *Gedenkschool der Hugenoten*, a school built in 1882 by another minister, the Reverend S. J. Du Toit, on the farm Kleinbosch in Daljosaphat, are other examples of Huguenot pride. As a pamphlet printed for the Huguenot Bicentenary in October 1885 explained, it was to disseminate the seed planted by the Huguenots two hundred years earlier that these schools had been built:

> The seed which God, amid such terrible siftings, had preserved, had brought into this quiet corner of the world, as into a safe garner, must be precious and of great price in God's sight. It is His will that that seed should now be scattered, that it may bring forth much fruit. And how can we better fulfil this purpose of God than by, on this sacred spot, where the Huguenots first found rest, and on their own soil might again worship God, establishing a school consecrated to their memory, to the preservation and dissemination of the faith for which they did not count their lives dear unto them, and so to the glory of God who counted us as worthy to be the descendants

of such a parentage, and hitherto preserved to us the precious legacy they left us.[61]

In 1888, the synod of the Dutch Reformed church decided to erect a "Huguenot memorial." That did not happen, but instead a church hall called *Huguenot-Gedenksaal* was built in Cape Town a few years later, in 1924. In 1938, the year of the centenary celebrations commemorating the Great Trek, the Huguenot rectory in Paarl was declared a historical museum. In 1939, a monument commemorating the Huguenots was unveiled in Wellington. The Huguenot Monument of Franschoek, which was inaugurated on 7 April 1948, six weeks before the poll which brought the National Party to power, is the best-known of all the Huguenot memorials. In 1957, a museum was established on the same site.

In 1983, the National Party government established a Huguenot Festival Committee whose task was to prepare a grandiose commemoration five years later. The third centenary of the arrival of the first Huguenots was celebrated with great pump in Saldanha, Cape Town, Paarl, and Franschhoek in April 1988. It was a strange celebration. The Afrikaner people celebrated their past glories while the country suffered under a state of emergency. The apartheid regime struggled for its survival amidst growing resistance. The same year, the Huguenot Tunnel was opened near Paarl, a sign that the tradition of giving a Huguenot name to national monuments was still alive.

The admirers of the Huguenots knew very well that their impact on South African history had been limited. Their influence on the economy of the country, with the possible exception of the wine industry, was minimal and their cultural role, after Pierre Simond's departure, almost non-existent. But their importance lay elsewhere. Diko van Zyl, a Stellenbosch academic who wrote the preface of a book published on the occasion of the Huguenot Festival, spoke of a "wider legacy" of the Huguenots which, he admitted, was "less tangible" than the material legacy. According to him, the Huguenots' main contribution to South Africa was their "spirit":

> Perhaps it means pride in the past, in forefathers who held firmly to their beliefs and were prepared to suffer for them. The tercentenary of the Huguenots' arrival at the Cape is a reminder that a country is blended from different human elements, each with its own contribution, both practical and spiritual.[62]

The historian Pieter Coertzen, who published a revised version of his doctoral thesis in the year of the Huguenot Festival, shared exactly the same vision: the "tangible" legacy of the Huguenots was less important than "the nobility of spirit which they brought with them to this country."[63] For an Afrikaner people isolated from the rest of the world and determined to maintain its identity in an environment perceived as hostile, the Huguenots represented an ideal model. Heroes of the faith, they chose to go into exile—another Great Trek—rather than to yield to the demands of an unjust ruler.

This vision of the Huguenots' legacy was not restricted to academics and ministers of religion. In a speech delivered during the Huguenot Festival, the Minister of Education, who was no other than F. W. De Klerk, the future State President, expressed the view that the Huguenots had influenced the (white) South African people by their blood which ran "in a substantial percentage" in their veins, by their liberty of spirit and their attachment to the Christian faith and by various skills which were reflected in the current achievements of the South African nation.[64]

South Africa has now entered another era. The Afrikaner people, who developed the Huguenot myth as a way of strengthening their identity, have lost their leading position in the government of the country. This new situation creates the conditions for a more critical appraisal of the role of the Huguenots in South African history.

Notes

1. The most important sources are to be found in the Royal General Archives in The Hague and in the Cape State Archives in Cape Town.

The Colonial Archives series (KA), found in the first of these two depositories, contains the correspondence between the Lords XVII (the Board of Governors of the Dutch East India Company), the Commander (later Governor) of the Cape Colony and the Huguenots during the first years of their stay in the colony (Algemeen Rijksarchief, Den Haag: KA 4005, fols. 85r–92v, 572r–631r; 4016, fols. 1298–1304).

The Cape State Archives hold the archives of the Drakenstein (now Paarl) Reformed Church, the old parish of the French refugees. Particularly important are the baptismal registers (1694–1880), the marriage registers (1717–1976), the membership lists (1715–1853), the acts of the consistory (1715–1968) and sundry correspondence (Cape State Archives: Nederduitsche Gereformeerde Kerkargief, G3/1, G3/3, G3/5). The Archives of the Master of the Supreme Court (MOOC), also held at the Cape State Archives, contains several pieces of interest to the history of the refugees, such as the journal of Gideon Le Grand, a French doctor practicing at the beginning of the eighteenth century, and the correspondence of Joseph de Grandpreez, a descendant of refugees, between 1757 and 1761 (Cape State Archives: MOOC 14/1 and 229. See also the correspondence of Pierre Joubert van Drakenstein MOOC 14/5). For the economic history of the Huguenot Refuge, the property titles of the French Protestants constitute the main source. They can be consulted at the Deeds Office in Cape Town (Deeds Office, Cape Town: Old Cape freeholds, II, 1 and 2, 1703–1717; Old Stellenbosch freeholds, II, 1 and 2, 1704–1785; Title deeds, Cape, 1685–1786; Title deeds, Drakenstein and Swellendam, 1689–1785).

Equally important are the diaries of French travelers to the Cape, which provide an eye-witness account of the daily life of the Huguenot communities in the colony (See G. Girelli, *Le cap de Bonne Espérance vu par les voyageurs français au XVIIe siècle* [Master's thesis, Université de Lyon III, 1983]; Xavier Beguin-Bille-cocq, *Les voyageurs français au Cape de Bonne Espérance* [French Travelers to the Cape of Good Hope] [Paris: Relations Internationales et Culture, 1996]). For the period under review, the most noteworthy is François Leguat's *Voyage et avantures*. A Huguenot nobleman chosen to prepare the foundation of a Protestant colony on the island of Bourbon (now Reunion), Leguat visited the Cape of Good Hope on two occasions, in 1691 and in 1698. His book was published in 1708 and was later translated into English (*Voyages et avantures de François Leguat & de ses Compagnons . . .*, 2 vols. [London: David Mortier, 1708]. English translation: *The voyage of Francois Leguat of Bresse to Rodriguez, Mauritius, Java, and the Cape of Good Hope*, edited and annotated by Pasfield Oliver, 2 vols. [London: Hakluyt Society, 1891]).

2. Of particular interest are the following books: Colin Graham Botha, *The French Refugees at the Cape* (1919; reprint, Cape Town: C. Struik, 1970); J. L. N. Franken, *Die Hugenote aan die Kaap* (Pretoria: Die Staatsdrukker, 1978): Pieter Coertzen, "Die Franse Hugenote in Suid-Afrika: 'n kerhistoriese studie'" (Ph.D. diss., Stellenbosch University, 1976) (popular edition under the title *The Huguenots of South Africa, 1688–1988* [Cape Town: Tafelberg, 1988]).

3. See Johannes August Heese and Roelof Theunis Johannes Lombard, ed., *Suid Afrikaanse Geslagregisters* (South African Genealogies), 4 vols. to date (Pretoria: Human Science Research Council, 1986–). According to a bibliography compiled by the Huguenot Memorial Museum (*Genealogical Sources in the Huguenot Memorial Museum* [Franschhoek, 1996]), 171 South African families, mostly of Huguenot origin, have compiled their genealogies, either in a manuscript or in a printed form.

4. The least unsatisfactory study so far is Anne Drabczuk's master's thesis: "Evolution de la communauté huguenote d'Afrique du Sud de 1688 à nos jours.

Problèmes de géographie historique" (Université de Paris-Sorbonne, 1983). See also Maurice Boucher's study of the refugees' European background: *French Speakers at the Cape in the First Hundred Years of Dutch East India Company Rule: The European Background* (Pretoria: University of South Africa, 1981). The author traces with great detail the whereabouts of each Huguenot family but fails to provide a full picture of the refugees' movements from France to Holland and from there to the Cape Colony.

5. On the Huguenots' contribution to agriculture: Coertzen, *Huguenots*, 106–22. On the history of the wine industry: D. J. Van Zyl, "Kaapse Wyn and Brandewyn, 1795–1860. Die geskiedenis van wynbou en wynhandel in die Kaapkolonie (Bellville: Maroela-Boeken, 1975).

6. See Randolph Vigne, "The Rev. Pierre Simond: 'lost leader' of the Huguenots at the Cape," *Journal of Theology for Southern Africa* 65 (December 1988): 14–26; "Pierre Simond, pasteur du refuge et traducteur des Psaumes. Une esquisse biographique," *Psaume. Bulletin de la Recherche sur le Psautier Huguenot* 14 (November 1997): 3–9. On church life in the Huguenot community see: Coertzen, *Huguenots*, 122–39; Jonathan Neil Gerstner, *The Thousand Generation Covenant: Dutch Reformed Covenant Theology and Group Identity in Colonial South Africa, 1652–1814* (Leiden: E. J. Brill, 1991), 219–39.

7. See Roy Henry Pheiffer, *Die gebroke Nederlands van Franssprekendes aan die Kaap in die eerste helfte van die 18de eeu.* (Cape Town: Academia, 1980); Marilet Sienaert-van Reenen, *Die Franse bydrae tot Africana literatuur, 1622–1902* (Pretoria and Cape Town: Human and Rousseau, 1989).

8. Botha, *French Refugees.* The book includes extracts of the Drakenstein baptismal register (1694–1713); a list of members (1715); a map of the farms allocated to the refugees; and various letters to or from the Lords XVII and the Chambers of Commerce in Holland (1685–1724). Several documents relative to the history of the Huguenot community in the Cape Colony are published in Cornelis Spoelstra, *Bouwstoffen voor de Geschiedenis der Nederduitsche-Gereformeerde Kerken in Zuid-Afrika*, vol. 2: Afdeeling, parts 2–6: *Brieven van de Classis Amsterdam et andere Kerkelijke Vergaderingen aan de Kaapsche Kerken (1651–1804), en verdere Archivalia op de geschiedenis van die tijdvak betrekking hebbende* (Amsterdam, 1907).

9. Three letters of Pierre Simond, dated 6 February 1698, 3 April 1700, and 20 March 1702 respectively, are already published. See Hendrik Carel V. Leibbrandt, *Precis of the Archives of the Cape of Good Hope. Letters dispatched, 1696–1708* (Cape Town, 1896), 65–66, 151, 192–93.

10. Paul Roux, *Belydenis des geloofs*, copy made on 8 May 1743 by H. C. von Wieding (Cape State Archives: G 3/5a).

11. The most comprehensive is to be found in Coertzen, *Huguenots*, 155–70. It includes 280 names.

12. Coertzen, *Huguenots*, 75.

13. The story of his journey was first published by Nathanael Weiss ("Les aventures de Guillaume Chenu de Chalezac, seigneur de Laujardière, au pays des Cafres, 1686–1689," *Bulletin de la Société de l'Histoire du Protestantisme Français* 80 (1921). The original manuscript was kept in the Magdeburg Library but disappeared during World War II. English translation with historical introduction and notes: Randolph Vigne, ed., *Guillaume Chenu de Chalezac, the "French Boy." The narrative of his experience as a Huguenot refugee, as a castaway among the Xhosa, his rescue with the* Stavenisse *survivors by the* Centaurus, *his service at the Cape and return to Europe, 1686–9*, 2nd ser., vol. 22 (Van Riebeeck Society, Cape Town, 1993).

14. Botha, *French Refugees*, 26.

15. See Randolph Vigne, "Rev. Pierre Simond (1651–1713?): The Family Background in the Dauphiné," *Africana Notes and News* 29, no. 7 (September 1991): 249–50.

16. The text of the oath is published by Botha, *French Refugees*, 4–5. See also Sienaert-van Reenen, *Franse bydrae*, 26.

17. See Gerstner, *The Thousand Generation Covenant*, 222.

18. Algemeen Rijksarchief, Den Haag: KA 4016, fols. 1298–1304. Extracts in Vigne, "Rev. Pierre Simond," 16–17.

19. Lords XVII, Resoluties, (28 November 1689), in Spoelstra, *Bouwstoffen*, 2:600–601. See Vigne, "Rev. Pierre Simond," 19.

20. Lords XVII, Resoluties, (28 November 1690), in Spoelstra, *Bouwstoffen*, 2:601. See Vigne, "Rev. Pierre Simond," 20.

21. In 1691, the commander of the Cape Colony had been promoted to the rank of governor.

22. Abbé Nicolas Louis de La Caille, *Journal Historique du Voyage du Cap de Bonne Espérance* (Paris, 1763).

23. François Le Vaillant, *Travels from the Cape of Good Hope into the Interior Part of Africa* (London, 1790), 1:196.

24. On the Cape Huguenots' demography, see Coertzen, *Huguenots*, 81–82; Drabczuk, *Evolution*, 63–69.

25. See about them Boucher, *French Speakers*, 290–97.

26. Figures for 1700. See Gerrit Schutte, "Company and Colonists at the Cape, 1652–1795," in *The Shaping of South African Society, 1652–1840*, ed. Richard Elphick and Hermann Giliomee, 2nd ed. (Cape Town: Maskew Miller Longman, 1989), 295.

27. Boucher, *French Speakers*, 103–289: Drabczuk, *Evolution*, 39–43.

28. Drabczuk, *Evolution*, 111.

29. Ibid., 64, 68. This study covers the period from 1688 to 1850.

30. François Valentyn, *Beschryvinge van de Kaap der Goede Hoope, met de zaaken daar toe behoerende* (Amsterdam, 1722; reprint, Cape Town: Van Riebeeck Society, 1973), 2:259. See Richard Elphick and Hermann Giliomee, "The Origins and Entrenchment of European Dominance at the Cape, 1652–c.1840," in Elphick and Giliomee, ed., *Shaping*, 527.

31. For a discussion of the Cape Huguenots' religious motivation, see Gerstner, *The Thousand Generation Covenant*, 219–21.

32. Lords XVII, Resoluties, (28 November 1689), in Spoelstra, *Bouwstoffen*, 2:600–601.

33. Vigne, "The Rev. Pierre Simond," 18.

34. The documents relative to this dispute are published in Franken, *Hugenote*, 34–51. See also Coertzen, *Huguenots*, 135–36; Vigne, "Rev. Pierre Simond," 17–18.

35. Valentyn, *Beschryvinge*, 1:163. See Coertzen, *Huguenots*, 124.

36. Cape State Archives: G 3/5a. For a description of this catechism, see Coertzen, *Huguenots*, 129–30, 182; Gerstner, *The Thousand Generation Covenant*, 221.

37. Jacques de Savoye and Guillaume Loree. See Gerstner, *The Thousand Generation Covenant*, 224–26.

38. See Coertzen, *Huguenots*, 131.

39. Haarlem: H. F. Buys, 1707. I am indebted to Mr. Randolph Vigne, the president of the Huguenot Society of London, for giving me a copy of this very rare pamphlet, a copy of which he found at the Bibliothèque Wallonne in The Hague. A handwritten copy, together with a Dutch translation, is kept in the Cape Town Dutch Reformed Archives (P 18), which are housed in the Cape Town State Archives. A translation of the sermon in Afrikaans appeared in *Die Kerkbode* (13 September 1939): 495–98. See Boucher, *French Speakers*, 358; Sienaert-van Reenen, *Franse bydrae*, 27–28; Coertzen, *Huguenots*, 134–35.

40. On the controversy regarding the new translation of the Psalms in the Huguenot Refuge, see Myriam Yardeni, "La querelle de la nouvelle version des Psaumes dans le refuge huguenot," in *Foi, fidélité, amitié en Europe à la période moderne. Mélanges offerts à Robert Sauzet*. Ed. Brigitte Maillard (Tours: Publications de l'Université de Tours, 1995), 2:457–63.

41. See Jean-Daniel Candaux, "Le psautier huguenot chez les imprimeurs néerlandais: concurrence ou spécialisation?" in *Le Magasin de l'Univers. The Dutch Republic as the Centre of the European Book Trade. Papers presented at the International Colloquium, held at Wassenaar, 5–7 July 1990*, ed. Christiane Berkvens-Stevenlinck et al. (Leiden: E. J. Brill, 1992), 79.

42. Yardeni, "La querelle," 461.

43. "Articles résolus au Synode de Rotterdam, le neuvième Septembre et jours suivants de l'année dix-sept cens." See Coertzen, *Huguenots*, 137.

44. [Pierre Simond], Preface to *Les Veilles afriquaines ou les Pseaumes de David, mis en vers François* (Amsterdam: pour l'auteur, chez Cornelle de Hoogenhuisen, 1704). National Library of Russia, St. Petersburg, Russia: 6.52.11.35. (microfilm, Bibliographie du Psautier, Institut Claude Longeon, Saint-Etienne, France). The preface and a few psalms are reproduced in *Psaume. Bulletin de la Recherche sur le Psautier Huguenot* 14 (November 1997): 9–17. See also Philippe Denis, "A Late Seventeenth Century Translation of the Psalms," in *The Bible in Africa: Transactions, Trends, and Trajectories*, ed. Gerald West (Leiden: E. J. Brill, 2000), 205–22.

45. See Coertzen, *Huguenots*, 136.

46. "Articles résolus au Synode des Eglises Wallonnes des Provinces Unies des Pays-Bas, assemblé à Utrecht le 3 May et jours suivans, 1703," art. 42. In Coertzen, *Huguenots*, 137.

47. Psalms 1–51, 74, 79, 103, 130, 137, and 143.

48. See note 44.

49. *Les six voyages de Jean-Baptiste Tavernier, écuyer, baron d'Aubonne, qu'il a faits en Turquie, en Perse et aux Indes* (Paris, 1679), 51–52.

50. *Voyages et avantures de François Leguat*, 149–53.

51. Algemeen Rijksarchief, Den Haag: KA 4016, fols. 1298–1304. Copy in the Cape State Archives: VC 168.

52. Contrary to what Drabczuk (*Evolution*, 85–96, 200–203) believes, the Huguenots' French did not exercise any influence on Afrikaans. The French expressions, which are abundant in Afrikaans, were introduced by the Dutch settlers. They were common in the dialects they used to speak in Holland before their arrival in the Cape. The Huguenots did influence Afrikaans but in a different way. According to Pheiffer (*Die gebroke Nederlands*, passim), their broken Dutch sped up the evolution of the settlers' language, contributing, in this way, to the development of Afrikaans. On this, see Sienaert-van Reenen, *Franse bydrae*, 33–37.

53. On the Drakenstein schism, see Gerstner, *The Thousand Generation Covenant*, 234–39.

54. For instance Calais, Laborie (La Brie), La Motte, Lourmarin, Picardie, La Provence, St. Omer. For a list of Huguenot farms, see Coertzen, *Huguenots*, 171–75.

55. Such as Coligny (Gauteng), Marseilles, Calais, Cabriere and Parys (Free State), La Plaisante, Le Chasseur, Lourdes, Malmaison, and Roux (Cape). See Drabczuk, *Evolution*, 96–97.

56. Coertzen, *Huguenots*, 145.

57. Heese, "Die herkoms van de Afrikanervolk," in *Mens en land*, ed. Pieter Willem Grobbelaar, *Die Afrikaner en sy kultuur*, part 1 (Cape Town and Johannesburg: Tafelberg, 1974), 52. See Sienaert-van Reenen, *Franse bydrae*, 29.

58. More than 30 percent, according to Heese. See Coertzen, *Huguenots*, 145.

59. On the Huguenot celebrations and monuments, see Coertzen, *Huguenots*, 146–52.

60. See Eric Hobsbawm, "Introduction: Inventing Tradition," in *The Invention of Tradition*, ed. Eric Hobsbawm and Terence Ranger (Cambridge: Cambridge University Press, 1992), 1–2.

61. *Souvenir of the Huguenot Bicentenary, 22nd October 1885*. Issued by the Huguenot Seminary, Wellington, 29 October, 1–2. Cape State Archives: P 18.

62. Lynne Bryer and François Theron, *The Huguenot Heritage. The story of the Huguenots at the Cape* (Diep River: Chameleon, 1988), 5.

63. Coertzen, *Huguenots*, 152.

64. N. P. Badenhorst, appendix 3 in *Verslag Hugenote Fees 1988* (Pretoria: Department van Onderwijs en Kultuur), 1991.

FIFTEEN

Frenchmen by Birth, Huguenots by the Grace of God

Some Aspects of the Huguenot Myth

Bernard Cottret

To speak of a "Huguenot myth" may sound provocative: the pursuit of truth seems to be the common venture of the historian and of the man of faith. How could we then define the object of history as imaginary and possibly fake? Recent trends in the history of immigration have tended to highlight the weight of economic, versus purely spiritual incentives. A recent study of early Huguenot immigrants to the Carolinas provides some remarkable insights. Issues like settlement and naturalization could be regarded as a *monnaie d'échange*, the result of a political deal between the proprietors and the French settlers.[1]

This renewal of Huguenot studies is not entirely economic. If religious, or for that matter ideological, factors can hardly be treated in isolation from more worldly pursuits, this does not imply a narrow concentration on private interest. Religion is not a mere ex post facto rationalization, or the opium of the people. It often serves to enhance a sense of community and belonging, which is still reinforced by the Christian concept of the church. Not all religions have churches, though all have communities. Islam, for example, has a community of believers and a deep sense of charity and mutual obligation between the faithful; the Christian idea of the church rests on Christ's two natures. The Christian community is literally a "body politic," as it impersonates the Redeemer.[2]

Religious groups, therefore, have a distinct world picture. Whatever the importance of economic motives, the history of the Huguenots has to be understood in cultural terms. The links between "law, memory, history and identity" are absolutely crucial.[3] The Calvinist consistory acted as an essential mediator in cases of interpersonal quarrels and violence. They fashioned behavior and references. A fine study of Saint-Jean-du-Gard, in the south of France, comes to similar conclusions, though the author aptly concludes that of its three main activities—control, guidance and management—management played an increasing role in the years leading up to the Revocation of the Edict of Nantes.[4] Torn between their loyalty to church and state, and to King and Country, many Huguenots could only flee their homeland.

The pace of adaptation to a host society is the next major issue tackled by historians of the Refuge. Individual communities may not have followed the same patterns of development, even though they were in the same country.[5] The relationship between Reformed Gallicanism and Episcopalianism still awaits its historian, though some work was done for a later period on the links between Paris and Canterbury.[6] But the American case is no less illuminating as conforming Huguenots often joined the Anglican fold while more recently the Huguenot community in Charleston has a distinct Episcopalian heritage and flavor.

My own contention would be that a number of Huguenots were ready to embrace Episcopalianism *before* landing in another country.[7] There is a discreet but distinguishable insistence on the role of bishops in the theology of Pierre Dumoulin in the first half of the seventeenth century. Some High-Church Huguenots became Low-Church Anglicans, who readily accepted episcopal ordination.[8]

From Reform to Revision

The revisionist trend in contemporary studies has been greatly influenced by Herbert Butterfield's bold attack on "Whig History."[9] Likewise, the French anthropologist Claude Lévi-Strauss emphasized the mythical nature of history. Whether they wished it or not, in spite of all their deserving efforts to free themselves, the best historians remained under that spell. History as seen by Lévi-Strauss is very much a captivity narrative.[10]

How to cope with this lasting dilemma? The best answer for historians is indeed to analyze their own myths. The study of patriotism, for example, provides one of the best hunting grounds to grasp the links between the past and the present: national identities involve an active process of selection. Simon Schama, Linda Colley, or Maurice Agulhon—to give but a few names—have all deciphered the myths and symbols which "forged" the Dutch, the French, and the "British nation" from the sixteenth up to the nineteenth century—though the existence of a British nation remains controversial to this day.[11]

To speak of a historical myth, therefore, does not imply the idea of forgery. But rather, to study a historical myth is to see how a political or religious experience is handled in cultural terms. In a recent survey, David Bell emphasized the possibility to define a nation in ethnic or civic terms. The first approach rests on exclusion, while the second is more universal: "Although this 'ethnic-civic' distinction is a familiar one, the extent to which the two vocabularies reflect highly divergent visions of the national community and its place in the world deserve further exploration. Ethnic representations are, by their nature, exclusionary: a community bound together by blood or language is a sharply bounded community, hostile or indifferent to outsiders, fearful of pollution. A community bound together by civic ties, by contrast, is at least potentially universal, open to all comers."[12]

The Huguenot experience provides an excellent example as it is both national and international, religious and political. There are therefore several interacting versions of that myth which cannot be all studied here. One may distinguish a definite German "Huguenot" tradition as it were, which was splendidly documented by Michèle Magdelaine and Rudolf von Thadden's 1985 collection of essays.[13] I have likewise stressed how, in the British case, Huguenot history provided an excellent sample of a living "Whig" tradition, still awaiting its social anthropologists.[14] Huguenot history has tended so far to be both retrospective and judgment-oriented: it clearly displayed, at one point, the ways of Providence in the epic of God's chosen people. The French, by contrast, have been more secular, incorporating the Huguenot myth into the Republican model—leaving aside Protestant integration in *Ancien Régime* society after the 1598 Edict of Nantes.[15]

Jean-Jacques Calet, French by Birth, English by the Grace of God

In their priceless collections of eighteenth-century pamphlets, a number of institutions house a strange narrative. Jean-Jacques Calet is the supposed author of *A True and Minute Account of the Destruction of the Bastile: by Jean-Jacques Calet, a French Protestant: who had been a prisoner there upwards of twenty years, and who recovered his Liberty on, and who assisted at the DEMOLITION of that INFAMOUS PRISON.*[16]

As far as we know no Jean-Jacques Calet was held prisoner at the Bastille at the time of its seizure by the Parisian crowd on 14 July 1789. The "infamous prison," with its eight towers overlooking the *faubourg Saint-Antoine*, had become a symbol of arbitrary government and despotism.[17] Linguet, Latude, and a flock of lesser writers had published endless memoirs of their confinement which instantaneously turned its would-be martyrs into heroes. Though somewhat uncomfortable, a stay in the state prison was highly respectable, not to say fashionable, in the small world of philosophy.

But no Jean-Jacques Calet was ever worthy of that consideration. In spite of the translator's claim to have met Monsieur Calet, we suspect the author simply did not exist. Or he may well have been an English gentleman from the country. If he had existed, Monsieur Calet would have deserved to be English: "Monsieur Calet is a French gentleman by birth and education: by religion a Protestant: in his ideas of liberty an Englishman."

Liberty, at the time, was thought to be an English characteristic.[18] Though a genuine Protestant, Jean-Jacques Calet himself had acquired his sense of public virtue during a stay abroad in the 1760s, at the time of the Wilkes' riots in London: "I was in London when the contest subsisted between Mr. Wilkes, or rather between the Public and the then Ministers of State, concerning the abolition of General Warrants. And as I came over to England wholly for pleasure, and as London was at that time a scene of riot and confusion, in which my interference would have been useless and impertinent, I returned to France."[19]

The English experience opened his eyes. When he came back to France, he imparted his experience to a friend: "Amongst other topics the conversation of course turned upon my late excursion to England, and the effort the nation was then making to abolish *General Warrants*, which I described to the Company as nearly analogous to *Lettres de Cachet.*"[20] But this was too much for his compatriots, and the poor Calet was arrested: "Behold reader, (and glory at once in your King and Constitution), a wretched man for no crime whatever reduced from the summit of happiness, to the depth of misery."[21]

The wretched man was then sent to jail with a broken heart, and his family could not survive the loss of their honor. In the mean time, Calet had the opportunity to ponder on the situation of his country: "Poor, wretched, degraded France! Poor do I say? Under a liberal government it would become the richest country in the world."[22]

At the time of the storming of the Bastille, 317 prisoners were set free, according to the author. The prison was finally destroyed to the shouts of *"Vive le roi, vive la liberté, vive la nation."* But worse was in store, as the new regime proved even more tyrannical than the old one. The ordeal of the royal family during the revolution, according to Calet, was clearly a providential punishment for the part the French had taken in the American war of independence: "I cannot myself (I may perhaps be singular in my opinion) forbear thinking that the French court is now suffering in its turn for the many acts of cruelty and perfidy it has been repeatedly guilty of towards a part of its subjects, which, on all occasions, has lived in the most orderly manner under that cruel and oppressive government. I mean the Protestants."[23]

The French revolutionaries were as fanatical and cruel as the Catholics had been during the Wars of Religion in the sixteenth century. Calet mentions the 1572 massacre though he wrongly ascribes it to François II, instead of Charles IX:[24]

> Poor France! wast thou cruel and perfidious more than two centuries ago. When wilt thou secure thyself from slavery and superstition? Condemned and convicted of meanness and treachery from the mouth, and recorded as base by the pen of thy native, learn honour and integrity from thy enemies. Compare with the candour and dignity of the British court suffering thy Navy at the present crisis to lay secure in it's harbour: thine own pitiful proceedings during the American war! Can Britain so far forgive as not to—But I will say no more of my country: my country! I disclaim the appellation! Beggar and vagabond as I am, France shall never have the honour of relieving me: having secured to itself my property: I will secure to myself my person under the very standard of Liberty itself, the British Scepter.

Where could the poor Calet immigrate but to England? As he himself put it: "Where was I to, to fly but to this land of Liberty and Peace: a land which heaven has thrust from other lands in order to bless it beyond comparison." England, of all countries, is "blessed in its climate, in its productions, in its liberty, religion and laws: blessed in its inhabitants, in its constitution and king."[25]

Expostulating the advantages of English weather, Calet heaves a sigh at Louis XVI. He kindly wishes that a "king once mine" be "speedily" restored "on honourable conditions, to the affections of his people, and be the means of bestowing upon them the greatest of all possible earthly benefits, the blessing of civil and religious liberty."[26]

The last word in the copy now held in the Huguenot library in London is a reader's comment in the margin: "Finis"? No: "Louis XVI was guillotined 21 January 1793."

Unfortunately, Jean-Jacques Calet was a fictitious character. The name "Calet" itself clearly refers to the city of Calais—which the English lost to the French in 1558. While "Jean-Jacques," although a very common first name, probably echoes Jean-Jacques Rousseau.

From Grace to Race
Huguenot Genes from the Civil War to the Present

The foundation of the Huguenot Society of South Carolina coincided with the anniversary of the Revocation in 1885. It followed a letter from the Huguenot Society of America in New York—which had been set up two years earlier in 1883. We read in the February 1885 issue of the *Charleston News and Courier* how on Thursday, 19 October, "all descendants (male and female) of the Huguenots of this state (South Carolina) are convened to meet at the French Protestant Church in Charleston."

Several Huguenot families were present, among them the Légarés, Manigaults, Lesesnes, DeSaussures, Gaillards, Ravenels, Gourdins, etc. A Huguenot Society emerged a few days later and was to adopt its constitution on 2 April. Its first principle was to "perpetuate the memory and to foster and promote the principles and virtues of the Huguenots." Among other assignments, the society had to commemorate the "principal events" in Huguenot history, and to constitute a library. Membership, as outlined in the 3 April 1885 issue of the *Charleston News and Courier,* extended to four categories: 1) "descendants in the direct male or female lines of the Huguenot families which emigrated to America" before the Edict of Toleration of 1787; 2) "other French families" professing the Protestant faith before that date; 3) pastors; 4) writers and historians studying the Huguenot past, whatever their nationality.[27]

Self-celebration served to promote the links between descendants, funeral sermons and addresses being among the most fruitful rhetorical devices: extolling the dead could hardly be regarded as flattery. The

Reverend Charles S. Vedder, in a sermon preached on 13 April 1889, set side-by-side the Huguenot epic and other glorious remembrances in the English-speaking world.[28] It is therefore possible to study in the "annals of the Huguenots" the "characteristics of their faith and race." Unfortunately, though, the "cause of protestantism was lost in France." But the "seed" will reappear in a "glorious harvest," in "distant lands"—like America.[29]

On Monday, 14 April 1889, at the Academy of Music, many prominent citizens of Charleston, including the mayor, were able to attend a celebration marking the visit of Thomas F. Bayard.[30] W. St. Julien Jervey, president of the Huguenot Society, greeted him as

> a gentleman who occupies a high niche in the glorious column
> of American statesmanship, and whose name is already a familiar
> word in our households. He is one whose family for generations has
> illustrated those characteristics and virtues which have made it an
> honorable distinction to be a Huguenot; one who, by his able and
> fearless exposition of the principles which actuated the South in
> 1861, and who by his eloquence and untiring defense of our people
> during the unhappy days of reconstruction, has endeared himself to
> the heart of every true Carolinian; one, in short, in honoring whom,
> Charleston honors herself.[31]

The Honorable Thomas F. Bayard's address that very afternoon may have met all the expectations of his hosts: "We may feel the glow of patriotic pride and a grateful reverence for the part played by the descendants of the Huguenots in the formation and administration of the Government of the United States. . . . Throughout the war of the Revolution, from Georgia to Massachusetts, the roll of military heroism contains the names of the Huguenot descendants, and as two of the signers of the first treaty by which our independence as a nation was granted by Great Britain, appear the names of Henry Laurens of South Carolina, and John Jay, of New York."[32]

Yet the study of Huguenot kith and kin may lead to some unpleasant conclusions, as a later author explained: "the Protestant Frenchman was a Frenchman just the same, his new religion did not change his Celtic blood and nature. We are prone to think of him as a French Puritan, substantially identical with the English Puritans; as a fact, he was not essentially different from a Catholic Frenchman, except that he averaged higher."[33]

The survival of the fittest provides a key to Huguenot endurance. The Reverend Robert Wilson, president of the Huguenot Society, had declared in April 1911: "We recall with pardonable pride the generation from whom we derive our descent, not only to do honor to their memories, but to quicken the hereditary life which never dies except with the extinction—if there be a true extinction—of a race . . . We are living the very lives of our Huguenot ancestors, with the very strongest elements of those lives as their legacy to us, *for it is only the strongest elements that persist, the weaker being merged and lost in the stronger lives with which they have mingled.*"[34]

Let us now turn to the Huguenot Society of London, at a critical stage in its history. In 1920, the Reverend William George Cazalet underlined the role played by Huguenot descendants in the battles of World War I. Addressing the Huguenot Society of London, now the Huguenot Society of Great Britain and Ireland, he insisted on the physical characteristics of some of the British soldiers: "Many of their descendants to this day bear the facial French type, and presumably French characteristics also."[35] He went on that the Huguenots who had settled in Britain in the seventeenth century were usually well educated and intelligent. They had therefore joined the army and the royal navy.

The Huguenot theme was also taken up to promote Anglo-American relations. In 1924, Sir Robert McCall, president of the Huguenot Society, wanted to develop "a new bond in the alliance of the English-speaking people on both sides of the Atlantic."[36] But very little was said at the time of all the German Huguenots. Huguenot history was largely an English concern, extending to the New World as a former colony: "Huguenot history roughly divides itself into two eras: the history of our predecessors in France, and the history of our emigrants in Britain."[37] The anti-German feeling was at its highest in 1921, when president Wyatt Wyatt-Paine described German racial characteristics:

> It seems probable that Rome gave not only her creed but also many political institutions and civil concepts to mediaeval and renaissance France. And this seems so in spite of the fact that centuries of territorial occupation by those Teutonic Franks who, issuing from the

mysterious depths of the Hercynian forest, must have infused into the Gallic, Burgundian and Lombardic tribes occupying that fair Frankland or France, as it is called to-day, not only a strong blend of Teutonic blood but also a considerable knowledge of the general principles and working of Teutonic law. As for the Franks themselves, their origin, like the origin of their name, is lost in the obscurity of the ages that have since elapsed. They came from the East, they imposed their Salic laws and strong-handed sway over widespread dominions in the West, and then, after many decades of conquest, as if haunted by some racial nostalgia, reverted as a nation to that land from whence they came, there to be reabsorbed in one or other of those later Teutonic waves, from which sprang, *as a degenerate type*, the modern Germanic race.[38]

Racial theorists were faced with a dilemma after the war. The Whig political tradition had usually insisted on the common ancestry of the Saxons and early Germans. Most eighteenth-century historians had turned to Tacitus and his *De origine et situ Germanorum* to find an accurate description of "Gothick" liberties. This passion for antiquity was also to be found in America; Benjamin Franklin exclaimed with pride: "Britain was formerly the America of the Germans."[39]

How could then the Germans be regarded as "degenerate"? The kinship between the English Huguenot descendants and the Germans had been further reinforced by French migrations to Prussia, in the wake of the Revocation of the Edict of Nantes. German military skills and drills were often due to the influence of Huguenot officers. A new sense of discipline had emerged during Louis XIV's reign, and was largely due to Louvois.

The anti-German feeling, after the war, led some to disown all past links between Britain and its former enemy. Hence the insistence on the "degeneracy of the German race," which was both unscientific and unsound. Conversely, the merits of the "Huguenot race" had chiefly benefited the British: "For the freedom of our time, as compared with the era of St. Bartholomew, for the progress of civilisation and the civilising effect of trade, the English-speaking world and the world at large may well recognise that some of this great development is due to the devotion, the industry, the steadfastness and the toleration of the Huguenot race."[40]

Though highly exclusive, this notion of "race" differs from other racial theories. Instead of propounding some sort of racial purity, based on blood, it defends the mixture of the "best" races. The British are a mixed breed: "In our own island the Briton, the Celt, the Roman, the Anglo-Saxon, the Norman, by coalescing, have edified a stalwart race in body and in mind which, in spite of its many frailties and imperfections, is nevertheless one of the most healthful and progressive in the world."[41]

If racial purity should neither be defended nor envisaged, one has to choose carefully one's allies. Some mixtures are better than others. The fusion of French and Dutch genes produced the South-African settler: "Such, ladies and gentlemen, were some of the adventures of these pilgrim fathers of the French Reformed Church in South Africa who, by importing a Latino-Gallic element into the phlegmatic Batavian stock, improved and built up the European race in its new environment."[42]

The overall importance of genetic factors in the history of Huguenot descendants was recently taken up by Robin Gwynn's *Huguenot Heritage* in 1985. The book, which was issued at the time of the anniversary of the Revocation of the Edict of Nantes, asserted the unique contribution of French Protestants to the development of the British Isles. Unlike English Catholics and Quakers, who had already been the butt of Macaulay's criticism, the Huguenots had exerted a positive and lasting influence on their new fatherland.[43] Gwynn resented all endeavors to show that France had not been completely ruined and poverty-stricken by the massive departure of Protestant *émigrés*.[44] The ways of the Lord may escape the attention of the best historians. He likewise mentioned the "genetic factors" which "may have helped determine which French Huguenots [*sic*] possessed the combination of faith, resolution, endurance, and a will to work for a new future which led him to seek refuge in strange lands."[45] But in a later discussion he disowned that influence.[46] Religious faith is definitely not a genetic factor.

The French "Republican" Model
Michelet as myth-maker

In France, the Huguenot myth has evolved in opposite directions. It has been politically, rather than genetically correct. With few exceptions, it tends to be liberal and progressive, versus conservative, and insists on the Protestant legacy to the Republic.[47]

This may partly explain the success of Jean Baubérot's analysis of the links between the secularization of society and the Protestant minority.[48] "Secularization"? One should rather say "laicization" or *laïcité*, to use the French concept. Church and state have to be separated; likewise, there are very few references, if any, to God or providence in public life. No prayers are to be said in public schools, which are usually defined as *laïques*, or secular. Likewise, the French Republic usually appeals to the principles of the 1789 Revolution; its motto, *Liberté, égalité, fraternité,—* liberty, equality and fraternity—is supposedly based on that precedent.

Protestantism itself often remains shrouded in mystery for the general public. In January 1996, *Le Point*, a well-known French magazine, mentioned tongue-in-cheek, the "great revenge of the Protestants." One of the best religious journalists, Christian Makarian, devoted a whole article to the obvious influence of the Protestant minority on the rest of society and its system of values. While extolling the Protestant work ethic, Makarian expressed some doubts about the received imagery of Huguenot harsh austerity. Another analyst, Alain Duhamel insisted in the same issue that the Protestants who had been "persecuted, crushed, defeated or exiled" before the 1789 Revolution had since recovered their position with the advent of the Republic."[49]

In other words, the failure of *Ancien Régime* Protestants had permitted their later success and adaptation. Likewise, the French Republic had greatly benefited from their sway and prestige. The problem is yet to know if Protestantism has fulfilled its historical mission by transmitting its values to the rest of society—as Baubérot argues—or if French society has acculturated Calvinism.

In itself, Reformed Protestantism is neither particularly democratic nor tolerant. Neither is it "Republican" or progressive. Those labels are the outcome of a long, troublesome, and even contradictory history. It can even be argued that the word "Republic" has changed its meaning since the sixteenth century, and that the Huguenot concept was purely aristocratic at first.[50] The very idea of a Reformation is conservative and rests on the rejection of novelty. In the nineteenth century, Michelet was one of the actors who forged the progressive imagery of Protestantism versus "reactionary" Catholicism.[51] But this leads him to treat a number of notorious Catholics as would-be Protestants: Shakespeare and Bacon, Descartes and Galileo were equally regarded by him as Protestants.[52] But this rests on no evidence whatever in the case of

Descartes and Galileo. In turn this identification was handed down to primary schools.[53] The Protestant faith was assimilated to a secularized version of Christianity.

From fusion to confusion, the Protestant experience has become one of the lasting myths of the French Republic. What exactly was the source of Michelet's hijacking of the Huguenot heritage? The answer is to be found in his opponents: counter-revolutionary thinkers were among the first to identify the Reformation and the 1789 Revolution. Bonald considered that the Reformation had ushered in all the major wars and rebellions which had turned Europe into a battlefield. This right-wing assimilation had immediate left-wing effects. Edgar Quinet contributed to the codification of those links in his seminal studies of the French Revolution, recently unearthed by François Furet.[54]

All history, old or new, Whig or revisionist, may one day appear as mythical. The Huguenot experience does not contradict this assertion: the French Protestant epic has lent itself to a number of national or even local histories. There is a distinct French Huguenot myth, a British and an American one—though it remains to be seen if it is absolutely identical in the state of New York and in South Carolina.[55] Huguenot societies did nonetheless contribute to the reconciliation of the North and South after the American Civil War. Whether literary or historical, myths have therefore an essential function to perform. They should be maintained to allow historians to exist. Or maybe, to use an economic argument, to let them keep body and soul together.

Notes

1. Bertrand Van Ruymbeke, "L'émigration huguenote en Caroline du Sud sous le régime des Seigneurs Propriétaires: étude d'une communauté du Refuge dans une province britannique d'Amérique du Nord (1680–1720)" (Ph.D. diss., Université de la Sorbonne Nouvelle, 1995), 2 vols., passim. Ibid., "Crossing the Rubicon: The South Carolina Huguenots and the Issue of Naturalization." Paper presented at the Conference "Out of Babylon: The Huguenots and Their Diaspora," Charleston, 1997.

2. This mystical element was taken up by Calvin in his definition of the Lord's Supper. See Bernard Cottret, "Pour une sémiotique de la Réforme. Le *Consensus Tigurinus* de Calvin," *Annales Economie, Société, Civilisation* 39 (1984): 265–85 and Ibid., *Calvin: A Biography* (Grand Rapids, Mich.: W. B. Eerdmans, 2000).

3. Diane C. Margolf, "Adjudicating Memory: Law and Religious Difference in Early Seventeenth-Century France," *Sixteenth-Century Journal* 27 (1996):

399–418. The relationship between Law and Grace does in fact condition the Calvinist emphasis on the wholeness of revelation. For Calvin, the Jewish Torah is an integral part of God's revelation to Man, hence the renewed emphasis on the Old Testament.

4. Didier Poton, "De l'édit à sa révocation: Saint-Jean-de-Gardonnenque, 1598–1686" 2 vols. (Ph.D. diss., Université de Montpellier III, 1988), 1:377.

5. Bernard Cottret, *The Huguenots in England: Immigration and Settlement, c. 1550–1700* (New York: Cambridge University Press, 1991), 18 ff.

6. Leonard Adams, ed., 2 vols. *William Wake's Gallican Correspondence and Related Documents, 1716–1731* (New York: P. Lang, 1989); J. Grès-Gayer, *Paris-Cantorbéry (1717–1720). Le dossier d'un premier oecuménisme* (Paris: Beauchesne, 1989).

7. Bernard Cottret, *1598: l'Édit de Nantes. Pour en finir avec les guerres de religion,* (Paris: Perrin, 1997) 304 ff.

8. Nonetheless they did not go so far as to believe in apostolic succession. Jean-Marie Mayeur et al., ed., "De la chrétienté à l'Europe. Les Églises face aux relations internationales," in *L'âge de raison (1620/30–1750)*, vol. 9 of *Histoire du christianisme*, ed. M. Venard (Paris: Desclée, 1997) 157–206.

9. Herbert Butterfield, *The Whig Interpretation of History* (1931; reprint, New York: Scribner's, 1951).

10. Claude Lévi-Strauss, *Mythologiques* 3 vols. (Paris: Plon, 1964–68), 1:21.

11. Maurice Agulhon, *Marianne au combat* (Paris: Flammarion, 1979); Simon Schama, *The Embarrassment of Riches. An Interpretation of Dutch Culture in the Golden Age* (New York: A. A. Knopf, 1987); Linda Colley, *Britons. Forging the Nation, 1707–1837* (London: Pimlico, 1994); David Bell, "*Lingua Populi, Lingua Dei*: Language, Religion, and the Origins of French Revolutionary Nationalism," *American Historical Review* 100 (1995): 1403–37; Bernard Cottret, *Bolingbroke's Political Writings. The Conservative Enlightenment* (New York: St. Martin's Press, 1997), 47*ff.* "The Swan's Song: A Patriot King or None!" For a Scottish assessment, see Murray G. H. Pittock, *Poetry and Jacobite Politics in Eighteenth-Century Britain and Ireland*, Cambridge Studies in Eighteenth-Century English Literature and Thought (Cambridge: Cambridge University Press, 1994).

12. Bell, "Recent Works on Early Modern French National Identity," *Journal of Modern History* 68 (March 1996): 89–90.

13. Michèle Magdelaine and Rudolf von Thadden ed., *Le refuge huguenot* (Paris: A. Colin, 1985); *Die Huguenotten* (Munich: C. H. Beck, 1985).

14. Bernard Cottret, "The Huguenots as Whig-Makers: A Rejoinder," *Proceedings of the Huguenot Society of Great Britain and Ireland* (hereafter *HSP*) 26 (1995): 367–70; Bernard Cottret and Bertrand Van Ruymbeke, "Le destin huguenot, entre l'universel et le singulier," in *L'Autre dans l'Europe du Nord-Ouest*

à travers l'histoire, ed. Jean-Pierre Jessenne (Lille: Presses Universitaires de Lille, 1996), 149–62.

15. Bernard Cottret, *1598: l'Édit de Nantes*

16. Jean-Jacques Calet, *A True and Minute Account of the Destruction of the Bastile: by Jean-Jacques Calet, a French Protestant: who had been a prisoner there upwards of twenty years, and who recovered his Liberty on, and who assisted at the DEMOLITION of that INFAMOUS PRISON*, translated from the French by an English Gentleman (London: W. Browne and J. Warren, 1789). The copy I used is now kept in the Huguenot Library in London: bookshelf 2 f. Other editions include *A True and Minute Account of the Destruction of the Bastile . . .* , (Norwich, 1796) and *A True and Minute Account of the Destruction of the Bastile . . .* , (Medford, Mass., 1800).

17. Monique Cottret, *La Bastille à prendre, histoire et mythe de la forteresse royale* (Paris: Presses Universitaires de France, 1986).

18. In Mozart's opera *Die Entführung aus dem Serail*, Blonde, being English, has a natural taste for freedom. This leads her to exclaim: "Ich bin eine Engländerin und zur Freiheit geboren."

19. *A True and Minute Account of the Destruction of the Bastile. . .* , 3.

20. Ibid., 4.

21. Ibid., 12.

22. Ibid., 22.

23. Ibid., 56.

24. Ibid., 58–59.

25. Ibid., 60.

26. Ibid., 61.

27. *Charleston Post and Courier,* 3 April, 1885.

28. *Transactions of the Huguenot Society of South Carolina* 2 (1889): 17: "In what shall be said there is no purpose to shadow the glory of other nationalities, in whom a like faith wrought its gracious work. Worthy of undying remembrance are those whose patent of Christian nobility dates from the immortal defence of Londonderry, and has lost no lustre since; or from the lowlands of Scotland; worthy of exultant thankfulness to their descendants is the inheritance left by the little colony of the Mayflower, and those who in the Netherlands wrested their liberties from the strongest nation then on the globe, and others like them, who loved truth and freedom more than life."

29. *Transactions of the Huguenot Society of South Carolina* 2 (1889): 25, 27.

30. Thomas Francis Bayard (1828–98): Democrat; Senator from Delaware (1869–85); candidate for presidential nomination (1880, 1884); U.S. secretary of state (1885–1889); ambassador to Great Britain (1893–1897).

31. *Transactions of the Huguenot Society of South Carolina* 2 (1889): 35.

32. Ibid., 61–62.

33. Ibid., 19 (1912): 29.

34. Ibid., 18 (1911): 8–9. My italics.

35. "Huguenot War Records 1914–1919," *HSP* 12 (1920): 289.

36. Ibid., 13 (1924): 12.

37. Ibid., 12.

38. Ibid., 12 (1921): 335. My italics.

39. *Gentleman's Magazine*, October 1773.

40. Samuel Kliger, *The Goths in England. A Study in Seventeenth-Century and Eighteenth-Century Thought* (Cambridge, Mass.: Harvard University Press, 1952). *Gentleman's Magazine*, October 1773.

41. *HSP* 13 (1924–1925): 96–97.

42. Ibid., 12 (1920): 244.

43. Ibid., 12 (1920): 243–44:

44. Robin D. Gwynn, *Huguenot Heritage* (London: Routledge and Kegan Paul, 1985), 2.

45. Ibid., 157–59. Warren Candler Scoville, *The Persecution of Huguenots and French Economic Development* (Berkeley: University of California Press, 1960).

46. Ibid., 175. For a somewhat different approach, see Cottret, *The Huguenots in England*.

47. On the memory of Protestantism, see Bernard Cottret, "'Le protestanisme Français,' un protestantisme en mal d'acte(s) fondateur(s)" *Bulletin de la Société de l'Histoire du Protestantisme Français* 148 (2002): 819–32, and Ibid., "Histoire et Mémoire du protestantisme," *Libre Sens, Bulletin du CPED* 116 (June 2002): 2–10.

48. *Huguenot Society Proceedings* 26 (1995): 370.

49. Jean Baubérot, *Le protestantisme doit-il mourir?* (Paris: Le Seuil, 1988).

50. Christian Makarian, "La grande revanche des protestants," *Le Point*, 1219, (27 janvier 1996): 70–79.

51. Arthur Herman, "The Huguenot Republic and Antirepublicanism in Seventeenth-Century France," *Journal of the History of Ideas* 53 (1992): 255.

52. Jules Michelet, *Histoire de France*, 12 vols., ed. Claude Mettra (Lausanne: Editions Rencontre, 1965–66), 7:457.

53. Ibid., 458.

54. É. Fauquet, *Michelet ou la gloire du professeur d'histoire* (Paris: Le Cerf, 1990), 431; Paul Viallaneix, "Réformation et Révolution dans l'historiographie française du XIXe siècle," in *Réforme et révolutions. Aux origines de la démocratie moderne* (Montpellier: Presses du Languedoc, 1990), 171.

55. Edgar Quinet, *Le christianisme et la révolution* (1845); idem, *Philosophie de l'Histoire de France* (1857); and idem, *Révolution* (1865). See François Furet, *Marx and the French Revolution* (Chicago: University of Chicago Press, 1988).

Contributors

Bertrand Van Ruymbeke is professor of American studies at the Université de Toulouse. Author of the introduction to a reprint of Arthur H. Hirsch's *The Huguenots of Colonial South Carolina* (1999), he has published in the fields of the Huguenot diaspora, early South Carolina history, and the Anglo-American Atlantic world. He is currently completing a history of the Huguenots in proprietary South Carolina.

Randy J. Sparks is associate professor of history at Tulane University. He is the author of *On Jordan's Stormy Banks: Evangelicalism in Mississippi* (1994), *Religion in Mississippi* (2000), and *Atlantic Odyssey: The Two Princes of Calabar and the 18th Century Atlantic World* (forthcoming), and co-editor of *Money, Trade, and Power: The Evolution of South Carolina's Plantation Society* (2001).

Lucien Abénon is professor of early modern history at the Université des Antilles et de la Guyane. He is the author of *La Guadeloupe de 1671 à 1759* (1987) and co-author of *Les Français en Amérique. Histoire d'une colonisation* (1993). His research interests include the French Revolution in the West Indies, the Huguenot immigration to the French Antilles, and Caribbean historical demography.

Jon Butler is William Robertson Coe Professor of American Studies and History and professor of religious studies at Yale University. He received his Ph.D. from the University of Minnesota. Among his books are *The Origins of American Denominational Order* (1978); *The Huguenots in America: A Refugee People in New World Society* (1983); *Awash in a Sea of Faith: Christianizing the American People* (1990); and *Becoming America: The Revolution before 1776* (2000). He is currently writing a book on urban religion in Manhattan between the Civil War and World War II.

Carolyn Lougee Chappell is professor of history and chair of the history department at Stanford University. She is author of *Le Paradis des Femmes:*

Women, Salons and Social Stratification in Seventeenth-Century France (1976). She is currently working on the family politics of the Revocation of the Edict of Nantes.

Leslie Choquette, L'Institut français Professor of Francophone Cultures and director of the French Institute at Assumption College, is the author of *Frenchmen into Peasants: Modernity and Tradition in the Peopling of French Canada* (1997).

Bernard Cottret was educated at the École Normale Supérieure de Saint-Cloud, near Paris. He is professor of British studies at the University of Versailles-Saint-Quentin and founder (and former chairman) of its department of humanities. He has held a seminar titled "Center and Periphery: Religion and Society in the British Isles and in Colonial America" at the Sorbonne and now at the Protestant Faculty in Paris since 1992, and taught a summer course at the University of Charleston in 1994. He has published extensively on the Protestant Reformation and early modern European history. His recent books include *The Huguenots in England* (1991); *Bolingbroke's Political Writings* (1997); and *John Calvin. A Biography* (2000) available in French, German, Spanish, Polish, and Georgian, and *Une histoire de la Révolution américaine: la poursuite du bonheur* (2003).

Philippe Denis, who received his Ph.D. in history from the Université de Liège, Belgium, in 1983, has since 1993 been professor of history of Christianity at the School of Theology, University of Natal, South Africa. His main areas of study are the Protestant Reformation, African Christianity, and oral history in Africa.

Timothy Fehler is associate professor of history at Furman University, Greenville, South Carolina, where he teaches early modern European history. His work on Emden includes *Poor Relief and Protestantism: The Evolution of Social Welfare in Sixteenth-Century Emden* (1999) and "Diakonenamt und Armenfürsorge bei a Lasco: Theologischer Impuls und praktische Wirklichkeit," in *Johannes a Lasco (1499–1560). Polnischer Baron, Humanist und europäischer Reformator*, ed., Christoph Strohm (2000), 173–85.

Willem Frijhoff is professor of early modern history at the Free University, Amsterdam. He has published extensively in cultural history, memory, intellectual history, popular religion, and sorcery. Educated in France, he is the author of *Wegen van Evert Willemsz. Een Hollands weeskind op zoek naar zichzelf,*

1607–1647 (The quest of Evert Willemsz: a Dutch orphan in search of himself) (1995) and *Embodied Belief: Ten Essays on Religious Culture in Dutch History* (2002), co-author of *1650: Bevochten eendracht* (1999), and co-editor of *Erasmus of Rotterdam, the Man and the Scholar* (1988), *Witchcraft in the Netherlands from the Fourteenth to the Twentieth Century* (1991), and *Lieux de mémoire et identités nationales* (1993).

Joyce D. Goodfriend, professor of history at the University of Denver, is the author of *Before the Melting Pot: Society and Culture in Colonial New York City, 1664–1730* (1992) and numerous articles on the colonial Dutch. Her most recent works on the Huguenots are "Seventeenth-Century New York City: Fertile Ground for Planting a Huguenot Community," in *D'un Rivage à l'Autre. Villes et Protestantisme dans l'Aire Atlantique XVIe-XVIIe siècle*, eds., G. Martinière, D. Poton, and F. Souty (1999), and "The Last of the Huguenots: John Pintard and the Memory of the Diaspora in the Early American Republic," *Journal of Presbyterian History* 78 (fall 2000): 181–92.

Gérard Lafleur has a Ph.D in history and is in charge of the educational department at the Archives départementales de la Guadeloupe. His research interests include religious and ethnic minorities in the French Antilles and the history of Guadeloupe. He is the author of *Les protestants aux Antilles françaises du Vent sous l'ancien régime* (1988), *Les Caraibes des Petites Antilles* (1992), *Les Libanais et les Syriens de Guadeloupe* (1992), *Saint-Claude: histoire d'une commune de la Guadeloupe* (1993), and *Gourbeyre: une commune de Guadeloupe* (1997)

Charles Littleton received his Ph.D. from the University of Michigan in 1996 for his dissertation, "Geneva on Threadneedle Street: The French Church of London and its Congregation, 1560–1625." From 1997 to 2001 he worked with Professor Michael Hunter at Birkbeck College, University of London on a project to publish the complete "workdiaries" of the seventeenth-century scientist Robert Boyle (http://www.bbk.ac.uk/boyle/workdiaries). He is now employed as a Research Associate at the History of Parliament Trust, where he is conducting research on the House of Lords, 1660–1832.

Keith P. Luria is associate professor of history at North Carolina State University, in Raleigh. He is author of *Territories of Grace: Cultural Change in the Seventeenth-Century Diocese of Grenoble* (1991) and is currently working on a book titled *Sacred Boundaries: Protestants and Catholics in Seventeenth-Century France*.

Diane C. Margolf received her Ph.D. from Yale University and is currently associate professor of history at Colorado State University. Her research interests include religion, law, and culture in early modern France and Europe, and her book, *Religion and Royal Justice in Early Modern France: The Paris Chambre de l'Edit 1598–1665* will be published in the series Sixteenth Century Essays and Studies.

Raymond A. Mentzer holds the Daniel J. Krumm Family Chair in Reformation Studies (Department of Religious Studies) at the University of Iowa. He is the author of *Heresy Proceedings in Languedoc, 1500–1560* (1984) and *Blood and Belief: Family Survival and Confessional Identity among the Provincial Huguenot Nobility* (1994). *Blood and Belief* won the 1995 National Huguenot Society Book Prize. He co-edited *Society and Culture in the Huguenot World, 1559–1685* (2002). His current research focuses on social discipline and the French Reformed community in the sixteenth and seventeenth centuries.

John Miller is professor of history at Queen Mary, University of London. He studied at Jesus College, Cambridge, and has been Research Fellow at Gonville and Caius College, Cambridge, 1971–1975. He joined the history faculty at Queen Mary College, University of London, in 1975 and has been professor of history since 1989. His publications include biographies of James II (1978, 1989, 2000 editions) and Charles II (1991). His latest book, *After the Civil Wars: English Politics and Government in the Reign of Charles II*, was published in 2000.

R. C. Nash, B.A., University of East Anglia, Ph.D. University of Cambridge, has been lecturer in economic history at the University of Manchester since 1975. His research interests are in British, European, and American colonial history, 1500–1800. He has recently published articles on colonial South Carolina history and economy and his latest work is a chapter on European economy in the *Short Oxford History of Europe: Seventeenth Century* (2000).

Index